Volume 2 Topics 5–8

Authors

Robert Q. Berry, III
Associate Professor of Mathematics Education, Department of Curriculum, Instruction and Special Education, University of Virginia, Charlottesville, Virginia

Zachary Champagne
Assistant in Research
Florida Center for Research in Science, Technology, Engineering, and Mathematics (FCR-STEM)
Jacksonville, Florida

Eric Milou
Professor of Mathematics
Rowan University, Glassboro, New Jersey

Jane F. Schielack
Professor Emerita
Department of Mathematics
Texas A&M University
College Station, Texas

Jonathan A. Wray
Mathematics Instructional Facilitator, Howard County Public Schools, Ellicott City, Maryland

Randall I. Charles
Professor Emeritus
Department of Mathematics
San Jose State University
San Jose, California

Francis (Skip) Fennell
L. Stanley Bowlsbey Professor of Education and Graduate and Professional Studies, McDaniel College
Westminster, Maryland

Glenview, Illinois Boston, Massachusetts Chandler, Arizona New York, New York

Mathematician Reviewers

Gary Lippman, Ph.D.
Professor Emeritus
Mathematics and Computer Science
California State University, East Bay
Hayward, California

Karen Edwards, Ph.D.
Mathematics Lecturer
Arlington, MA

PEARSON

ISBN-13: 978-0-328-88187-1
ISBN-10: 0-328-88187-2
14 20

CONTENTS

TOPICS

KEY

 Major Cluster

 Supporting Cluster

 Additional Cluster

DIGITAL RESOURCES

Go Online | PearsonRealize.com

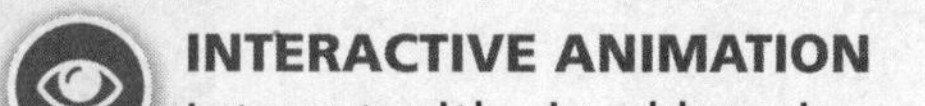

INTERACTIVE ANIMATION
Interact with visual learning animations

ACTIVITY
Use with ***Solve & Discuss It, Explore It,*** and ***Explain It*** activities and Examples

VIDEOS
Watch clips to support ***3-Act Mathematical Modeling*** Lessons and ***STEM Projects***

PRACTICE
Practice what you've learned and get immediate feedback

TUTORIALS
Get help from ***Virtual Nerd*** any time you need it

KEY CONCEPT
Review important lesson content

GLOSSARY
Read and listen to English and Spanish definitions

ASSESSMENT
Show what you've learned

MATH TOOLS
Explore math with digital tools

GAMES
Play math games to help you learn

ETEXT
Access your book online

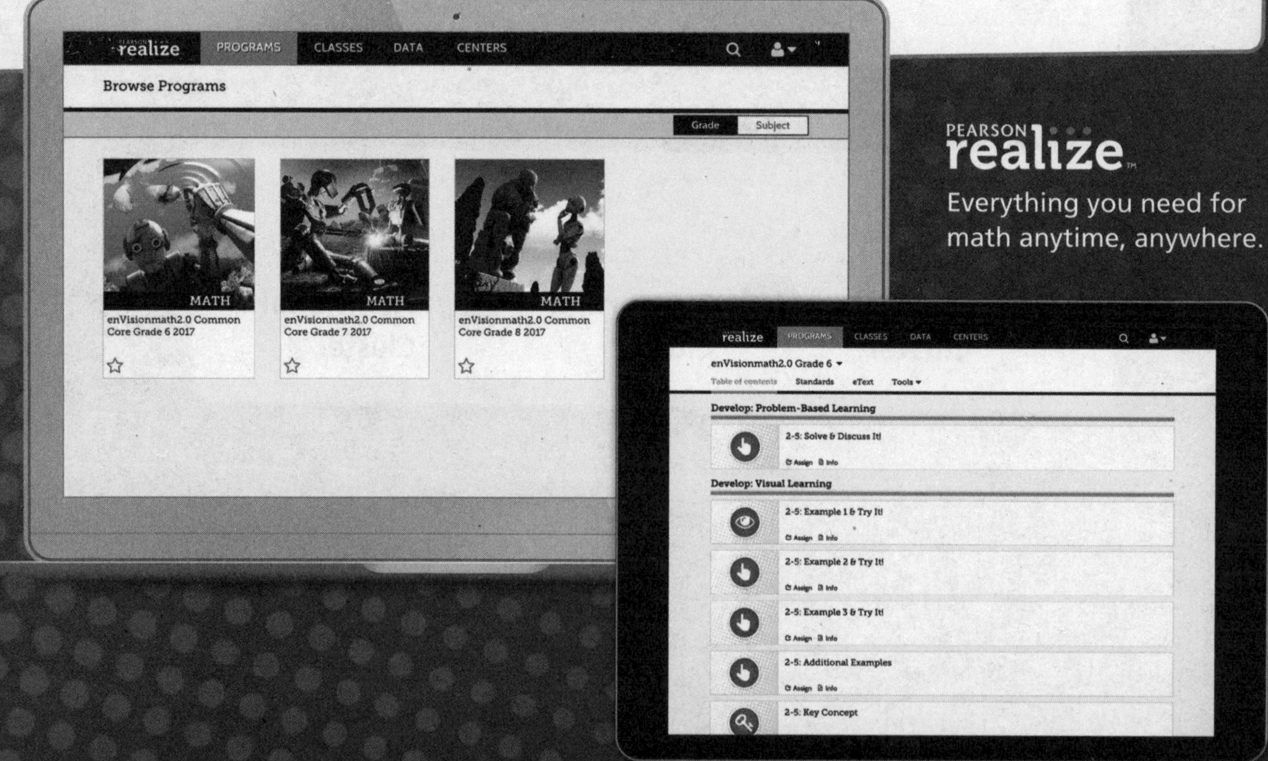

PEARSON realize™
Everything you need for math anytime, anywhere.

TOPIC 5

Understand and Use Ratio and Rate

TOPIC 6

Understand and Use Percent

TOPIC 7

Solve Area, Surface Area, and Volume Problems

TOPIC 8

Display, Describe, and Summarize Data

GRADE 6

COMMON CORE STATE STANDARDS

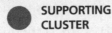

 MAJOR CLUSTER  SUPPORTING CLUSTER  ADDITIONAL CLUSTER

Standards for Mathematical Content

DOMAIN 6.RP RATIOS AND PROPORTIONAL RELATIONSHIPS

MAJOR CLUSTER 6.RP.A

Understand ratio concepts and use ratio reasoning to solve problems.

6.RP.A.1 Understand the concept of a ratio and use ratio language to describe a ratio relationship between two quantities.

6.RP.A.2 Understand the concept of a unit rate a/b associated with a ratio $a:b$ with $b \neq 0$, and use rate language in the context of a ratio relationship.[1]

6.RP.A.3 Use ratio and rate reasoning to solve real-world and mathematical problems, e.g., by reasoning about tables of equivalent ratios, tape diagrams, double number line diagrams, or equations.

6.RP.A.3a Make tables of equivalent ratios relating quantities with whole-number measurements, find missing values in the tables, and plot the pairs of values on the coordinate plane. Use tables to compare ratios.

6.RP.A.3b Solve unit rate problems including those involving unit pricing and constant speed.

6.RP.A.3c Find a percent of a quantity as a rate per 100 (e.g., 30% of a quantity means 30/100 times the quantity); solve problems involving finding the whole, given a part and the percent.

6.RP.A.3d Use ratio reasoning to convert measurement units; manipulate and transform units appropriately when multiplying or dividing quantities.

DOMAIN 6.NS THE NUMBER SYSTEM

MAJOR CLUSTER 6.NS.A

Apply and extend previous understandings of multiplication and division to divide fractions by fractions.

6.NS.A.1 Interpret and compute quotients of fractions, and solve word problems involving division of fractions by fractions, e.g., by using visual fraction models and equations to represent the problem.

ADDITIONAL CLUSTER 6.NS.B

Compute fluently with multi-digit numbers and find common factors and multiples.

6.NS.B.2 Fluently divide multi-digit numbers using the standard algorithm.

6.NS.B.3 Fluently add, subtract, multiply, and divide multi-digit decimals using the standard algorithm for each operation.

6.NS.B.4 Find the greatest common factor of two whole numbers less than or equal to 100 and the least common multiple of two whole numbers less than or equal to 12. Use the distributive property to express a sum of two whole numbers 1–100 with a common factor as a multiple of a sum of two whole numbers with no common factor.

[1]Expectations for unit rates in this grade are limited to non-complex fractions

MAJOR CLUSTER
SUPPORTING CLUSTER
ADDITIONAL CLUSTER

Standards for Mathematical Content

MAJOR CLUSTER 6.NS.C

Apply and extend previous understandings of numbers to the system of rational numbers.

6.NS.C.5 Understand that positive and negative numbers are used together to describe quantities having opposite directions or values (e.g., temperature above/below zero, elevation above/below sea level, credits/debits, positive/negative electric charge); use positive and negative numbers to represent quantities in real-world contexts, explaining the meaning of 0 in each situation.

6.NS.C.6 Understand a rational number as a point on the number line. Extend number line diagrams and coordinate axes familiar from previous grades to represent points on the line and in the plane with negative number coordinates.

6.NS.C.6a Recognize opposite signs of numbers as indicating locations on opposite sides of 0 on the number line; recognize that the opposite of the opposite of a number is the number itself, e.g., $-(-3) = 3$, and that 0 is its own opposite.

6.NS.C.6b Understand signs of numbers in ordered pairs as indicating locations in quadrants of the coordinate plane; recognize that when two ordered pairs differ only by signs, the locations of the points are related by reflections across one or both axes.

6.NS.C.6c Find and position integers and other rational numbers on a horizontal or vertical number line diagram; find and position pairs of integers and other rational numbers on a coordinate plane.

6.NS.C.7 Understand ordering and absolute value of rational numbers.

6.NS.C.7a Interpret statements of inequality as statements about the relative position of two numbers on a number line diagram.

6.NS.C.7b Write, interpret, and explain statements of order for rational numbers in real-world contexts.

6.NS.C.7c Understand the absolute value of a rational number as its distance from 0 on the number line; interpret absolute value as magnitude for a positive or negative quantity in a real-world situation.

6.NS.C.7d Distinguish comparisons of absolute value from statements about order.

6.NS.C.8 Solve real-world and mathematical problems by graphing points in all four quadrants of the coordinate plane. Include use of coordinates and absolute value to find distances between points with the same first coordinate or the same second coordinate.

DOMAIN 6.EE
EXPRESSIONS AND EQUATIONS

MAJOR CLUSTER 6.EE.A

Apply and extend previous understandings of arithmetic to algebraic expressions.

6.EE.A.1 Write and evaluate numerical expressions involving whole-number exponents.

6.EE.A.2 Write, read, and evaluate expressions in which letters stand for numbers.

6.EE.A.2a Write expressions that record operations with numbers and with letters standing for numbers.

6.EE.A.2b Identify parts of an expression using mathematical terms (sum, term, product, factor, quotient, coefficient); view one or more parts of an expression as a single entity.

6.EE.A.2c Evaluate expressions at specific values of their variables. Include expressions that arise from formulas used in real-world problems. Perform arithmetic operations, including those involving whole-number exponents, in the conventional order when there are no parentheses to specify a particular order (Order of Operations).

6.EE.A.3 Apply the properties of operations to generate equivalent expressions.

6.EE.A.4 Identify when two expressions are equivalent (i.e., when the two expressions name the same number regardless of which value is substituted into them).

MAJOR CLUSTER
SUPPORTING CLUSTER
ADDITIONAL CLUSTER

Standards for Mathematical Content

MAJOR CLUSTER 6.EE.B

Reason about and solve one-variable equations and inequalities.

6.EE.B.5 Understand solving an equation or inequality as a process of answering a question: which values from a specified set, if any, make the equation or inequality true? Use substitution to determine whether a given number in a specified set makes an equation or inequality true.

6.EE.B.6 Use variables to represent numbers and write expressions when solving a real-world or mathematical problem; understand that a variable can represent an unknown number, or, depending on the purpose at hand, any number in a specified set.

6.EE.B.7 Solve real-world and mathematical problems by writing and solving equations of the form $x + p = q$ and $px = q$ for cases in which p, q and x are all nonnegative rational numbers.

6.EE.B.8 Write an inequality of the form $x > c$ or $x < c$ to represent a constraint or condition in a real-world or mathematical problem. Recognize that inequalities of the form $x > c$ or $x < c$ have infinitely many solutions; represent solutions of such inequalities on number line diagrams.

MAJOR CLUSTER 6.EE.C

Represent and analyze quantitative relationships between dependent and independent variables.

6.EE.C.9 Use variables to represent two quantities in a real-world problem that change in relationship to one another; write an equation to express one quantity, thought of as the dependent variable, in terms of the other quantity, thought of as the independent variable. Analyze the relationship between the dependent and independent variables using graphs and tables, and relate these to the equation.

DOMAIN 6.G GEOMETRY

SUPPORTING CLUSTER 6.G.A

Solve real-world and mathematical problems involving area, surface area, and volume.

6.G.A.1 Find the area of right triangles, other triangles, special quadrilaterals, and polygons by composing into rectangles or decomposing into triangles and other shapes; apply these techniques in the context of solving real-world and mathematical problems.

6.G.A.2 Find the volume of a right rectangular prism with fractional edge lengths by packing it with unit cubes of the appropriate unit fraction edge lengths, and show that the volume is the same as would be found by multiplying the edge lengths of the prism. Apply the formulas $V = \ell wh$ and $V = bh$ to find volumes of right rectangular prisms with fractional edge lengths in the context of solving real-world and mathematical problems.

6.G.A.3 Draw polygons in the coordinate plane given coordinates for the vertices; use coordinates to find the length of a side joining points with the same first coordinate or the same second coordinate. Apply these techniques in the context of solving real-world and mathematical problems.

6.G.A.4 Represent three-dimensional figures using nets made up of rectangles and triangles, and use the nets to find the surface area of these figures. Apply these techniques in the context of solving real-world and mathematical problems.

Standards for Mathematical Content

MAJOR CLUSTER
SUPPORTING CLUSTER
ADDITIONAL CLUSTER

DOMAIN 6.SP
STATISTICS AND PROBABILITY

ADDITIONAL CLUSTER 6.SP.A
Develop understanding of statistical variability.

6.SP.A.1 Recognize a statistical question as one that anticipates variability in the data related to the question and accounts for it in the answers.

6.SP.A.2 Understand that a set of data collected to answer a statistical question has a distribution which can be described by its center, spread, and overall shape.

6.SP.A.3 Recognize that a measure of center for a numerical data set summarizes all of its values with a single number, while a measure of variation describes how its values vary with a single number.

ADDITIONAL CLUSTER 6.SP.B
Summarize and describe distributions.

6.SP.B.4 Display numerical data in plots on a number line, including dot plots, histograms, and box plots.

6.SP.B.5 Summarize numerical data sets in relation to their context, such as by:

6.SP.B.5a Reporting the number of observations.

6.SP.B.5b Describing the nature of the attribute under investigation, including how it was measured and its units of measurement.

6.SP.B.5c Giving quantitative measures of center (median and/or mean) and variability (interquartile range and/or mean absolute deviation), as well as describing any overall pattern and any striking deviations from the overall pattern with reference to the context in which the data were gathered.

6.SP.B.5d Relating the choice of measures of center and variability to the shape of the data distribution and the context in which the data were gathered.

Math Practices and Problem Solving Handbook

CONTENTS

Common Core State Standards

Standards for Mathematical Practice

MP.1 Make sense of problems and persevere in solving them.

Mathematically proficient students:

- can explain the meaning of a problem
- look for entry points to begin solving a problem
- analyze givens, constraints, relationships, and goals
- make conjectures about the solution
- plan a solution pathway
- think of similar problems, and try simpler forms of the problem
- evaluate their progress toward a solution and change pathways if necessary
- can explain similarities and differences between different representations
- check their solutions to problems.

MP.2 Reason abstractly and quantitatively.

Mathematically proficient students:

- make sense of quantities and their relationships in problem situations:
  - They *decontextualize*—create a coherent representation of a problem situation using numbers, variables, and symbols; and
  - They *contextualize* – attend to the meaning of numbers, variables, and symbols in the problem situation
- know and use different properties of operations to solve problems.

MP.3 Construct viable arguments and critique the reasoning of others.

Mathematically proficient students:

- use definitions and problem solutions when constructing arguments
- make conjectures about the solutions to problems
- build a logical progression of statements to support their conjectures and justify their conclusions
- analyze situations and recognize and use counterexamples
- reason inductively about data, making plausible arguments that take into account the context from which the data arose
- listen or read the arguments of others, and decide whether they make sense
- respond to the arguments of others
- compare the effectiveness of two plausible arguments
- distinguish correct logic or reasoning from flawed, and—if there is a flaw in an argument—explain what it is
- ask useful questions to clarify or improve arguments of others.

MP.4 Model with mathematics.

Mathematically proficient students:

- can develop a representation—drawing, diagram, table, graph, expression, equation–to model a problem situation
- make assumptions and approximations to simplify a complicated situation
- identify important quantities in a practical situation and map their relationships using a range of tools
- analyze relationships mathematically to draw conclusions
- interpret mathematical results in the context of the situation and propose improvements to the model as needed.

MP.5 Use appropriate tools strategically.

Mathematically proficient students:

- consider appropriate tools when solving a mathematical problem
- make sound decisions about when each of these tools might be helpful
- identify relevant mathematical resources, and use them to pose or solve problems
- use tools and technology to explore and deepen their understanding of concepts.

MP.6 Attend to precision.

Mathematically proficient students:

- communicate precisely to others
- use clear definitions in discussions with others and in their own reasoning
- state the meaning of the symbols they use
- specify units of measure, and label axes to clarify their correspondence with quantities in a problem
- calculate accurately and efficiently
- express numerical answers with a degree of precision appropriate for the problem context.

MP.7 Look for and make use of structure.

Mathematically proficient students:

- look closely at a problem situation to identify a pattern or structure
- can step back from a solution pathway and shift perspective
- can see complex representations, such as some algebraic expressions, as single objects or as being composed of several objects.

MP.8 Look for and express regularity in repeated reasoning.

Mathematically proficient students:

- notice if calculations are repeated, and look both for general methods and for shortcuts
- maintain oversight of the process as they work to solve a problem, while also attending to the details
- continually evaluate the reasonableness of their intermediate results.

MP.1 Make sense of problems and persevere in solving them.

Jon earns $15.50 per week for helping his dad deliver newspapers. He has helped his dad for 3 weeks. Jon uses part of his earnings to buy a new video game that costs $42.39, including tax. How much of his earnings does he have left?

What am I asked to find? How much money Jon has left.

What are the quantities and variables? How do they relate? The cost of the video game is an expense.

The amount Jon earned by helping his father is income.

What can I do if I get stuck? Start by finding out how much money Jon earned in two weeks, then in three weeks.

What is a good plan for solving the problem? Find the total Jon earned in three weeks. Then subtract the cost of the video game.

Other questions to consider:

- **Have I solved a similar problem before?**
- **What information is necessary and what is unnecessary?**
- **How can I check that my answer makes sense?**
- **How is my solution pathway the same as or different from my classmate's?**

MP.2 Reason abstractly and quantitatively.

Next, Jon decides that he wants to save for a new bicycle that costs $210. He will also need to pay sales tax of $13.13. How many weeks will he need to work to earn enough for the bike?

How can I represent this problem situation using numbers, variables, and symbols? I can write an equation with a variable for the number of weeks Jon needs to work.

What do the numbers, variables, and symbols in the expression or equation mean/represent in the problem situation? 15.5*x* represents the amount Jon earns after *x* weeks.

210 + 13.13 = 223.13
the total cost of the bike
223.13 = 15.5x
14.40 = x
the number of weeks Jon needs to help his father
Jon needs to work 15 weeks to earn enough money

Math Practices and Problem Solving Handbook

MP.3 Construct viable arguments and critique the reasoning of others.

Jacie needs to buy 24 drinks for an after-school club. She can buy a 6-pack of juice drinks for $4.50 or an 8-pack of juice drinks for $6.25. Which packs of juice should she buy?

The 8-pack is a better deal. I need to buy 3 8-packs. If I bought the 6-packs, I would need to buy 4.

What assumptions can I make when constructing an argument? The unit prices for a 6-pack and an 8-pack may be the same or different.

What questions can I ask to understand other people's thinking? Why does Jacie think the cost of 3 8-packs will be less than 4 6-packs?

What flaw, if any, do I note in her thinking? She didn't take into account the unit price for each option.

How can I justify my conclusions? I can find the total cost of 4 6-packs and 3 8-packs.

Other questions to consider:

- How can I determine the accuracy (truth) of my conjectures?
- What arguments can I present to defend my conjectures?
- What conjectures can I make about the solution to the problem?
- Which argument do I find more plausible?

MP.4 Model with mathematics.

What representation can I use to show the relationships between quantities and variables?
A double number line can help me see the relationships between quantities.

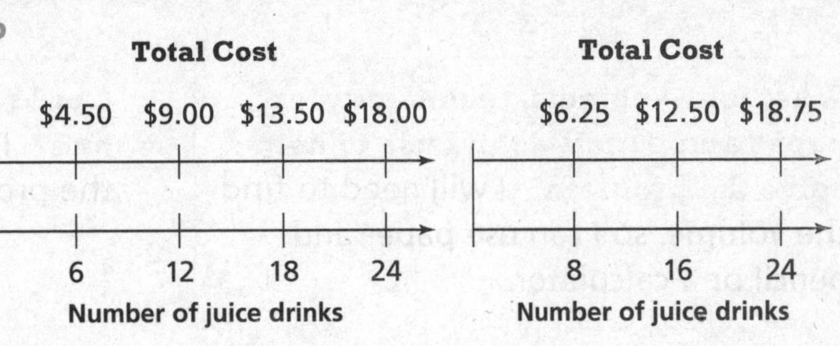

Other questions to consider:

- **Can I use a drawing, diagram, table, graph, or equation to model the problem?**
- **How can I make my model better if it doesn't work?**
- **What assumptions can I make about the problem situation to simplify the problem?**
- **Does my solution or prediction make sense?**
- **Is there something I have not considered or forgotten?**

MP.5 Use appropriate tools strategically.

Maddy's father makes and sells custom golf balls. Each golf ball is packaged in a specially designed $1\frac{1}{2}$-inch cube. He needs to order shipping boxes to ship 12, 18, and 24 balls. What should be the dimensions of the different shipping boxes?

What tool—objects, technology, or paper and pencil—can I use to help solve the problem? I will need to find the volume, so I can use paper and pencil or a calculator.

Could I use a different tool? Which one? I could build cubes to model the problem situation.

Other questions to consider:

- How can technology help me with a solution strategy?
- What other resources can I use to help me reach and understand my solution?

Math Practices and Problem Solving Handbook

MP.6 Attend to precision.

Have I stated the meaning of the variables and symbols I am using? I'm looking for volume, so the variables in my equation represent the dimensions of the shipping boxes.

Have I specified the units of measure I am using? The units in the problem are inches and volume is cubic inches, so I need to specify cubic inches in my solution.

Have I calculated accurately? I can check my worked-out solution on a calculator.

Other questions to consider:

- **Is my work precise/exact enough?**
- **Am I using the definitions precisely?**
- **Did I provide carefully formulated explanations?**
- **Am I using accurate vocabulary to communicate my reasoning?**

MP.7 Look for and make use of structure.

A rancher is building a fence on a 200-foot stretch of field. He has 30 posts and 225 feet of fencing. He plans to place one post every 6 feet. Will he have enough posts to build the fence as planned?

Can I see a pattern or structure in the problem or solution strategy?
I can see that one post is needed for every 6 feet.

How can I use the pattern or structure I see to help me solve the problem?
I can write an equation that finds the number of posts needed for 200 feet.

Other questions to consider:

- Are there attributes in common that help me?
- Can I see the expression or equation as a single object or as a composition of several objects?

MP.8 Look for and express regularity in repeated reasoning.

Do I notice any repeated calculations or steps? Each post covers a 6-foot distance.

Are there general methods that I can use to solve the problem? I can divide the total distance to be fenced by the distance between posts.

Other questions to consider:

- **What can I generalize from one problem to another?**
- **Can I derive an equation from a series of data points?**
- **How reasonable are the results that I am getting?**

Bar Diagrams with Operations

You can draw bar diagrams to show how quantities are related and to write an equation to solve the problem.

Add To

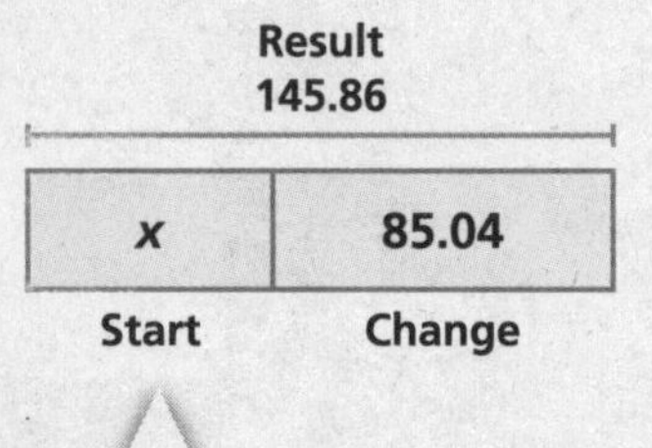

The start is unknown, so this is a variable.

Take From

The start is unknown, so this is a variable.

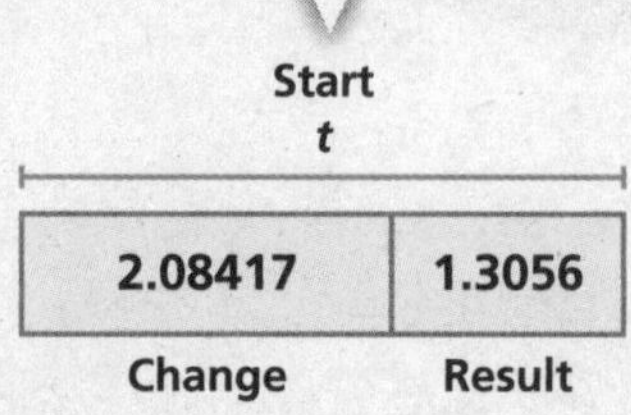

Put Together/Take Apart

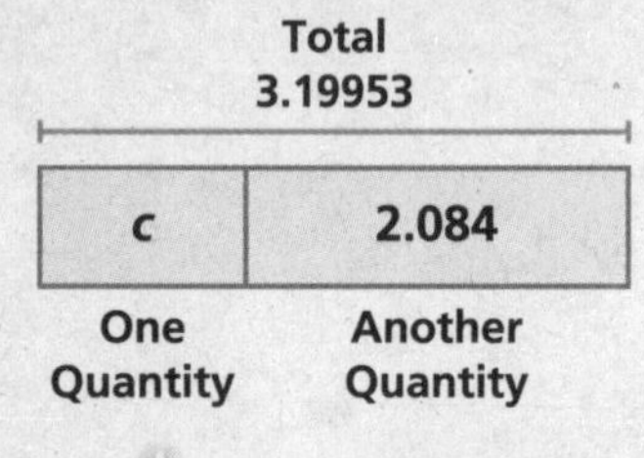

One of the quantities is unknown, so this is a variable.

Compare: Addition and Subtraction

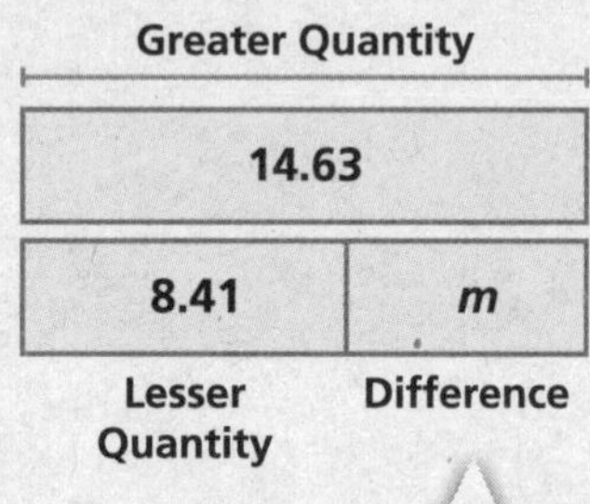

The difference is unknown, so this is a variable.

Equal Groups: Multiplication and Division

The number of equal groups is unknown, so this is a variable.

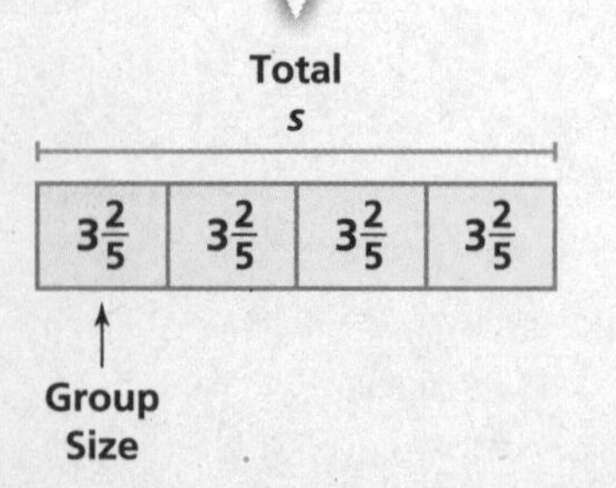

Compare: Multiplication and Division

The bigger quantity is unknown, so this is a variable.

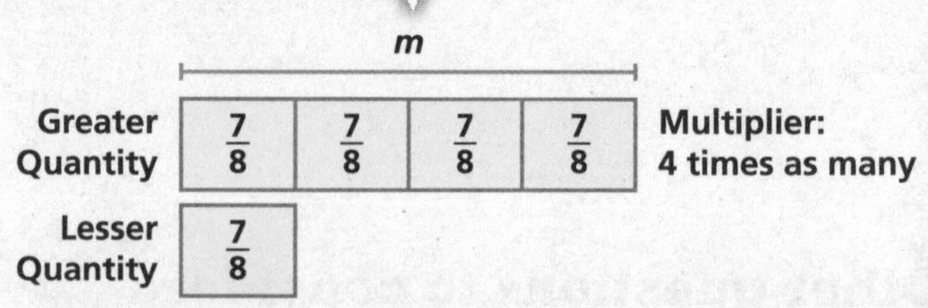

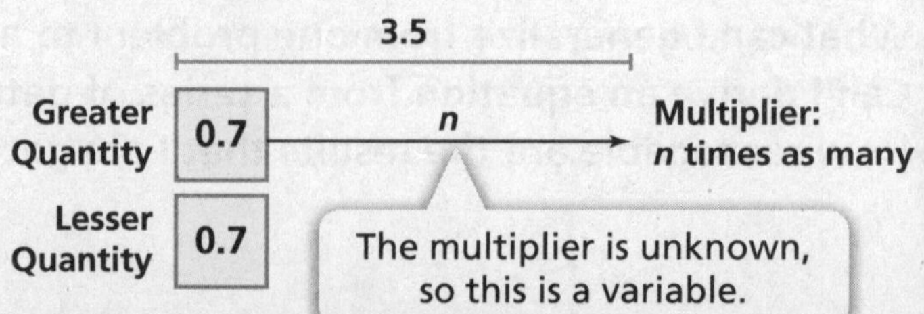

The multiplier is unknown, so this is a variable.

Bar Diagrams in Proportional Reasoning

You can draw bar diagrams to show how quantities are related in proportional relationships.

Ratios and Rates

Draw this bar diagram to show ratios and rates.

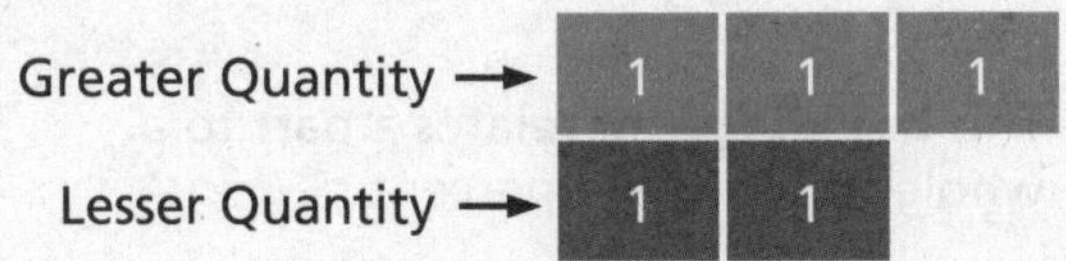

This **bar diagram** represents the ratio **3 : 2**.

Greater Quantity Unknown

For every 3 cashews in a snack mix, there are 5 almonds. A package contains 42 cashews. How many almonds are in the same package?

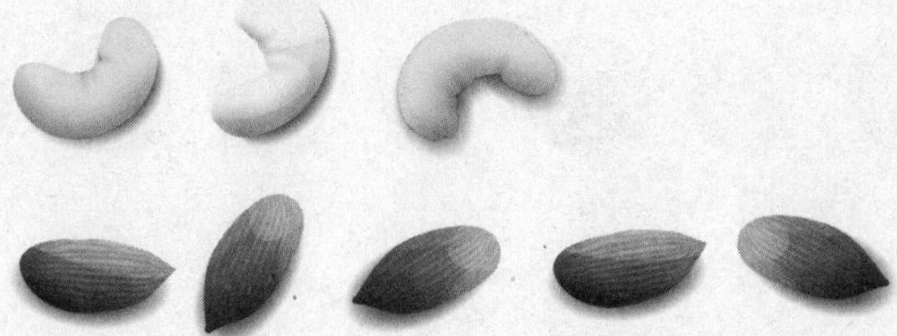

Draw a bar diagram to represent the ratio of cashews to almonds.

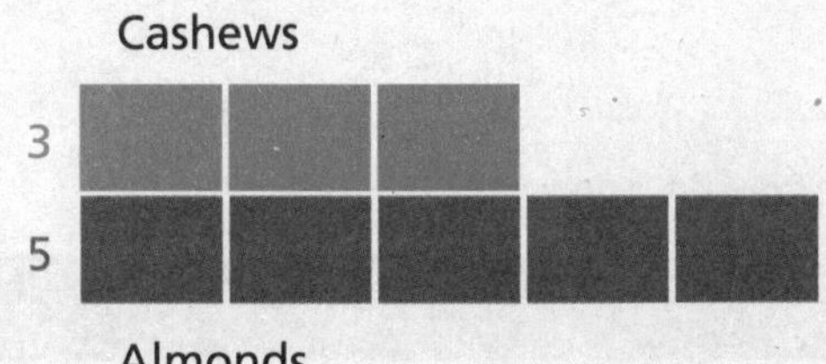

Use the same diagram to represent 42 cashews and to determine the number of almonds.

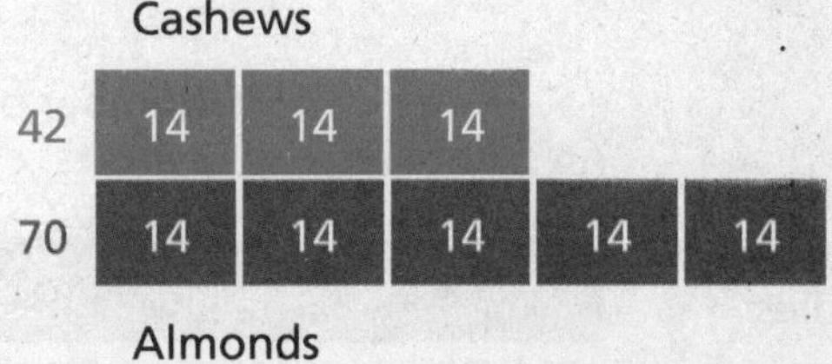

There are 70 almonds in the package.

Math Practices and Problem Solving Handbook BAR DIAGRAMS

Bar Diagrams in Proportional Reasoning

You can draw bar diagrams to show how quantities are related in proportional relationships.

Percents

Draw this bar diagram to show percents.

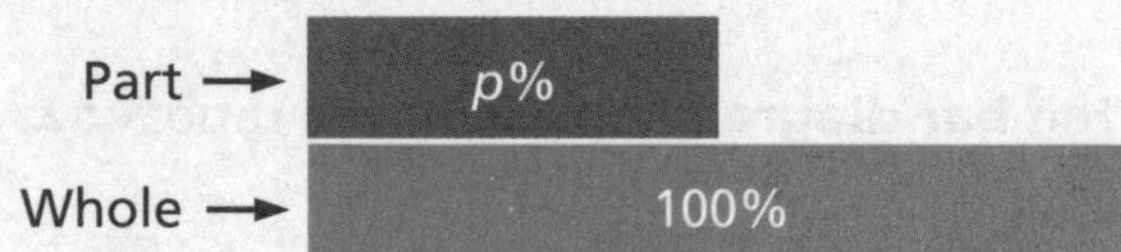

This **bar diagram** relates a part to a whole to represent percent.

Part Unknown

A candy company creates batches of colored candies so that, on average, 30% of the candies are orange. About how many orange candies should be included in a batch of 1,500 candies?

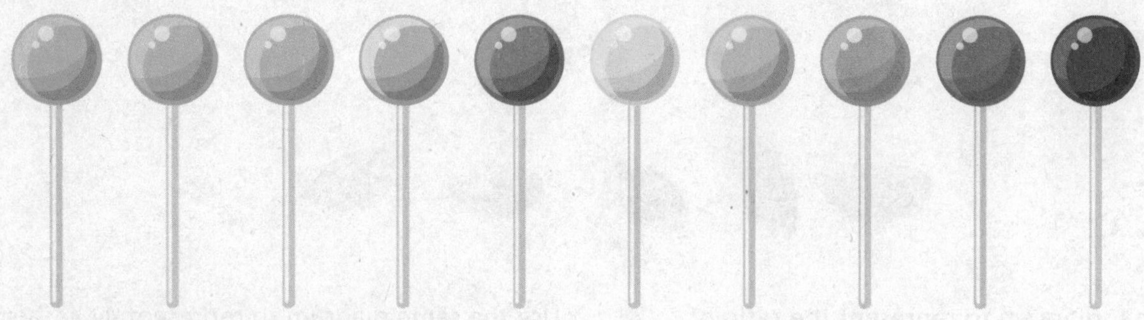

Use the bar diagram to write an equation.

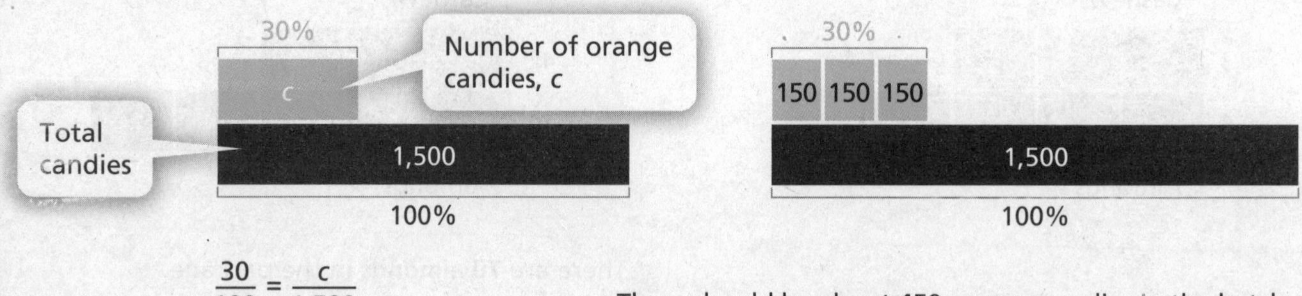

$$\frac{30}{100} = \frac{c}{1{,}500}$$

There should be about 450 orange candies in the batch.

Bar Diagrams in Quantitative Reasoning

You can use bar diagrams to solve one-variable equations.

Solve for x: $2x + 5 = 19$

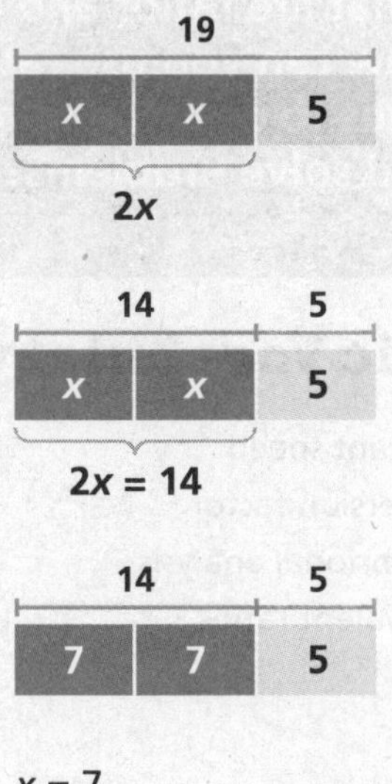

$x = 7$

Solve for y: $4(y - 2) = 24$

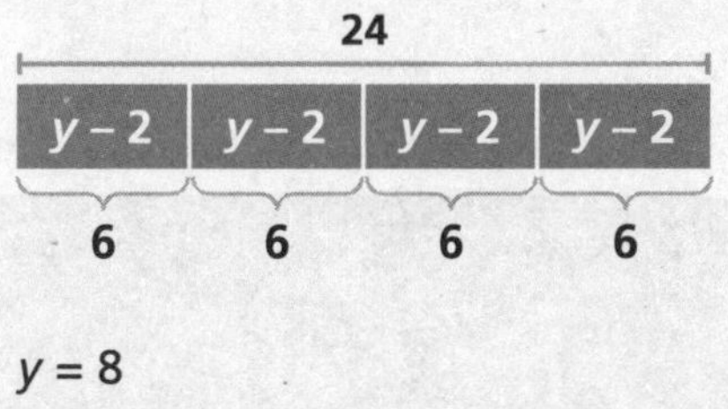

$y = 8$

Solve for m: $4m + 2 = 3m + 4$

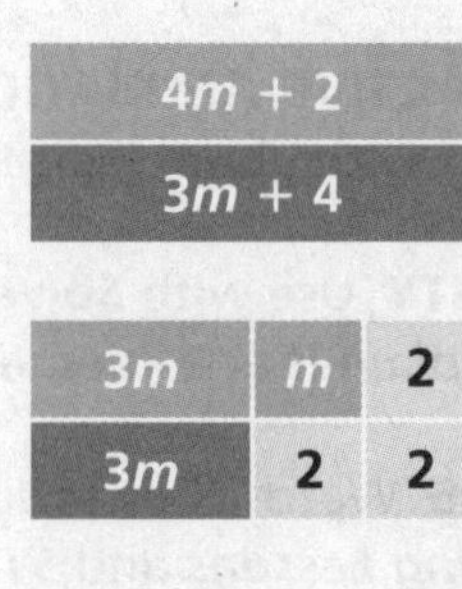

$m = 2$

Andy's brother can spend \$80 each month on his cable bill. The local cable company charges a \$45 monthly fee for basic cable and \$8 per month for each premium channel a customer orders.

How many premium channels can Andy's brother order?

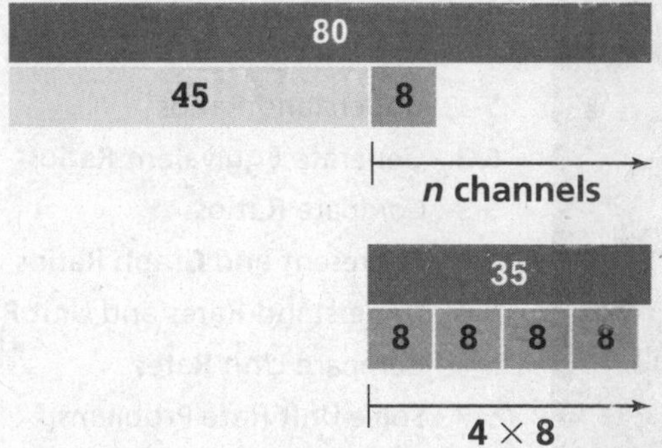

He can order 4 premium channels.

Ella opens a savings account with the \$150 she got for her birthday. She plans to deposit \$25 each month.

Assuming she does not withdraw any money, how much will she have saved after 2 years?

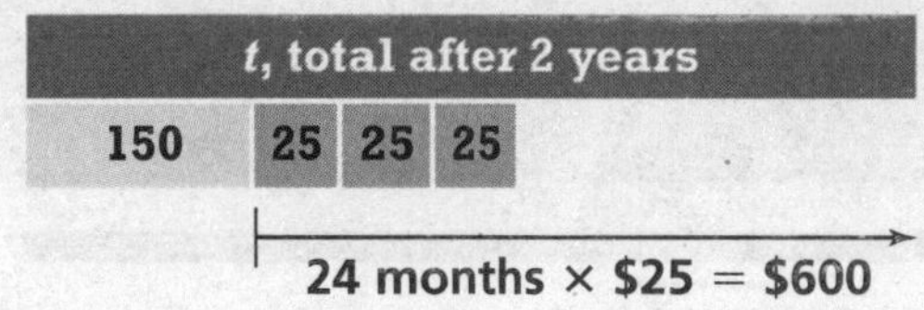

24 months × \$25 = \$600

\$600 + \$150 = \$750

She will have saved \$750 after 2 years.

TOPIC 5

UNDERSTAND AND USE RATIO AND RATE

? Topic Essential Question

What are ratios and rates? How can you use ratios and rates to describe quantities and solve problems?

Topic Overview

- 5-1 Understand Ratios
- 5-2 Generate Equivalent Ratios
- 5-3 Compare Ratios
- 5-4 Represent and Graph Ratios
- 5-5 Understand Rates and Unit Rates
- 5-6 Compare Unit Rates
- 5-7 Solve Unit Rate Problems
- 3-Act Mathematical Modeling: Get in Line
- 5-8 Ratio Reasoning: Convert Customary Units
- 5-9 Ratio Reasoning: Convert Metric Units
- 5-10 Relate Customary and Metric Units

Topic Vocabulary

- constant speed
- conversion factor
- dimensional analysis
- equivalent ratios
- rate
- ratio
- term
- unit price
- unit rate

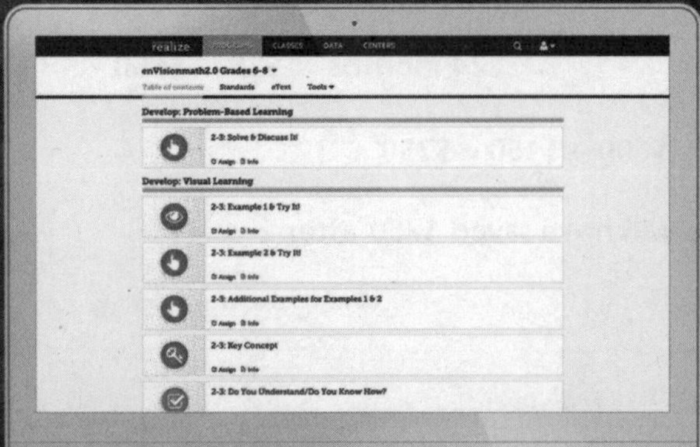

Go online | **PearsonRealize.com**

Lesson Digital Resources

INTERACTIVE ANIMATION Interact with visual learning animations.

ACTIVITY Use with ***Solve & Discuss It***, ***Explore*** and ***Explain It*** activities, and to explore Exampl

VIDEOS Watch clips to support ***3-Act Mathem*** ***Modeling Lessons*** and ***STEM Projects***.

PRACTICE Practice what you've learned.

Get in Line

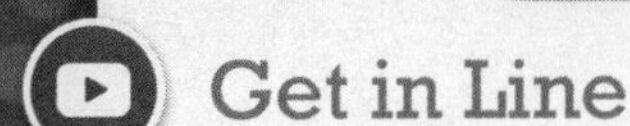

Get in Line

It is hard to call it a freeway when you are stuck in the middle of a traffic jam. To keep vehicles moving on the freeway, some on-ramps have traffic signals. Controlling when cars enter the freeway is not only about reducing delays. It can decrease air pollution and collisions.

These ramp meters typically have alternating green and red lights. The time for one cycle depends on the time of day and the amount of traffic on the freeway. Think about this during the 3-Act Mathematical Modeling lesson.

TUTORIALS Get help from ***Virtual Nerd***, right when you need it.

KEY CONCEPT Review important lesson content.

GLOSSARY Read and listen to English/Spanish definitions.

ASSESSMENT Show what you've learned.

Additional Digital Resources

MATH TOOLS Explore math with digital tools.

GAMES Play Math Games to help you learn.

ETEXT Interact with your Student's Edition online.

TOPIC 5

STEM Project

Did You Know?

Gears are found in the mechanisms of many common objects, such as cars, bicycles, analog watches, and wind turbines.

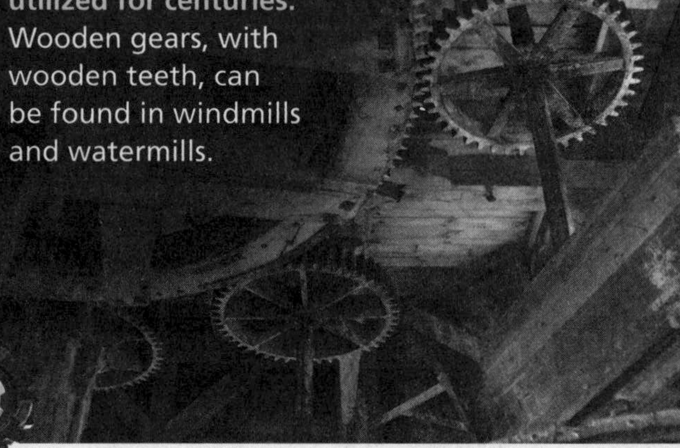
Gears have been utilized for centuries. Wooden gears, with wooden teeth, can be found in windmills and watermills.

Gears have equally spaced teeth that enable them to interlock with other gears.

The gears of a bicycle are connected and driven by a chain.

Bicycles often have multiple gears that allow riders to make adjustments to power output and speed.

Riders back in the 19th century were not as lucky—no gears meant a lot of pedaling!

Your Task: Get into Gear

Cyclists strive to achieve efficiency during continuous riding. But, which pairing of gears is the best or most efficient? And does the answer change depending on the terrain? You and your classmates will explore gear ratios and how they can affect pedaling and riding speeds.

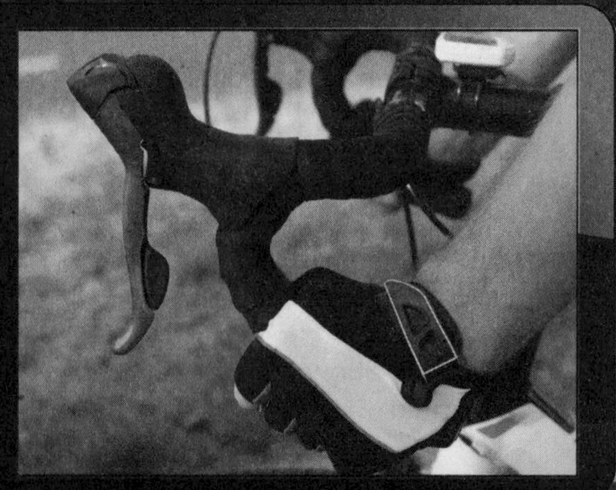

Review What You Know!

Vocabulary

Choose the best term from the box to complete each definition.

common factor
common multiple
equivalent fractions
fraction

1. Fractions that name the same amount are called equivalent fractions.

2. The number 3 is a common factor of 9 and 12.

3. A number that can be used to describe a part of a set or a part of a whole is a(n) common multiple.

Equivalent Fractions

Write two fractions equivalent to the given fraction.

4. $\frac{3}{4}$ **5.** $\frac{7}{8}$ **6.** $\frac{12}{5}$

7. $\frac{1}{2}$ **8.** $\frac{8}{9}$ **9.** $\frac{2}{3}$

Equations

Write an equation that represents the pattern in each table.

10.

x	2	3	4	5	6
y	16	24	32	40	48

11.

x	2	4	6	8	10
y	5	7	9	11	13

Units of Measure

Choose the best unit of measure by writing *inch, foot, yard, ounce, pound, ton, cup, quart,* or *gallon*.

12. serving of trail mix **13.** height of a person

14. weight of a newborn kitten **15.** gasoline

Measurement Conversions

16. Michael is 4 feet tall. Explain how Michael could find his height in inches. Then explain how he could find his height in yards.

Prepare for Reading Success

Before you begin the topic, predict whether each statement is true or false. Write *True* or *False* in the first column. After you finish each lesson, write *True* or *False* in the second column based on what you learned. When you finish the topic, see how many of your predictions were correct.

Prediction	Text	Statement
__________	__________	5-1 When writing a ratio, order does not matter. The ratio of dogs to cats is the same as the ratio of cats to dogs.
__________	__________	5-2 You can use a table to find equivalent ratios.
__________	__________	5-3 You can only compare part to whole ratios, not part to part ratios.
__________	__________	5-4 The ratio 5:2 can be represented as the ordered pair (5, 2).
__________	__________	5-5 A unit rate is a rate in which the first term is 1.
__________	__________	5-6 A rate of 5 miles in 2 minutes is faster than a rate of 4 miles in 1 minute.
__________	__________	5-7 You can use the unit price for oranges in dollars per pound to find the price of 10 pounds of oranges.
__________	__________	5-8 One method for converting customary units is to use dimensional analysis.
__________	__________	5-9 The methods for converting metric units are the same as the methods for converting customary units.
__________	__________	5-10 When converting between customary and metric units, all conversions will be approximate.

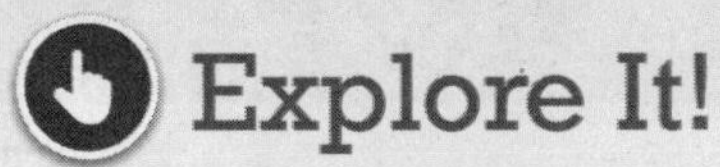

Explore It!

Lesson 5-1 Understand Ratios

Go Online | PearsonRealize.com

I can...
use a ratio to describe the relationship between two quantities.

Common Core Content Standards
6.RP.A.1, 6.RP.A.3

Mathematical Practices
MP.1, MP.2, MP.3, MP.4

A band just released an album that contains both pop songs and R&B (rhythm and blues) songs.

BEST OF THE 90's
Pop
1 British Pop
2 Chamber Pop
3 Dance Pop
4 Dream Pop
5 Electro Pop
6 Orchestral
7 Pop/Rock
8 Soft Rock
9 Teen Pop
R&B
10 Contemporary
11 Funk
12 Modern Soul
13 Motown
14 Psychedelic Soul
15 Soul Blues
POP and R&B

A. How can you describe the relationship between the number of pop songs and the number of R&B songs on the album?

B. How does the bar diagram represent the relationship between the number of pop songs and the number of R&B songs?

Pop Songs | | |
R&B Songs | |

Focus on math practices

Reasoning Another album has 2 pop songs and 10 R&B songs. Draw a bar diagram that you could use to represent the relationship between the number of pop songs and the number of R&B songs. MP.2

Essential Question What is a mathematical way to compare quantities?

EXAMPLE 1  Write Ratios to Compare Quantities

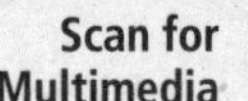
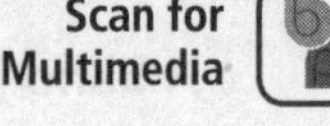

Tom's Pet Service takes care of cats and dogs. Currently, there are more dogs than cats. Compare the number of cats to the number of dogs. Then compare the number of cats to the total number of pets at Tom's Pet Service.

A **ratio** is a relationship in which for every x units of one quantity there are y units of another quantity.

A ratio can be written three ways.

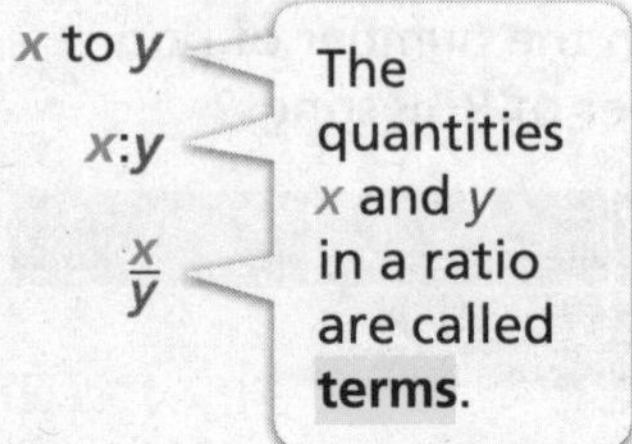

x to y
x:y
$\frac{x}{y}$
The quantities x and y in a ratio are called **terms**.

Use a ratio to compare the number of cats to the number of dogs.

14 to 17

14:17

$\frac{14}{17}$

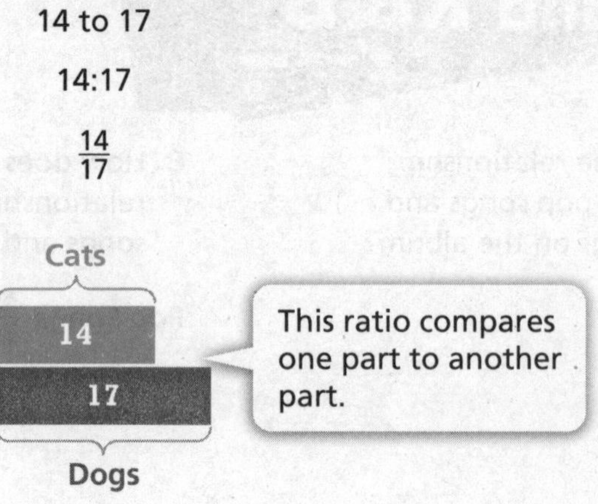

Use a ratio to compare the number of cats to the total number of pets.

14 to 31

14:31

$\frac{14}{31}$

Cats

14	
14	17

Total Number of Pets

This ratio compares one part to the whole.

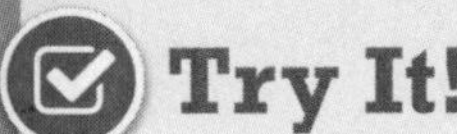 Try It!

What are three ways to write the ratio of the number of dogs to the total number of pets?

Convince Me! Is the ratio of dogs to cats the same as the ratio of cats to dogs? Explain.

EXAMPLE 2  Use a Bar Diagram to Solve a Ratio Problem

ACTIVITY ASSESS

The ratio of footballs to soccer balls at a sporting goods store is 5 to 3. If the store has 100 footballs in stock, how many soccer balls does it have?

Use a bar diagram to show the ratio 5:3.

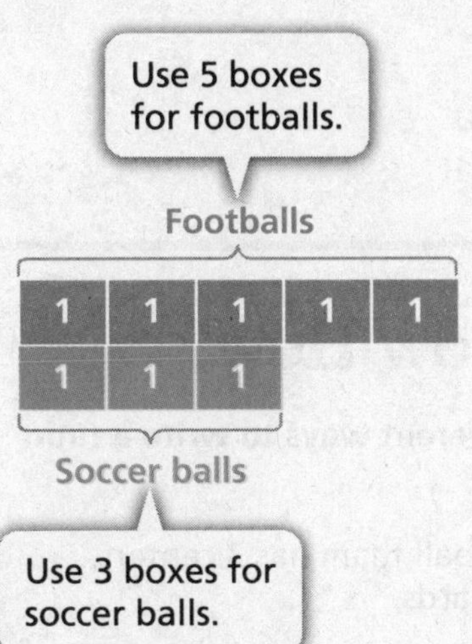

Use the same diagram to represent 100 footballs.

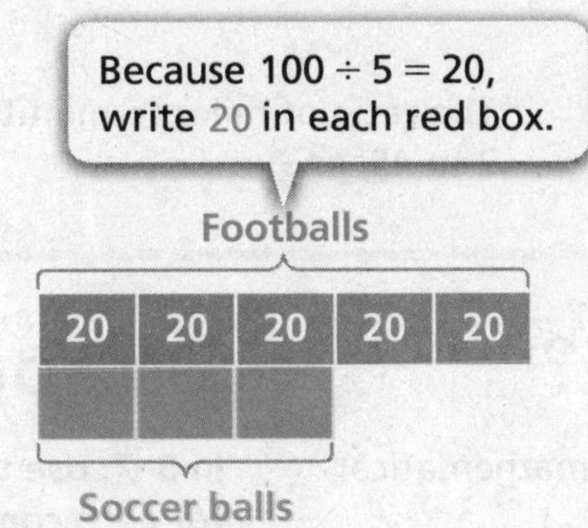

Each box represents the same value. Write 20 in each green box.

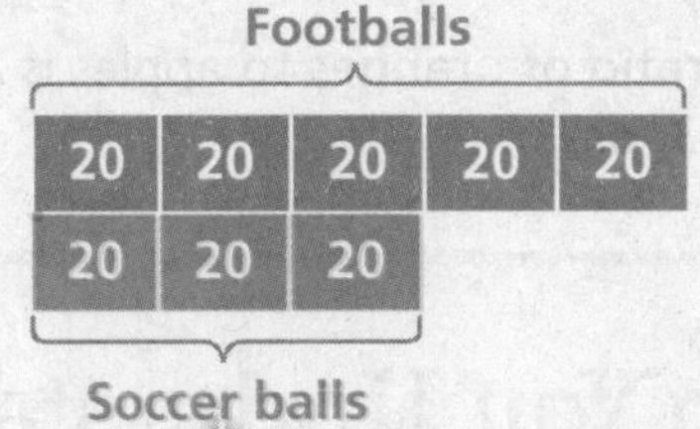

There are 3 green boxes, so the total number of soccer balls is 3×20, or 60.

The sporting goods store has 60 soccer balls in stock.

EXAMPLE 3  Use a Double Number Line Diagram to Solve a Ratio Problem

Chen can ride his bike 3 miles in 15 minutes. At this rate, how long will it take Chen to ride his bike 18 miles?

Use a double number line diagram. Show 15 minutes for every 3 miles.

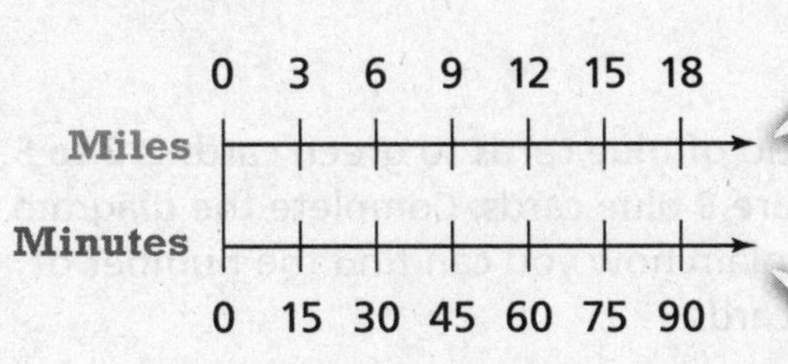

Count by 3s along the top number line until you get to 18 miles.

Count by 15s for the same number of spaces along the bottom number line.

Chen can ride 18 miles in 90 minutes.

Model with Math A double number line diagram can represent a constant relationship between two values with different units. MP.4

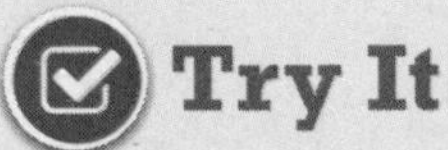

Try It!

Chen's friend Alisa can ride her bike 2 miles in 7 minutes. Use a bar diagram or a double number line diagram to find how long it would take Alisa to ride 10 miles if she rides at the same rate.

KEY CONCEPT

A ratio compares two quantities. A ratio can be written 3 ways: *x* to *y*, *x*:*y*, or $\frac{x}{y}$. Ratios can be represented using bar diagrams and double number line diagrams.

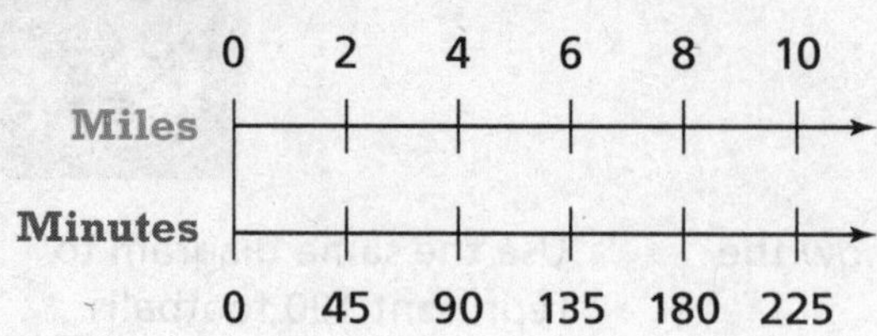

The ratio of oranges to apples is 2:3, 2 to 3, or $\frac{2}{3}$.

The ratio of miles to minutes is 2:45, 2 to 45, or $\frac{2}{45}$.

Do You Understand?

1. **Essential Question** What is a mathematical way to compare quantities?

2. **Reasoning** What are two different types of comparisons that a ratio can be used to make? MP.2

3. A science classroom has 5 turtles and 7 frogs. What is the ratio of frogs to total animals?

4. Tye is making trail mix with 3 cups of nuts for every 4 cups of granola. If Tye has 6 cups of nuts, how many cups of granola should he use?

Do You Know How?

In 5–7, use three different ways to write a ratio for each comparison.

A sixth-grade basketball team has 3 centers, 5 forwards, and 6 guards.

5. Forwards to guards

6. Centers to total players

7. Guards to centers

8. The ratio of blue cards to green cards is 2 to 5. There are 8 blue cards. Complete the diagram and explain how you can find the number of green cards.

Blue cards

Green cards

Name:

Practice & Problem Solving

Scan for Multimedia 

In 9–14, use the data to write a ratio for each comparison in three different ways.

A person's blood type is denoted with the letters A, B, and O, and the symbols + and −. The blood type A+ is read as *A positive*. The blood type B− is read as *B negative*.

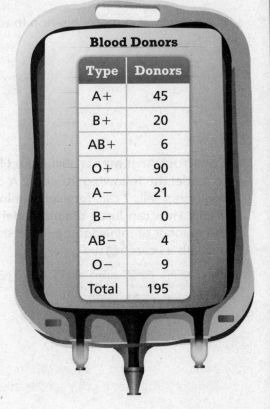

Blood Donors

Type	Donors
A+	45
B+	20
AB+	6
O+	90
A−	21
B−	0
AB−	4
O−	9
Total	195

9. O+ donors to A+ donors

10. AB− donors to AB+ donors

11. B+ donors to total donors

12. O− donors to A− donors

13. A+ and B+ donors to AB+ donors

14. A− and B− donors to AB− donors

15. Which comparison does the ratio $\frac{90}{9}$ represent?

16. Which comparison does the ratio 20:21 represent?

17. Sam is packing gift boxes with fruit. For each apple, he packs 3 plums and 5 oranges. If he puts 3 apples in a box, how many plums and oranges will Sam put in the box? Draw a diagram to solve the problem.

18. Write a ratio that compares the number of teal squares to the total number of squares in the quilt.

19. Reasoning Rita's class has 14 girls and 16 boys. How does the ratio 14:30 describe Rita's class? MP.2

20. A math class surveyed students about their musical preferences and recorded the results in the table. Use the data to write a ratio for each comparison in three different ways.

Favorite Music

Music Type	Number of Students
Rock	10
Classical	4
Techno	12
Hip-Hop	15
Country	8
Alternative	4

a. Students who prefer classical to students who prefer techno

b. Students who prefer hip-hop to total number of students surveyed

21. **Construct Arguments** Justin used blocks to model the following situation: A car dealership sells 7 cars for every 4 minivans it sells. How can Justin use his model to find the number of minivans the dealership sells if it sells 35 cars? MP.3

22. **Make Sense and Persevere** The ratio of adult dogs to puppies at a park on Monday was 3:2. There were 12 puppies there that day. On Tuesday, 15 adult dogs were at the park. What is the difference between the number of adult dogs at the park on Monday and Tuesday? MP.1

23. **Higher Order Thinking** At 9:30 A.M., Sean started filling a swimming pool. At 11:30 A.M., he had filled 1,800 gallons. At what time will the pool be full?

Assessment Practice

24. Of the students taking a foreign language class, 8 students take Spanish for every 5 students who take French. This is represented in the diagram below.

Spanish: 8 boxes
French: 5 boxes

Explain how you can use the diagram to find the number of students who are taking French if there are 72 students taking Spanish.

Lesson 5-2
Generate Equivalent Ratios

Go Online | PearsonRealize.com

I can... use multiplication and division to find equivalent ratios.

Common Core Content Standards
6.RP.A.3a

Mathematical Practices
MP.2, MP.3, MP.5, MP.7, MP.8

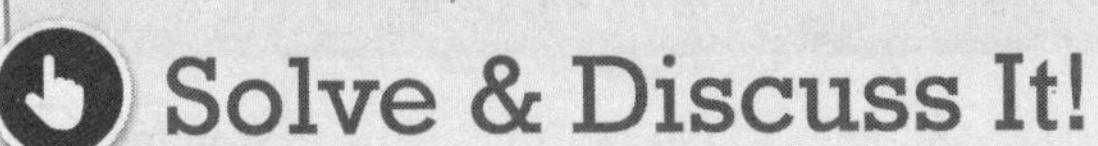

Solve & Discuss It!

Sally used all of the paint shown below to make a certain tint of orange paint. How many pints of red paint should be mixed with 24 pints of yellow paint to make the same tint of orange?

Look for Relationships How can you use the relationship between the number of pints of yellow paint and the number of pints of red paint to answer the question? MP.7

Focus on math practices

Reasoning If Sally uses the same ratio of yellow paint to red paint, how many pints of yellow paint should she mix with 16 pints of red paint? MP.2

Essential Question How can you find equivalent ratios?

EXAMPLE 1  Use Multiplication to Find Equivalent Ratios

Scan for Multimedia 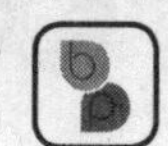

For every 16 basketball players in Crystal County schools, there are 48 soccer players. If the ratio remains constant and there are 64 basketball players, how many soccer players are there?

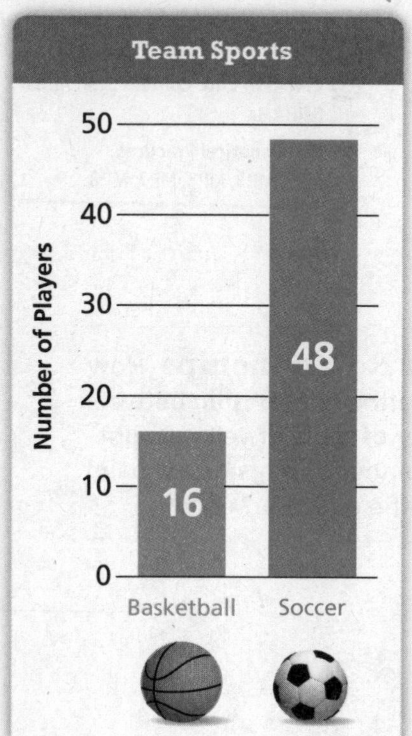

ONE WAY Make a table with equivalent ratios.

Equivalent ratios are ratios that express the same relationship.

Multiply both terms of the original ratio by the same number to find an equivalent ratio.

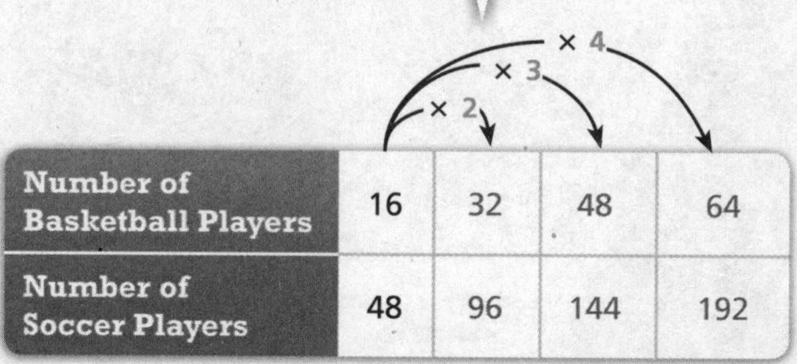

Number of Basketball Players	16	32	48	64
Number of Soccer Players	48	96	144	192

There are 192 soccer players when there are 64 basketball players.

ANOTHER WAY Use multiplication. Multiply both terms by the same nonzero number.

Multiply 16 × 4 for the 64 basketball players.

$$\frac{16 \times 4}{48 \times 4} = \frac{64}{192}$$

Multiply 48 × 4 to find the number of soccer players.

There are 192 soccer players when there are 64 basketball players.

Try It!

If you extend the table above, how would you find the next ratio of basketball players to soccer players? MP.7

Convince Me! What is the relationship between the number of basketball players and the number of soccer players in each column in the table?

EXAMPLE 2  Use Division to Find Equivalent Ratios

ACTIVITY

ASSESS

Sarah made baskets on some of her shots in a basketball game. If she continues to make baskets at the same rate, how many baskets will Sarah make in her next 6 shots?

ONE WAY Make a table with equivalent ratios.

Divide both terms of the original ratio by the same number to find an equivalent ratio.

÷ 3, ÷ 2

Number of Shots Taken	6	9	18
Number of Baskets Made	4	6	12

Sarah will make 4 baskets in her next 6 shots.

ANOTHER WAY Use division.

Reasoning By what number do you need to divide 18 to get 6? Divide 12 by the same number. MP.2

$$\frac{18 \div 3}{12 \div 3} = \frac{6}{4}$$

Divide both terms by the same nonzero number.

Sarah will make 4 baskets in her next 6 shots.

Try It!

Rashida uses 8 cups of tomatoes and 3 cups of onions to make salsa. How many cups of onions should Rashida use if she uses only 4 cups of tomatoes?

EXAMPLE 3  Find Equivalent Ratios

Which of the following ratios are equivalent to 9:12?

3:4, 2:3, 6:9, 12:16

Make tables of equivalent ratios.

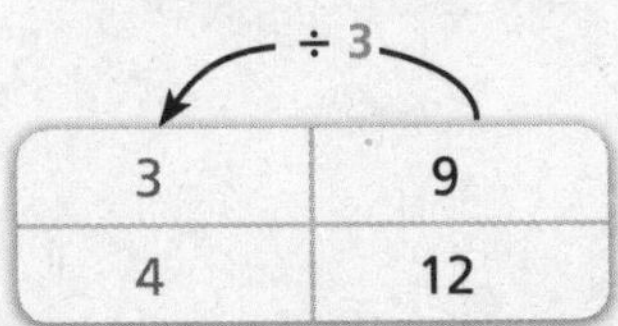

3	9
4	12

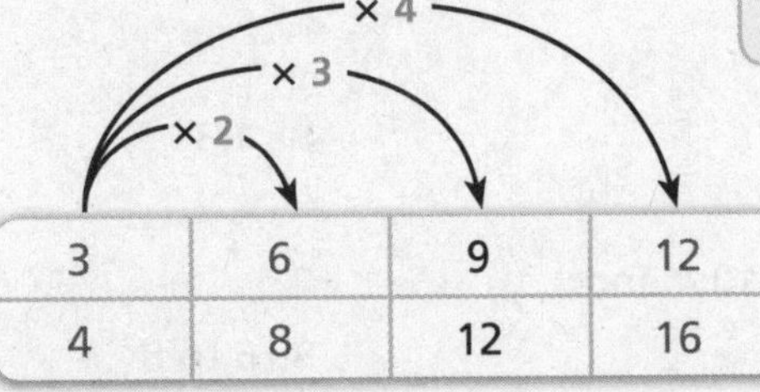

3	6	9	12
4	8	12	16

The ratios 3:4 and 12:16 are equivalent to 9:12.

Generalize If 3:4 is equivalent to 9:12, then any other ratio that is equivalent to 3:4 is also equivalent to 9:12. MP.8

Try It!

Which of the following ratios are equivalent to 16:20?

2:3, 4:5, 18:22, 20:25

KEY CONCEPT

You can multiply or divide both terms of a ratio by the same nonzero number to find equivalent ratios.

Multiply both terms by the same nonzero number.

$$\frac{30 \times 2}{40 \times 2} = \frac{60}{80}$$

Divide both terms by the same nonzero number.

$$\frac{30 \div 10}{40 \div 10} = \frac{3}{4}$$

Do You Understand?

1. **Essential Question** How can you find equivalent ratios?

2. **Critique Reasoning** Deshawn says that the ratios 3:5 and 5:7 are equivalent ratios because by adding 2 to both terms of 3:5 you get 5:7. Is Deshawn correct? Explain. MP.3

3. What are two ways you can find an equivalent ratio for $\frac{12}{16}$?

4. How can you show that the ratios 10:4 and 15:6 are equivalent?

Do You Know How?

5. Complete the table using multiplication to find ratios that are equivalent to 4:5.

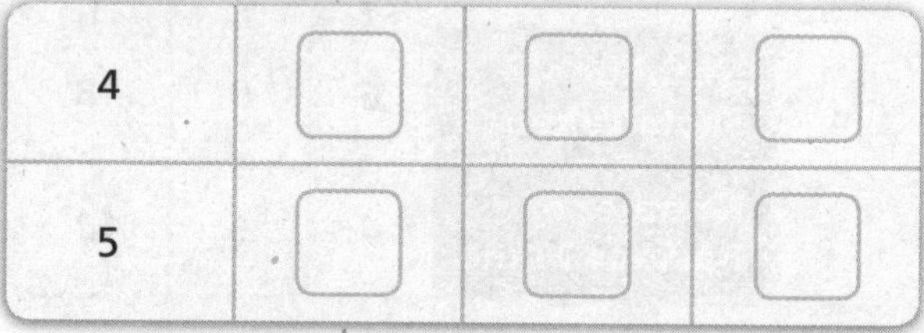

4	☐	☐	☐
5	☐	☐	☐

6. Complete the table using division to find ratios that are equivalent to 40:28.

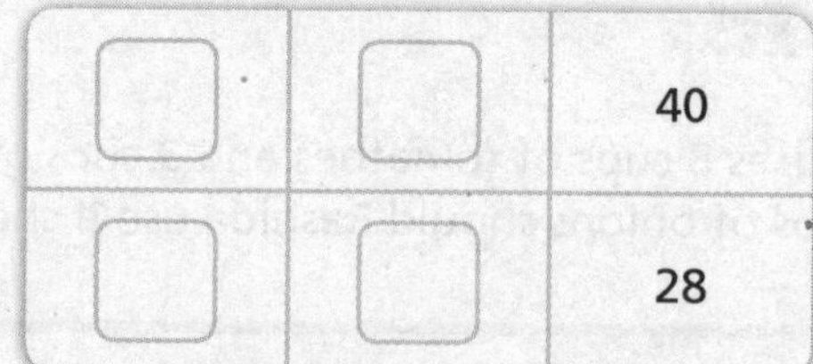

☐	☐	40
☐	☐	28

In 7–10, write an equivalent ratio for each given ratio.

7. $\frac{12}{21}$

8. 1:3

9. 6 to 8

10. 15:10

Name: ____________________

Practice & Problem Solving

Scan for Multimedia

11. Eva is making French toast. How many ounces of milk should Eva use with 10 eggs?

The recipe calls for 5 ounces of milk for every 2 eggs.

Milk (oz)	5	☐	☐	☐	☐
Eggs	2	4	6	8	10

In 12–15, write three ratios that are equivalent to the given ratio.

12. $\frac{6}{7}$

13. $\frac{9}{5}$

14. 8:14

15. 7:9

16. A teacher kept track of what students consumed at a school picnic. For three grades, the ratios of the amount of water consumed to the amount of fruit juice consumed were equivalent. Complete the table.

Grade	Water (gallons)	Juice (gallons)
5th	6	7
6th	24	☐
7th	18	☐

17. The attendant at a parking lot compared the number of hybrid vehicles to the total number of vehicles in the lot during a weekend. The ratios for the three days were equivalent. Complete the table.

Day	Hybrids	Total
Fri.	4	9
Sat.	☐	63
Sun.	32	☐

18. Shiloh is sharing jellybeans. The jar of jellybeans has the ratio shown. If Shiloh keeps the ratio the same and gives his friend 7 pink jellybeans, how many green jellybeans should he also share?

32 green jellybeans
56 pink jellybeans
Jellybeans

Green Jellybeans	☐	☐	☐	32
Pink Jellybeans	7	☐	☐	56

19. **Use Appropriate Tools** Equivalent ratios can be found by extending pairs of rows or columns in a multiplication table. Write three ratios equivalent to $\frac{2}{5}$ using the multiplication table. MP.5

X	0	1	2	3	4	5	6
0	0	0	0	0	0	0	0
1	0	1	2	3	4	5	6
2	0	2	4	6	8	10	12
3	0	3	6	9	12	15	18
4	0	4	8	12	16	20	24
5	0	5	10	15	20	25	30
6	0	6	12	18	24	30	36

20. If 5 mi ≈ 8 km, about how many miles would be equal to 50 km? Explain.

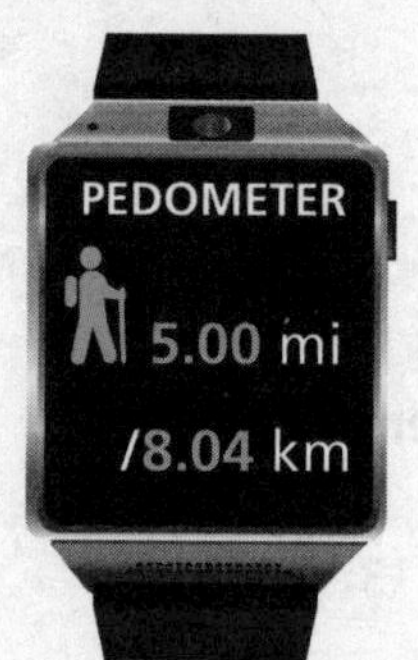

21. **Vocabulary** How is the word *term* defined when used to describe a ratio relationship? How is the word *term* defined in the context of an expression?

22. **Higher Order Thinking** Three sisters are saving for a special vacation. The ratio of Ada's savings to Ellie's savings is 7:3, and the ratio of Ellie's savings to Jasmine's savings is 3:4. Together all three girls have saved $56. How much has each girl saved? Complete the table. Explain how the table can be used to solve the problem.

Ada's savings	$7	☐	$21	☐
Ellie's savings	☐	$6	☐	☐
Jasmine's savings	$4	☐	☐	$16

Assessment Practice

23. Select all the ratios that are equivalent to 18:8.

☐ 9:4

☐ 6:3

☐ $\frac{48}{24}$

☐ $\frac{90}{40}$

☐ 36 to 16

24. Select all the ratios that are equivalent to 3:5.

☐ 5 to 7

☐ 2:4

☐ 9:15

☐ $\frac{18}{30}$

☐ 5:3

Lesson 5-3
Compare Ratios

Go Online | PearsonRealize.com

I can...
compare ratios to solve problems.

Common Core Content Standards
6.RP.A.3a
Mathematical Practices
MP.2, MP.4, MP.7

Solve & Discuss It!

ACTIVITY

Scott is making a snack mix using almonds and raisins. For every 2 cups of almonds in the snack mix, there are 3 cups of raisins. Ariel is making a snack mix that has 3 cups of almonds for every 5 cups of sunflower seeds. If Scott and Ariel each use 6 cups of almonds to make a batch of snack mix, who will make a larger batch?

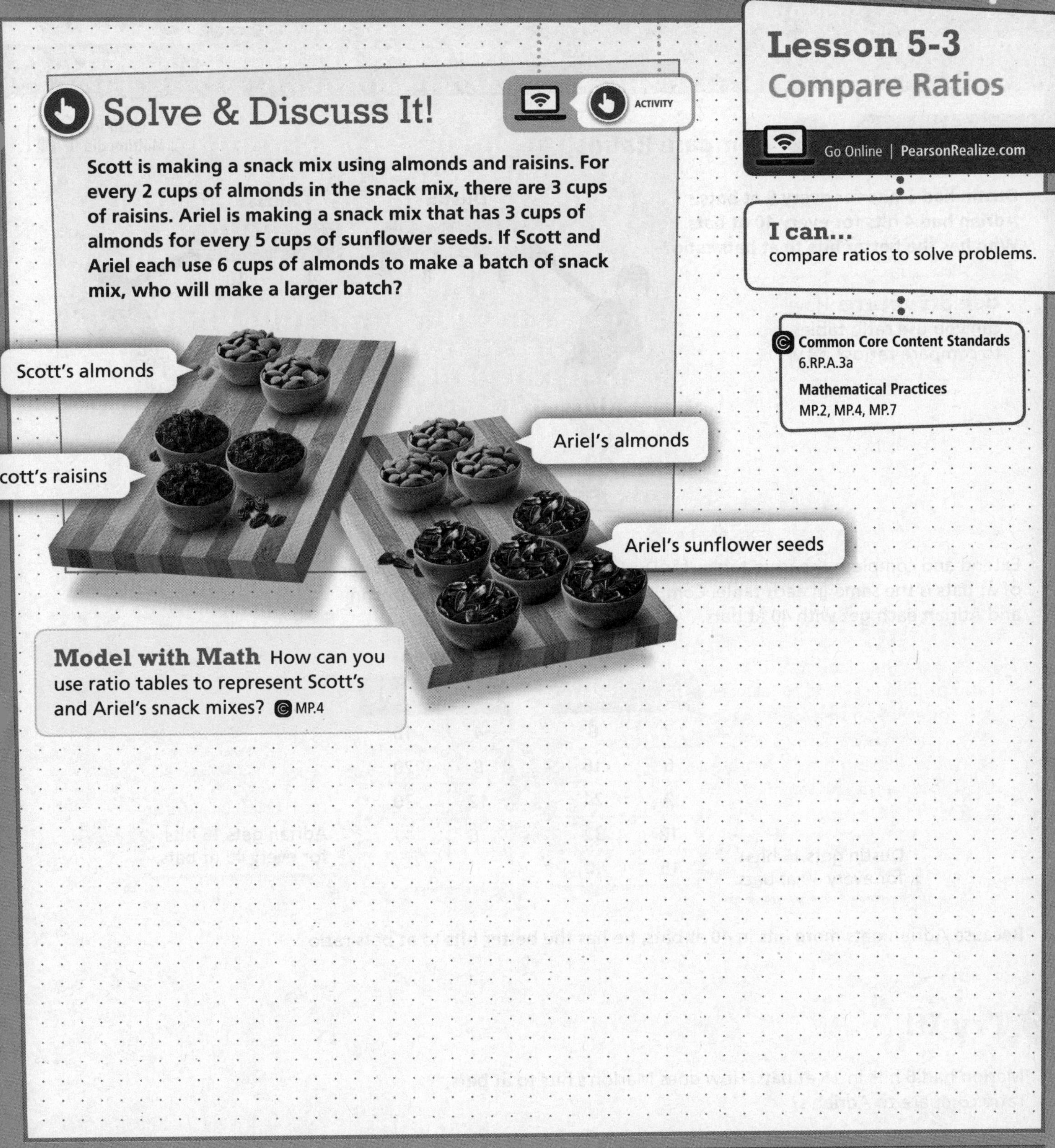

Model with Math How can you use ratio tables to represent Scott's and Ariel's snack mixes? MP.4

Focus on math practices

Look for Relationships Scott and Ariel want to make as much snack mix as possible, but no more than 25 cups of mix. If they can use only full cups of ingredients, who can make more mix without going over? MP.7

? Essential Question How can you compare ratios to solve a problem?

INTERACTIVE ANIMATION

ASSESS

EXAMPLE 1  Compare Ratios

Scan for Multimedia 

Dustin had 3 hits for every 8 at bats. Adrian had 4 hits for every 10 at bats. Who has the better hits to at bats ratio?

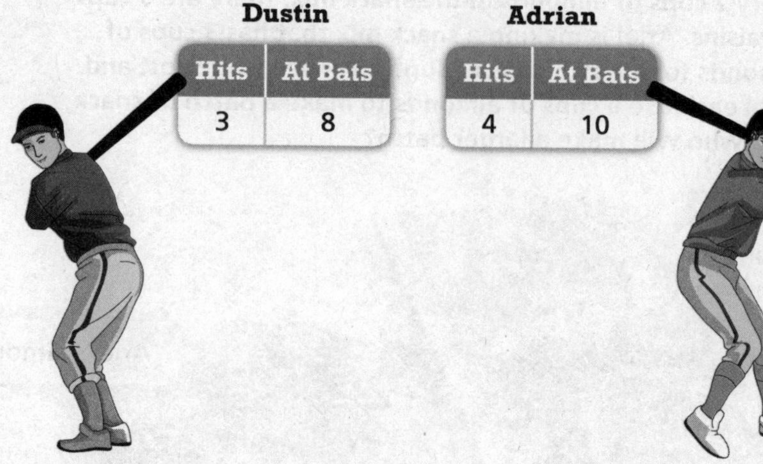

Dustin

Hits	At Bats
3	8

Adrian

Hits	At Bats
4	10

Use Structure How can you use ratio tables to compare ratios? MP.7

Extend and complete the ratio tables for Dustin and Adrian until the number of at bats is the same in each table. Compare the number of hits that Dustin and Adrian each get with 40 at bats.

Dustin

Hits	At Bats
3	8
6	16
9	24
12	32
15	40

Dustin gets 15 hits for every 40 at bats.

Adrian

Hits	At Bats
4	10
8	20
12	30
16	40

Adrian gets 16 hits for every 40 at bats.

Because Adrian gets more hits in 40 at bats, he has the better hits to at bats ratio.

Try It!

Marlon had 6 hits in 15 at bats. How does Marlon's hits to at bats ratio compare to Adrian's?

Convince Me! Based on their hits to at bats ratios, who would you expect to have more hits in a game, Marlon or Dustin? Explain.

EXAMPLE 2 Compare Ratios to Solve Problems

Due to compatibility and size restrictions, only certain types of fish can live together in an aquarium. If there are 15 mollies in each tank with the ratios shown at the right, which tank has more fish?

STEP 1

Make a table to show the ratio of guppies to mollies in Tank 1.

Guppies	Mollies
4	5
8	10
12	15
16	20
20	25

There are 12 guppies for every 15 mollies.

STEP 2

Make a table to show the ratio of angelfish to mollies in Tank 2.

Angelfish	Mollies
2	3
4	6
6	9
8	12
10	15

There are 10 angelfish for every 15 mollies.

STEP 3

Add to find the total number of fish in each aquarium.

Tank 1: 12 guppies $+$ 15 mollies $=$ 27 fish

Tank 2: 10 angelfish $+$ 15 mollies $=$ 25 fish

$27 > 25$

Tank 1 has more fish.

Try It!

Tank 3 has a ratio of 3 guppies for every 4 angelfish. Complete the ratio table to find the number of angelfish in Tank 3 with 12 guppies.

Using the information in Example 2 and the table at the right, which tank with guppies has more fish?

Guppies	3			
Angelfish	4			

KEY CONCEPT 

You can use ratio tables to compare ratios when one of the corresponding terms is the same.

Theresa's Purple Paint Mixture

Cups of Blue Paint	2	4	6
Cups of Red Paint	5	10	15

Hala's Purple Paint Mixture

Cups of Blue Paint	3	6	9
Cups of Red Paint	7	14	21

Theresa used more cups of red paint than Hala.

Do You Understand?

1. **Essential Question** How can you compare ratios to solve a problem?

2. In Example 1, how many hits would Adrian have in 50 at bats? Explain.

3. **Reasoning** During the first week of a summer camp, 2 out of 3 campers were boys. During the second week, 3 out of 5 campers were boys. There were 15 total campers each week. During which week were there more boy campers? Explain. MP.2

Do You Know How?

4. To make plaster, Kevin mixes 3 cups of water with 4 pounds of plaster powder. Complete the ratio table. How much water will Kevin mix with 20 pounds of powder?

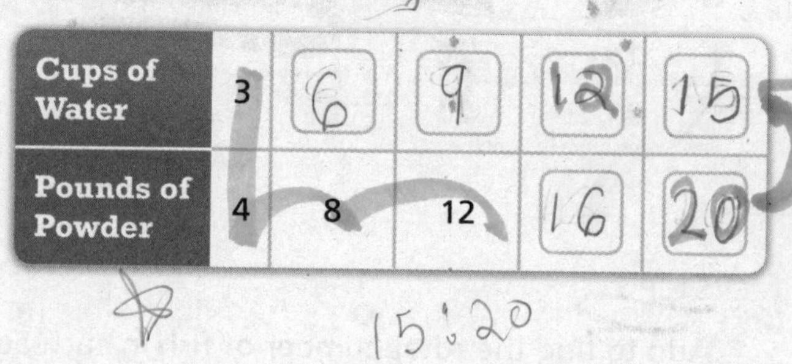

Cups of Water	3				
Pounds of Powder	4	8	12		

5. Jenny makes plaster using a ratio of 4 cups of water to 5 pounds of plaster powder. Whose plaster recipe uses more water? Use the ratio table here and in Exercise 4 to compare.

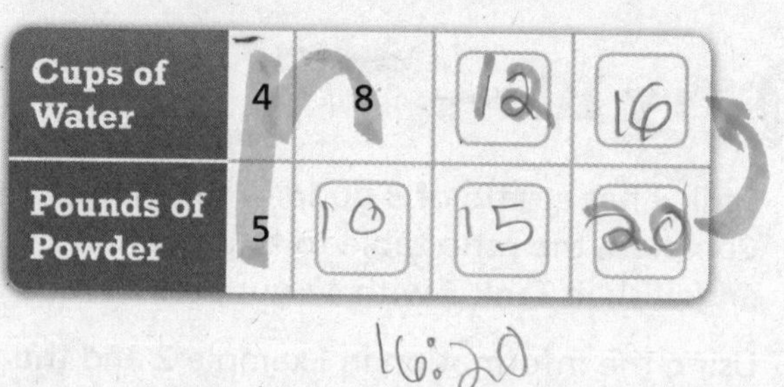

Cups of Water	4	8		
Pounds of Powder	5			

6. Kevin and Jenny each use 12 cups of water to make plaster. Who will make more plaster? Explain.

Name: Madelyn Zink

Practice & Problem Solving

Scan for Multimedia 

In 7–10, use the ratio table at the right.

7. Local radio station *WMTH* schedules 2 minutes of news for every 20 minutes of music. Complete the ratios shown in the table at the right.

Minutes of Music	20	?	40	?	60
Minutes of News	2	3	?	5	?

↑ No Radios look Like this!

8. What is the ratio of minutes of music to minutes of news?

9. Radio station *WILM* broadcasts 4 minutes of news for every 25 minutes of music. Which radio station broadcasts more news each hour?

10. Which station will have to be on the air longer to broadcast 4 minutes of news? Explain.

11. Reasoning The ratio tables at the right show the comparison of books to games for sale at Bert's Store and at Gloria's Store. Complete the ratio tables. Which store has the greater ratio of books to games? Explain. MP.2

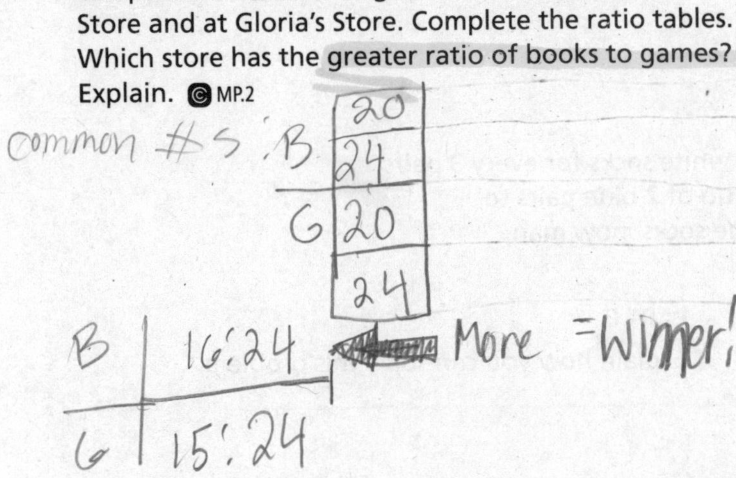

Bert's Store

Books	4	8	12	16	20
Games	6	12	18	24	30

Gloria's Store

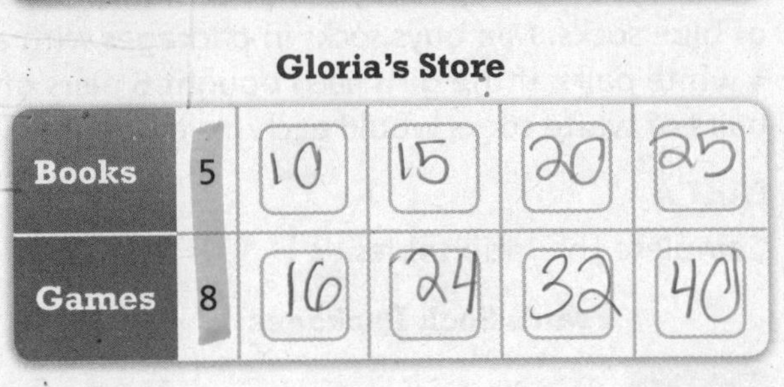

Books	5	10	15	20	25
Games	8	16	24	32	40

12. The ratio of soy sauce to lime juice in a homemade salad dressing is 7:6. The ratio of soy sauce to lime juice in a store-bought dressing is 11:9. Which dressing has the greater ratio of soy sauce to lime juice?

Homemade Salad Dressing

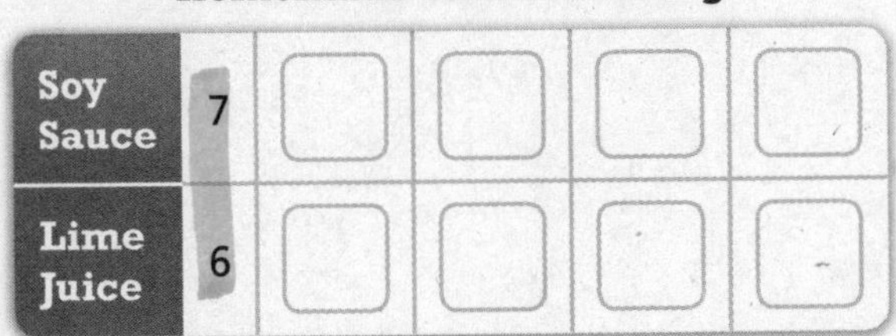

Soy Sauce	7				
Lime Juice	6				

Store-Bought Salad Dressing

Soy Sauce	11				
Lime Juice	9				

13. One bouquet of flowers has 3 roses for every 5 carnations. Another bouquet has 4 carnations for every 5 daisies. If both bouquets have 20 carnations, which bouquet has more flowers?

Roses and Carnations

Roses	3				
Carnations	5				

Carnations and Daisies

Carnations	4				
Daisies	5				

14. **Higher Order Thinking** Lauren can drive her car 320 miles on 10 gallons of gasoline. Melissa can drive her car 280 miles on 8 gallons of gasoline. Who can drive farther on 40 gallons of gasoline? Complete the ratio tables to justify your solution.

Lauren's Car

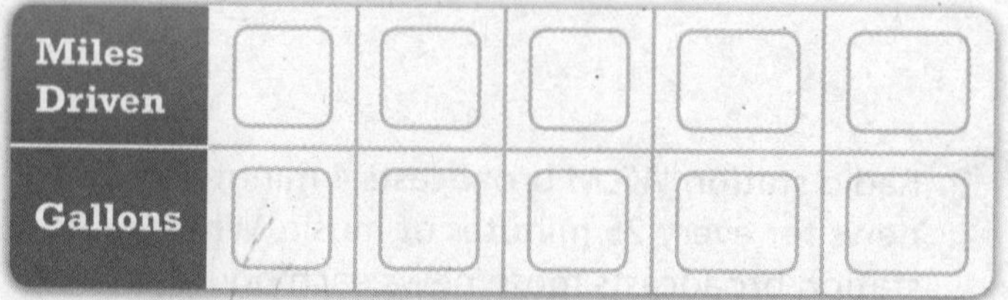

Miles Driven					
Gallons					

Melissa's Car

Miles Driven					
Gallons					

Assessment Practice

15. Fran buys socks in packages that contain 9 pairs of white socks for every 3 pairs of blue socks. Mia buys socks in packages with a ratio of 2 blue pairs to 4 white pairs. If the girls each bought 6 pairs of blue socks, how many pairs of white socks would each have bought?

PART A

Complete the ratio tables.

Fran's Sock Packages

White Socks				
Blue Socks				

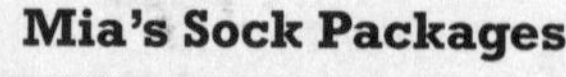

Mia's Sock Packages

White Socks				
Blue Socks				

PART B

Explain how you can solve this problem.

Lesson 5-4
Represent and Graph Ratios

Go Online | PearsonRealize.com

I can...
solve ratio problems by using tables and graphs to show equivalent ratios.

Common Core Content Standards
6.RP.A.3a

Mathematical Practices
MP.3, MP.4, MP.7

Solve & Discuss It!

ACTIVITY

For every 4 adults at the beach one afternoon, there were 3 children. How many children were at the beach if there were 8, 12, 16, or 20 adults at the beach?

Number of Adults	4	8	12	16	20
Number of Children	3	6	9	12	15

Model with Math How does the graph show the ratio? MP.4

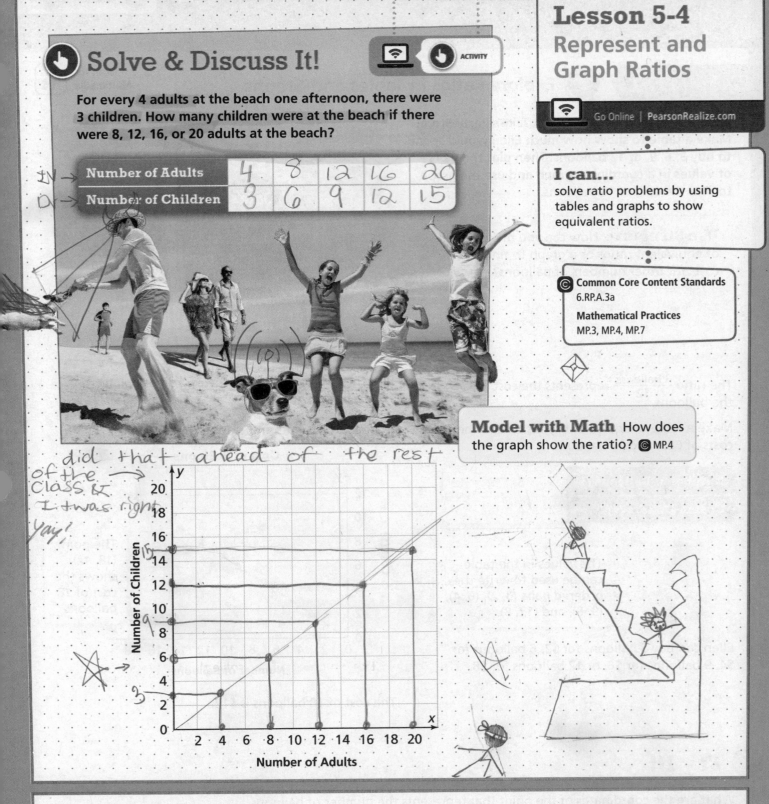

y

Number of Children

0, 2, 4, 6, 8, 10, 12, 14, 16, 18, 20

x

2, 4, 6, 8, 10, 12, 14, 16, 18, 20

Number of Adults

Focus on math practices

Critique Reasoning There were 25 children and 15 adults at the beach. Emery said that there were 5 children for every 3 adults. Is he correct? Explain. MP.3

? Essential Question How can you use tables and graphs to show equivalent ratios?

EXAMPLE 1  Explore Ratios in Tables and Graphs

Scan for Multimedia 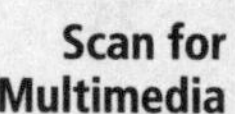

Ellen is shopping for supplies at Jake's Party Store. Make a table to show how much Ellen would spend to buy 3, 6, 9, or 12 balloons. Then plot the pairs of values in a coordinate graph and use the graph to find the cost of 18 balloons.

Use Structure How can you make a table of equivalent ratios or a graph to find the costs for other numbers of balloons? MP.7

The ratio $\frac{3 \text{ balloons}}{\$2}$ represents the cost of the balloons.

Make a table of equivalent ratios to find the costs of 6, 9, and 12 balloons.

Number of Balloons (x)	3	6	9	12
Cost in Dollars (y)	2	4	6	8

The values in the table can be used to write the ordered pairs (3, 2), (6, 4), (9, 6), and (12, 8).

Ellen can buy 3 balloons for $2, 6 balloons for $4, 9 balloons for $6, or 12 balloons for $8.

Plot the pairs of values on the coordinate plane for each ratio, x to y.

Connect the points and extend the line.

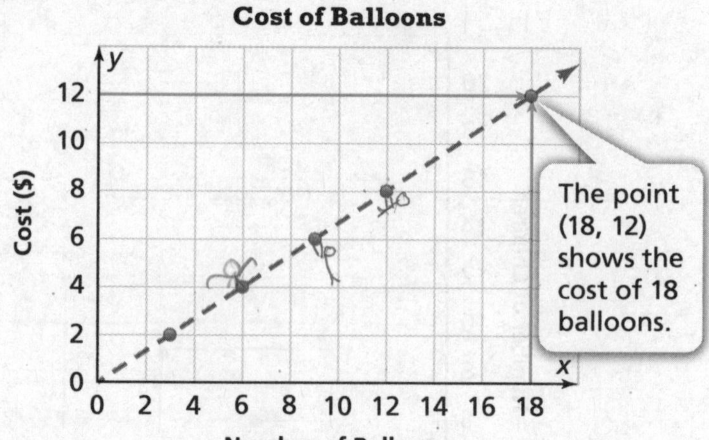

The cost of 18 balloons is $12.

Try It!

What are the coordinates of the point that represents the number of balloons you can buy for $6?

Convince Me! How can you use the graph to find the cost of 15 balloons?

EXAMPLE 2  Graph Ratios Using Repeated Addition

Jack is making juice. He has 25 celery sticks. If Jack uses all 25 celery sticks, how many apples will he need to make the juice?

Use repeated addition to complete the ratio table.

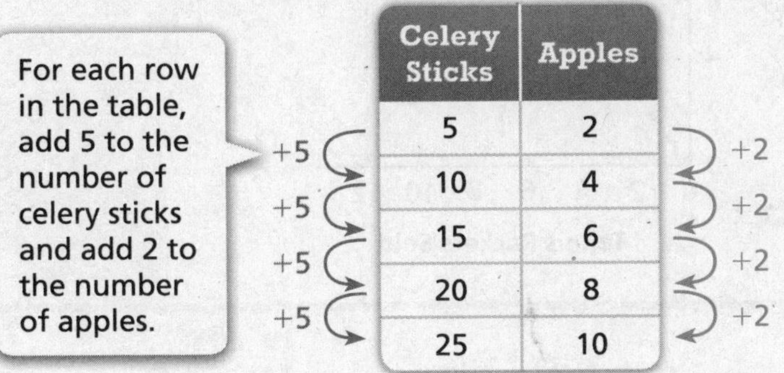

Celery Sticks	Apples
5	2
10	4
15	6
20	8
25	10

Plot the pairs of values on a coordinate plane.

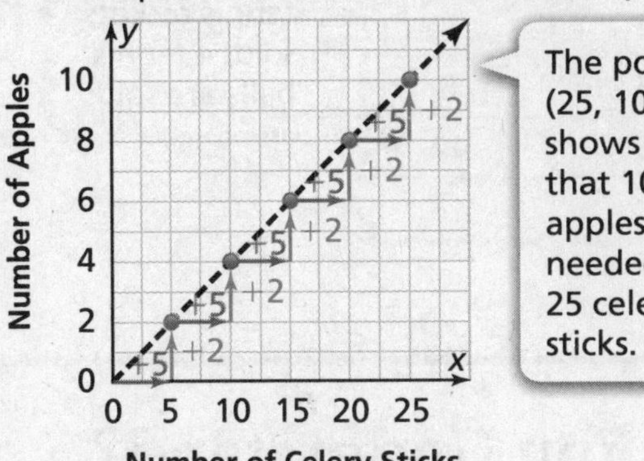

Jack needs 10 apples to make the juice.

EXAMPLE 3  Graph Ratios Using Repeated Subtraction

Tyrese lives 10 blocks from the library. He walks 3 blocks every 2 minutes towards the library. How far is he from the library after 5 minutes?

Use repeated subtraction to complete the table.

For each row in the table, add 2 to the number of minutes and subtract 3 from the number of blocks.

Time (min)	Distance from Library (blocks)
0	10
2	7
4	4
6	1

+ 2, + 2, + 2   − 3, − 3, − 3

Plot the pairs of values on a coordinate plane.

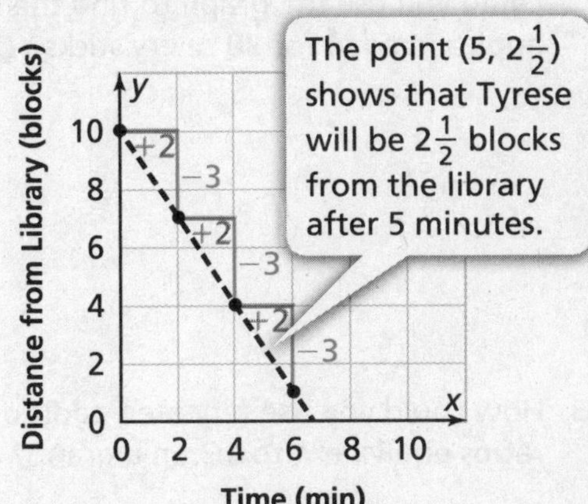

Tyrese will be $2\frac{1}{2}$ blocks from the library after 5 minutes.

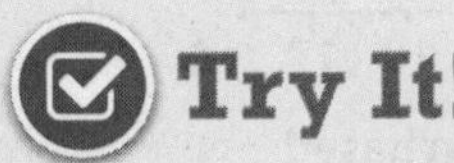

Try It!

How would the graph change if Tyrese walks 4 blocks every 2 minutes?

KEY CONCEPT 

You can use ratio tables and graphs to show equivalent ratios. When ordered pairs representing equivalent ratios are graphed as points in the coordinate plane, they form a line.

Tennis Rackets Sold	Tennis Balls Sold
3	4
6	8
9	12
12	16

For every 3 tennis rackets sold, 4 tennis balls are sold.

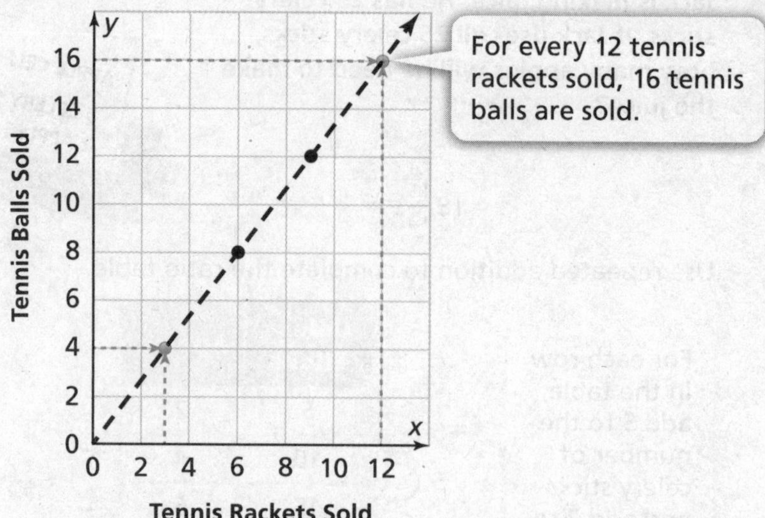

Do You Understand?

1. **Essential Question** How can you use tables and graphs to show equivalent ratios?

2. **Look for Relationships** In Example 2, how could you use the graph to find the number of apples needed for 30 celery sticks? MP.7

3. How could you use repeated addition to show ratios equivalent to 1:3 on a graph?

Do You Know How?

4. Complete the table to show equivalent ratios representing a cost of $8 for every 3 boxes. Then write the pairs of values as points to be plotted on a coordinate plane.

Number of Boxes	Cost of Boxes ($)
3	8
6	16
9	24

5. **Model with Math** Plot the equivalent ratios (3, 4), (6, 8), and (9, 12) on the graph. Use the graph to find the number of nonfiction books purchased if 10 fiction books are purchased. MP.4

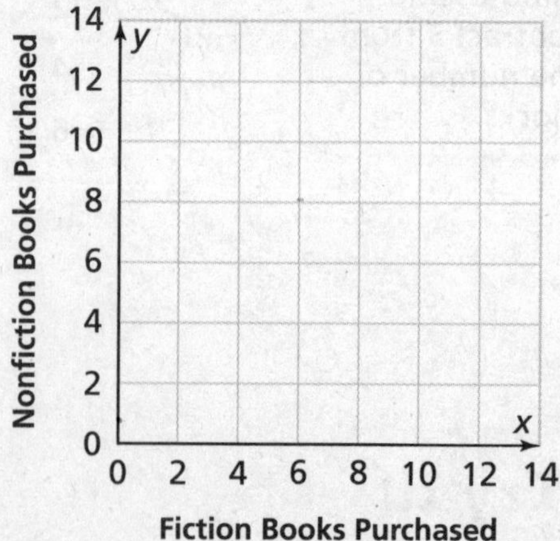

Name: ____________________

Practice & Problem Solving

Scan for Multimedia

Leveled Practice **In 6 and 7, complete the table and graph the pairs of values.**

6.

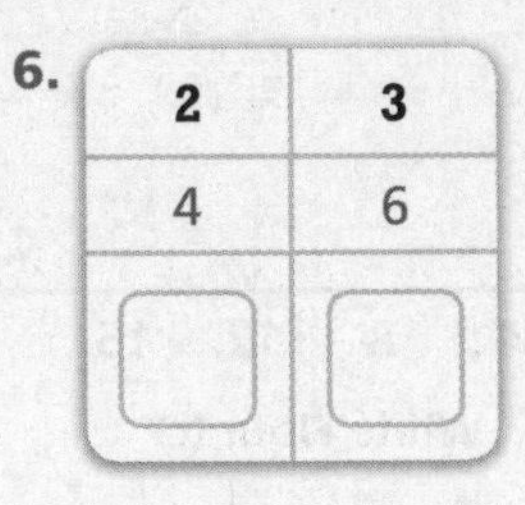

2	3
4	6
☐	☐

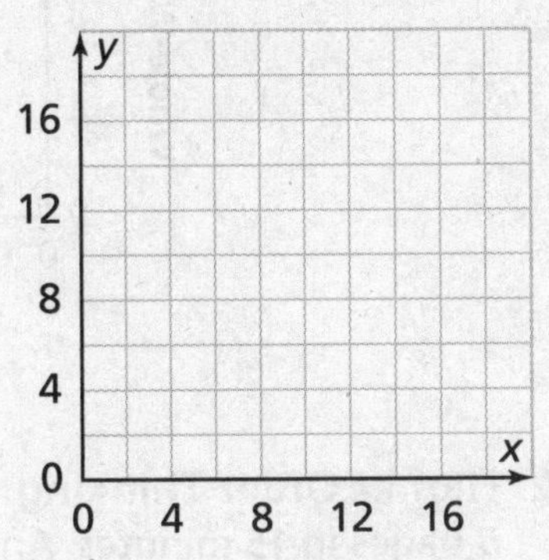

7.

5	2
25	10
☐	☐

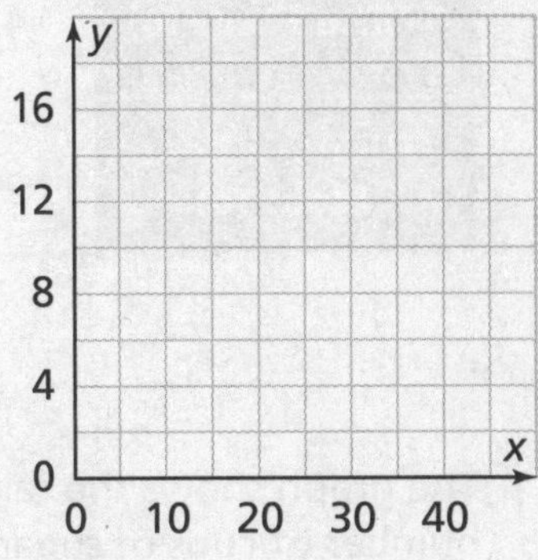

8. A student runs 2 minutes for every 10 minutes she walks.

a. Complete the table. Graph the pairs of values.

Running (min)	Walking (min)
2	10
4	20
☐	☐

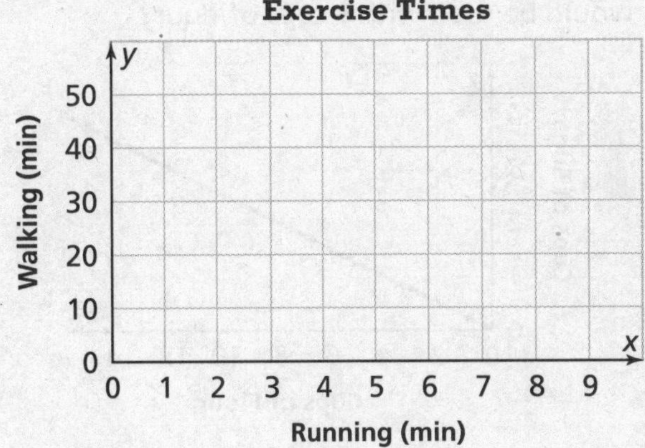

b. For how long would the student walk if she runs for 7 minutes?

9. A car magazine reports the number of miles driven for different amounts of gas for three cars. Which car travels the farthest on 1 gallon of gas? Explain.

Car C Gas Mileage

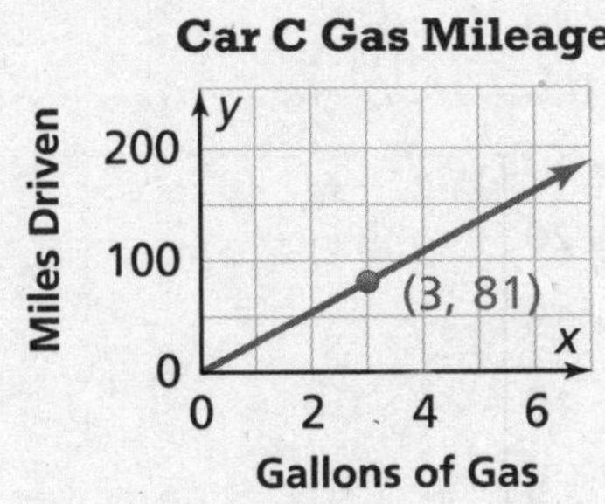

Car A

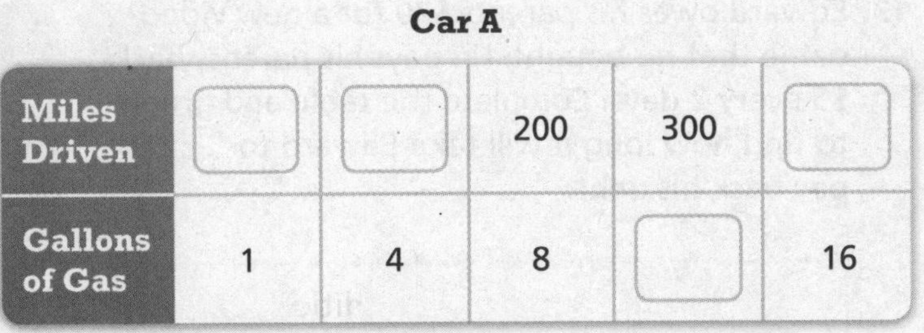

Miles Driven	☐	☐	200	300	☐
Gallons of Gas	1	4	8	☐	16

Car B can travel 140 miles for every 5 gallons of gas.

10. Model with Math A bread recipe calls for 4 cups of white flour for every 5 cups of whole-wheat flour. Complete the table to show how many cups of whole-wheat flour are needed to mix with 16 cups of white flour. Then graph the pairs of values. © MP.4

White Flour (c)	4	8	12	16
Whole-Wheat Flour (c)				

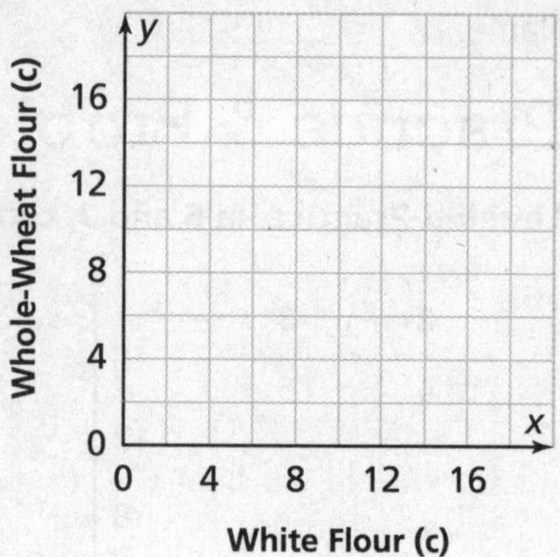

11. The graph shows the relationship between the number of cups of sugar and the number of cups of flour in a recipe. What point on the graph represents the number of cups of sugar that would be used with 8 cups of flour?

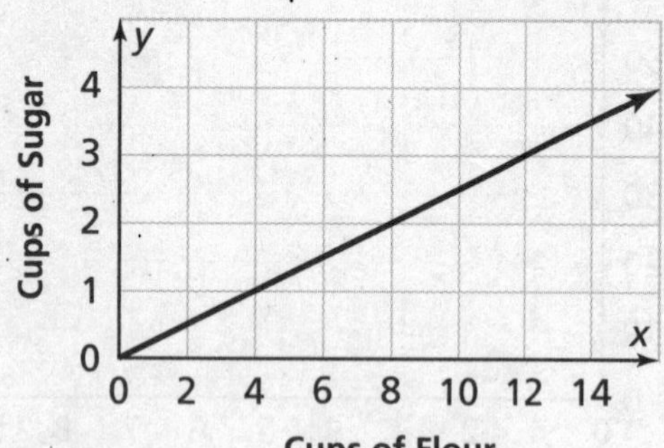

12. Higher Order Thinking Ishwar can read 5 pages in 15 minutes. Anne can read 15 pages in 1 hour. Explain how you could use a table or graph to find how much longer it would take Anne to read a 300-page book than Ishwar.

© Assessment Practice

13. Edward owes his parents $20 for a new video game that he bought. He pays his parents back $5 every 2 days. Complete the table and graph to find how long it will take Edward to pay back his debt.

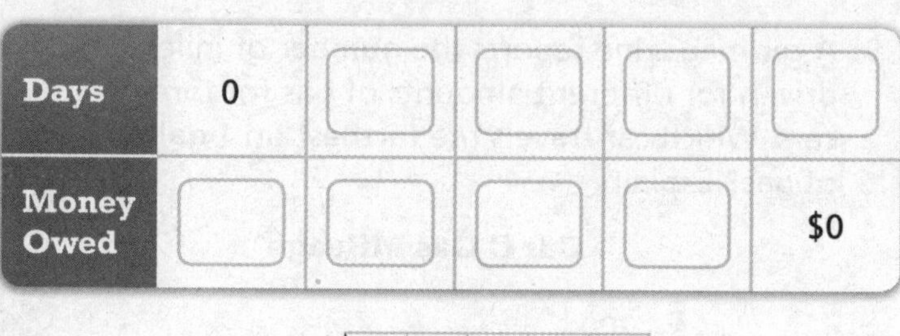

Days	0				
Money Owed					$0

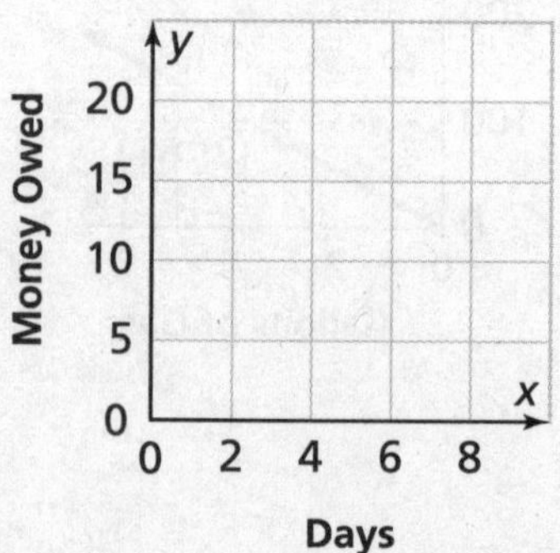

Name: ______________________________

MID-TOPIC CHECKPOINT

TOPIC 5

1. **Vocabulary** How can a *ratio* be used to compare quantities? *Lesson 5-1*

2. Elsie's math class has 11 female students and 10 male students. Write the ratio of female students to the total number of students in two different ways. *Lesson 5-1*

3. During the breakfast service, the D-Town Diner sells 12 cups of coffee for every 10 glasses of orange juice. How many cups of coffee would the diner have sold if 40 glasses of orange juice had been sold? Complete the table with equivalent ratios. *Lesson 5-2*

Cups of Coffee	12	☐	☐	☐
Glasses of Orange Juice	10	☐	☐	40

4. The ratio of cows to chickens at Old McDonald's Farm is 2:7. Which farms have a greater ratio of cows to chickens than Old McDonald's Farm? Select all that apply. *Lessons 5-3*

- ☐ Red's Farm: 3 cows for every 5 chickens
- ☐ Cluck & Moo Farm: 1 cow for every 5 chickens
- ☐ T Family Farm: 1 cow for every 3 chickens
- ☐ Pasture Farm: 2 cows for every 9 chickens
- ☐ C & C Farm: 3 cows for every 8 chickens

5. A package of 3 notebooks costs $5. Complete the ratio table and graph the pairs of values. How much will 18 notebooks cost? *Lesson 5-4*

Number of Notebooks	Cost ($)
3	5
☐	10
☐	15
☐	20
☐	25

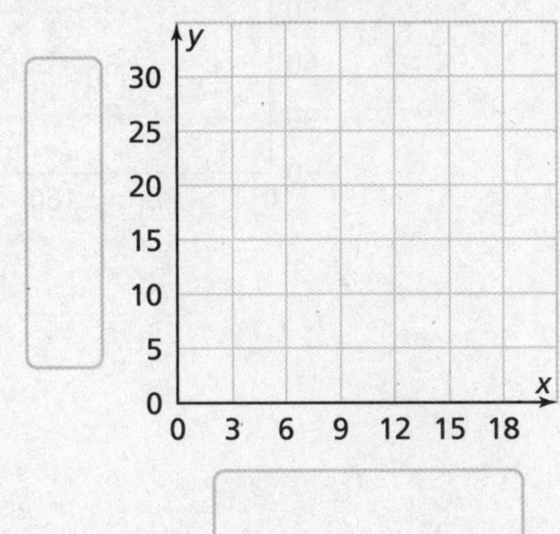

How well did you do on the mid-topic checkpoint? Fill in the stars. ☆☆☆

TOPIC 5

MID-TOPIC PERFORMANCE TASK

Hillsdale Orchard grows Fuji apples and Gala apples. There are 160 Fuji apple trees and 120 Gala apple trees in the orchard.

PART A

Hillsdale Orchard's owners decide to plant 30 new Gala apple trees. Complete the ratio table to find the number of new Fuji apple trees the owners should plant if they want to maintain the same ratio of Fuji apple trees to Gala apple trees.

Fuji Apple Trees	☐	☐	160
Gala Apple Trees	30	☐	120

PART B

Use the ratio table to complete a graph that shows the relationship between the number of Fuji apple trees and Gala apple trees at Hillsdale Orchard.

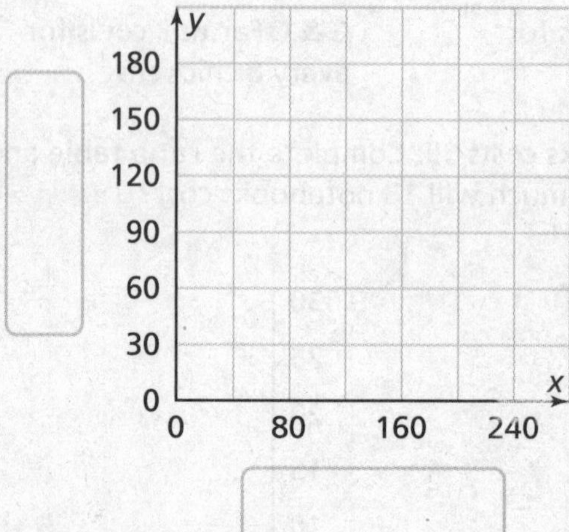

PART C

By the end of the next season, the owners of Hillsdale Orchard plan to have 240 Fuji apple trees. Explain how you could use the graph to find the total number of Fuji and Gala apple trees that Hillsdale Orchard will have if the owners achieve their goal.

Lesson 5-5
Understand Rates and Unit Rates

Go Online | PearsonRealize.com

I can...
solve problems involving rates.

Common Core Content Standards
6.RP.A.2, 6.RP.A.3a, 6.RP.A.3b

Mathematical Practices
MP.1, MP.2, MP.3, MP.8

Solve & Discuss It!

ACTIVITY

What is the cost of 10 bottles of fruit juice?

Make Sense and Persevere
How can you use tables or diagrams to make sense of the quantities in the problem? MP.1

Focus on math practices

Critique Reasoning Monica says, "If 4 bottles cost $10, then 2 bottles cost $5, and 8 bottles cost $20. So 10 bottles cost $5 + $20." Is Monica correct? Explain. MP.3

Essential Question What are rates and unit rates?

EXAMPLE 1  Find Equivalent Rates

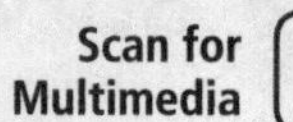

A rate is a special type of ratio that compares quantities with unlike units of measure.

If the race car continues to travel at the same rate, how long will it take it to travel 25 kilometers?

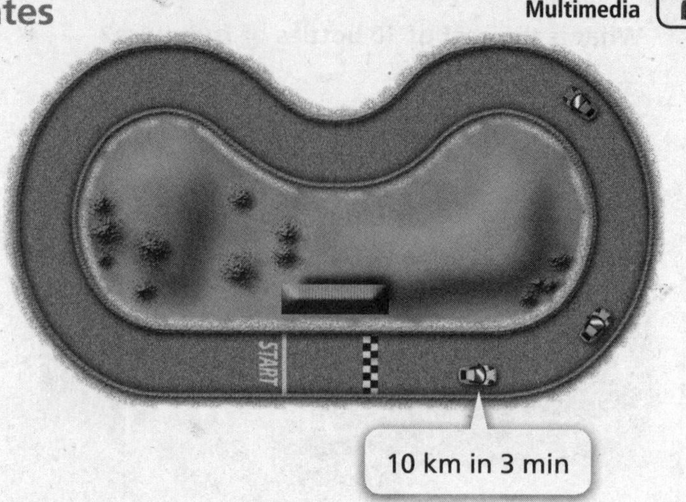

> **Generalize** You can find equivalent rates the same ways that you find equivalent ratios. MP.8

ONE WAY Use a ratio table to find rates that are equivalent to $\frac{10 \text{ km}}{3 \text{ min}}$.

Distance (km)	Time (min)
5	$1\frac{1}{2}$
10	3
15	$4\frac{1}{2}$
20	6
25	$7\frac{1}{2}$

It will take the race car $7\frac{1}{2}$ minutes to travel 25 kilometers.

ANOTHER WAY Write the rate as a fraction. Multiply both terms of the rate by the same number to find an equivalent rate.

Think, $10 \times ? = 25$.

$$\frac{10 \text{ km}}{3 \text{ min}} = \frac{25 \text{ km}}{x \text{ min}}$$

$$\frac{10 \text{ km} \times 2.5}{3 \text{ min} \times 2.5} = \frac{25 \text{ km}}{7.5 \text{ min}}$$

Multiply both terms by 2.5.

It will take the race car 7.5 minutes to travel 25 kilometers.

Try It!

At the same rate, how long would it take the car to travel 60 kilometers?

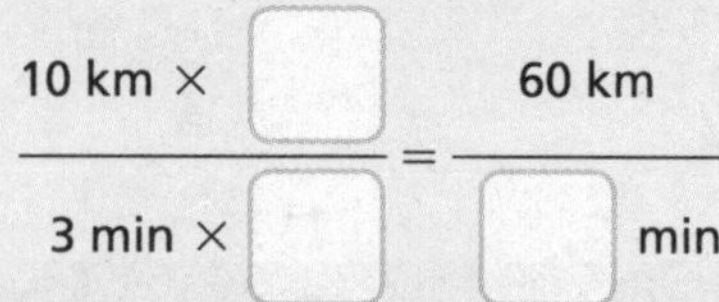

It will take the car ☐ minutes to travel ☐ kilometers.

Convince Me! Sal draws the double number line diagram at the right. He says it shows that at this rate the race car will travel 35 kilometers in 10.5 minutes. Critique Sal's reasoning. Is he correct? Explain.

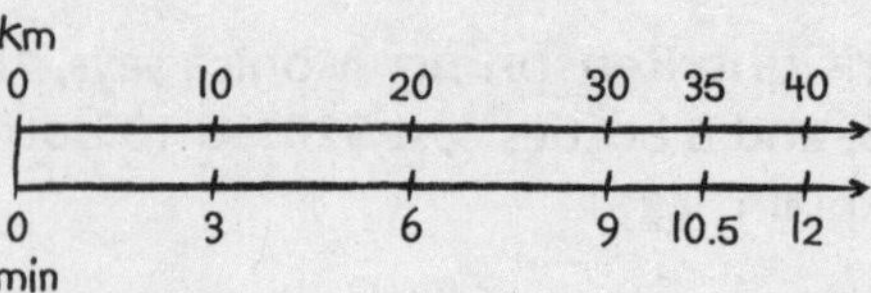

EXAMPLE 2  Compare Quantities in Two Ways

Harvest Market sells a crate of Fuji apples for $12.00. What are two different unit rates that could represent the situation?

Find the unit rate in pounds per dollar.

$\frac{15 \text{ pounds}}{\$12.00}$

$\frac{15 \text{ pounds} \div 12}{\$12.00 \div 12} = \frac{1.25 \text{ pounds}}{\$1.00}$

The unit rate in pounds per dollar is $\frac{1.25 \text{ pounds}}{\$1.00}$.

Find the unit rate in dollars per pound.

$\frac{\$12.00}{15 \text{ pounds}}$

$\frac{\$12.00 \div 15}{15 \text{ pounds} \div 15} = \frac{\$0.80}{1 \text{ pound}}$

The unit rate in dollars per pound is $\frac{\$0.80}{1 \text{ pound}}$.

 **Try It!**

A recipe for scrambled eggs uses 2 tablespoons of milk for every 3 eggs. What are two unit rates that could represent the recipe?

EXAMPLE 3  Use Unit Rates to Solve Problems

A unit rate is a rate in which the comparison is to 1 unit.

How far could the family travel in 8 hours if they maintain the same rate of speed?

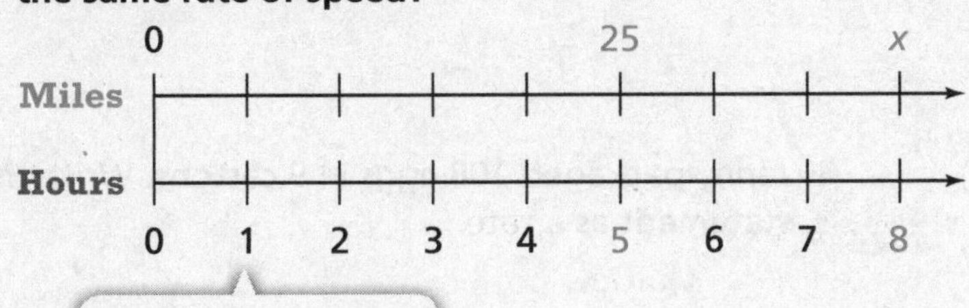

STEP 1

Find the unit rate in miles per hour.

$\frac{25 \text{ miles}}{5 \text{ hours}}$ or $\frac{25}{5}$

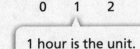

$\frac{25 \div 5}{5 \div 5} = \frac{5}{1}$

Write an equivalent rate with a denominator of 1.

The unit rate is $\frac{5}{1}$, or 5 miles per hour.

Generalize The unit rate is an equivalent rate with a denominator of 1. MP.8

STEP 2

Use the unit rate to find how far the family could travel in 8 hours.

$\frac{5 \times 8}{1 \times 8} = \frac{40}{8}$ or $\frac{40 \text{ miles}}{8 \text{ hours}}$

The family could travel 40 miles in 8 hours.

A canoeing club travels 78 miles in 3 days. How far could they travel in 5 days if they maintain the same speed?

KEY CONCEPT 

A rate compares quantities with unlike units of measure.

$$\frac{\$3.50}{7 \text{ oranges}}$$

A unit rate compares a quantity to 1 unit of another quantity.

$$\frac{\$3.50}{7 \text{ oranges}} = \frac{\$0.50}{1 \text{ orange}}$$

Do You Understand?

1. **Essential Question** What are rates and unit rates?

2. Be Precise Use what you know about ratios to describe a rate. MP.6

3. Reasoning A bathroom shower streams 5 gallons of water in 2 minutes. MP.2

a. Find the unit rate for gallons per minute and describe it in words.

b. Find the unit rate for minutes per gallon and describe it in words.

Do You Know How?

In 4 and 5, find the value of *n*.

4.

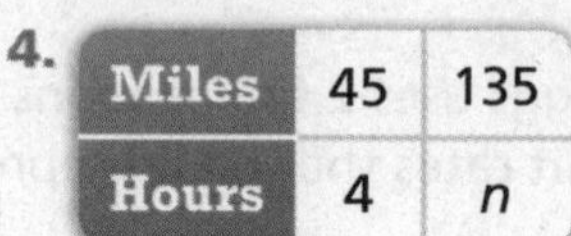

Miles	45	135
Hours	4	n

5.

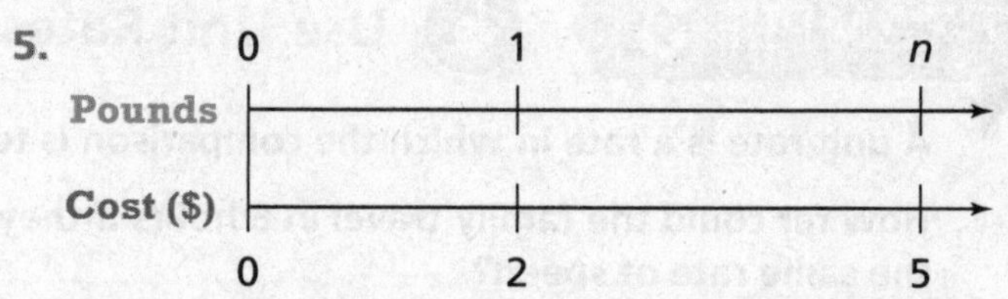

6. Jenny packaged 108 eggs in 9 cartons. Write this statement as a rate.

7. Anna Maria read 40 pages in 60 minutes. What is her unit rate in pages per minute?

In 8 and 9, use the unit rates that you found in Exercise 3.

8. How many gallons of water does the shower stream in 6 minutes?

9. How long can someone shower to use only 10 gallons of water?

Name: ______________________

Practice & Problem Solving

Scan for Multimedia

In 10 and 11, write each statement as a rate.

10. Jan saw 9 full moons in 252 days.

11. It took Hannah 38 minutes to run 8 laps.

In 12 and 13, find the value of *x*.

12.

Fish	16	48
Bowls	2	x

13.

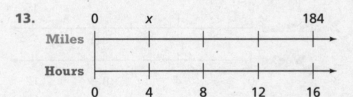

Miles	0	x			184
Hours	0	4	8	12	16

Leveled Practice **In 14 and 15, find the unit rate.**

14. $\frac{320 \text{ mi}}{16 \text{ gal}}$

$\frac{320 \div 16}{16 \div 16} = \frac{\square}{1}$

$\frac{\square \text{ mi}}{1 \text{ gal}}$

15. $\frac{75 \text{ cm}}{5 \text{ h}}$

$\frac{75 \div \square}{5 \div 5} = \frac{\square}{1}$

$\frac{\square \text{ cm}}{1 \text{ h}}$

In 16–19, complete each table.

16.

Pages	9			
Minutes	18	1	10	15

17.

Beans	186			
Bags	3	1	7	11

18.

Ounces		24.6		123
Bags	1	2	5	

19.

Miles	25		125	
Gallons		3	5	12

20. Which runner set the fastest pace? Explain.

Runner	Laps	Time
Martha	20	32 min
Allison	16	25 min
Rachel	17	27.2 min

21. **Model with Math** Over the summer, Alexis read 15 books in 12 weeks. The diagram below can be used to track her progress. If Alexis read at the same rate each week, how many books had she read in 4 weeks? In 8 weeks? Complete the diagram. MP.4

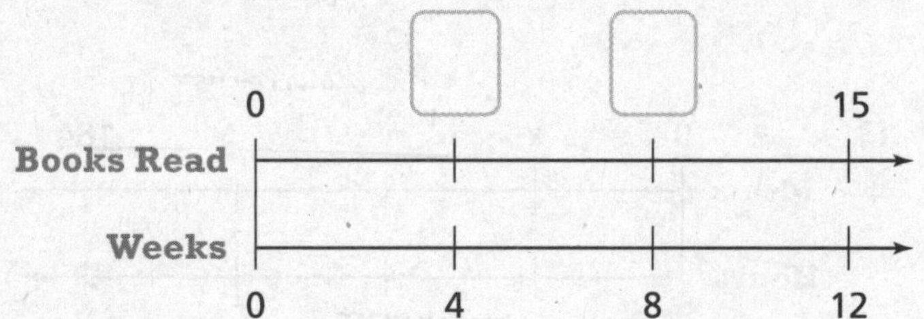

22. An elephant charges an object that is 0.35 kilometer away. How long will it take the elephant to reach the object?

Elephants can charge at speeds of 0.7 km per minute.

23. A machine takes 1 minute to fill 6 cartons of eggs. At this rate, how many minutes will it take to fill 420 cartons?

24. **Higher Order Thinking** How are the ratios $\frac{24 \text{ laps}}{1 \text{ hour}}$ and $\frac{192 \text{ laps}}{8 \text{ hours}}$ alike? How are they different?

Assessment Practice

25. A cook mixes 4 pounds of rice into 5 quarts of boiling water. Choose all the statements that are true.

- ☐ $\frac{0.8 \text{ lb rice}}{1 \text{ qt water}}$ is a unit rate for the mix.
- ☐ $\frac{1.25 \text{ qt water}}{1 \text{ lb rice}}$ is a unit rate for the mix.
- ☐ Using the same rate, the cook should mix 12.5 pounds of rice with 10 quarts of water.
- ☐ Using the same rate, the cook should mix 10 pounds of rice with 12.5 quarts of water.
- ☐ Using the same rate, the cook should mix 2.5 pounds of rice with 2 quarts of water.

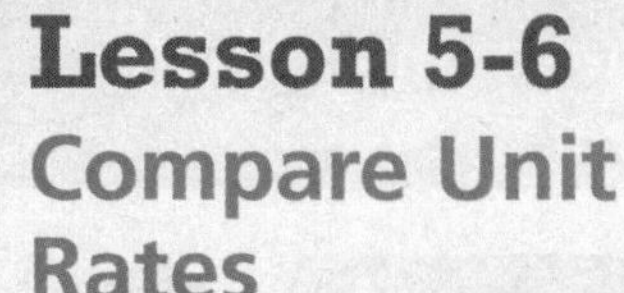

Lesson 5-6
Compare Unit Rates

Go Online | PearsonRealize.com

I can... compare unit rates to solve problems.

Common Core Content Standards 6.RP.A.3b, 6.RP.A.3a
Mathematical Practices MP.1, MP.2, MP.6

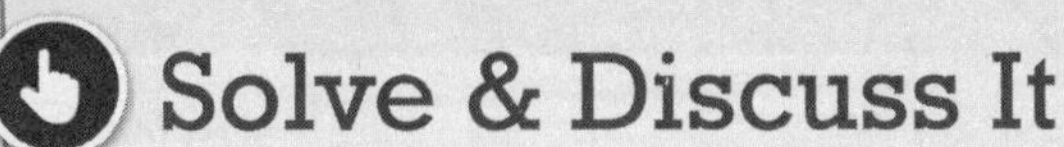

Solve & Discuss It!

ACTIVITY

Rick and Nikki own remote-control cars. They use a stopwatch to record the speed of each car. Whose car is faster?

Speed of Rick's Car

Distance (feet)	Time (seconds)
150	30

Speed of Nikki's Car

Distance (feet)	Time (seconds)
40	.10
80	20
120	

Be Precise Use precise numbers and units to describe and compare rates. MP.6

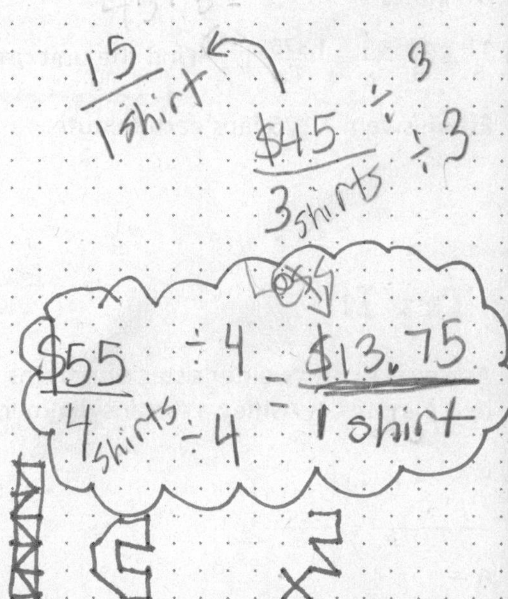

Focus on math practices

Make Sense and Persevere If each car maintains its rate of speed, how long will it take Rick's car to travel 300 feet? How long will it take Nikki's car to travel the same distance? Explain. MP.1

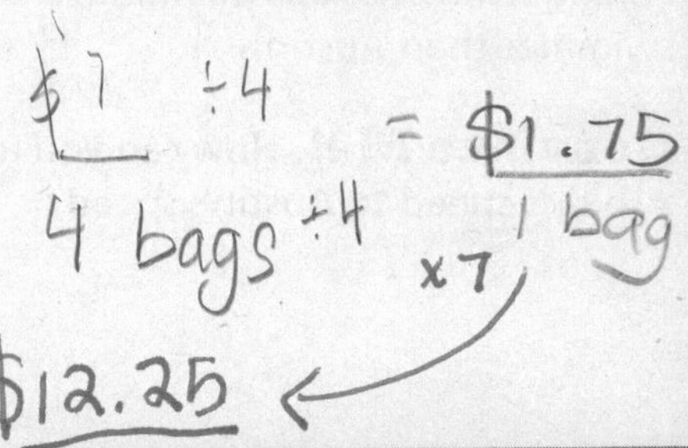

? **Essential Question** How can you use unit rates to make comparisons?

EXAMPLE 1 Compare to Find the Greater Unit Rate

Ethan swam 11 laps in the pool in 8 minutes. Austin swam 7 laps in the same pool in 5 minutes. Which boy swam at a faster rate?

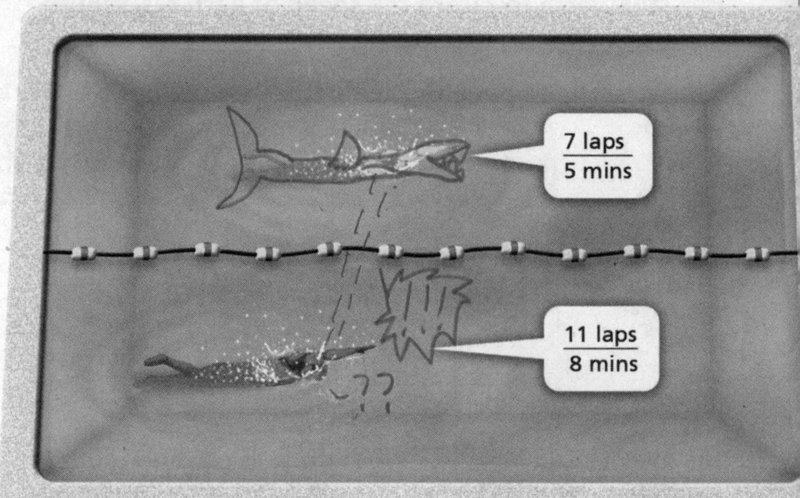

Make Sense and Persevere
Is the faster rate a fewer number of laps per minute or a greater number of laps per minute? MP.1

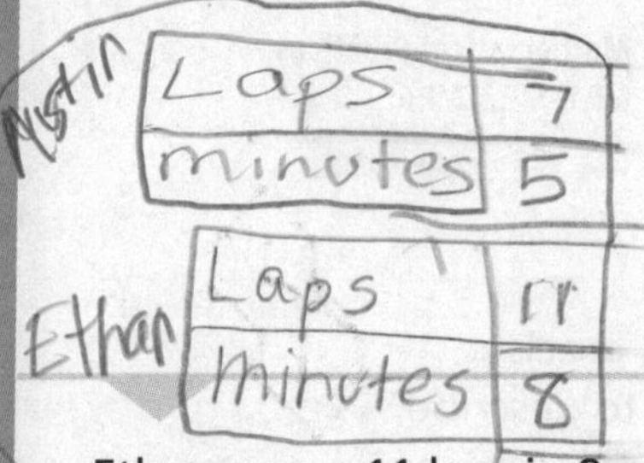

Ethan swam 11 laps in 8 minutes.

$\frac{11 \text{ laps}}{8 \text{ minutes}}$ or $\frac{11}{8}$

$\frac{11}{8} = \frac{11 \div 8}{8 \div 8} = \frac{1.375}{1}$ Find the unit rate.

Ethan swam 1.375 laps each minute.

Austin swam 7 laps in 5 minutes.

$\frac{7 \text{ laps}}{5 \text{ minutes}}$ or $\frac{7}{5}$

$\frac{7}{5} = \frac{7 \div 5}{5 \div 5} = \frac{1.4}{1}$ Find the unit rate.

Austin swam 1.4 laps each minute.

$1.4 > 1.375$, so Austin swam at a faster rate.

Try It!

Ashley is Austin's older sister. She trains in the same pool and can swim 9 laps in 6 minutes. Is Ashley a faster swimmer than Austin?

$\frac{9 \div \square}{6 \div \square} = \frac{\square}{\square}$

Ashley swims 1.5 laps per minute. Because ☐ ☐ 1.4, Ashley is a ☐ swimmer than Austin.

Convince Me! How can you use the unit rate in minutes per lap to compare Ashley's speed to Austin's speed?

EXAMPLE 2 Compare to Find the Lesser Unit Rate

Is the lunch special or the weekend special a better value? Find the unit price of each special.

A unit price is a unit rate that gives the price of one item.

> **Make Sense and Persevere**
> Is the lesser unit price or the greater unit price a better value? MP.1

Find the unit price of the lunch special.

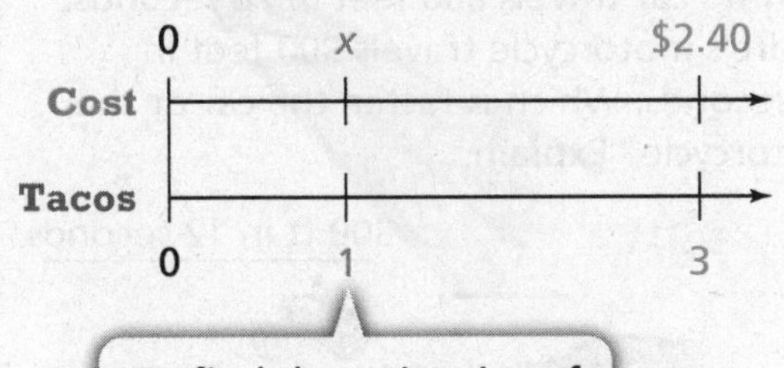

To find the unit price of the lunch special, find the cost of 1 taco.

$\frac{\$2.40}{3}$

$\frac{\$2.40}{3} \div \frac{3}{3} = \frac{\$0.80}{1}$ Find the unit rate.

The unit price for the lunch special is $0.80 per taco.

Find the unit price of the weekend special.

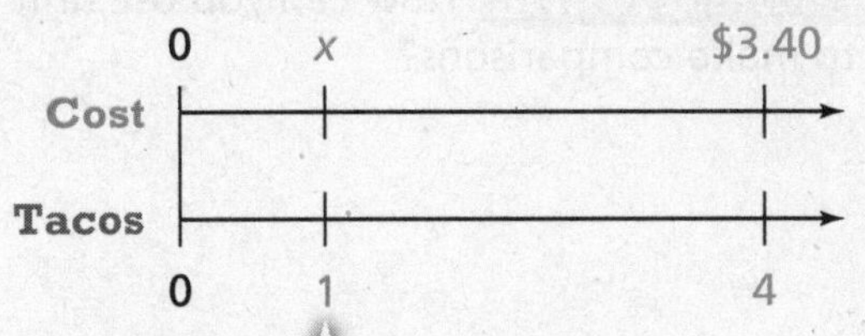

To find the unit price of the weekend special, find the cost of 1 taco.

$\frac{\$3.40}{4}$

$\frac{\$3.40}{4} \div \frac{4}{4} = \frac{\$0.85}{1}$ Find the unit rate.

The unit price for the weekend special is $0.85 per taco.

$0.80 per taco < $0.85 per taco, so the lunch special is a better value.

Try It!

Explain how to decide which is the better value, 4 greeting cards for $10 or 6 greeting cards for $14.

4 greeting cards for $10

6 greeting cards for $14

KEY CONCEPT 

You can use unit rates to make comparisons.

\$8.50 per hour > \$8.00 per hour

$\frac{7 \text{ laps}}{1 \text{ min}} < \frac{9 \text{ laps}}{1 \text{ min}}$

$\frac{32 \text{ cm}}{1 \text{ sec}} < \frac{45 \text{ cm}}{1 \text{ sec}}$

175 words per minute > 95 words per minute

Do You Understand?

1. **Essential Question** How can you use unit rates to make comparisons?

2. **Critique Reasoning** Paul says that a lower unit rate is a better value only if you can use all the items purchased to get the lower unit rate. Do you agree? Explain. MP.3

3. **Reasoning** Car A travels 115 miles on 5 gallons of gas. Car B travels 126 miles on 6 gallons of gas. How can you find which car gets better gas mileage? MP.2

Do You Know How?

4. Hakim's car travels 600 feet in 20 seconds. Andre's motorcycle travels 300 feet in 12 seconds. Which is faster, the car or the motorcycle? Explain.

300 ft in 12 seconds

600 ft in 20 seconds

a. Find the unit rates.

b. Compare the unit rates.

In 5 and 6, find each unit price.

5. 7 movie tickets for \$56

6. 12 fluid ounces of shampoo for \$2.76

7. Which is the better value, 2 books for \$15 or 6 books for \$45? Explain.

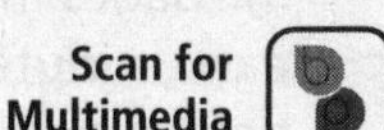

Name: ______________________________

Practice & Problem Solving

Scan for Multimedia

Leveled Practice **In 8 and 9, find each unit price.**

8. 9 pens for $3.60

$$\frac{\$3.60 \div 9}{9 \div 9} = \frac{\square}{1}$$

9. 15 ounces of canned beans for $2.25

$$\frac{\$2.25 \div \square}{15 \div \square} = \frac{\square}{\square}$$

In 10 and 11, determine which is the better value.

10. 3 kilograms of charcoal for $7.95 or 5 kilograms of charcoal for $12.50

11. 50 envelopes for $2.49 or 90 envelopes for $5.50

In 12–15, compare the rates to find which is greater.

12. 35 points in 20 minutes or 49 points in 35 minutes

13. 12 laps in 8 minutes or 16 laps in 10 minutes

14. 45 strikeouts in 36 innings or 96 strikeouts in 80 innings

15. 480 stickers on 6 sheets or 120 stickers on 2 sheets

In 16–18, compare the rates to find which is the better value.

16. $27 for 4 large pizzas or $32 for 5 large pizzas

17. $30 for 100 flyers or $65 for 250 flyers

18. 36 pictures for $8 or 24 pictures for $5

19. Model with Math Katrina and Becca exchanged 270 text messages in 45 minutes. An equal number of texts was sent each minute. The girls can send 90 more text messages before they are charged additional fees. Complete the double number line diagram. At this rate, for how many more minutes can the girls exchange texts before they are charged extra? MP.4

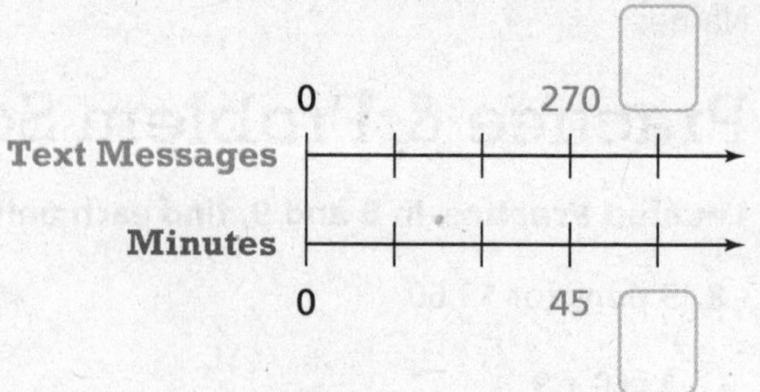

20. Reasoning Which container of milk would you buy? Explain. MP.2

21. Higher Order Thinking Amil and Abe rode in a bike-a-thon. Abe rode for 77 minutes at a faster rate per mile than Amil. Find Amil's unit rate. Then explain how you could use it to find a possible unit rate for Abe.

Assessment Practice

22. A food warehouse sells cans of soup in boxes. Bargain shoppers have four options. Complete the table to find the unit price for each option. Identify the best value.

Boxes of Soup	Unit Price
12 cans for $10.56	
16 cans for $13.60	
20 cans for $17.20	
24 cans for $21.36	

Lesson 5-7
Solve Unit Rate Problems

Go Online | PearsonRealize.com

I can...
use unit rates to solve problems.

Common Core Content Standards
6.RP.A.3b
Mathematical Practices
MP.2, MP.4, MP.7, MP.8

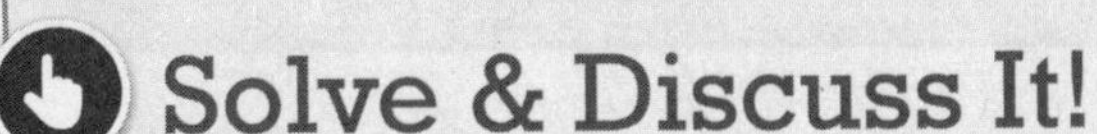

Solve & Discuss It!

Suppose you are traveling by train to visit a friend who lives 275 miles away. How long will the trip take? Moving at a constant speed, how long would it take the train to travel 385 miles?

The train travels at a constant speed of 55 miles per hour.

Model with Math How can you use what you know about unit rates to model and solve this problem? MP.4

Focus on math practices

Reasoning Suppose the train was traveling at a constant speed that is twice as fast as 55 miles per hour. How long would it take the train to go 275 miles? Explain. MP.2

? **Essential Question** How can you use unit rates to solve problems?

  INTERACTIVE ANIMATION  ASSESS

EXAMPLE 1  Solve Constant Speed Problems

Scan for Multimedia 

The jet flies at a constant speed.

Constant speed means that the speed stays the same over time.

If the jet continues to fly at the same rate, how far could it fly in 85 minutes?

The jet flies 175 miles in 7 minutes.

ONE WAY Use a table to record equivalent rates to find how far the jet could fly in 85 minutes.

Time (min)	Distance (mi)
1	25
7	175
25	625
50	1,250
85	2,125

×85 ×85

The jet could fly 2,125 miles in 85 minutes.

ANOTHER WAY Use the unit rate to find how far the jet could fly in 85 minutes.

$$\frac{175 \text{ miles} \div 7}{7 \text{ minutes} \div 7} = \frac{25 \text{ miles}}{1 \text{ minute}}$$

$$\frac{25 \text{ miles} \times 85}{1 \text{ minute} \times 85} = \frac{2{,}125 \text{ miles}}{85 \text{ minutes}}$$

Find an equivalent rate.

Look for Relationships The table and the equation represent the same relationship. MP.7

The jet could fly 2,125 miles in 85 minutes.

Try It!

At the same rate, how far would the jet fly in 75 minutes?

$$\frac{\square \text{ miles} \times \square}{1 \text{ minute} \times \square} = \frac{\square \text{ miles}}{75 \text{ minutes}}$$

The jet would fly ☐ miles.

Convince Me! How could you use the table from Example 1 to find how far the jet would fly in 75 minutes? Explain.

EXAMPLE 2  Solve Unit Price Problems

  ACTIVITY  ASSESS

Grocery Giant is having a sale on Swiss cheese. How much would it cost to buy 5 slices of cheese at the same rate?

Reasoning How can you use the unit price to solve the problem? MP.2

ONE WAY Use a ratio table to solve.

Slices	Price
1	$0.30
5	$1.50
24	$7.20

ANOTHER WAY Use the unit price to solve.

$$\frac{\$7.20 \div 24}{24 \text{ slices} \div 24} = \frac{\$0.30}{1 \text{ slice}}$$

$$\frac{\$0.30 \times 5}{1 \text{ slice} \times 5} = \frac{\$1.50}{5 \text{ slices}}$$

At this rate, it would cost $1.50 for 5 slices of cheese.

 **Try It!**

Jarod paid $13.80 for 5 tickets to the game. At the same rate, how much would 3 tickets cost?

EXAMPLE 3  Use an Equation to Represent Unit Rate Problems

A ferryboat travels at a constant speed of 57.5 miles in 2.5 hours. How long would it take the ferryboat to travel 92 miles at that rate?

STEP 1 Find the unit rate.

Time (h)	1	2.5
Distance (mi)	23	57.5

÷2.5 (both rows)

The ferryboat travels at a rate of 23 miles per hour.

STEP 2 Find the time.

$d = r \times t$ — The equation shows that distance is the product of rate and time.

$92 = 23t$ — Substitute 92 for distance and 23 for the rate.

$\frac{92}{23} = \frac{23t}{23}$

$t = 4$

It would take 4 hours for the ferryboat to travel 92 miles.

Generalize You can use a formula such as $d = r \times t$ to solve constant speed problems. MP.8

Try It!

A submarine travels 19 miles in $\frac{1}{2}$ hour. Write an equation to find out how long it would take the submarine to travel 57 miles at the same rate. Then find the time.

KEY CONCEPT

You can use ratio tables or unit rates to solve rate problems, including constant speed problems.

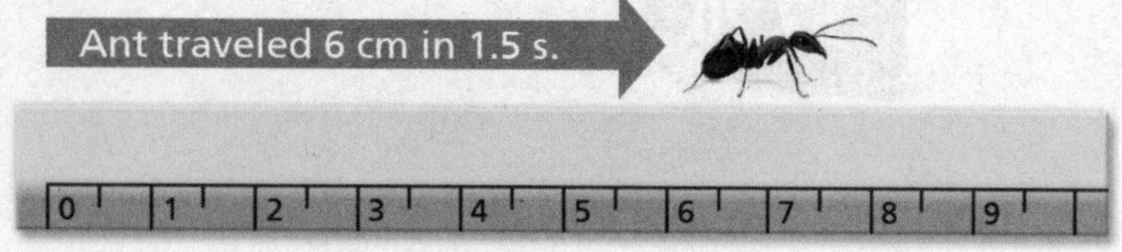

Time (s)	Distance (cm)
1	4
1.5	6
3	12
4.5	18
6	24

×6 ×6

Do You Understand?

1. **Essential Question** How can you use unit rates to solve problems?

2. **Construct Arguments** An ostrich runs 6 miles in 12 minutes at a constant speed. Explain how you can use a unit rate to find how far the ostrich could run in 40 minutes. MP.3

3. Bananas sell for \$0.58 per pound. How could you write an equation to show the relationship between the total cost, c, and the number of pounds of bananas, p?

Do You Know How?

In 4 and 5, use unit rates to solve.

4. A football player runs 80 yards in 25 seconds. If he maintains the same rate of speed, how far could he run in 60 seconds?

5. On a family vacation, Amy's dad drove the car at a constant speed and traveled 585 miles in 13 hours. At this rate, how long would it have taken the family to travel 810 miles? What was the car's rate of speed?

6. Look at Exercise 5. Write an equation to find the total distance, d, that Amy's family traveled after t hours.

Name: ______________________________

Practice & Problem Solving

Scan for Multimedia

Leveled Practice **In 7–9, solve the rate problems.**

7. A horse named Northern Dancer won the Kentucky Derby with a time of exactly 2 minutes. At this constant rate, how long would it take Northern Dancer to run the Belmont Stakes?

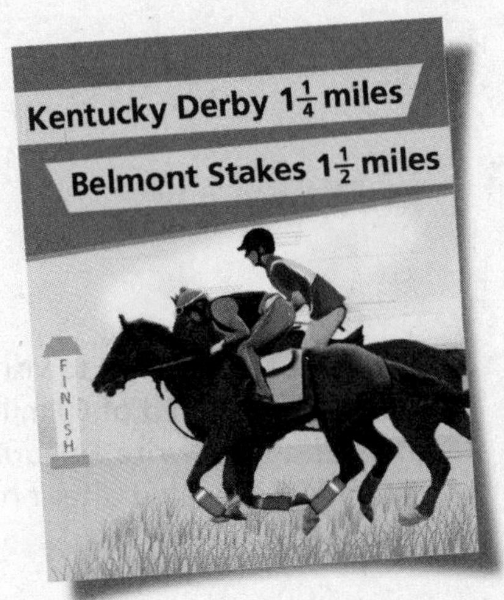

Use the unit rate. $\dfrac{1.25 \text{ miles} \div \square}{2 \text{ minutes} \div 2} = \dfrac{\square \text{ mile}}{1 \text{ minute}}$

Find an equivalent rate. $\dfrac{\square \text{ mile} \times 2.4}{1 \text{ minute} \times \square} = \dfrac{1.5 \text{ miles}}{\square \text{ minutes}}$

It would take Northern Dancer ☐ minutes to run the Belmont Stakes.

8. If a cyclist rides at a constant rate of 24 miles per hour, how long would it take the cyclist to ride 156 miles?

9. The price of an 8-minute phone call is $1.20. What is the price of a 17-minute phone call?

In 10 and 11, use the map at the right.

The Garcia family is driving from San Diego, California, to Bar Harbor, Maine. In 5 days, they have traveled 2,045 miles. At this rate, how long will it take them to travel from San Diego to Bar Harbor?

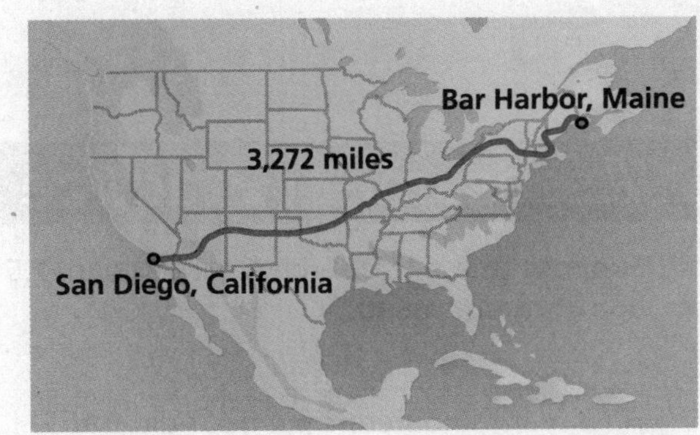

10. How can you use rate reasoning to solve this problem? Explain.

11. Be Precise Show how to use numbers, units, and symbols precisely to solve the problem. MP.6

12. Vik wrote the equation $470 \cdot h = 3{,}008$, where h is the number of hours it took a plane flying at a constant speed of 470 miles per hour to travel 3,008 miles. Solve for h.

13. A nursery owner buys 7 panes of glass to fix some damage to his greenhouse. The 7 panes cost $15.05. Unfortunately, he breaks 2 more panes while repairing the damage. What is the cost of another 2 panes of glass?

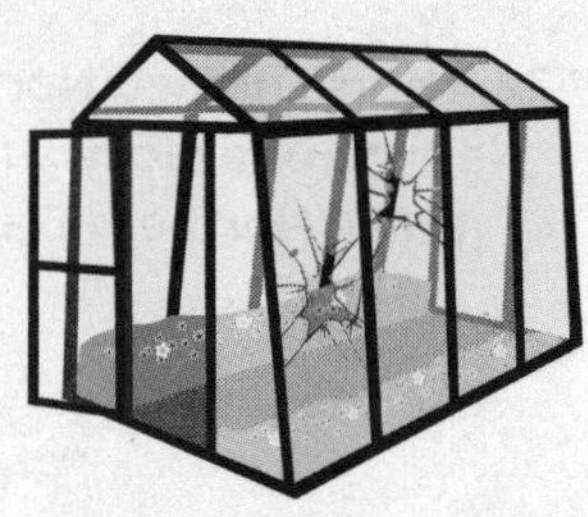

14. Cheyenne took a train to visit her aunt. The train traveled at a constant speed of 60 miles per hour. Complete the table, and then write an equation to find the total distance, d, traveled after t hours.

Time, t (hours)	1	2	3	4
Distance, d (miles)	60			

15. Jayden bought 70 feet of speaker wire for $18.20. He needs 30 more feet. If the unit price is the same, how much will Jayden pay for the extra 30 feet of wire? Explain.

16. **Higher Order Thinking** Sasha runs at a constant speed of 3.8 meters per second for $\frac{1}{2}$ hour. Then she walks at a constant rate of 1.5 meters per second for $\frac{1}{2}$ hour. How far did Sasha run and walk in 60 minutes?

Assessment Practice

17. Suppose that a leatherback turtle swam 7.5 kilometers in 3 hours at a constant speed.

PART A

How many kilometers per hour did the turtle swim?

PART B

At this rate, how long would it take the turtle to swim 10 kilometers?

3-ACT MATH

3-Act Mathematical Modeling: Get in Line

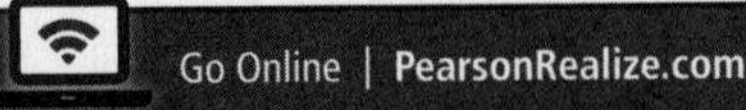

Common Core Content Standards
6.RP.A.2, 6.RP.A.3b

Mathematical Practices
MP.4

ACT 1

1. After watching the video, what is the first question that comes to mind?

2. Write the Main Question you will answer.

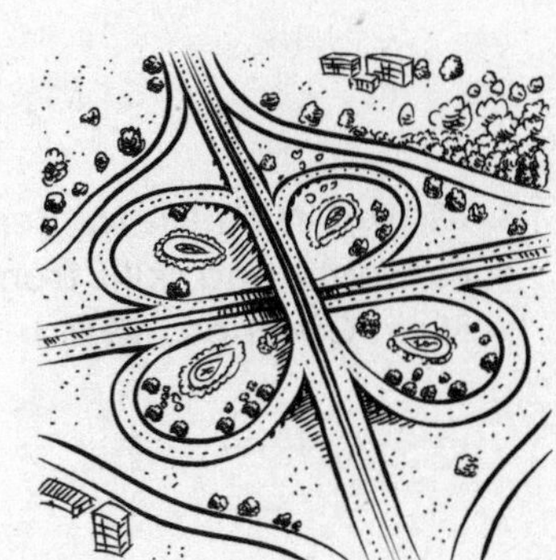

3. Construct Arguments Predict an answer to this Main Question. Explain your prediction. MP.3

4. On the number line below, write a number that is too small to be the answer. Write a number that is too large.

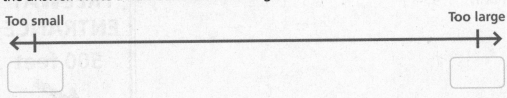

5. Plot your prediction on the same number line.

ACT 2

6. What information in this situation would be helpful to know? How would you use that information?

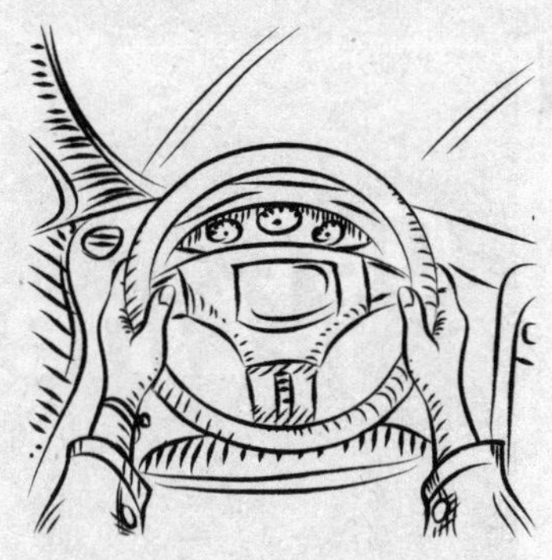

7. **Use Appropriate Tools** What tools can you use to get the information you need? Record the information as you find it. MP.5

8. **Model with Math** Represent the situation using the mathematical content, concepts, and skills from this topic. Use your representation to answer the Main Question. MP.4

9. What is your answer to the Main Question? Is it higher or lower than your prediction? Explain why.

ACT 3

10. Write the answer you saw in the video.

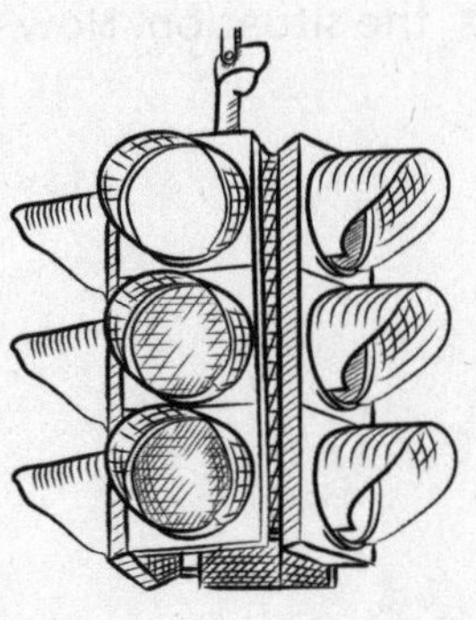

11. **Reasoning** Does your answer match the answer in the video? If not, what are some reasons that would explain the difference? MP.2

12. **Make Sense and Persevere** Would you change your model now that you know the answer? Explain. MP.1

ACT 3 Extension

Reflect

13. Model with Math Explain how you used a mathematical model to represent the situation. How did the model help you answer the Main Question? MP.4

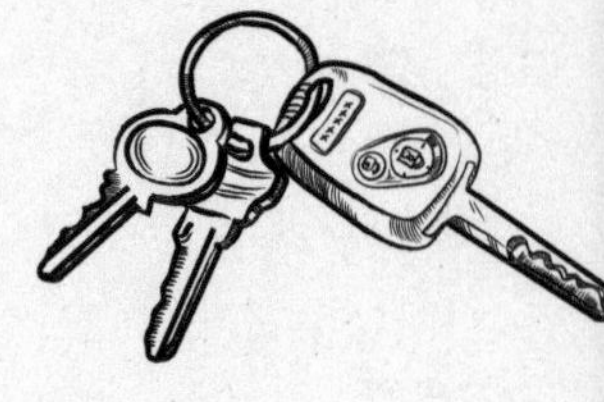

14. Generalize Will your model work on other lights? Explain your reasoning. MP.8

SEQUEL

15. Use Structure Later that week, it took between 20 and 21 minutes to get through the same light. How many cars were in line? MP.7

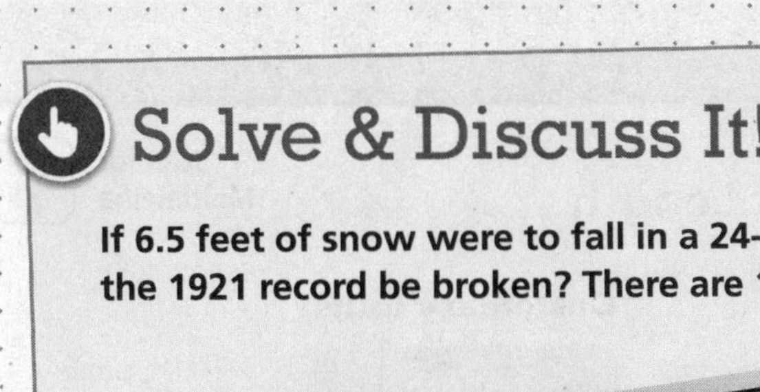

Solve & Discuss It!

If 6.5 feet of snow were to fall in a 24-hour period, would the 1921 record be broken? There are 12 inches in 1 foot.

THE NEWS
April 15, 1921
Silver Lake, Colorado
RECORD BREAKING SNOWFALL
75.8 INCHES IN 24 HOURS
BREAKING NEWS
Man digging his pickup truck out from snow.

Lesson 5-8

Ratio Reasoning: Convert Customary Units

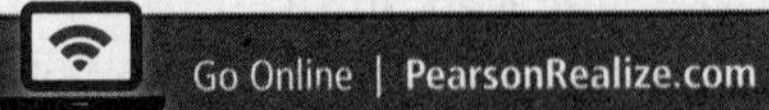

I can...
use ratio reasoning to convert customary measurements.

Common Core Content Standards
6.RP.A.3d

Mathematical Practices
MP.1, MP.2, MP.3, MP.4

Reasoning Use the relationship between inches and feet to solve the problem. MP.2

Focus on math practices

Make Sense and Persevere How many feet of snow would need to fall in Silver Lake, Colorado, to break the 1921 24-hour snowfall record from 1921? MP.1

? Essential Question How can you use ratios to convert customary units of measure?

INTERACTIVE ANIMATION

ASSESS

EXAMPLE 1  Convert Customary Units of Length

Scan for Multimedia 

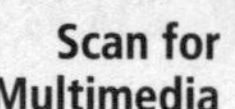

The sidewalk in front of a store is 4.5 feet wide. The city regulations establish a maximum width for sidewalks of 66 inches. Does the sidewalk meet the city regulations?

Customary Units

Length
1 ft = 12 in.
1 yd = 36 in.
1 yd = 3 ft
1 mi = 5,280 ft
1 mi = 1,760 yd

Model with Math The conversions in the table can be written as rates that compare equivalent measurements. MP.4

ONE WAY

Write the width of the sidewalk in inches.

Identify the conversion rate that relates feet to inches.

12 in. = 1 ft

Find an equivalent rate.

$\frac{12 \text{ in.} \times 4.5}{1 \text{ ft} \times 4.5} = \frac{54 \text{ in.}}{4.5 \text{ ft}}$

Multiply both terms of the rate by 4.5.

The sidewalk is 54 inches wide. It meets the city regulations.

ANOTHER WAY

Use **dimensional analysis** to convert measures by including measurement units when you multiply by a conversion factor. A **conversion factor** is a rate that compares equivalent measures.

$4.5 \not{\text{ft}} \times \frac{12 \text{ in.}}{1 \not{\text{ft}}}$

$= 4.5 \times 12 \text{ in.}$

$= 54 \text{ in.}$

Multiply by the conversion factor that relates the measures and leaves you with the units needed to solve the problem. Divide out the common units.

The sidewalk is 54 inches wide. It meets the city regulations.

Try It!

According to city regulations, how many feet wide is the maximum sidewalk width? Explain.

Convince Me! What conversion factor would you use when converting 66 inches to feet? Explain.

EXAMPLE 2  Convert Customary Units of Capacity

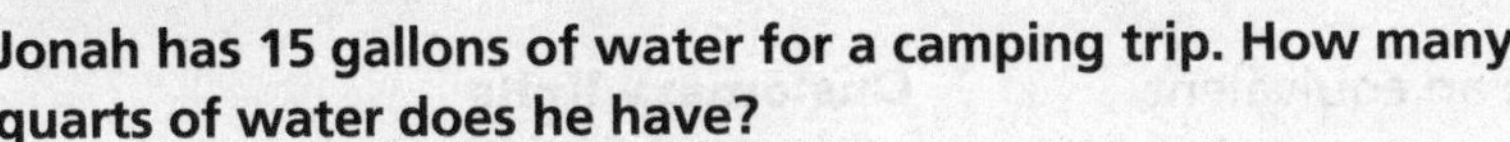

Jonah has 15 gallons of water for a camping trip. How many quarts of water does he have?

Customary Units

Capacity	
1 tbsp = 3 tsp	1 pt = 2 c
1 fl oz = 2 tbsp	1 qt = 2 pt
1 c = 8 fl oz	1 gal = 4 qt

ONE WAY Use an equivalent rate.

4 qt = 1 gal — Identify the conversion rate.

$\frac{4 \text{ qt} \times 15}{1 \text{ gal} \times 15} = \frac{60 \text{ qt}}{15 \text{ gal}}$ — Multiply both terms of the rate by 15.

Jonah has 60 quarts of water.

ANOTHER WAY Use dimensional analysis.

$15 \cancel{\text{gal}} \times \frac{4 \text{ qt}}{1 \cancel{\text{gal}}}$ — Multiply by the conversion factor. Divide out the common units.

$= 15 \times 4 \text{ qt}$

$= 60 \text{ qt}$

Jonah has 60 quarts of water.

Make Sense and Persevere
How can you use the conversion table to identify an appropriate conversion rate? MP.1

Try It!

Brandon is making bread. His recipe says to use $2\frac{1}{2}$ tablespoons of sugar. How many teaspoons of sugar should he use?

EXAMPLE 3  Convert Customary Units of Weight

The alpine pika is a small mammal in the rabbit family. How much does the alpine pika weigh in pounds?

Customary Units

Weight
1 lb = 16 oz
1 T = 2,000 lb

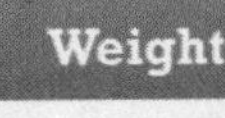

The number of ounces in the conversion rate is greater than the number of ounces that the pika weighs. Use division to find the equivalent rate.

ONE WAY Use an equivalent rate.

16 oz = 1 lb — Identify the conversion rate.

$\frac{16 \text{ oz} \div 1.6}{1 \text{ lb} \div 1.6} = \frac{10 \text{ oz}}{0.625 \text{ lb}}$ — Divide both terms of the rate by 1.6.

The alpine pika weighs 0.625 pound.

ANOTHER WAY Use dimensional analysis.

$10 \cancel{\text{oz}} \times \frac{1 \text{ lb}}{16 \cancel{\text{oz}}}$ — Multiply by the conversion factor. Divide out the common units.

$= \frac{10}{16} \text{ lb}$

$= 0.625 \text{ lb}$

The alpine pika weighs 0.625 pound.

Try It!

How many pounds does the elephant weigh?

KEY CONCEPT

You can convert customary measures by finding an equivalent rate or by using dimensional analysis.

Use an equivalent rate.

1 mi = 5,280 ft

$\frac{5,280 \text{ ft} \times 4.25}{1 \text{ mi} \times 4.25} = \frac{22,440 \text{ ft}}{4.25 \text{ mi}}$

Use dimensional analysis.

$4.25 \cancel{\text{mi}} \times \frac{5,280 \text{ ft}}{1 \cancel{\text{mi}}}$

$= 4.25 \times 5,280 \text{ ft}$

$= 22,440 \text{ ft}$

Customary Units

Length
1 ft = 12 in.
1 yd = 36 in.
1 yd = 3 ft
1 mi = 5,280 ft
1 mi = 1,760 yd

Do You Understand?

1. **Essential Question** How can you use ratios to convert customary units of measure?

2. What is a conversion factor that relates miles to yards?

3. **Construct Arguments** Jenna used the conversion factor $\frac{1 \text{ T}}{2,000 \text{ lb}}$ to convert 50 tons to pounds. Did she use the correct conversion factor? Explain. MP.3

4. How can you use the conversion rates of fluid ounces to cups, and cups to pints, to find the number of fluid ounces in a pint?

Do You Know How?

5. Convert 27 inches to yards by finding an equivalent rate.

6. Use dimensional analysis to convert 1.8 pounds to ounces.

7. **Critique Reasoning** Sam is tripling a recipe for an organic cleaning solution. The new recipe calls for 15 tsp of orange oil. To find how many tbsp this is, Sam converted this way:

Conversion factor: $\frac{3 \text{ tsp}}{1 \text{ tbsp}}$

$15 \cancel{\text{tsp}} \times \frac{3 \cancel{\text{tsp}}}{1 \text{ tbsp}} = \frac{45}{1} \text{ tbsp} = 45 \text{ tbsp}$

What error did Sam make? MP.3

Name: ______________________________

Practice & Problem Solving

Scan for Multimedia 

In 8–13, complete each conversion.

8. 5 pt = ☐ c

9. $2\frac{1}{2}$ gal = ☐ qt

10. 2,640 yd = ☐ mi

11. Convert 16 yards to feet. Use the conversion rate 3 feet = 1 yard.

12. Convert 10 pints to quarts. Use the conversion rate 1 quart = 2 pints.

13. Convert 12 ounces to pounds. Use the conversion rate 16 ounces = 1 pound.

14. Two neighbors in a rural area want to know the distance between their homes in miles. What should the neighbors use as a conversion factor to convert this distance to miles?

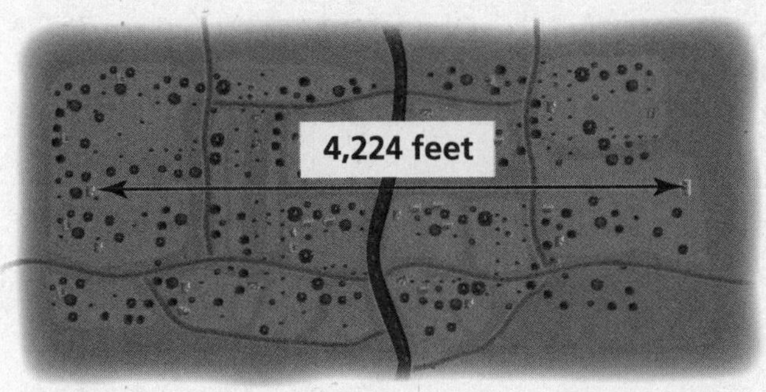

15. A school custodian discovered a leak in a water pipe. The custodian found that 1,920 fluid ounces of water had leaked out. How many gallons of water is this? Use the conversion factor $\frac{1 \text{ gallon}}{128 \text{ fluid ounces}}$.

16. Critique Reasoning Two students, Stella and Vladimir, complete the conversion statement 12 feet 8 inches = ________ inches.

Stella stated that 12 feet 8 inches = 152 inches.
Vladimir stated that 12 feet 8 inches = 9 inches.

Which student is incorrect? Explain. MP.3

17. The hole for a support post needs to be 6 feet deep. It is currently 1 foot 8 inches deep. How much deeper must the hole be? Use the conversion factor $\frac{12 \text{ inches}}{1 \text{ foot}}$.

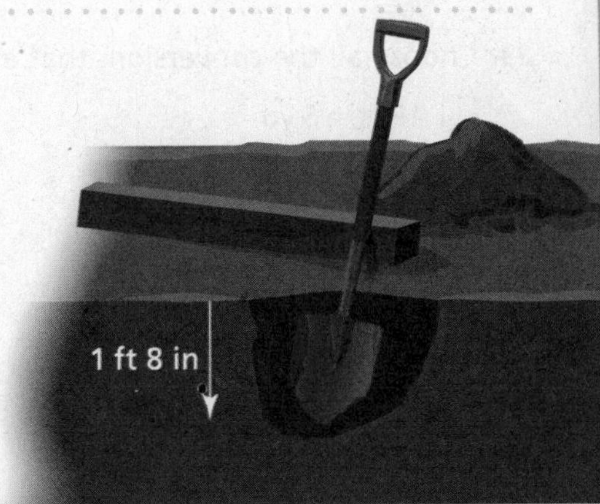

In **18** and **19**, use the recipe card.

Green Slime Recipe

- 1 pint water
- $\frac{1}{2}$ cup cornstarch
- Green food coloring

Add hot water to cornstarch and stir constantly. Then add green food coloring, and stir. Allow the slime to cool to room temperature. This makes a messy slime that goes from liquid to solid. Make sure to play with it on a plastic covered surface. Always have adult supervision when using hot water.

18. Look for Relationships Cheryl has measured 3 cups of water. Is this enough water for Cheryl to make a double recipe of green slime for a class project? Explain. MP.7

19. There are 16 tablespoons in 1 cup. How many tablespoons of cornstarch would Cheryl need to make the green slime recipe 15 times?

20. Make Sense and Persevere Len plans to run at least 3 miles each day to get ready for a cross-country race. One lap of the school track is 440 yards. If Len runs 10 laps each day, will he cover at least 3 miles? Explain. MP.1

21. Higher Order Thinking Hunter is splitting a quart of ice cream with 7 members of his family. If the quart is split evenly, how many cups will each family member get? Explain.

22. A fully loaded and fueled space shuttle can weigh close to 4.5 million pounds at liftoff. What is this weight expressed in tons?

Assessment Practice

23. Choose all the conversions that are true.

- ☐ 18 ft = 6 yd
- ☐ 18 yd = 6 ft
- ☐ 0.5 mi = 10,560 ft
- ☐ 0.5 mi = 2,640 ft
- ☐ $\frac{1}{2}$ mi = 880 yd

Customary Units

Length
1 ft = 12 in.
1 yd = 36 in.
1 yd = 3 ft
1 mi = 5,280 ft
1 mi = 1,760 yd

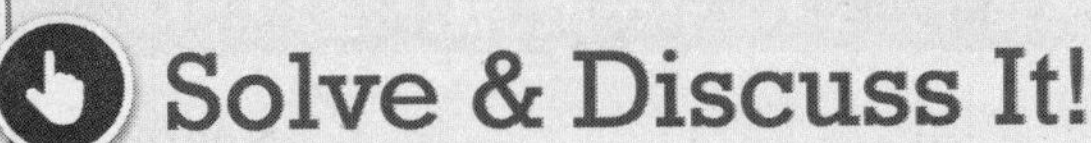

Solve & Discuss It!

Sam needs to fill a 5-liter water jug for his team. If Sam uses the water bottle to fill the jug, how many times does he need to fill the water bottle to fill the jug?

Lesson 5-9

Ratio Reasoning: Convert Metric Units

Go Online | PearsonRealize.com

I can...
use unit rates to convert metric measurements.

Common Core Content Standards
6.RP.A.3d

Mathematical Practices
MP.2, MP.3, MP.6, MP.7, MP.8

Reasoning How many milliliters are in 5 liters? MP.2

Metric Units of Capacity
1,000 milliliters (mL) = 1 liter (L)
100 centiliters (cL) = 1 liter
10 deciliters (dL) = 1 liter
1 dekaliter (daL) = 10 liters
1 hectoliter (hL) = 100 liters
1 kiloliter (kL) = 1,000 liters

Focus on math practices

Be Precise How many liters of water does Sam's water bottle hold when full? MP.6

? Essential Question How can you use ratios to convert metric units of measure?

EXAMPLE 1  Convert Metric Units of Length

Scan for Multimedia

Emelia is helping her father build a skate ramp. They cut a board 1.2 meters long to use as the back of the ramp. Is the length of the board as shown in centimeters correct?

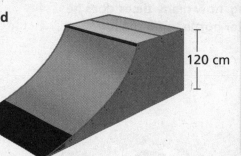

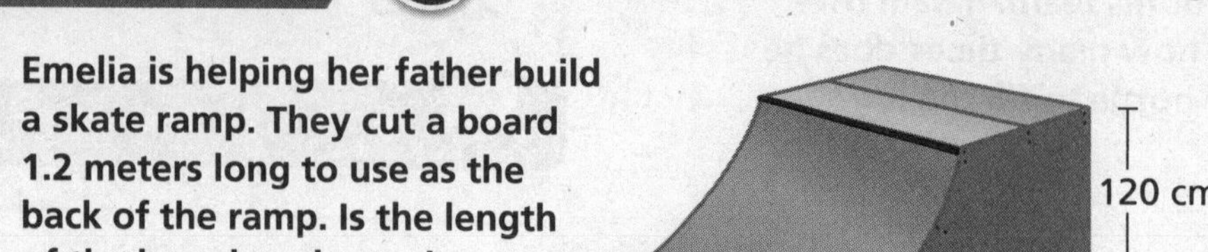

Metric Units of Length
1,000 millimeters (mm) = 1 meter (m)
100 centimeters (cm) = 1 meter
10 decimeters (dm) = 1 meter
1 dekameter (dam) = 10 meters
1 hectometer (hm) = 100 meters
1 kilometer (km) = 1,000 meters

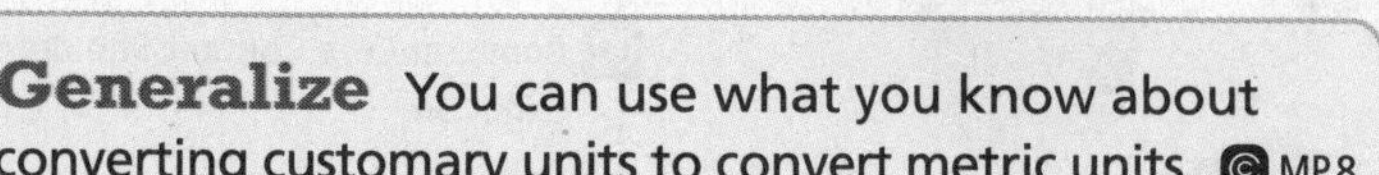

Generalize You can use what you know about converting customary units to convert metric units. MP.8

ONE WAY Use an equivalent rate to convert meters to centimeters.

100 cm = 1 m — Identify the conversion rate.

$\frac{100 \text{ cm} \times 1.2}{1 \text{ m} \times 1.2} = \frac{120 \text{ cm}}{1.2 \text{ m}}$ — Multiply both terms of the rate by 1.2.

1.2 m = 120 cm

The board is the correct length.

ANOTHER WAY Use dimensional analysis to convert meters to centimeters.

$1.2 \text{ m} \times \frac{100 \text{ cm}}{1 \text{ m}}$ — Multiply by the conversion factor. Divide out the common units.

$= 1.2 \times 100 \text{ cm}$

$= 120 \text{ cm}$

1.2 m = 120 cm

The board is the correct length.

Try It!

The middle of the skate ramp is 2.5 meters wide. Emelia and her father want to use a board that is 23.5 decimeters long. Is this board wide enough for them to use? Convert the decimeters to meters to explain.

Convince Me! How can you convert 2.5 meters to decimeters to determine whether the board is wide enough?

EXAMPLE 2  Convert Metric Units of Capacity

Raji poured 150 liters of water into an aquarium. How much more water does Raji need to fill the aquarium?

2.2 hectoliters total capacity

Metric Units of Capacity
1,000 milliliters (mL) = 1 liter (L)
100 centiliters (cL) = 1 liter
10 deciliters (dL) = 1 liter
1 dekaliter (daL) = 10 liters
1 hectoliter (hL) = 100 liters
1 kiloliter (kL) = 1,000 liters

ONE WAY Use an equivalent rate.

1 hectoliter = 100 liters

$\frac{1 \text{ hL} \times 2.2}{100 \text{ L} \times 2.2} = \frac{2.2 \text{ hL}}{220 \text{ L}}$

220 L − 150 L = 70 L — Subtract 150 L from the capacity of the aquarium.

Raji needs 70 more liters of water.

ANOTHER WAY Use dimensional analysis.

$2.2 \cancel{\text{hL}} \times \frac{100 \text{ L}}{1 \cancel{\text{hL}}}$

$= 2.2 \times 100 \text{ L}$

$= 220 \text{ L}$

220 L − 150 L = 70 L — Subtract 150 L from the capacity of the aquarium.

Raji needs 70 more liters of water.

EXAMPLE 3  Convert Metric Units of Mass

Lyle has a bowl that contains 0.8 kilogram of salt. He uses a spoon to remove 850 centigrams of salt. How much salt, in centigrams, remains?

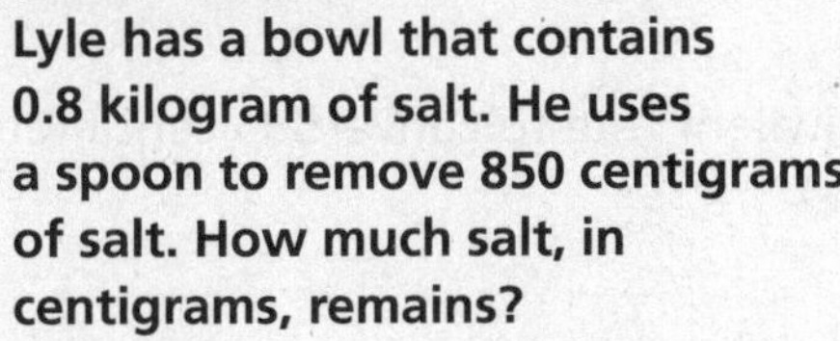

Metric Units of Mass
1,000 milligrams (mg) = 1 gram (g)
100 centigrams (cg) = 1 gram
10 decigrams (dg) = 1 gram
1 dekagram (dag) = 10 grams
1 hectogram (hg) = 100 grams
1 kilogram (kg) = 1,000 grams

Calculate the conversion rate of kilograms to centigrams.

$1 \text{ kg} = 1{,}000 \cancel{\text{g}} \times \frac{100 \text{ cg}}{1 \cancel{\text{g}}}$

$1 \text{ kg} = 1{,}000 \times 100 \text{ cg}$

$1 \text{ kg} = 100{,}000 \text{ cg}$

Convert 0.8 kilogram to centigrams.

$\frac{1 \text{ kg} \times 0.8}{100{,}000 \text{ cg} \times 0.8} = \frac{0.8 \text{ kg}}{80{,}000 \text{ cg}}$

80,000 cg − 850 cg = 79,150 cg — Subtract 850 cg from the original mass.

79,150 cg of salt remains in the bowl.

Look for Relationships
You could also convert kilograms to centigrams using dimensional analysis. MP.7

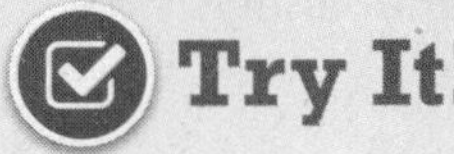

Try It!

To make violet paint, Iris mixes 0.25 liter of red paint, 0.25 liter of blue paint, and 4.5 centiliters of white paint. How many centiliters of paint are in the mixture?

KEY CONCEPT 

You can convert metric measures by finding an equivalent rate or by using dimensional analysis.

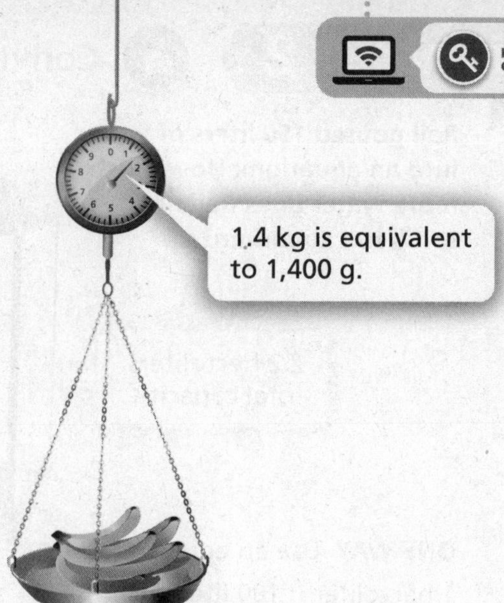

Use an equivalent rate.

$1 \text{ kg} = 1{,}000 \text{ g}$

$\frac{1 \text{ kg} \times 1.4}{1{,}000 \text{ g} \times 1.4} = \frac{1.4 \text{ kg}}{1{,}400 \text{ g}}$

Use dimensional analysis.

$1.4 \cancel{\text{kg}} \times \frac{1{,}000 \text{ g}}{1 \cancel{\text{kg}}}$

$= 1.4 \times 1{,}000 \text{ g}$

$= 1{,}400 \text{ g}$

Do You Understand?

1. **Essential Question** How can you use ratios to convert metric units of measure?

2. **Be Precise** How are the metric units kilometer and kilogram the same? How are they different? MP.6

3. **Reasoning** Which is greater, 250 m or 0.25 km? Justify your reasoning. MP.2

4. How can you find the conversion rate for milliliters to kiloliters?

Do You Know How?

5. What is the conversion factor when converting from liters to milliliters?

6. Use an equivalent rate to convert 35 centimeters to meters.

7. **Critique Reasoning** Maddy wants to know how many centigrams are in 0.75 gram. She converted 0.75 gram to its equivalent in centigrams as shown. Is her work correct? Explain. MP.3

$\frac{10 \text{ cg} \times 0.75}{1 \text{ g} \times 0.75} = \frac{7.5 \text{ cg}}{0.75 \text{ g}}$

8. Look at Exercise 7. Use dimensional analysis to convert 0.75 gram to centigrams.

PRACTICE

TUTORIAL

Name: ______________________

Practice & Problem Solving

Scan for Multimedia

Leveled Practice In 9 and 10, complete each conversion using an equivalent rate.

9. 4 m = ☐ cm

$$\frac{100 \text{ cm} \times \square}{1 \text{ m} \times \square} = \frac{\square \text{ cm}}{4 \text{ m}}$$

10. 800 mL = ☐ L

$$\frac{1{,}000 \text{ mL} \div \square}{1 \text{ L} \div \square} = \frac{800 \text{ mL}}{\square \text{ L}}$$

Leveled Practice In 11 and 12, complete each conversion using dimensional analysis.

11. 200 cL = ☐ L

$$200 \text{ cL} \times \frac{\square \text{ L}}{\square \text{ cL}} = \frac{\square}{\square} \text{ L} = \square \text{ L}$$

12. 2.5 kg = ☐ g

$$2.5 \text{ kg} \times \frac{\square \text{ g}}{\square \text{ kg}} = \frac{\square}{\square} \text{ g} = \square \text{ g}$$

In 13 and 14, complete each conversion.

13. 80 cm = ☐ m

14. 2.1 g = ☐ mg

In 15–17, use the table showing the amount of liquid that Whitney drinks each day.

Drink	Amount
Juice	250 mL
Milk	400 mL
Water	1,500 mL

15. How many liters of water does Whitney drink each day?

16. What is the total amount of liquid, in liters, that Whitney drinks each day?

17. Troy drinks 1.8 L of water each day. How many more milliliters of water does Troy drink each day than Whitney?

18. There are 10 millimeters in 1 centimeter, so about how many millimeters long is this dinosaur bone? Explain.

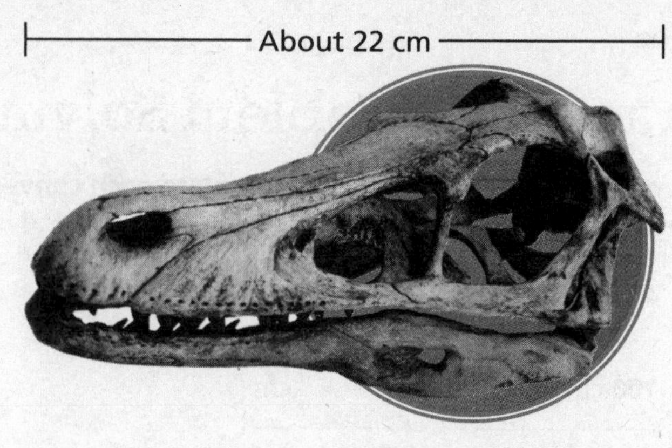

19. Critique Reasoning Savannah says that 1 kilogram is equivalent to 1,000,000 milligrams. Is Savannah correct? Explain. MP.3

20. Model with Math Lucas hiked 14,300 meters in the morning. After lunch he continued hiking. When he finished the hike, he had covered 31.5 kilometers in all. Write an equation that can be used to find how far Lucas hiked after lunch. MP.4

21. Tariq has a collection of 35 quarters that he wants to send to his cousin. What is the total weight of the quarters in kilograms?

22. Higher Order Thinking Louis has a bag of 25 pencils. Each pencil is 18 centimeters long. What is the combined length of the pencils in meters?

Assessment Practice

23. Choose all the conversions that are equivalent to the capacity of a 5.5-liter pitcher of lemonade.

- ☐ 0.0055 kL
- ☐ 55 mL
- ☐ 0.055 kL
- ☐ 550 mL
- ☐ 5,500 mL

24. Choose all the conversions that are equivalent to the mass of a 425-gram football.

- ☐ 42,000 mg
- ☐ 42,500 cg
- ☐ 450 dg
- ☐ 4.25 hg
- ☐ 0.425 kg

Explain It!

Lesson 5-10
Relate Customary and Metric Units

Go Online | PearsonRealize.com

I can...
convert between customary and metric units.

Common Core Content Standards
6.RP.A.3d

Mathematical Practices
MP.1, MP.2, MP.3, MP.8

Gianna and her friends are in a relay race. They have a pail that holds 1 liter of water. They need to fill the 1-liter pail, run 50 yards, and dump the water into the large bucket until it overflows. Gianna says that as long as they do not spill any of the water, they will need 7 trips with the 1-liter pail before the large bucket overflows.

Units of Capacity Conversion Chart	
1 gal ≈ 3.79 L	1 L ≈ 0.26 gal
1 gal = 4 qt	1 L ≈ 1.06 qt
1 qt ≈ 0.95 L	

The ≈ symbol means "about" or "approximately."

1 Liter

A. Which conversion factor could you use to determine whether Gianna is correct? Explain.

B. Critique Reasoning Gianna's friend Linus says that you cannot be certain how many trips it will take because the conversion is approximate. Is Linus's reasoning appropriate? Explain. MP.3

C. Construct Arguments Is Gianna correct that 7 trips are needed before the bucket overflows? If not, how many trips will it take? Use the table to justify your answer. MP.3

Focus on math practices

Construct Arguments Morgan says that 4 liters is less than 1 gallon. Construct an argument to show that Morgan is incorrect. MP.3

Essential Question How can you use ratios to convert customary and metric units of measure?

  INTERACTIVE ANIMATION  ASSESS

EXAMPLE 1  Convert from Metric Units to Customary Units

Scan for Multimedia 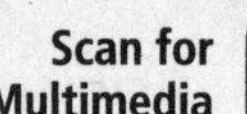 

Tyrel is using a kit to build a robot. The directions use metric units and describe the robot's height as 2 meters tall. About how many inches is 2 meters? Round to the nearest tenth.

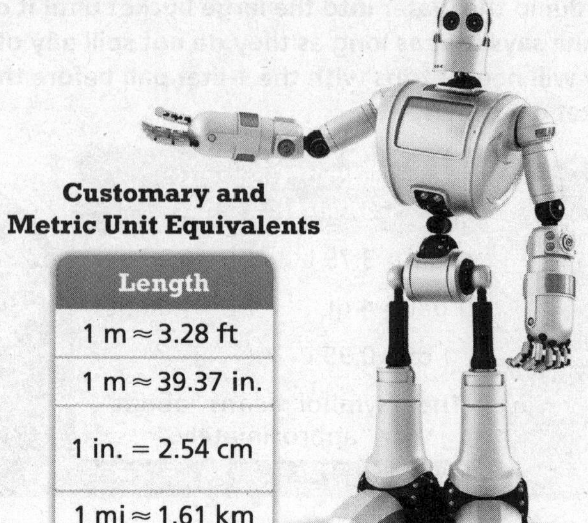

Make Sense and Persevere When relating customary and metric units, exact whole-number conversions are rare. The table shows approximate equivalents. MP.1

Customary and Metric Unit Equivalents

Length
1 m ≈ 3.28 ft
1 m ≈ 39.37 in.
1 in. = 2.54 cm
1 mi ≈ 1.61 km

ONE WAY Find an equivalent rate to convert meters to inches.

1 m ≈ 39.37 in.

$\frac{39.37 \text{ in.} \times 2}{1 \text{ m} \times 2} = \frac{78.74 \text{ in.}}{2 \text{ m}}$ Multiply both terms of the rate by 2.

78.74 ≈ 78.7 Round to the nearest tenth of an inch.

So, 2 m ≈ 78.7 in.

ANOTHER WAY Use dimensional analysis to convert meters to inches.

$2 \cancel{m} \times \frac{39.37 \text{ in.}}{1 \cancel{m}}$ Multiply by the conversion factor. Divide out the common units.

2 × 39.37 in. = 78.74 in.

78.74 ≈ 78.7 Round to the nearest tenth of an inch.

So, 2 m ≈ 78.7 in.

Try It!

Jacob is building a robot named T3-X that is 75 inches tall. To the nearest tenth, how many centimeters tall is T3-X?

1 in. = ☐ cm

$75 \cancel{\text{in.}} \times \frac{☐ \text{ cm}}{1 \cancel{\text{in.}}} = 75 \times ☐ \text{ cm} = ☐ \text{ cm}$

T3-X is ☐ cm tall.

Convince Me! If you want to find the height of T3-X in meters, will you get the same answer if you convert inches to centimeters, and then centimeters to meters, as you would if you convert inches to feet, and then feet to meters? Explain.

EXAMPLE 2  Convert from Customary Units to Metric Units

  ACTIVITY  ASSESS

Jenna's Alaskan husky weighs 21 pounds. What is her husky's approximate weight in kilograms? Round to the nearest tenth.

Generalize When relating customary and metric units, use what you know about converting within one measurement system. MP.8

Customary and Metric Unit Equivalents

Weight/Mass
1 oz ≈ 28.35 g
1 kg ≈ 2.20 lb
1 metric ton (t) ≈ 1.102 T

Use dimensional analysis.

$21\ \cancel{lb} \times \frac{1\text{ kg}}{2.20\ \cancel{lb}}$

$\frac{21\text{ kg}}{2.20} \approx 9.5\text{ kg}$ — Divide to simplify. Round to the nearest tenth.

Jenna's Alaskan husky weighs about 9.5 kilograms.

EXAMPLE 3  Convert Using Two Steps

If Deva drank all the water in her bottle, how many cups of water did she drink? Round to the nearest tenth.

Convert liters to quarts, and then quarts to cups.

H2O Ultra 0.75 liter

Customary and Metric Equivalents	Customary Units
Capacity	Capacity
1 gal ≈ 3.79 L	1 tbsp = 3 tsp
1 qt ≈ 0.95 L	1 fl oz = 2 tbsp
1 L ≈ 0.26 gal	1 c = 8 fl oz
1 L ≈ 1.06 qt	1 pt = 2 c
	1 qt = 2 pt
	1 gal = 4 qt

STEP 1

1 L ≈ 1.06 qt

$0.75\ \cancel{L} \times \frac{1.06\text{ qt}}{1\ \cancel{L}}$ — Multiply by the conversion factor. Divide out the common units.

$0.75 \times 1.06 = 0.795$

0.75 L ≈ 0.795 qt

STEP 2

1 qt = 4 c — Identify the conversion factors: 1 qt = 2 pt and 2 pt = 4 c.

$0.795\ \cancel{qt} \times \frac{4\text{ c}}{1\ \cancel{qt}}$ — Multiply by the conversion factor. Divide out the common units.

$0.795 \times 4 = 3.18\text{ c}$ — Multiply the remaining factors.

To the nearest tenth, Deva drank about 3.2 cups of water.

Try It!

Find the length of a 100-yard football field in meters. Use 1 yard = 3 feet and 1 meter ≈ 3.28 feet. Round to the nearest tenth.

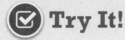

KEY CONCEPT

You can use what you know about converting within one measurement system to relate customary and metric units. You can convert measures with customary and metric units by finding an equivalent rate or using dimensional analysis.

Use an equivalent rate.

$1 \text{ kg} \approx 2.20 \text{ lb}$

$\frac{1 \text{ kg} \times 5}{2.20 \text{ lb} \times 5} = \frac{5 \text{ kg}}{11 \text{ lb}}$

$5 \text{ kg} \approx 11 \text{ lb}$

Use dimensional analysis.

$5 \text{ kg} \times \frac{2.20 \text{ lb}}{1 \text{ kg}}$

$5 \times 2.20 = 11 \text{ lb}$

$5 \text{ kg} \approx 11 \text{ lb}$

Do You Understand?

1. **Essential Question** How can you use ratios to convert customary and metric units of measure?

2. **Reasoning** When converting centimeters to inches, do you multiply or divide by 2.54? Explain. MP.2

3. **Use Structure** How can you find the approximate number of liters in 1 pint? MP.7

   Remember: 1 quart = 2 pints

4. How is the conversion from inches to centimeters different from other conversions between customary and metric units?

Do You Know How?

In 5–8, find the equivalent measure. Round to the nearest tenth.

5. 5 in. = ☐ cm

6. 2 mi ≈ ☐ km

7. 113 g ≈ ☐ oz

8. 14 kg ≈ ☐ lb

9. Convert 30 gallons to liters by finding an equivalent rate.

10. Approximately how many ounces are equivalent to 1 kilogram?

Name: ______________________________

Practice & Problem Solving

Scan for Multimedia

In 11–18, find the equivalent measure. Round to the nearest tenth.

11. 9 qt ≈ ☐ L

12. 2 gal ≈ ☐ L

13. 2 in. ≈ ☐ cm

14. 5 km ≈ ☐ mi

15. 10 L ≈ ☐ qt

16. 5.5 t ≈ ☐ T

17. 50 lb ≈ ☐ kg

18. 10 oz ≈ ☐ g

19. A chef at a restaurant uses 12 pounds of butter each day. About how many grams of butter does the chef use each day? Use the conversion factors $\frac{16 \text{ ounces}}{1 \text{ pound}}$ and $\frac{28.35 \text{ grams}}{1 \text{ ounce}}$.

20. Reasoning Simone wants to know whether a new chest of drawers will fit next to her bed. The chest she would like to buy is 73 centimeters wide. She knows that her room is 86 inches wide. The bed is 76 inches wide. Will the chest fit next to her bed? Explain. MP.2

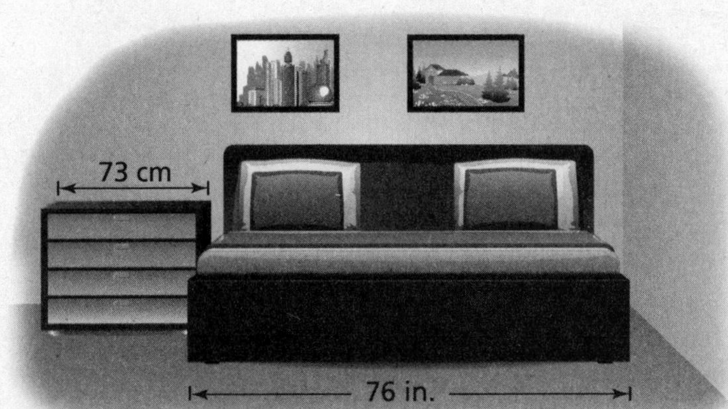

21. Be Precise Denali is the highest mountain in the United States. What is its height in meters? Round to the nearest whole number. MP.6

Denali is approximately
20,320 ft high.

22. Construct Arguments Francesca wants to convert 1 foot to centimeters. Use what you know about customary units to explain how she can do this. MP.3

23. Higher Order Thinking At the state fair, a person must be at least 138 centimeters tall to ride the roller coaster. Billy wants to ride the coaster. He is 4 feet 7 inches tall. Is Billy tall enough to ride the coaster? Explain.

24. Paul's car holds a maximum of 19 gallons of gas. About how many liters of gas does Paul need to fill his gas tank?

9
gallons
remaining

Assessment Practice

25. The posted speed limit is 65 miles per hour. Choose all the metric measures that are faster than 65 miles per hour.

- ☐ 65 km per hour
- ☐ 97.5 km per hour
- ☐ 104 km per hour
- ☐ 105.7 km per hour
- ☐ 120.3 km per hour

26. Boys competing in the long jump event must jump at least 15 feet to qualify for the state track and field meet. Choose all the metric measures that are less than 15 feet.

- ☐ 6.5 m
- ☐ 5.0 m
- ☐ 4.5 m
- ☐ 3.92 m
- ☐ 3.5 m

? Topic Essential Question

What are ratios and rates? How can you use ratios and rates to describe quantities and solve problems?

Vocabulary Review

Complete each definition and then provide an example of each vocabulary word.

Vocabulary	constant speed	conversion factor	rate
	ratio	term	unit price

Definition	Example
1. A relationship in which there are *y* units of a quantity for every *x* units of a quantity is a ___________.	
2. The price of a single item is called a ___________.	
3. A ratio that compares quantities with unlike units of measure is a ___________.	

Use Vocabulary in Writing

Explain how you can convert 52 ounces to pounds. Use vocabulary words in your explanation.

Concepts and Skills Review

LESSON 5-1 Understand Ratios

Quick Review

A ratio is a relationship in which for every *x* units of one quantity there are *y* units of another quantity. A ratio can be written using the word "to," a colon, or a fraction bar to separate the two terms.

Example

The ratio of men to women at a small wedding is 6:4. If there are 16 women at the wedding, how many men are at the wedding?

Draw a diagram to represent the ratio. Because 4 boxes represent 16 women, each box represents 4 women.

There are 24 men at the wedding.

Practice

A florist uses 5 red roses for every 2 white roses in her bouquets.

1. Write the ratio of white roses to red roses in three different ways.

2. Write the ratio of red roses to the total number of flowers in three different ways.

3. If the florist uses 10 red roses in a bouquet, how many white roses does she use?

4. If the florist uses 10 white roses in an arrangement, how many red roses does she use?

LESSON 5-2 Generate Equivalent Ratios

Quick Review

You can multiply or divide both terms of a ratio by the same nonzero number to find equivalent ratios.

Example

Find two ratios that are equivalent to $\frac{21}{126}$.

One Way

Multiply.

$$\frac{21 \times 2}{126 \times 2} = \frac{42}{252}$$

Another Way

Divide.

$$\frac{21 \div 3}{126 \div 3} = \frac{7}{42}$$

Practice

In 1–4, find two ratios equivalent to the given ratio.

1. $\frac{5}{12}$

2. 14:32

3. 3 to 4

4. $\frac{7}{8}$

5. For every 4 bagels sold at a bakery, 7 muffins are sold. How many muffins are sold when the bakery sells 24 bagels? Complete the table.

Bagels	4	8	12	16	20	24
Muffins	7					

LESSON 5-3 Compare Ratios

Quick Review

To compare ratios, make a table to show each ratio and then find a value in which one of the terms is the same in both tables.

Example

Erica

Math Facts	Seconds
25	30
50	60
75	90
100	120
125	150

Klayton

Math Facts	Seconds
38	50
76	100
114	150
152	200
190	250

Erica can complete more facts than Klayton.

Practice

1. The school soccer team buys 3 soccer balls for every 2 players. The school volleyball team buys 7 volleyballs for every 5 players. Which team buys more balls per player?

2. Jenna walks 12 miles in 5 days. Alex walks 7 miles in 3 days. Who walks more miles per day?

LESSON 5-4 Represent and Graph Ratios

Quick Review

You can solve some ratio problems by making a table of equivalent ratios and then graphing the pairs of values on a coordinate plane.

Example

Days of Rain	1	2	3	n
Days of Sun	2	4	6	8

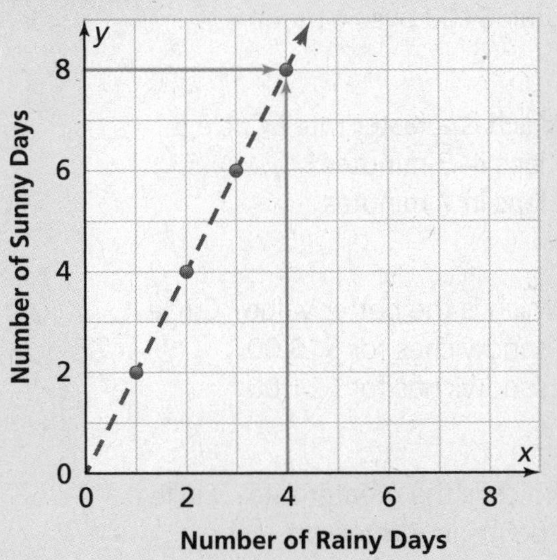

There will be 4 rainy days if there are 8 sunny days.

Practice

1. In gym class, the sixth graders walk 2 laps for every 3 laps they run. If the students run 12 laps, how many laps will they walk? Complete the table. Then plot the pairs of values on the coordinate plane.

Run (laps)	3	6	9	12
Walk (laps)	2			

y: 12, 10, 8, 6, 4, 2, 0

x: 0, 2, 4, 6, 8, 10, 12

LESSON 5-5 Understand Rates and Unit Rates

Quick Review

A rate is a ratio that relates two quantities with different units. A unit rate relates a quantity to 1 unit of another quantity. You can use what you know about dividing fractions to write a ratio of fractions as a unit rate.

Example

Write 20 meters in 4 minutes as a rate and as a unit rate.

Rate:

$$\frac{20 \text{ meters}}{4 \text{ minutes}}$$

Unit Rate:

$$\frac{20 \text{ meters} \div 4}{4 \text{ minutes} \div 4} = \frac{5 \text{ meters}}{1 \text{ minute}}$$

The unit rate is an equivalent rate with a denominator of 1 unit.

Practice

Write each statement as a unit rate.

1. 78 miles on 3 gallons

2. 18 laps in 6 minutes

3. 48 sandwiches for 16 people

4. 49 houses in 7 blocks

5. 6 desks in 2 rows

LESSON 5-6 Compare Unit Rates

Quick Review

A unit rate compares a quantity to 1 unit of another quantity. To compare unit rates, compare the first terms.

Example

On Pet Day, Meg's turtle crawled 30 feet in 6 minutes, and Pat's turtle crawled 25 feet in 5 minutes. Whose turtle crawled at a faster rate?

Write each rate.

Meg's turtle $\frac{30 \text{ ft}}{6 \text{ min}}$ $\frac{25 \text{ ft}}{5 \text{ min}}$ Pat's turtle

Find each unit rate.

$$\frac{5 \text{ ft}}{1 \text{ min}} \quad \frac{5 \text{ ft}}{1 \text{ min}}$$

Both turtles crawled at the same rate.

Practice

1. Which is the better value? Circle it.
$5.00 for 4 mangoes
$6.00 for 5 mangoes

2. Who earned more each month? Circle it.
Atif: $84 over 3 months
Jafar: $100 over 4 months

3. Which is a faster rate? Circle it.
3 laps in 5 minutes
4 laps in 7 minutes

4. Which is the better value? Circle it.
3 sandwiches for $15.00
4 sandwiches for $21.00

5. Which is the greater rate? Circle it.
6 points in 3 attempts
15 points in 5 attempts

LESSON 5-7 Solve Unit Rate Problems

Quick Review

You can use a ratio table or a unit rate to solve problems involving ratios or rates.

Example

A plane travels at a rate of 780 miles in 2 hours. At this rate, how far will it travel in 3.5 hours?

Find the unit rate.

$$\frac{780 \text{ miles} \div 2}{2 \text{ hours} \div 2} = \frac{390 \text{ miles}}{1 \text{ hour}}$$

Find an equivalent rate.

$$\frac{390 \text{ miles} \times 3.5}{1 \text{ hour} \times 3.5} = \frac{1{,}365 \text{ miles}}{3.5 \text{ hours}}$$

The plane will travel 1,365 miles in 3.5 hours.

Practice

1. Doug has 5 hours to make an on-time delivery 273 miles away. Doug drives at a constant speed of 55 miles per hour. Will Doug make the delivery by the deadline? Explain.

2. Marie has 8 hours to write a 45-page chapter for her book. Marie writes at a constant speed of 4 pages per hour. Will Marie complete the chapter in time? Explain.

LESSON 5-8 Ratio Reasoning: Convert Customary Units

Quick Review

You can convert customary measures by finding equivalent rates or by using dimensional analysis.

Example

How many pints are equivalent to 4 quarts?

Find an equivalent rate:

2 pints = 1 quart .... Identify the conversion rate.

$$\frac{2 \text{ pints} \times 4}{1 \text{ quart} \times 4} = \frac{8 \text{ pints}}{4 \text{ quarts}}$$

Use dimensional analysis:

$$4 \text{ quarts} \times \frac{2 \text{ pints}}{1 \text{ quart}} = 8 \text{ pints}$$ .... Multiply by the conversion factor.

So, 8 pints are equivalent to 4 quarts.

Practice

In 1–4, complete each conversion.

1. 2 mi = ☐ ft

2. 144 in. = ☐ yd

3. 4 oz = ☐ lb

4. 3 gal = ☐ qt

5. The hippo at the zoo weighs 1.5 tons. How many pounds does the hippo weigh?

LESSON 5-9 Ratio Reasoning: Convert Metric Units

Quick Review

To convert metric units, use the same methods used for converting customary units. Either use the conversion rate to find an equivalent rate or use dimensional analysis.

Example

Tariq rode his bike 15,100 meters. How many kilometers did he ride his bike?

Find an equivalent rate:

1,000 meters = 1 kilometer

$$\frac{1{,}000 \text{ m} \times 15.1}{1 \text{ km} \times 15.1} = \frac{15{,}100 \text{ m}}{15.1 \text{ km}}$$

Use dimensional analysis:

$$15{,}100 \cancel{\text{m}} \times \frac{1 \text{ km}}{1{,}000 \cancel{\text{m}}} = \frac{15{,}100}{1{,}000} \text{ km} = 15.1 \text{ km}$$

Tariq rode 15.1 kilometers.

Practice

In 1–4, complete each conversion.

1. 3 m = ☐ mm

2. 3,520 mm = ☐ cm

3. 4.2 kg = ☐ g

4. 300 mL = ☐ L

5. Li needs to buy 2 kilograms of apples. If she buys 9 apples that each weigh approximately 150 grams, will she have enough? Explain.

LESSON 5-10 Relate Customary and Metric Units

Quick Review

To convert between metric and customary units, use the conversion rate and find an equivalent rate, or use dimensional analysis. Most conversions will be approximate because, except in the case of inches to centimeters, the conversion rates are approximate.

Example

Gwen has a cooler that holds 3 quarts. About how many liters does the cooler hold?

1 qt ≈ 0.95 L

$$3 \cancel{\text{qt}} \times \frac{0.95 \text{ L}}{1 \cancel{\text{qt}}} = (3 \times 0.95) \text{ L} = 2.85 \text{ L}$$

Gwen's cooler holds approximately 2.85 liters.

Practice

In 1–4, find the equivalent measure. Round to the nearest tenth.

1. 100 g ≈ ☐ oz

2. 6 ft ≈ ☐ m

3. 57 gal ≈ ☐ L

4. 27 km ≈ ☐ mi

5. The science class is raising monarch caterpillars. One of the caterpillars weighs 2.3 ounces. About how many grams does the caterpillar weigh? Round to the nearest tenth.

Pathfinder

Shade a path from START to FINISH. Follow the sums and differences in which the digit in the ones place is greater than the digit in the tenths place. You can only move up, down, right, or left.

I can...
add and subtract multidigit decimals. 6.NS.B.3

START

$31.2 - 5.73$	$1.84 + 19.26$	$25 - 8.53$	$2 - 0.95$	$12.3 - 4.81$
$14.27 + 4.9$	$7.29 - 0.8$	$12.95 + 9.06$	$1.07 + 0.27$	$4.22 + 2.8$
$18 + 4.301$	$3.007 - 1.71$	$8.38 - 6.42$	$10 - 8.94$	$21 - 3.303$
$43.397 + 17.81$	$15.75 - 8.8$	$4.02 - 3.83$	$17.54 + 6.82$	$3.8 + 1.89$
$2.35 + 1.08$	$1.035 - 0.641$	$29.06 + 2.87$	$28.12 - 5.016$	$0.62 + 5.38$

FINISH

UNDERSTAND AND USE PERCENT

Topic Essential Question

What is the meaning of percent? How can percent be estimated and found?

Topic Overview

6-1 Understand Percent
6-2 Relate Fractions, Decimals, and Percents
6-3 Represent Percents Greater Than 100 or Less Than 1
6-4 Estimate to Find Percent
6-5 Find the Percent of a Number
6-6 Find the Whole Given a Part and the Percent
3-Act Mathematical Modeling: Ace the Test

Topic Vocabulary

- percent

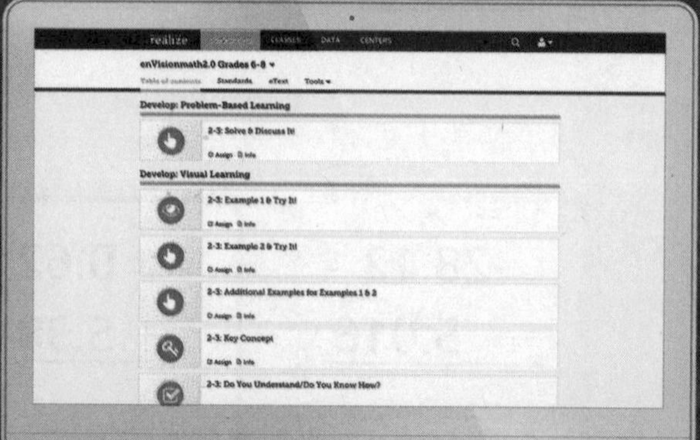

Go online | PearsonRealize.com

Lesson Digital Resources

INTERACTIVE ANIMATION Interact with visual learning animations.

ACTIVITY Use with ***Solve & Discuss It***, ***Explore I*** and ***Explain It*** activities, and to explore Example

VIDEOS Watch clips to support ***3-Act Mathema Modeling Lessons*** and ***STEM Projects***.

PRACTICE Practice what you've learned.

3-ACT MATH

Ace the Test

Ace the Test

Numbers, percents, letters—teachers use grades as a language to help explain how you are doing in class. When you know how your grade is determined, it is easier to understand your teacher's expectations. Think about this during the 3-Act Mathematical Modeling lesson.

TUTORIALS Get help from ***Virtual Nerd***, right when you need it.

KEY CONCEPT Review important lesson content.

GLOSSARY Read and listen to English/Spanish definitions.

ASSESSMENT Show what you've learned.

Additional Digital Resources

MATH TOOLS Explore math with digital tools.

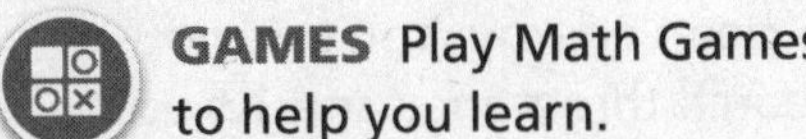

GAMES Play Math Games to help you learn.

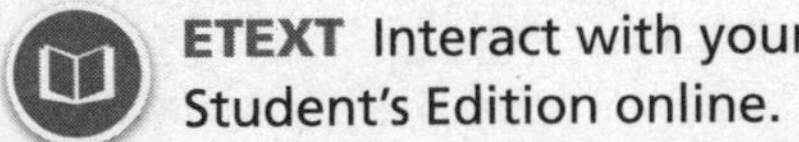

ETEXT Interact with your Student's Edition online.

TOPIC 6

STEM Project

Did You Know?

Extinction normally occurs at a rate of about one to five species per year. The earth is now **losing species** at 1,000 to 10,000 times that rate, with dozens going extinct every day.

There are 1,373 species of birds identified as **threatened**.

13% of all bird species threatened

Polar Bears need ice floes to rest when they travel long distances to find food or migrate. Due to **melting ice**, the population will likely decrease by more than **30%** in the next three generations.

Scientists estimate that the **population** of nearly 17,000 eastern lowland gorillas has **declined** by more than **50%**.

Conservation efforts helped the total number of **black rhinos** to grow from 2,410 to 4,880 in 15 years.

According to the Chinese government, the population of wild giant pandas has reached 1,864, up from 1,596 at last count.

In **100 years**, the number of the world's tigers **declined** from 100,000 to 3,200.

Your Task: Engineering to Prevent Extinction

Engineers help to to prevent extinction with both direct and indirect solutions. Materials engineers develop wood alternatives. Mechanical and chemical engineers produce clean energy. You and your classmates will research threatened species and identify ways that engineers can help to prevent the extinction of these species.

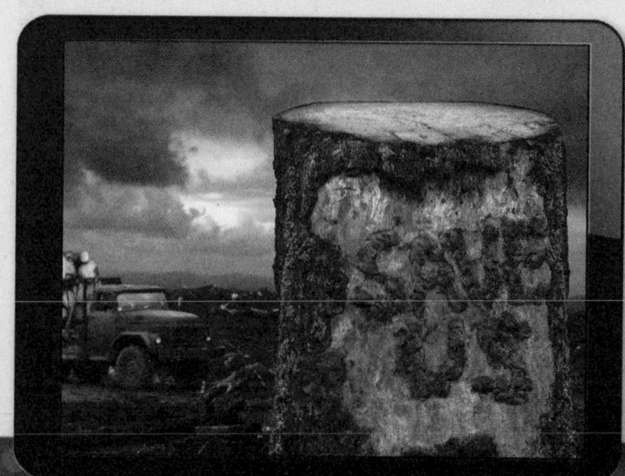

Review What You Know!

Vocabulary

Choose the best term from the box to complete each definition.

decimal
fraction
ratio
term

1. A ______________ can be written as x to y, x:y, or $\frac{x}{y}$.

2. The number 2.25 is a ______________.

3. A number that can be used to describe a part of a whole is a ______________.

Rates

Write an equivalent rate.

4. $\frac{60 \text{ mi}}{1 \text{ hr}} = \frac{\square \text{ mi}}{5 \text{ hr}}$

5. $\frac{8 \text{ hr}}{2 \text{ days}} = \frac{28 \text{ hr}}{\square \text{ days}}$

6. $\frac{16 \text{ limes}}{\square \text{ bags}} = \frac{40 \text{ limes}}{5 \text{ bags}}$

7. $\frac{\square \text{ cups}}{9 \text{ boxes}} = \frac{24 \text{ cups}}{4 \text{ boxes}}$

8. $\frac{\square \text{ m}}{3 \text{ s}} = \frac{135 \text{ m}}{15 \text{ s}}$

9. $\frac{36 \text{ lb}}{\$\square} = \frac{9 \text{ lb}}{\$6}$

Decimal Computation

Find each product or quotient.

10. $21 \div 0.05$

11. 18×1.25

12. $10.2 \div 1.2$

13. 150×0.625

14. $4 \div 100$

15. 0.25×0.1

Equivalent Ratios

Write three equivalent ratios for each ratio.

16. $\frac{8}{12}$

17. $\frac{15}{35}$

18. $\frac{30}{48}$

19. What are two ways to find an equivalent ratio for $\frac{10}{25}$?

Prepare for Reading Success

Before you begin this topic, read through the lessons. Outline the lessons by writing statements that you think are important about each lesson's content. After you finish each lesson, re-read the statements you wrote and correct or change anything that you had not understood.

Lesson Title	Outline Statements	Changes, If Needed
Understand Percent		
Relate Fractions, Decimals, and Percents		
Represent Percents Greater Than 100 or Less Than 1		
Estimate to Find Percent		
Find the Percent of a Number		
Find the Whole Given a Part and the Percent		

Lesson 6-1
Understand Percent

Go Online | PearsonRealize.com

I can...
represent and find the percent of a whole.

Common Core Content Standards
6.RP.A.3c

Mathematical Practices
MP.2, MP.3, MP.4, MP.7

Explain It!

ACTIVITY

Tom made a vegetable pizza and a pepperoni pizza. He cut the vegetable pizza into 5 equal slices and the pepperoni pizza into 10 equal slices. Tom's friends ate 2 slices of vegetable pizza and 4 slices of pepperoni pizza.

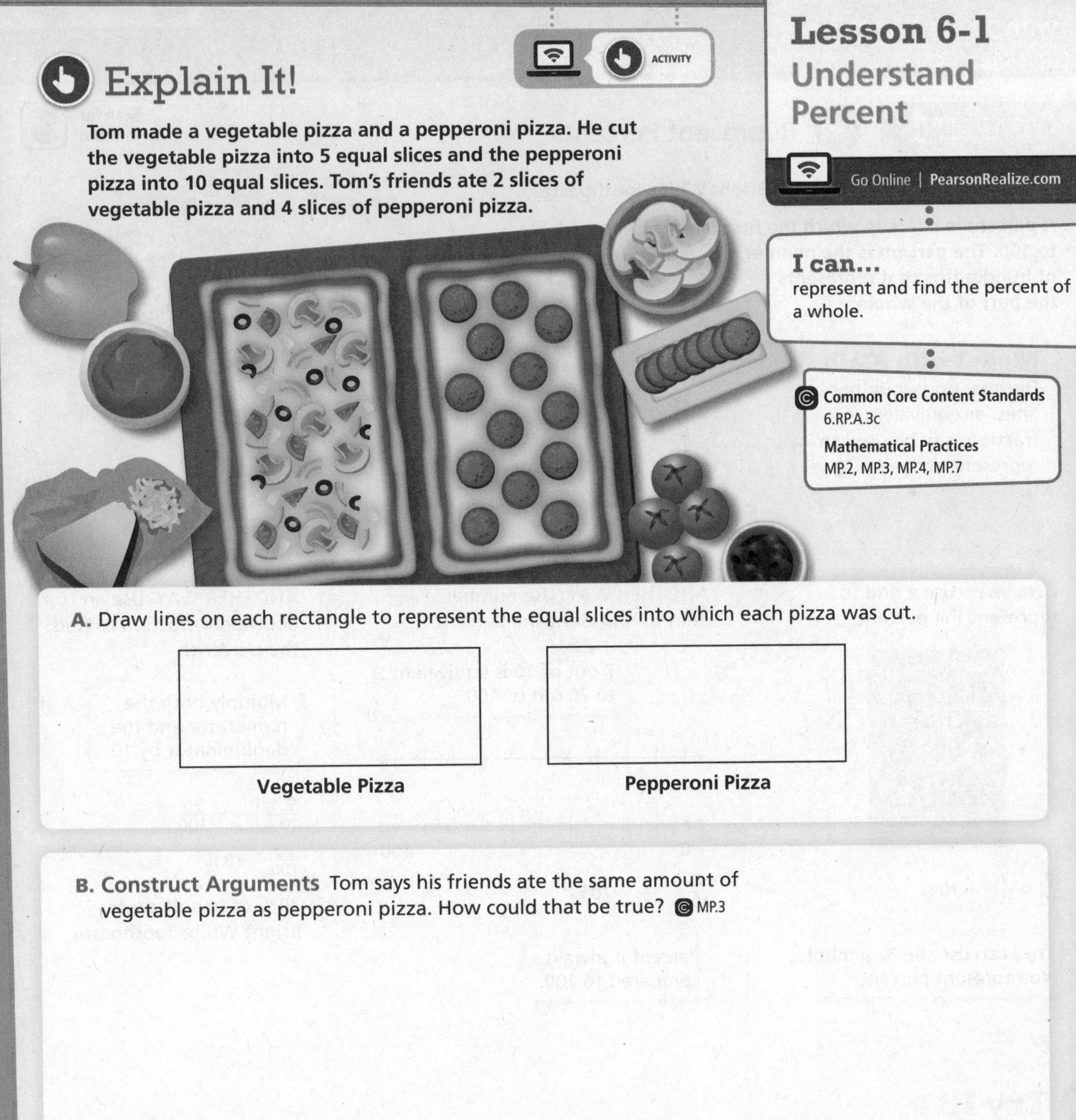

A. Draw lines on each rectangle to represent the equal slices into which each pizza was cut.

Vegetable Pizza **Pepperoni Pizza**

B. Construct Arguments Tom says his friends ate the same amount of vegetable pizza as pepperoni pizza. How could that be true? MP.3

Focus on math practices

Model with Math What if Tom's friends ate $\frac{6}{10}$ of the pepperoni pizza? How could you use the rectangles above to find an equal amount of vegetable pizza? MP.4

? Essential Question How can you represent a rate with 100 as the whole?

EXAMPLE 1 Represent Percents

Scan for Multimedia

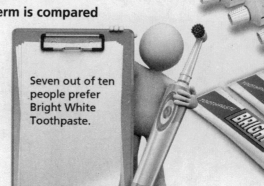

What percent of people prefer Bright White Toothpaste?

A percent is a rate in which the first term is compared to 100. The percent is the number of hundredths that represents the part of the whole.

Model with Math
Decimal grids, number lines, or equivalent fractions can be used to represent percents. MP.4

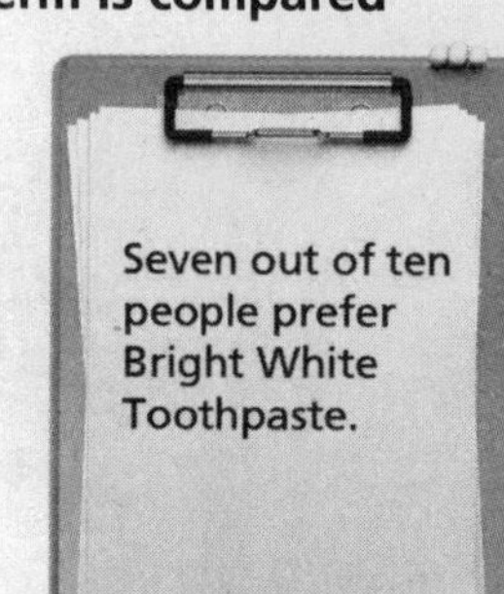

Seven out of ten people prefer Bright White Toothpaste.

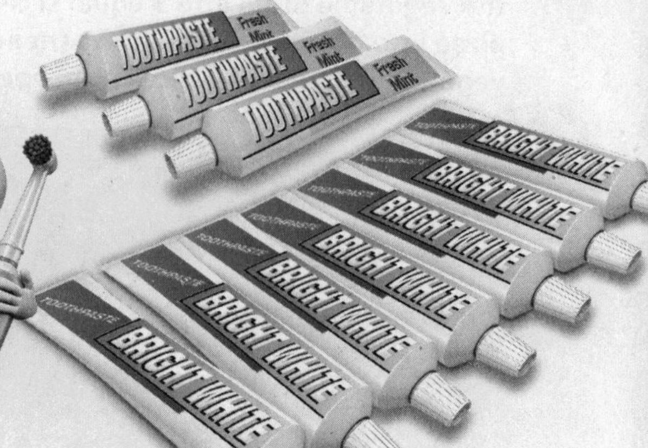

ONE WAY Use a grid to represent the percent.

$\frac{7}{10} = \frac{70}{100} = 70\%$

You can use the % symbol to represent percent.

ANOTHER WAY Use number lines to represent the percent.

7 out of 10 is equivalent to 70 out of 100.

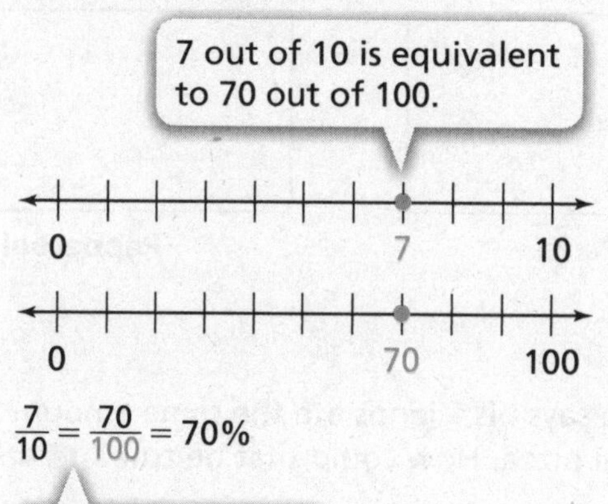

$\frac{7}{10} = \frac{70}{100} = 70\%$

Percent is always compared to 100.

ANOTHER WAY Use an equivalent fraction to find the percent.

Multiply both the numerator and the denominator by 10.

$\frac{7 \times 10}{10 \times 10} = \frac{70}{100}$

$\frac{70}{100} = 70\%$

70% of people prefer Bright White Toothpaste.

Try It!

Jane won 9 out of the 10 video games she played. What percent of the video games did Jane win?

Convince Me! When using an equivalent fraction to find a percent, why do you write 100 as the denominator?

EXAMPLE 2  Examine Percents and Wholes

Each line segment represents 100%, but the segments are not the same length. Use equivalent rates to find the percent, or part, of each line segment that points *A* and *B* represent.

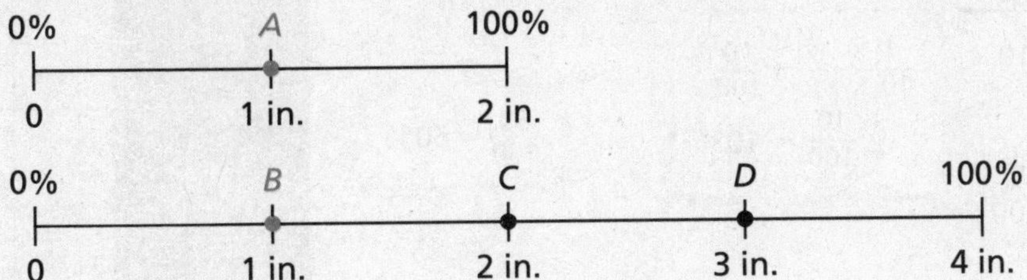

Point *A* is at $\frac{1}{2}$ of the line segment.

$\frac{1 \times 50}{2 \times 50} = \frac{50}{100} = 50\%$

2 × 50 = 100, so multiply the numerator and the denominator by 50.

Point $A = 50\%$

Point *B* is at $\frac{1}{4}$ of the line segment.

$\frac{1 \times 25}{4 \times 25} = \frac{25}{100} = 25\%$

4 × 25 = 100, so multiply the numerator and the denominator by 25.

Point $B = 25\%$

 Try It!

Which point represents 50% on the second line segment? Explain.

EXAMPLE 3  Use Percents

You can use percent and mental math to find the length of a line segment.

A. If $\overline{CD}$ represents 10%, what is the length of a line segment that is 100%?

100% is 10 × 10%, so the length of the line segment is 10 × 4 inches, or 40 inches.

B. If $\overline{EF}$ represents 200%, what is the length of a line segment that is 100%?

E F

6 in.

100% is $\frac{1}{2}$ of 200%, so the length of the line segment is $\frac{1}{2}$ of 6 inches, or 3 inches.

Try It!

If $\overline{CD}$ represents 100%, what is the length of a line segment that is 25%? Explain.

KEY CONCEPT

A percent is a rate that compares a part to a whole. The second term in the rate is always 100. The whole is 100%.

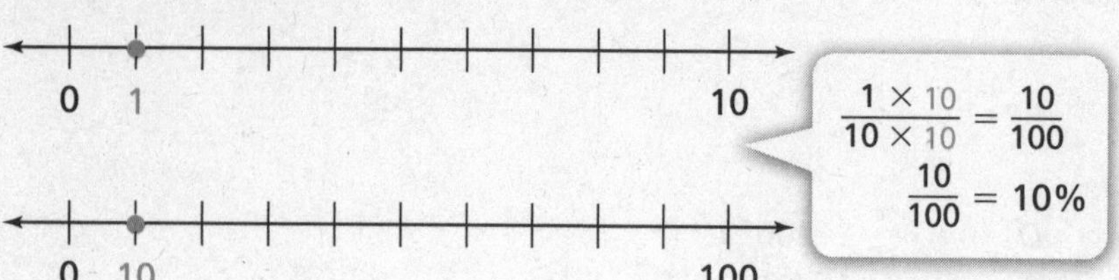

$\frac{1 \times 10}{10 \times 10} = \frac{10}{100}$

$\frac{10}{100} = 10\%$

$\frac{60}{100} = 60\%$

Do You Understand?

1. **Essential Question** How can you represent a rate with 100 as the whole?

2. When writing a percent as a fraction, what number do you write as the whole, or denominator?

3. Why are tenths, fifths, fourths, and halves easy to express as percents?

4. Why is the grid in Example 1 a good way to represent a percent?

5. **Look for Relationships** If $\overline{CD}$ in Example 3 represents 100%, is the length of a line segment that is 300% longer or shorter than 4 inches? Explain. MP.7

Do You Know How?

In 6 and 7, write the percent of each figure that is shaded.

6. 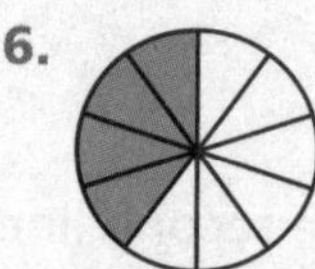

7. 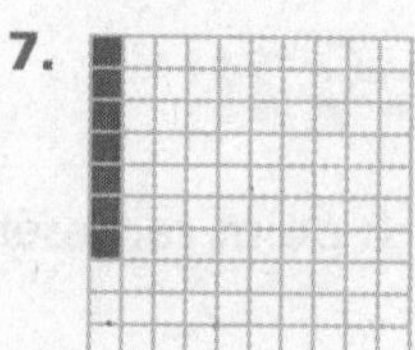

In 8–10, find the percent.

8. $\frac{1 \times \square}{5 \times \square} = \frac{20}{\square} = \square\%$

9. $\frac{3 \times \square}{10 \times \square} = \frac{30}{\square} = \square\%$

10. $\frac{11 \times \square}{20 \times \square} = \frac{55}{\square} = \square\%$

11. Find the percent of the line segment that point D represents in Example 2.

Name: ______________________________

Practice & Problem Solving

Scan for Multimedia

In 12 and 13, shade each model to represent the percent.

12. 14%

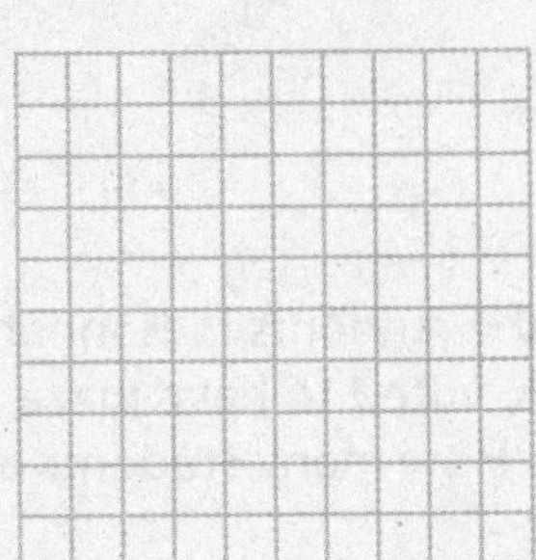

13. 20%

In 14 and 15, use $\overline{AB}$.

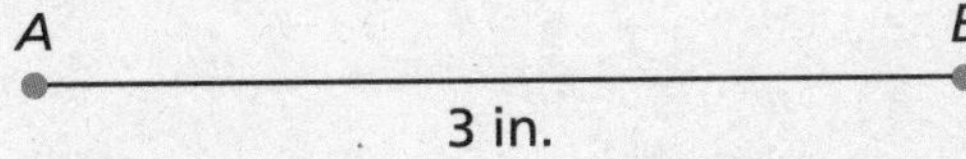

14. If $\overline{AB}$ represents 50%, what is the length of a line segment that is 100%?

15. If $\overline{AB}$ is 300%, what is the length of a line segment that is 100%?

16. Your friend shows you a coin collection. In it, $\frac{45}{50}$ of the coins are quarters. What percent of the coins are quarters?

17. Use Structure In a race, 19 out of 50 runners finished in fewer than 30 minutes. What percent of the runners finished in fewer than 30 minutes? Write an equivalent fraction to find the percent. MP.7

18. A basketball player made 63 out of 100 attempted free throws. What percent of free throws did the player make?

19. Harry kept a weather journal for September. The sun was shining on 4 out of every 5 days. On what percent of the days was the sun not shining?

In **20** and **21**, use the line segment.

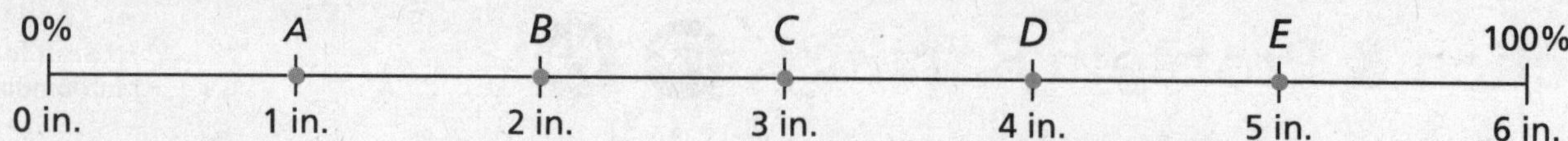

20. What percent of the line segment is 6 inches long?

21. What percent of the line segment does point *C* represent?

22. Critique Reasoning Kyle solved 18 of 24 puzzles in a puzzle book. He says that he can use an equivalent fraction to find the percent of puzzles in the book that he solved. How can he do that? What is the percent? MP.3

23. Reasoning Twenty of the students in Hannah's class, or 80% of the class, voted to have pizza for lunch every Wednesday. How many students are in Hannah's class? MP.2

24. According to a survey of workers, $\frac{2}{20}$ of the workers walk to work, $\frac{1}{20}$ bike, $\frac{4}{20}$ carpool, and $\frac{13}{20}$ drive alone. What percent of the workers walk or bike to work?

25. Higher Order Thinking From Monday through Friday, James works in the library on 2 days and in the cafeteria on another day. On Saturday and Sunday, James washes cars 50% of the days. How many days does James work in a week? What percent of the days from Monday through Friday does he work?

Assessment Practice

26. Select all the figures that are shaded to represent 20% of the whole.

☐ 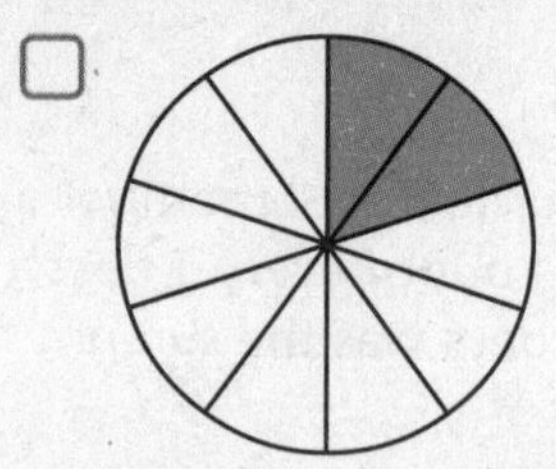

☐ 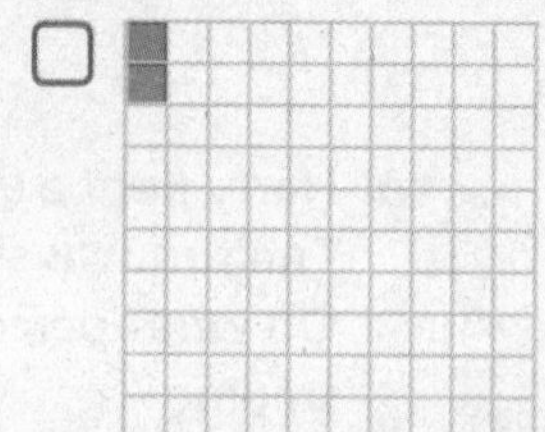

☐ 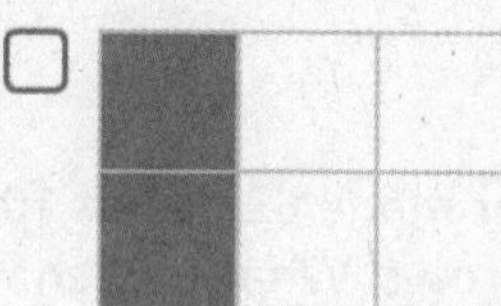

☐ 

☐ 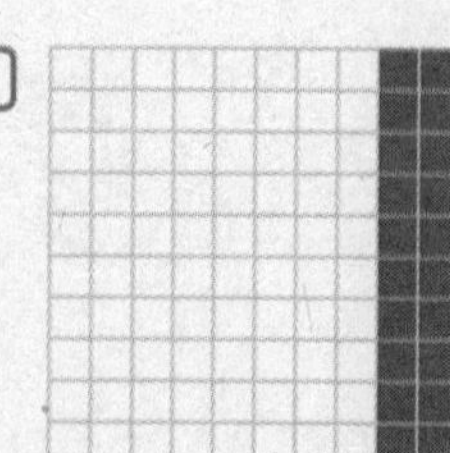

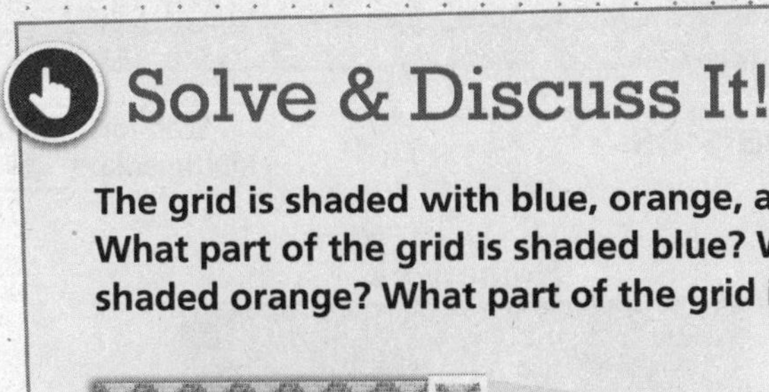

Solve & Discuss It!

The grid is shaded with blue, orange, and yellow. What part of the grid is shaded blue? What part is shaded orange? What part of the grid is shaded?

Lesson 6-2
Relate Fractions, Decimals, and Percents

Go Online | PearsonRealize.com

I can...
write equivalent values as fractions, decimals, or percents.

Common Core Content Standards
6.RP.A.3c

Mathematical Practices
MP.2, MP.3, MP.7, MP.8

Use Structure Look for patterns in the grid to help count parts that are shaded in blue and in orange. MP.7

Focus on math practices

Reasoning Write the part of the grid that is shaded yellow as a decimal and a percent. How are the decimal and the percent alike and how are they different? MP.2

Essential Question How are fractions, decimals, and percents related?

EXAMPLE 1 Express Percents and Decimals as Parts of a Whole

The portion of the time that Teddy spends doing homework for each subject is shown in the bar diagram.

How can you write the amount of time Teddy spends on reading or science as a fraction, decimal, and percent?

Homework

Whole		
Percent 30%	Fraction $\frac{3}{5}$	Decimal ← 0.10
Reading	Math	Science

Reasoning Fractions, decimals, and percents are three ways to show parts of a whole. How can you use reasoning to write quantities as a fraction, a decimal, or a percent? MP.2

Write 30% as a fraction and as a decimal.

$30\% = \frac{30}{100}$ or $\frac{3}{10}$ — Write the percent as a fraction with 100 as the denominator.

$\frac{30}{100} = 0.30$ — Write a fraction with a denominator of 10 or 100 as a decimal.

$\frac{3}{10} = 0.3$

30% can be written as $\frac{30}{100}$ or $\frac{3}{10}$ and 0.30 or 0.3.

Write 0.10 as a fraction and as a percent.

$0.10 = \frac{10}{100}$

$\frac{10}{100} = 10\%$ — The number compared to 100 is the percent.

$\frac{10 \div 10}{100 \div 10} = \frac{1}{10}$ — You can also write an equivalent fraction.

0.10 can be written as $\frac{10}{100}$ or $\frac{1}{10}$ and 10%.

Try It!

Ana spends 0.45 of her homework time reading. What is 0.45 as a percent? Explain.

Convince Me! What relationship do you see when comparing the equivalent fraction and percent?

EXAMPLE 2 Express Fractions as Parts of a Whole

Teddy spends $\frac{3}{5}$ of his homework time doing math problems. Write $\frac{3}{5}$ as a decimal and as a percent.

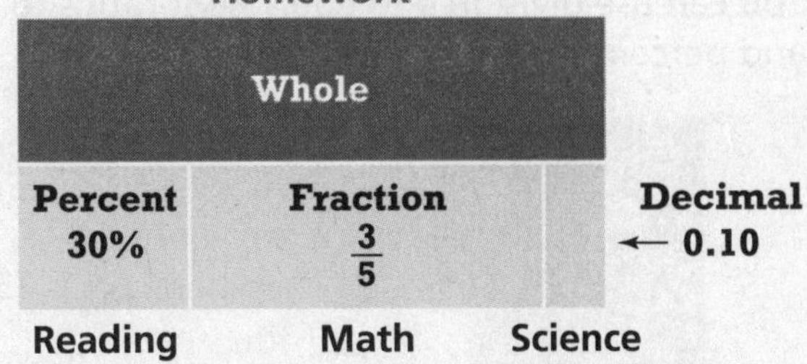

Look for Relationships If the denominator of a fraction is not 100, how can you express the fraction as a decimal and as a percent? MP.7

Use division to find the decimal.

$\frac{3}{5} = 3 \div 5$

$$\begin{array}{r} 0.6 \\ 5\overline{)3.0} \\ -30 \\ \hline 0 \end{array}$$

Insert a decimal point and annex a zero to divide.

$\frac{3}{5}$ can be written as 0.6 or 0.60.

Use an equivalent rate to find the percent.

$\frac{3}{5} = \frac{x}{100}$

$\frac{3 \times 20}{5 \times 20} = \frac{60}{100}$

$5 \times 20 = 100$, so multiply the numerator and the denominator by 20.

$\frac{60}{100} = 60\%$

$\frac{3}{5}$ can be written as 60%.

EXAMPLE 3 Use Division with Equivalent Rates to Express Fractions as Part of a Whole

Teddy's friend Jacob spends $\frac{5}{8}$ of his homework time doing math problems. Write $\frac{5}{8}$ as a decimal and as a percent.

Homework

Whole	
$\frac{5}{8}$	$\frac{3}{8}$
Math	Science

Use division to find the decimal.

$\frac{5}{8} = 5 \div 8$

$$\begin{array}{r} 0.625 \\ 8\overline{)5.000} \\ -48 \\ \hline 20 \\ -16 \\ \hline 40 \\ -40 \\ \hline 0 \end{array}$$

Insert a decimal point and annex zeros to divide.

$\frac{5}{8}$ can be written as 0.625.

Use the decimal to find an equivalent rate.

$0.625 = \frac{625}{1,000}$

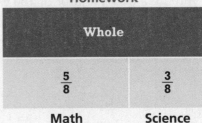

$\frac{625 \div 10}{1,000 \div 10} = \frac{62.5}{100}$

$1,000 \div 10 = 100$, so divide the numerator and the denominator by 10.

$\frac{62.5}{100} = 62.5\%$

$\frac{5}{8}$ can be written as 62.5%.

Try It!

Isabel spends $\frac{3}{8}$ of her homework time on reading. What is $\frac{3}{8}$ as a decimal and as a percent?

KEY CONCEPT

You can use division and equivalent ratios to express fractions, decimals, and percents in equivalent forms.

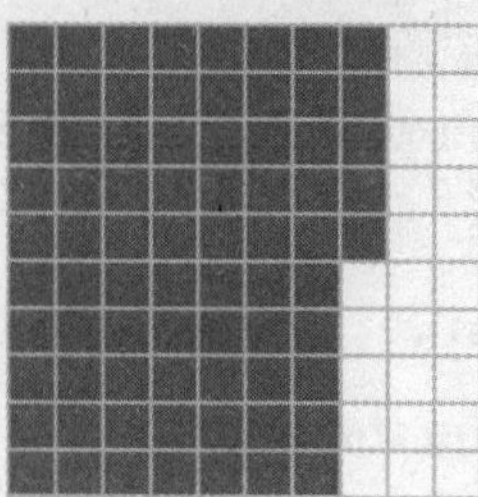

$0.75 = \frac{75}{100}$

$\frac{75}{100} = 75\%$

$0.75 = \frac{75}{100} = 75\%$

Whole
0.75

Do You Understand?

1. **Essential Question** How are fractions, decimals, and percents related?

2. Why do you use a denominator of 100 when you write a percent as a fraction?

3. **Look for Relationships** How do you use the digits in a hundredths decimal to write a percent? MP.7

4. How do you write a fraction with a denominator of 20 as a decimal?

Do You Know How?

In 5–7, write each number in equivalent forms using the two other forms of notation: fraction, decimal, or percent.

5. 27%

6. 0.91

7. $\frac{6}{100}$

8. Greek yogurt has 25% of the calcium that most people need in a day. What is 25% as a decimal?

25%
Daily
Calcium

9. Linda received $\frac{4}{5}$ of the votes in the election for student council president. What percent of the votes did Linda receive?

Name: ______________________________

Practice & Problem Solving

Scan for Multimedia

Leveled Practice In 10–15, write each number in equivalent forms using the two other forms of notation: fraction, decimal, or percent.

10. 0.25

$$0.25 = \frac{\square}{100} = \square\%$$

$$0.25 = \frac{\square \div 25}{100 \div \square} = \frac{\square}{4}$$

11. $\frac{2}{2}$

$$\frac{2}{2} = \frac{2 \times \square}{2 \times \square} = \frac{100}{100} = \square\%$$

$$\frac{2}{2} = 2 \div \square = \square.0$$

12. 7%

$$7\% = \frac{\square}{100}$$

$$7\% = \frac{\square}{100} = 0.\square$$

13. 38%

14. $\frac{7}{8}$

15. 0.04

16. Devon answered 23 out of 25 problems on a math test correctly. What percent of the problems did Devon answer correctly?

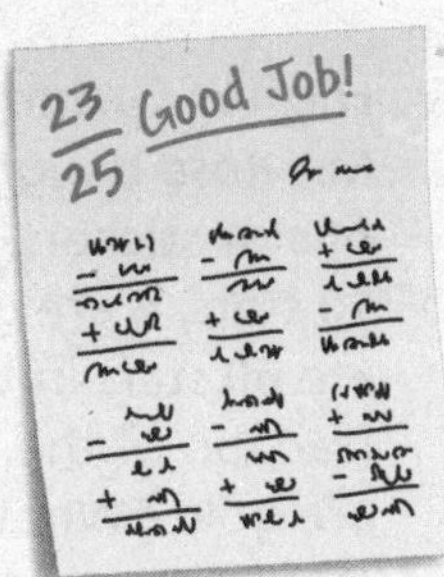

17. Reasoning How could you write $\frac{4}{8}$ as a percent without dividing? MP.2

In 18–21, use the circle graph.

18. Many chemical elements can be found in Earth's atmosphere. What fraction of Earth's atmosphere is made up of nitrogen?

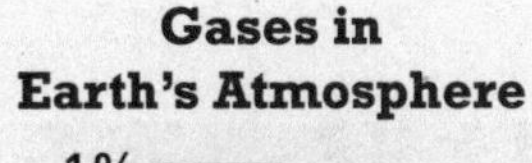

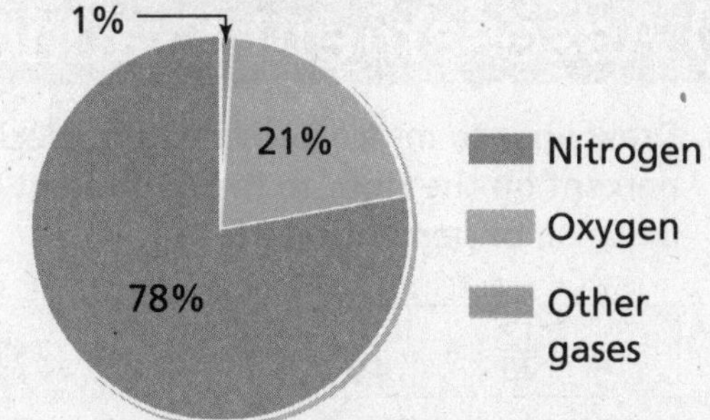

19. How much of Earth's atmosphere is made up of oxygen? Write the part as a decimal.

20. What percent of gases in Earth's atmosphere does the whole circle graph represent?

21. What fraction of the gases in Earth's atmosphere are gases other than nitrogen and oxygen?

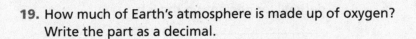

04/05/2021 madelyn zinck

22. Look for Relationships All T-shirts in a store are on sale as shown. Is this markdown greater than or less than a markdown of $\frac{1}{5}$ off the original price? Explain. © MP.7

23. Critique Reasoning Enrollment at Jackson Middle School increased by 3% this year. Sofia says that the increase, written as a decimal, is 0.3. Is Sofia correct? Explain. © MP.3

24. Generalize What are the attributes of fractions that are equivalent to 100%? © MP.8

25. The cost of building a new library is 0.85 of the cost of remodeling the old library. What is the cost as a percent?

26. Nine out of every 20 people walking out of a movie theater say that they would recommend the movie to a friend. What percent of the people would recommend the movie to a friend?

27. Higher Order Thinking Ms. Rose bought a package of star stickers. Out of every 10 stars, 4 are gold. If there are 60 stars in the pack, what fraction of the stars in the pack are gold? What percent of the stars in the pack are gold?

© Assessment Practice

28. Draw lines to match each fraction, decimal, or percent on the right to the equivalent fraction, decimal, or percent on the left.

$\frac{12}{25}$

4%

$\frac{3}{4}$

$\frac{11}{50}$

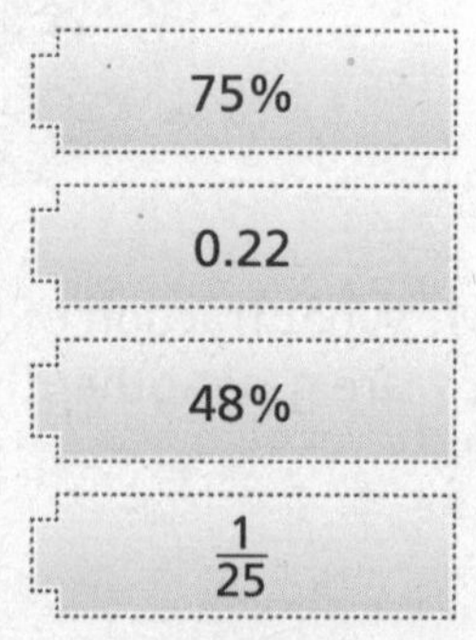

29. Draw lines to match each fraction, decimal, or percent on the right to the equivalent fraction, decimal, or percent on the left.

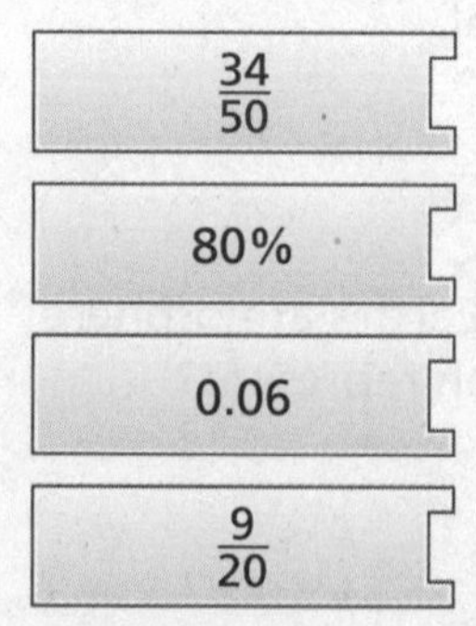

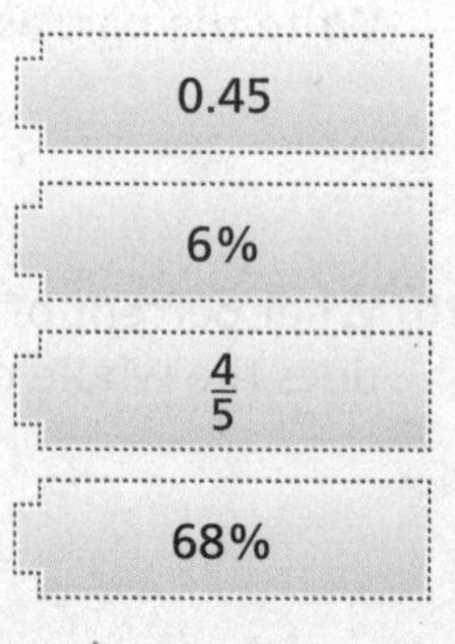

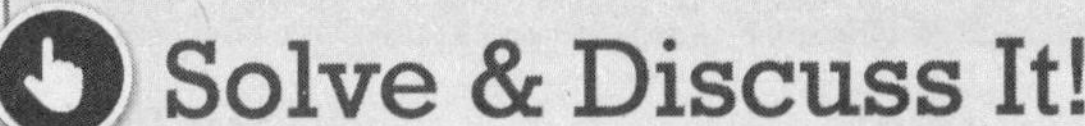

Solve & Discuss It!

Marci, Bobby, and Max began their homework at the same time. Marci finished her homework in 60 minutes. Bobby finished his homework in 50% of the time it took Marci to finish. Max finished his homework in 150% of Marci's time. How long did each of them work?

Lesson 6-3
Represent Percents Greater Than 100 or Less Than 1

Go Online | PearsonRealize.com

I can...
write percents that are greater than 100 or less than 1.

Common Core Content Standards
6.RP.A.3c

Mathematical Practices
MP.2, MP.3, MP.4, MP.7

Model with Math How can you use a model to represent a part that is greater than a whole? MP.4

Focus on math practices

Reasoning Did Max spend more time or less time on his homework than Marci? Explain. MP.2

? Essential Question How can you write a percent greater than 100 or less than 1 as a fraction and as a decimal?

EXAMPLE 1  Write a Percent Greater Than 100 as a Fraction and as a Decimal

Scan for Multimedia 

Jan and Kim built model cars for a science project. Kim's car traveled 140% as far as Jan's car. How can you write 140% as a fraction and as a decimal?

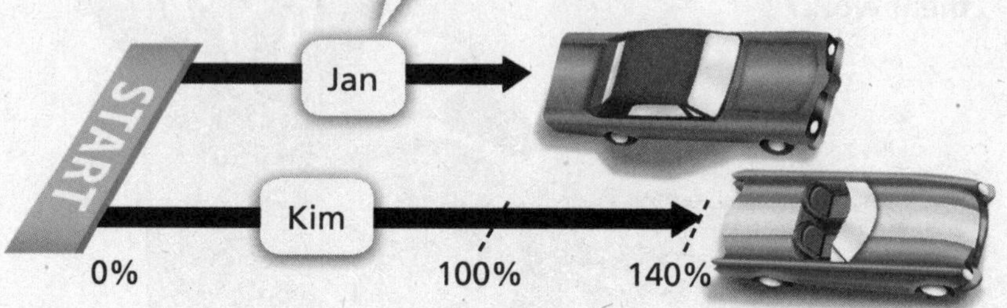

Write 140% as a fraction compared to 100.

$$140\% = \frac{140}{100}$$

Use division to write an equivalent fraction.

$$140\% = \frac{140 \div 20}{100 \div 20} = \frac{7}{5}$$

140% can be written as $\frac{140}{100}$ or $\frac{7}{5}$.

The fraction equivalent of a percent greater than 100 has a numerator greater than the denominator.

You can use reasoning or division to write 140% as a decimal.

Use reasoning.

$$140\% = \frac{140}{100} = \frac{14}{10} = 1.4$$

Use division.

$$\begin{array}{r} 1.4 \\ 100\overline{)140.0} \\ -100 \\ \hline 400 \\ -400 \\ \hline 0 \end{array}$$

Insert a decimal point and annex a zero to divide.

140% can be written as 1.4.

A decimal value greater than 1 will always be a percent greater than 100%.

Try It!

The area of a new movie theater is 225% of the area of the old theater. What is 225% as a fraction and as a decimal?

Convince Me! How would you write 1.75 as a percent? Give an example in which you would use a percent that is greater than 100.

EXAMPLE 2  Write a Fraction Percent Less Than 1 as a Fraction and as a Decimal

  ACTIVITY  ASSESS

Write $\frac{1}{2}$% as a fraction and as a decimal.

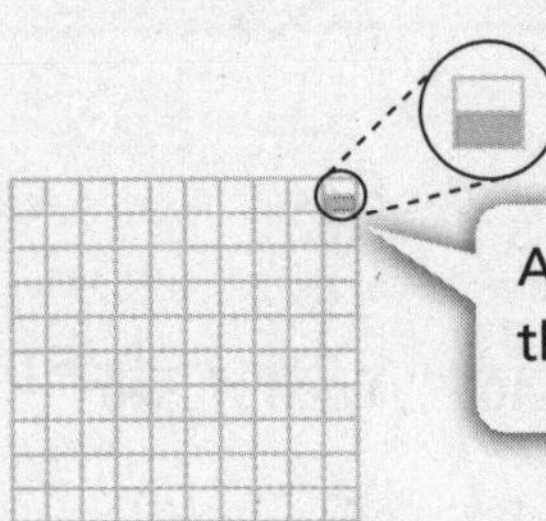

A percent less than 1 is less than $\frac{1}{100}$ of the whole.

Write $\frac{1}{2}$% as a fraction.

$\frac{1}{2}\% = \frac{\frac{1}{2}}{100}$

Percent means out of 100. Divide $\frac{1}{2}$ by 100.

$= \frac{1}{2} \div 100$

$= \frac{1}{2} \times \frac{1}{100}$

$= \frac{1}{200}$

$\frac{1}{2}$% can be written as $\frac{1}{200}$.

Write $\frac{1}{2}$% as a decimal.

$\frac{1}{2}\% = 0.5\%$

$= \frac{0.5}{100}$

$= \frac{5}{1{,}000} = 0.005$

$\frac{1}{2}$% can be written as 0.005.

EXAMPLE 3  Write a Decimal Percent Less Than 1 as a Fraction and as a Decimal

Write the percent of the solution that is water as a fraction and as a decimal.

0.9% of this solution is water.

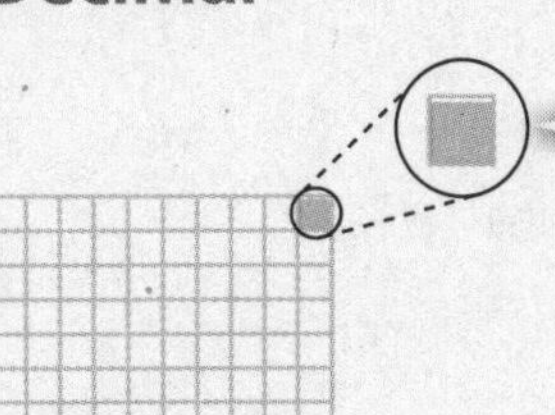

0.9% is less than 1%.

Write 0.9% as a fraction.

$0.9\% = 0.9 \div 100$

$= \frac{0.9}{100}$

$= \frac{9}{1{,}000}$

0.9% can be written as $\frac{9}{1{,}000}$.

Write 0.9% as a decimal.

$0.9\% = 0.9 \div 100$

$\frac{0.9}{100} = \frac{9}{1{,}000}$

$= 0.009$

0.9% can be written as 0.009.

Try It!

Write each percent as a fraction and as a decimal.

a. $\frac{2}{5}$%

b. 0.3%

KEY CONCEPT

You can express percents greater than 100 or less than 1 in equivalent forms.

$275\% = \frac{275}{100}$

$\frac{275 \div 25}{100 \div 25} = \frac{11}{4}$

$275\% = \frac{11}{4} = 2.75$

$\frac{1}{5}\% = 0.2\%$

$\frac{0.2}{100} = \frac{2}{1{,}000}$ or $\frac{1}{500} = 0.002$

$\frac{1}{5}\% = \frac{1}{500} = 0.002$

Do You Understand?

1. **Essential Question** How can you write a percent greater than 100 or less than 1 as a fraction and as a decimal?

2. **Reasoning** Explain why $\frac{3}{4}$ is less than 100%. MP.2

3. **Reasoning** Why is the numerator greater than the denominator in a fraction that is equivalent to a percent greater than 100? MP.2

4. Explain the difference between $\frac{1}{2}$ and $\frac{1}{2}\%$.

Do You Know How?

In 5–7, write each percent as a fraction and as a decimal.

5. 150%

6. $\frac{3}{10}\%$

7. 0.24%

8. Kelly saved $\frac{4}{5}\%$ of her allowance. What is this percent expressed as a fraction and as a decimal?

9. Mrs. Sanchez sold her house for 250% of the amount she paid for it. What is this percent expressed as a fraction and as a decimal?

Name: ____________________

Practice & Problem Solving

Scan for Multimedia 

Leveled Practice **In 10–15, write each percent as a fraction and as a decimal.**

10. $\frac{3}{5}\% = \frac{3}{5} \div \square$

$= \frac{3}{5} \times \frac{1}{\square}$

$= \frac{3}{\square} = \square$

11. $\frac{3}{4}\% = 0.\square\%$

$= \frac{\square}{100}$

$= \frac{\square}{10{,}000} = \square$

12. $0.1\% = 0.1 \div 100$

$= \frac{0.1}{\square} = \frac{1}{\square}$

$= \square$

13. $0.4\% = 0.4 \div 100$

$= \frac{0.4}{\square} = \frac{4}{\square}$

$= \square$

14. 322%

15. 210%

16. **Reasoning** Use the art at the right. How do you express the length of the *Queen Mary 2* as it compares to the height of the Washington Monument as a fraction and as a decimal? MP.2

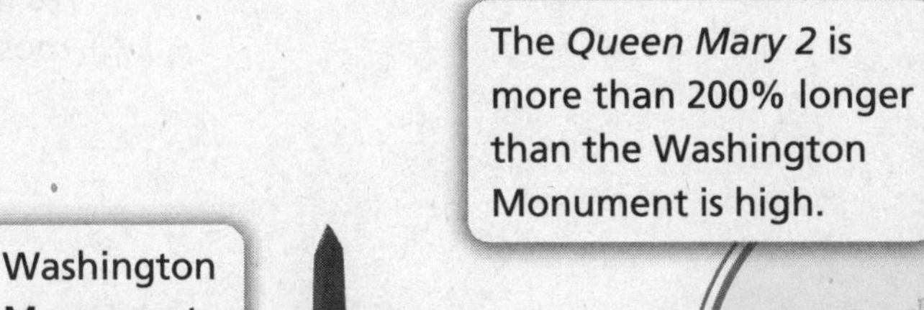
The *Queen Mary 2* is more than 200% longer than the Washington Monument is high.
Washington Monument

17. About $\frac{7}{10}\%$ of the passengers on a cruise ship swam in the ship's pool on the first day of the cruise. How would you express this number as a decimal and as a percent?

18. The fastest boat can reach speeds more than 710% as fast as the *Queen Mary 2*. How would you express this number as a fraction and as a decimal?

19. The weight of the Washington Monument is about 105% as much as the *Queen Mary 2*. Write this percent as a fraction and as a decimal.

20. Students set a goal for the number of cans to collect for the canned food drive. They reached 120% of their goal. What is 120% expressed as a fraction and as a decimal?

21. **Use Structure** Popcorn sales at a Saturday afternoon matinee were 108% of the sales at the 8:00 showing of the movie. Calvin expressed 108% as 10.8. Is Calvin correct? Explain. MP.7

22. **Construct Arguments** There are 350% more students enrolled in Spanish class than Latin class. How does expressing 350% as a decimal prove that more than 3 times as many students are enrolled in Spanish class as are enrolled in Latin class? MP.3

23. **Critique Reasoning** Free round-trip tickets to Hawaii were given to 0.4% of the people staying at a hotel. Larry says that tickets were given to $\frac{4}{10}$ of the people at the hotel. What did Larry do wrong when he calculated 0.4% as a fraction? What is the correct fraction? MP.3

24. The unemployment rate decreased by $\frac{1}{10}$% in one month. Write $\frac{1}{10}$% as a fraction and as a decimal.

25. **Higher Order Thinking** A photo of a mosquito in a science book is magnified to 635% of the mosquito's actual size. If the mosquito is 16 millimeters long, what is the length of the mosquito in the picture?

16 mm

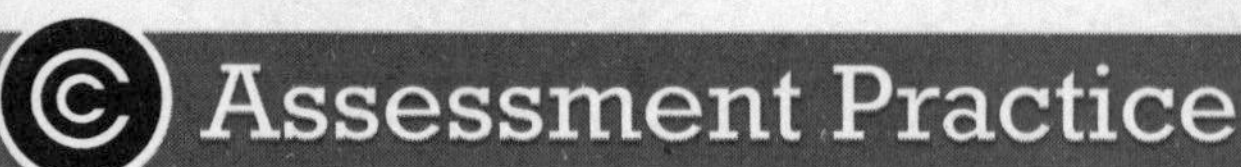

Assessment Practice

26. Cooper weighs 20 pounds. When he is an adult dog, he will weigh about 315% of his current weight. Write 315% as a fraction and as a decimal.

27. The results of a survey show that 0.32% of the people in the survey have never sent a text message. What is 0.32% expressed as a fraction and as a decimal?

Name: ____________________

MID-TOPIC CHECKPOINT

TOPIC 6

1. **Vocabulary** Explain how fractions, decimals, and percents are related. *Lesson 6-2*

2. Draw a line to match each fraction to the equivalent percent. *Lessons 6-1 and 6-3*

$\frac{4}{5}$	35%
$\frac{7}{20}$	2.5%
$\frac{9}{4}$	80%
$\frac{25}{1,000}$	225%

3. Which number is equivalent to 40%? Select all that apply. *Lesson 6-2*

☐ $\frac{40}{100}$ ☐ 0.04 ☐ 0.4
☐ $\frac{2}{5}$ ☐ 40

4. Complete the table. *Lessons 6-2 and 6-3*

Percent	Fraction	Decimal
70%	☐	☐
☐	☐	1.25
☐	$\frac{11}{20}$	☐
0.2%	☐	☐

5. A basketball player made 17 out of 20 free throws at practice. What percent of the free throws did the player miss? *Lesson 6-1*

6. A section of rope 5 inches long represents 20% of the length of the entire rope. How long is the rope? *Lesson 6-1*

How well did you do on the mid-topic checkpoint? Fill in the stars. ☆☆☆

TOPIC 6

MID-TOPIC PERFORMANCE TASK

The students in Mr. Anderson's class conducted a survey of 1,000 people. They asked each person to name his or her favorite color. The results are shown in the table.

Color	Number
Blue	450
Red	300
Orange	50
Yellow	10
White	5

PART A

Complete the table to write each result as a fraction, a decimal, and a percent.

Color	Number	Fraction	Decimal	Percent
Blue	450			
Red	300			
Orange	50			
Yellow	10			
White	5			

PART B

Green was chosen by 18% of the people. Which number is equivalent to 18%? Select all that apply.

- ☐ $\frac{18}{1,000}$
- ☐ 0.18
- ☐ $\frac{9}{5}$
- ☐ $\frac{18}{100}$
- ☐ 0.018

PART C

Cecilia noticed that not all of the survey responses were recorded in the table. What percent of the responses were not recorded in the table? Explain.

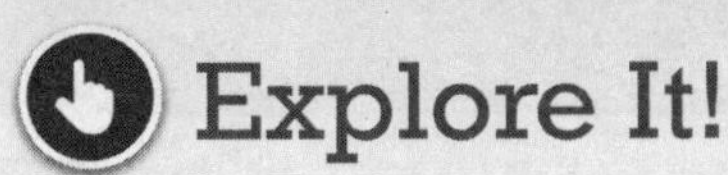

Explore It!

Sarah wants to score 78% on her next test. She knows that the test will have 40 questions.

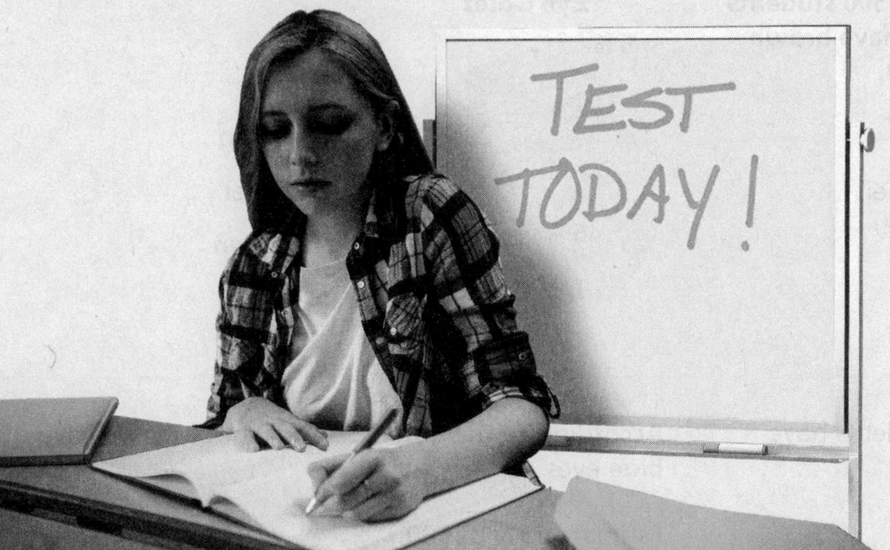

Lesson 6-4
Estimate to Find Percent

Go Online | PearsonRealize.com

I can...
estimate the percent of a number using equivalent fractions, rounding, or compatible numbers.

Common Core Content Standards
6.RP.A.3c

Mathematical Practices
MP.1, MP.2, MP.7

A. How can Sarah represent the situation to help her determine how many questions she needs to answer correctly?

1	2	3	4	5	6	7	8	9	10
11	12	13	14	15	16	17	18	19	20
21	22	23	24	25	26	27	28	29	30
31	32	33	34	35	36	37	38	39	40

B. How could you use the model to help solve the problem?

Focus on math practices

Use Structure On her last test, Sarah answered 82% of 60 questions correctly. About how many questions did Sarah answer correctly? Use estimation. MP.7

Essential Question How can you estimate to find the percent of a number?

EXAMPLE 1 Use Equivalent Fractions to Estimate

Scan for Multimedia

This graph shows the eye colors among 500 students at a school. About how many students have brown eyes? About how many have blue eyes?

Use Structure How can you use what you know about percents and their fraction equivalents to estimate? MP.7

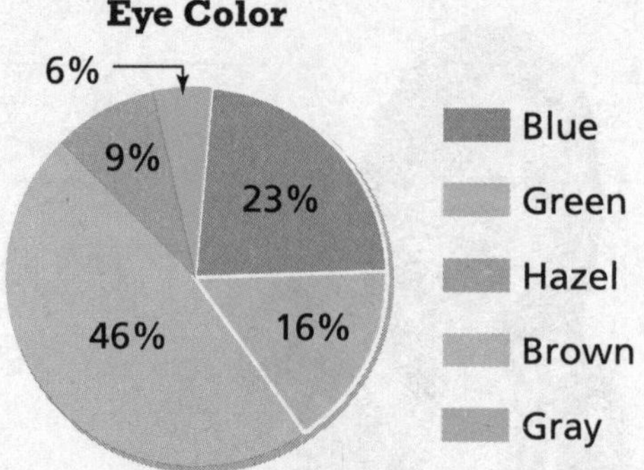

According to the graph, 46% of the students have brown eyes.

Estimate 46% of 500.

$46\% \approx 50\%$ and $50\% = \frac{1}{2}$

So, 46% of 500 is about $\frac{1}{2}$ of 500.

$$\frac{1}{2} \times 500 = 250$$

About 250 students have brown eyes.

According to the graph, 23% of the students have blue eyes.

Estimate 23% of 500.

$23\% \approx 25\%$ and $25\% = \frac{1}{4}$

So, 23% of 500 is about $\frac{1}{4}$ of 500.

$$\frac{1}{4} \times 500 = 125$$

About 125 students have blue eyes.

Try It!

Suppose the graph shows eye colors among 120 students in sixth grade. About how many sixth grade students would have green eyes? Explain how you can use estimation to find the answer.

Convince Me! How does understanding fraction equivalents help you estimate how many students in sixth grade have green eyes?

EXAMPLE 2  Use Rounding and Compatible Numbers to Estimate

  ACTIVITY  ASSESS

Use the results of the survey shown to the right. About how many high school students plan to get a summer job?

Reasoning You can use rounding or compatible numbers to find a reasonable estimate of how many students plan to get a summer job. MP.2

53% of 94 students surveyed plan to get a summer job.

ONE WAY Use rounding to estimate 53% of 94.

53% of 94 — 94 rounds to 90.

53% ≈ 50% and 50% = $\frac{1}{2}$

$\frac{1}{2} \times 90 = 45$

About 45 students plan to get a summer job.

ANOTHER WAY Use compatible numbers to estimate 53% of 94.

53% of 94 — 100 is a compatible number for 94.

53% ≈ 50% and 50% = $\frac{1}{2}$

$\frac{1}{2} \times 100 = 50$

About 50 students plan to get a summer job.

Both 45 and 50 are good estimates for the number of students who plan to get a summer job.

Try It!

Students in another survey were asked whether they plan to attend summer camp. Out of the 56 students in the survey, 44% said yes. Use rounding and compatible numbers to estimate how many students plan to attend summer camp.

Use rounding to estimate 44% of 56.

44% ≈ 40% and 40% = $\frac{4}{\square}$ or $\frac{2}{\square}$

56 rounds to ☐.

$\frac{2}{\square} \times \square = \square$

About ☐ students plan to attend summer camp.

Use compatible numbers to estimate 44% of 56.

44% ≈ 40% and 40% = $\frac{4}{\square}$ or $\frac{2}{\square}$

☐ is a compatible number for 56.

$\frac{2}{\square} \times \square = \square$

About ☐ students plan to attend summer camp.

KEY CONCEPT

Fraction equivalents, rounding, or compatible numbers can be used to estimate the percent of a number.

$8\% \approx 10\%$ and $10\% = \frac{1}{10}$

8% of 300,000 is about 30,000.

$\frac{1}{10} \times 300{,}000 = 30{,}000$

$27\% \approx 25\%$ and $25\% = \frac{1}{4}$

300 is a compatible number for 297.

27% of 297 is about 75.

$\frac{1}{4} \times 300 = 75$

Do You Understand?

1. **Essential Question** How can you estimate to find the percent of a number?

2. Is there more than one fraction you could use to estimate 27% of 200? Explain.

3. What compatible number could you use to estimate 75% of 35? Why is this number compatible with 75%?

4. **Use Structure** Out of 195 students, 9% have hazel eyes. How can you estimate the number of students with hazel eyes? MP.7

Do You Know How?

In 5–8, estimate the percent of each number.

5. 47% of 77

47% ≈ ☐ 77 ≈ ☐

☐ of ☐ = ☐

6. 18% of 48

18% ≈ ☐ 48 ≈ ☐

☐ of ☐ = ☐

7. 73% of 800

8. 31% of 94

9. Tara sent party invitations to 98 people. Eighty-two percent of the people said they will come to the party. About how many people said they will come to the party? Explain.

Name: ____________________

Practice & Problem Solving

Scan for Multimedia

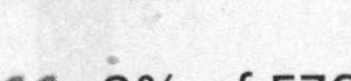

Leveled Practice **In 10–15, estimate the percent of each number.**

10. 74% of 63

74% ≈ ☐ 63 ≈ ☐

☐ of ☐ = ☐

11. 8% of 576

8% ≈ ☐ 576 ≈ ☐

☐ of ☐ = ☐

12. 34% of 55

13. 27% of 284

14. 65% of 89

15. 4% of 802

16. There are about 320 million residents in the United States. If 38% of them live in the South, estimate how many live in other areas of the United States.

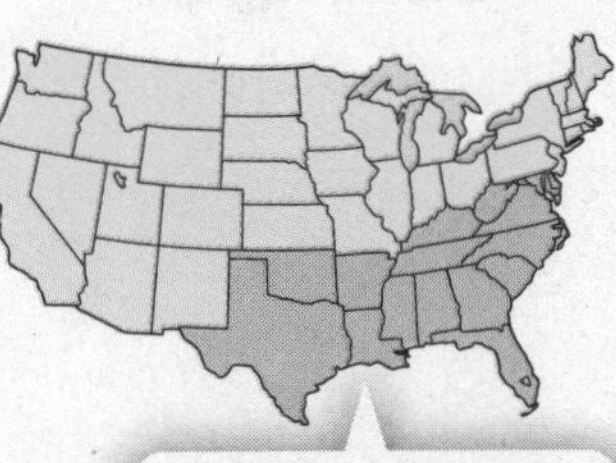

38% of the U.S. population lives in this region.

17. Lisa and Bill made 60 magnets for a craft fair. They sold 55% of the magnets. Lisa says that they sold about 30 magnets. Bill says that they sold about 36 magnets. Could they both be correct? Explain.

18. Make Sense and Persevere Roland has 180 coins in his collection. Approximately 67% of the coins are quarters. About how much money does Roland have in quarters? Explain. MP.1

19. Out of 9,799 whistles that a company manufactured, some were rejected for shipment to stores because they did not pass the quality control standards of the company. Estimate the number of whistles that did not pass.

19% of the whistles were rejected.

20. There are 8,249 people registered to vote in the town of Mayfield. About how many people voted in the election? Explain.

21. Higher Order Thinking Lea spent 25% of x hours at her part-time job. What is x if 25% of x is about 30 hours? Explain how you estimated and which property of equality you used to find x.

22. Reasoning Vanessa scored 78% on a test with 120 questions. What benchmark fraction would you use to estimate the number of questions that Vanessa answered correctly? Explain. MP.2

23. Jason has saved 41% of what he needs to buy a skateboard. About how much has Jason saved? Explain.

Assessment Practice

24. There were 240 shoppers at an electronics store on opening day. The specials that day allowed 24% of shoppers to receive a free set of earbuds and 20% of shoppers to receive $10 off their first purchase.

PART A

About how many shoppers received a free set of earbuds? Use an equivalent fraction to estimate.

PART B

About how many shoppers received $10 off their first purchase? Use an equivalent fraction and rounding to estimate.

Lesson 6-5
Find the Percent of a Number

Go Online | PearsonRealize.com

I can...
solve problems involving percents.

Common Core Content Standards
6.RP.A.3c

Mathematical Practices
MP.1, MP.4, MP.5, MP.6, MP.8

Solve & Discuss It!

ACTIVITY

Lauren bought a jacket that was on sale for 60% off. She paid 40% of the original price of $75. How much did Lauren pay for the jacket?

Model with Math
How can you use a model to represent problems involving percents? MP.4

Focus on math practices

Generalize When finding the percent of a number, how can you tell whether your answer is reasonable? Will the answer be greater than or less than the original amount? Explain. MP.8

 **Essential Question** How can you find percents?

EXAMPLE 1  Estimate and Find Percent

Scan for Multimedia 

The fourth, fifth, and sixth graders at Great Oaks School are taking a field trip. Of the 575 students attending the field trip, how many are sixth graders?

Make Sense and Persevere The percents in the circle graph sum to 100%, which represents 575 total students, or the whole. MP.1

Percent of Students in Each Grade Attending the Field Trip

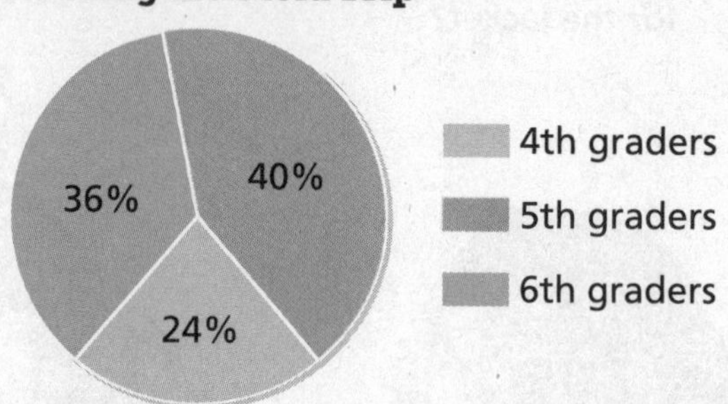

Use a double number line diagram and benchmark fraction equivalents to estimate 36% of 575.

$36\% \approx 33\frac{1}{3}\% = \frac{1}{3}$ and $575 \approx 600$

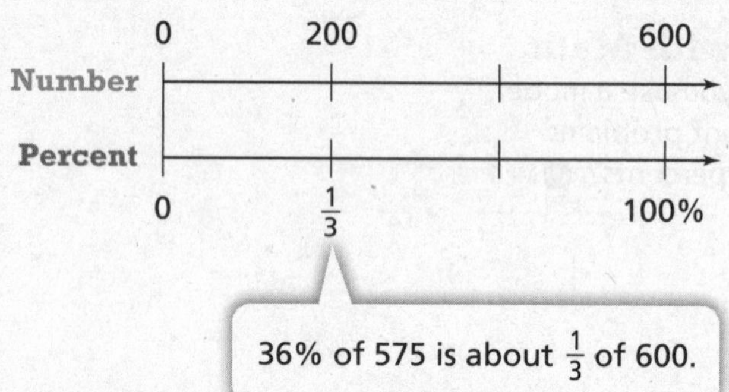

About 200 sixth graders are attending.

Use the decimal form of a percent to find 36% of 575.

The decimal form of 36% is 0.36.

$0.36 \times 575 = 207$

You can also use a calculator.

Enter: 0.36 × 575 =

Display: 207.

207 is close to 200.
The answer is reasonable.

There are 207 sixth graders attending the field trip.

Try It!

Suppose 68% of the students attending the field trip were boys. How can you use the double number line diagram above to find the number of boys and to check whether your answer is reasonable?

Convince Me! In finding the percent of a number, when might you want to use the fraction form of the percent instead of the decimal form?

EXAMPLE 2  Find the Part

D'wayne plans to wallpaper 72.5% of a 60-square-foot wall. How many square feet of the wall does D'wayne plan to wallpaper? Find 72.5% of 60.

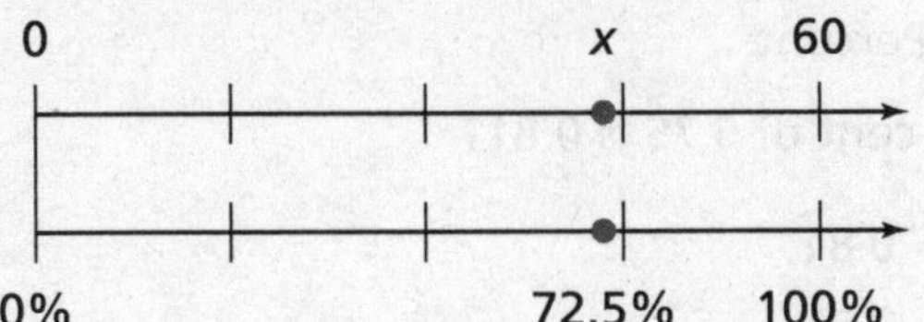

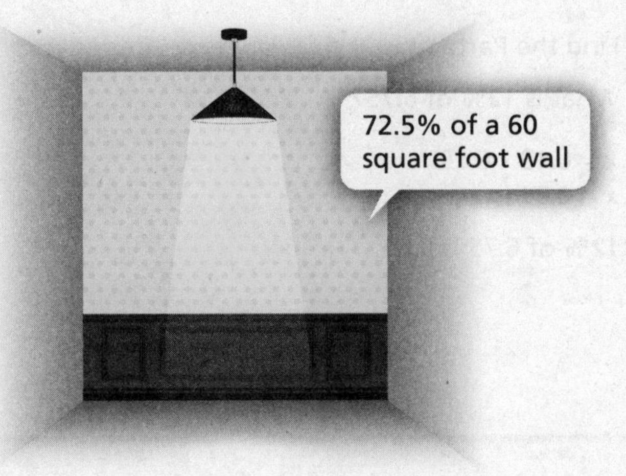

Model with Math You can use a double number line diagram to help write an equation to find the part in a percent problem. MP.4

Write an equation.

$x = 0.725 \cdot 60$ — x represents 72.5% of 60. Multiply 72.5% by 60 to find x.

$x = 43.5$

So, 43.5 is 72.5% of 60.

D'wayne plans to wallpaper 43.5 square feet.

 **Try It!**

What is 0.8% of 35?

EXAMPLE 3  Find the Percent

What percent of 92 is 11.5?

Write an equation.

$p \cdot 92 = 11.5$ — p represents the percent value 11.5 is of 92. Divide 11.5 by 92 to find p.

$92p = 11.5$

$\frac{92p}{92} = \frac{11.5}{92}$

$p = 0.125$ or 12.5%

So, 11.5 is 12.5% of 92.

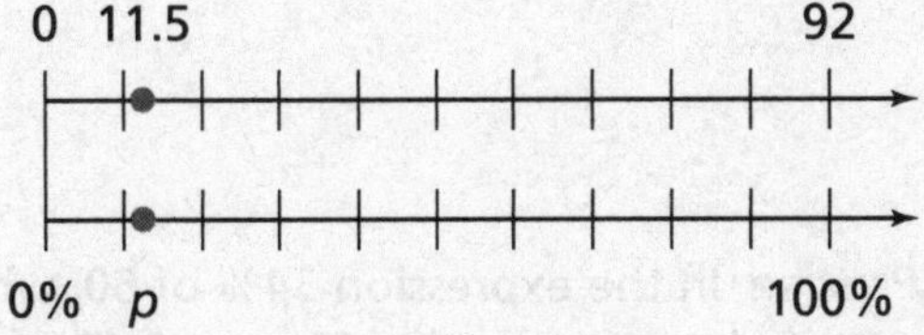

Model with Math You can use a double number line diagram to help write an equation to find the percent of a number. MP.4

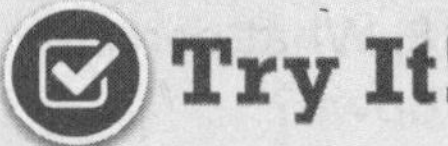

What percent of 120 is 72?

CONCEPT 

Percent equations have a part, a whole, and a percent. You can use the equation to solve for the part, the whole, or the percent.

Find the Part:

What is 12% of 6.75?

$x = 0.12 \cdot 6.75$

$x = 0.81$

12% of 6.75 is 0.81.

Find the Percent:

What percent of 6.75 is 0.81?

$p \cdot 6.75 = 0.81$

$6.75p = 0.81$

$\frac{6.75p}{6.75} = \frac{0.81}{6.75}$

$p = 0.12$ or 12%

12% of 6.75 is 0.81.

Do You Understand?

1. **Essential Question** How can you find percents?

2. Describe the equation you use to find the unknown part in a percent problem.

3. Describe the equation you use to find the percent value in a percent problem.

4. **Be Precise** In the expression 34% of 60, what operation does the word "of" mean? MP.6

5. **Use Appropriate Tools** How can you use a calculator to find what percent of 180 is 108? MP.5

Do You Know How?

In 6 and 7, find the part.

6. What is 26% of 50?

7. What is 2.1% of 60?

In 8 and 9, find the percent.

8. What percent of 315 is 126?

9. What percent of 120 is 28.8?

10. An electronics company has 450 employees. The company plans to increase its staff by 30%. How many new employees will the company hire?

11. The original price of a computer game is \$45. The price is marked down by \$18. What percent of the original price is the markdown?

Name: ____________________

Practice & Problem Solving

Scan for Multimedia

Leveled Practice **In 12–17, find each part or percent.**

12. What is 5% of 210?

$x = \square \times 210$

$x = \square$

13. What is 8.2% of 500?

$x = \square \times 500$

$x = \square$

14. What percent of 32 is 5.6?

$p \cdot 32 = \square$

$32p = \square$

$\frac{32p}{32} = \frac{\square}{32}$

$p = \square = \square\%$

15. What is 35% of 10?

16. What percent of 75 is 33?

17. What is 2.25% of 24?

18. The meal tax at a restaurant is 5.5%. What is the meal tax on a dinner that costs $24?

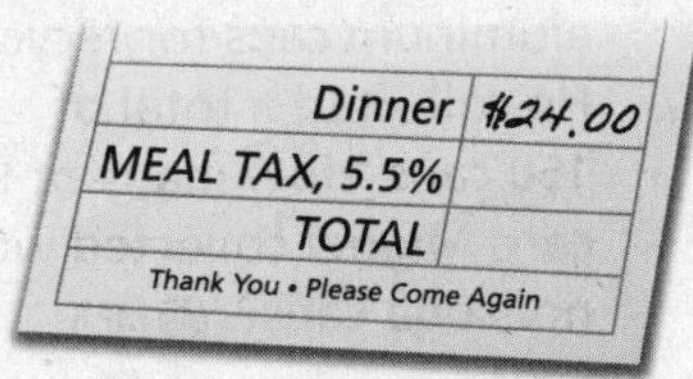

19. An electronics store donated a percentage of every sale to charity. The total sales were $7,150, of which the store donated $429. What percent of $7,150 was donated to charity?

In 20–22, use the circle graph.

There are 180 cars in a parking lot. The colors of the cars are represented in the circle graph.

Cars in Parking Lot

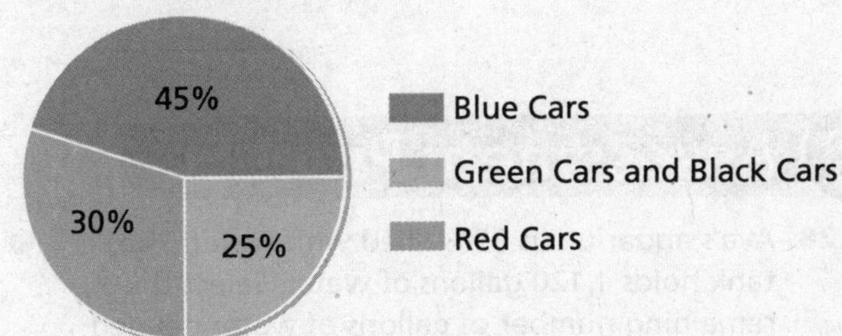

20. How many blue cars are there?

21. How many red cars are there?

22. Reasoning There are 27 more green cars than black cars in the parking lot. What percentage of the cars in the parking lot are green? What percent are black? MP.2

23. The bank contains pennies, nickels, dimes, and quarters. There are 4 more nickels than pennies. How much money does the bank contain?

Of the 50 coins, 10% are pennies and 42% are dimes.

24. Model with Math How can you use the double number line diagram to find what percent of 450 is 270? MP.4

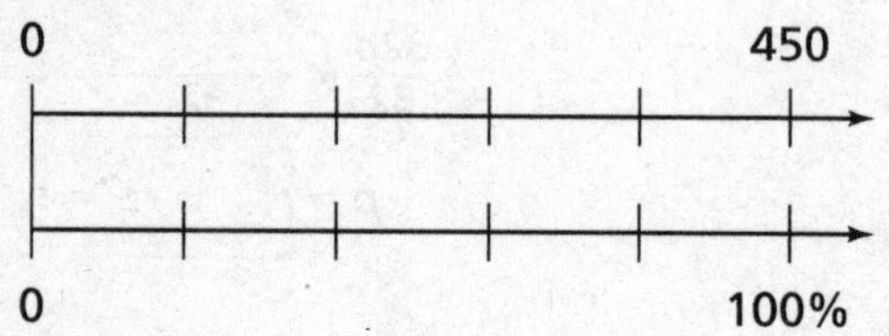

25. Make Sense and Persevere A movie complex is showing the same movie in three theaters. In theater A, 112 of the 160 seats are filled. In theater B, 84 seats are filled and 56 seats are empty. In theater C, 63 of the 180 seats are empty. Which theater has the greatest percent of its seats filled? MP.1

26. Higher Order Thinking Thomas has an album that holds 600 baseball cards. Each page of the album holds 6 cards. If 45% of the album is empty, how many pages are filled with baseball cards?

27. Be Precise Miguel collected aluminum cans for recycling. He collected a total of 150 cans. How many of the cans Miguel collected were not soda cans? MP.6

58% of the cans collected were soda cans.

Assessment Practice

28. Ava's aquarium is 95% filled with water. The tank holds 1,120 gallons of water. Select the remaining number of gallons of water needed to fill the aquarium to the top.

Ⓐ 1,120 gallons

Ⓑ 1,010 gallons

Ⓒ 101 gallons

Ⓓ 56 gallons

29. Students set a goal of collecting 900 cans for the canned food drive. The number of cans they have collected so far is 82% of their goal. How many more cans do the students need to collect to reach their goal?

Ⓐ 162 cans

Ⓑ 180 cans

Ⓒ 720 cans

Ⓓ 738 cans

Lesson 6-6
Find the Whole Given a Part and the Percent

Go Online | PearsonRealize.com

I can...
find the whole amount when given a part and the percent.

Common Core Content Standards
6.RP.A.3c
Mathematical Practices
MP.1, MP.2, MP.4, MP.6, MP.7

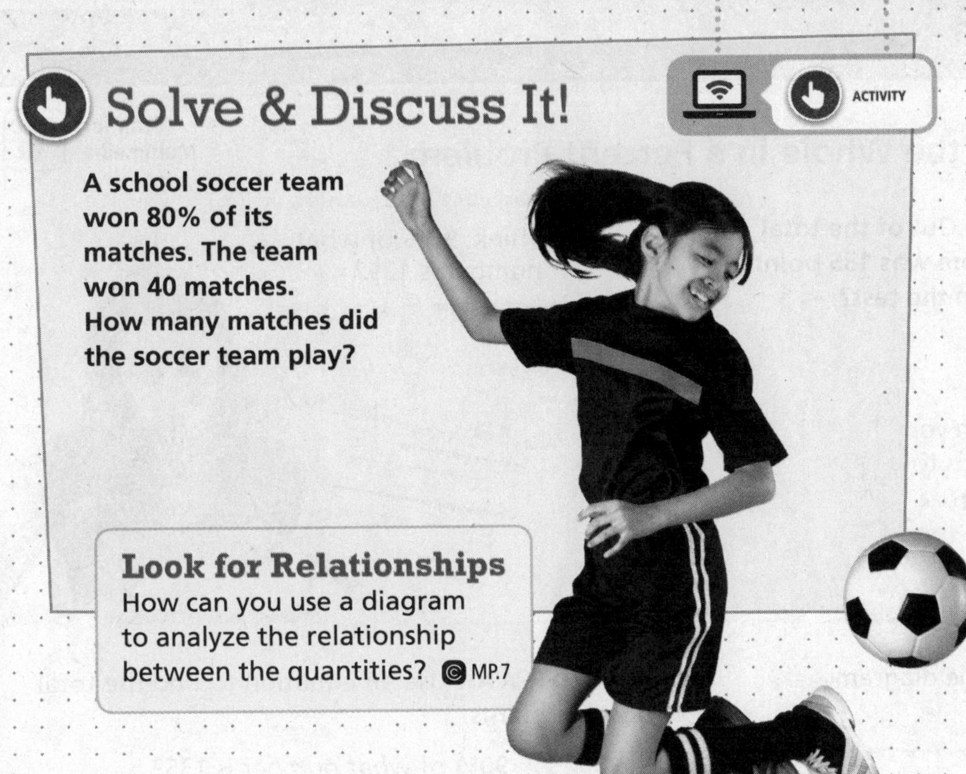

Solve & Discuss It!

ACTIVITY

A school soccer team won 80% of its matches. The team won 40 matches. How many matches did the soccer team play?

Look for Relationships
How can you use a diagram to analyze the relationship between the quantities? MP.7

Focus on math practices

Model with Math Write an equation to find the total number of matches played by the soccer team. Let *m* represent the total number of matches. MP.4

  INTERACTIVE ANIMATION  ASSESS

? Essential Question How can you find the whole in a percent problem?

EXAMPLE 1  Find the Whole in a Percent Problem

Scan for Multimedia 

Bree scored 90% on her math test. Out of the total possible points on the test, her score was 135 points. How many points were possible on the test?

Think: 90% of what number is 135?

Model with Math How can you draw pictures and write equations to find the total possible points? MP.4

ONE WAY Use a double number line diagram to find the total possible points.

Bree scored 135 points, which was 90%.

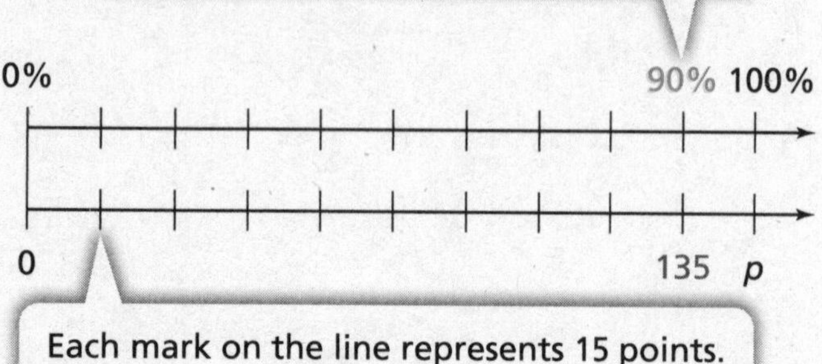

Add to find the total possible points, p.

$$135 + 15 = 150$$

There were 150 total possible points on the test.

ANOTHER WAY Use an equation to find the total possible points.

90% of *what number* is 135?

Let p = the total number of possible points.

$$90\% \cdot p = 135$$

$$90\% = \frac{90}{100} = 0.90$$

Write 90% as a decimal.

Solve the equation.

$$0.90p = 135$$

$$p = 135 \div 0.90$$

$$p = 150$$

There were 150 total possible points on the test.

Try It!

Bree took another math test and scored 152 points, which was 95% of the total possible points on the test. What was the total number of possible points?

Convince Me! How could you use a double number line diagram to check your answer?

EXAMPLE 2  Find the Whole When the Percent Is Greater Than 100

ACTIVITY

ASSESS

The students in one classroom sold tickets to the talent show. They sold 200% of the amount of tickets that they sold last year. How many tickets did the students sell last year? Find the number of which 200% is 40.

One classroom sold a total of 40 tickets.

ONE WAY Use a double number line diagram.

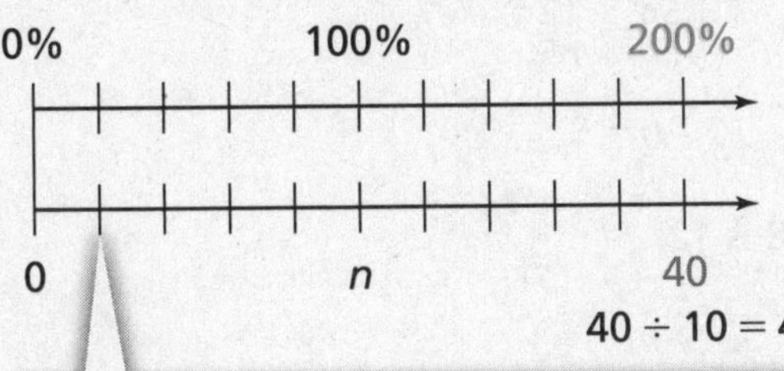

$40 \div 10 = 4$

Each mark represents an increase of 4.

So, 100% is 20.

200% of 20 is 40.

The students sold 20 tickets last year.

ANOTHER WAY Write and solve an equation.

$$200\% \cdot n = 40$$

Write 200% as a whole number.

$$2n = 40$$

$$\frac{2n}{2} = \frac{40}{2}$$

$$n = 20$$

200% of 20 is 40.

200% is the same as 2 times 100%.

The students sold 20 tickets last year.

EXAMPLE 3  Find the Whole When the Percent Is a Decimal

62.5% of what number is 30?

ONE WAY Use a double number line diagram.

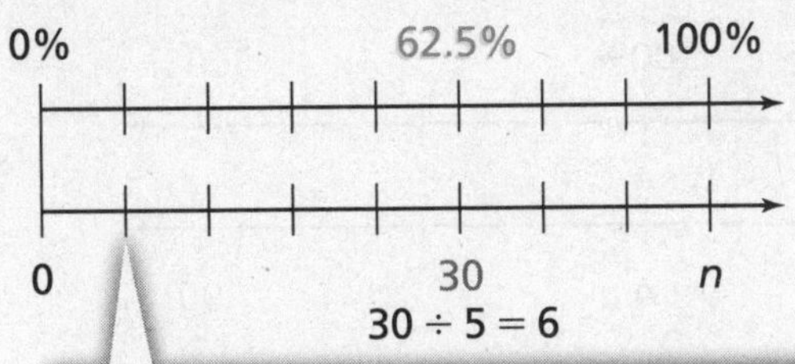

$30 \div 5 = 6$

Each mark represents an increase of 6.

62.5% of 48 is 30.

ANOTHER WAY Write and solve an equation.

$$62.5\% \cdot n = 30$$

$$0.625n = 30$$

$$\frac{0.625n}{0.625} = \frac{30}{0.625}$$

$$n = 48$$

62.5% of 48 is 30.

Try It!

a. 300% of what number is 180?

b. 0.3% of what number is 24?

KEY CONCEPT

You can use a double number line diagram or an equation to find the whole when the percent and a part are known.

Use a diagram.

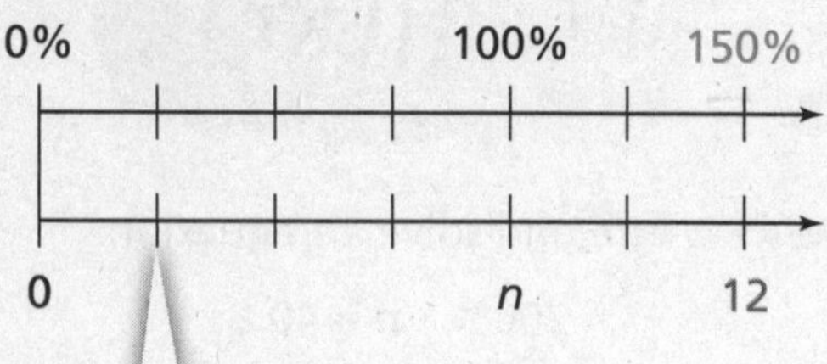

Each mark represents an increase of 2.

150% of 8 is 12.

Use an equation.

Let n = the whole.

$$150\% \cdot n = 12$$

$$1.5n = 12$$

$$\frac{1.5n}{1.5} = \frac{12}{1.5}$$

$$n = 8$$

150% of 8 is 12.

Do You Understand?

1. **Essential Question** How can you find the whole in a percent problem?

2. When you write an equation for a problem such as *300% of what number is 180*, what do you use to represent the phrase 'what number'?

3. When you find the whole in a percent problem in which the percent is greater than 100%, is the whole less than or greater than the part?

4. **Be Precise** Tony participated in 6 races, or 10% of the events. Do the 6 races represent the part, the percent, or the whole? Tell what the others represent. MP.6

Do You Know How?

5. 40% of what number is 80?

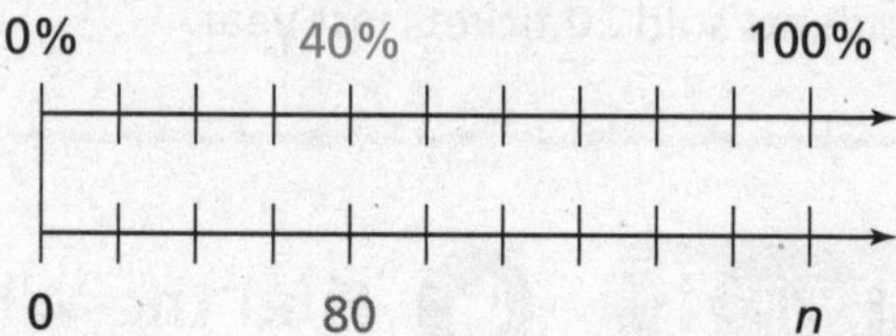

6. 300% of what number is 90?

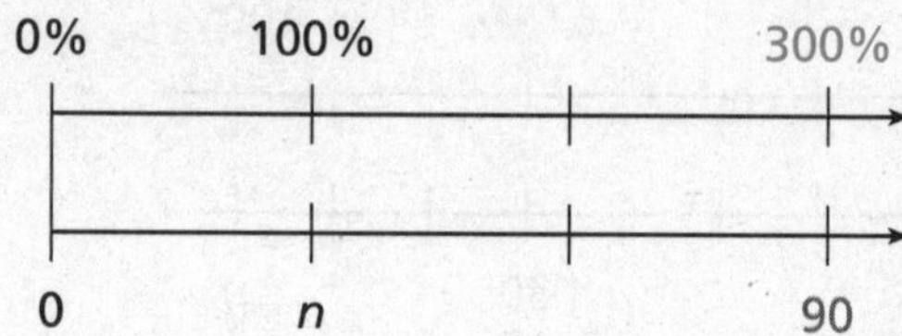

7. 70% of what number is 112?

8. 35% of what number is 28?

9. 7.5% of what number is 15?

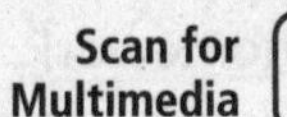

Name: ____________________

Practice & Problem Solving

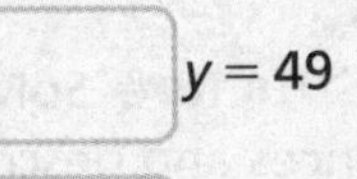

Scan for Multimedia

Leveled Practice **In 10–15, find each whole.**

10. 35% of what number is 91?

35% • $a = 91$

$0.35a = \square$

$\frac{0.35a}{\square} = \frac{\square}{\square}$

$a = \square$

35% of $\square$ is 91.

11. 125% of what number is 45?

125% • $n = 45$

$1.25n = \square$

$\frac{1.25n}{\square} = \frac{\square}{\square}$

$n = \square$

125% of $\square$ is 45.

12. 87.5% of what number is 49?

87.5% • $y = 49$

$\square\, y = 49$

$\frac{\square\, y}{\square} = \frac{49}{\square}$

$y = \square$

87.5% of $\square$ is 49.

13. 700% of what number is 1,540?

14. 0.7% of what number is 35?

15. 56% of what number is 14?

In 16–18, use the list of state taxes.

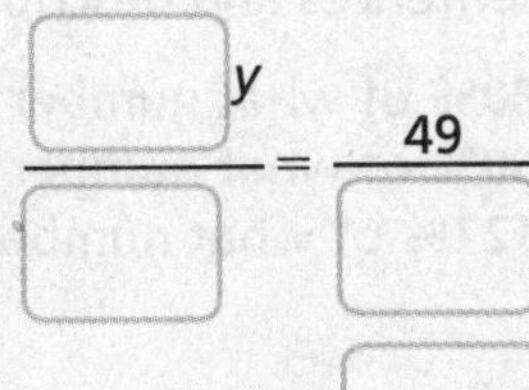

STATE TAXES

Sales tax:	3.5%
Income tax:	5%
Meal tax:	4.5%

16. Reasoning Otis had a salad for $4.50, a sandwich for $6.25, and a drink at his favorite restaurant. The tax for the entire meal was $0.54. What was the price of the drink? MP.2

17. Jill paid a sales tax of $1.40 when she bought a vest. What was the price of the vest not including the tax?

18. Rachel paid $46 in tax for the money she earned as a camp counselor. How much money did Rachel earn?

19. A restaurant wants to study how well its salads sell. The circle graph shows the sales of salads during the past few days. If 5 of the salads sold were Caesar salads, how many total salads did the restaurant sell?

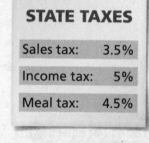

Salads Sold

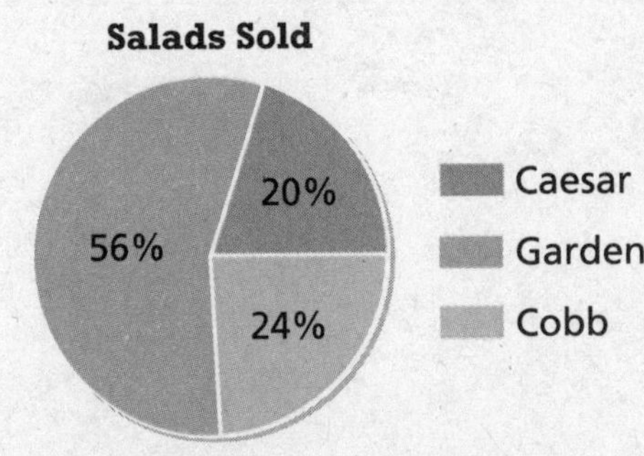

20. **Make Sense and Persevere** Sydney completed 60% of the math problems assigned for homework. She has 4 more problems to finish. How many math problems were assigned for homework? MP.1

21. **Reasoning** Carrie gave her hair stylist a \$4.20 tip. The tip was 15% of the cost of the haircut. Write an equation to find h, the cost of the haircut. MP.2

22. **Use Structure** Solve each of the number sentences and describe the pattern. MP.7

80% of what number is 80?
60% of what number is 60?
127% of what number is 127?

23. **Higher Order Thinking** An hour before show time, only 105 people have arrived for a concert. According to ticket sales, 95% of the people have yet to arrive. How many tickets were sold for the concert? Explain.

24. Nineteen students named lacrosse as their favorite sport. Explain how to use the circle graph to find the total number of students surveyed.

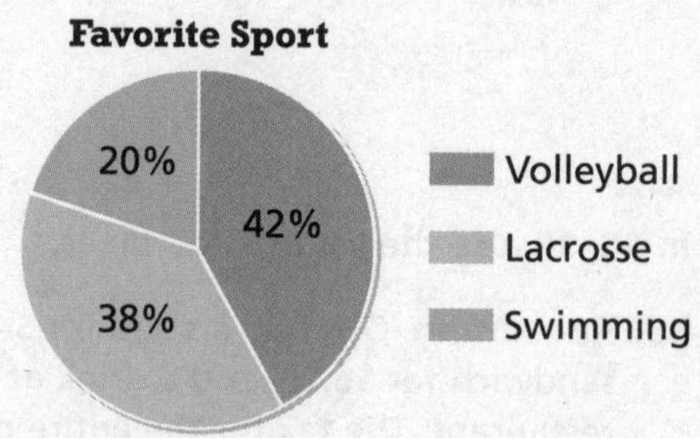

Assessment Practice

25. People use water to cook, clean, and drink every day. It is estimated that 16.8% of the water used each day is for cleaning. If a family uses 67.2 gallons of water per day for cleaning, how many total gallons do they use per day? Explain.

26. Martha has a budget for groceries, fuel, and utilities. She spent 20% of her budget on groceries. If Martha spent \$42.00 on groceries, how much is her budget?

3-ACT MATH

3-Act Mathematical Modeling:
Ace the Test

Go Online | PearsonRealize.com

Common Core Content Standards
6.RP.A.1, 6.RP.A.3c

Mathematical Practices
MP.4

ACT 1

1. After watching the video, what is the first question that comes to mind?

2. Write the Main Question you will answer.

3. Predict an answer to this Main Question.

4. Construct Arguments Explain how you arrived at your prediction. MP.3

5. What information in this situation would be helpful to know? How would you use that information?

6. **Use Appropriate Tools** What tools can you use to get the information you need? Record the information as you find it. © MP.5

7. **Model with Math** Represent the situation using the mathematical content, concepts, and skills from this topic. Use your representation to answer the Main Question. © MP.4

8. What is your answer to the Main Question? Does it differ from your prediction? Explain.

9. Write the answer you saw in the video.

10. **Reasoning** Does your answer match the answer in the video? If not, what are some reasons that would explain the difference? MP.2

11. **Make Sense and Persevere** Would you change your model now that you know the answer? Explain. MP.1

ACT 3 Extension

Reflect

12. Model with Math Explain how you used a mathematical model to represent the situation. How did the model help you answer the Main Question? MP.4

13. Be Precise Why are percents more useful in this situation than the number of correct answers? MP.6

SEQUEL

14. Reasoning Suppose each test has 3 additional questions, and she gets 2 of them correct. How will that affect the answer? MP.2

? Topic Essential Question

What is the meaning of percent? How can percent be estimated and found?

Vocabulary Review

Complete each definition with a vocabulary word.

Vocabulary	compatible numbers	fraction	percent	ratio

1. A ratio of a quantity to 100 is a ________.

2. A ________ compares two numbers or the number of items in two groups.

3. ________ are numbers that are easier to compute mentally.

Draw a line to match each *fraction*, *decimal*, or *percent* in Column A to the equivalent value in Column B.

Column A	Column B
4. $\frac{40}{50}$	$1\frac{3}{4}$
5. 13%	$1\frac{11}{20}$
6. 1.75	0.13
7. 155%	80%

Use Vocabulary in Writing

Out of 230 students surveyed, 11% chose gymnastics as their favorite sport. Explain how you can estimate the number of students who chose gymnastics. Use vocabulary words in your explanation.

Concept and Skills Review

LESSON 6-1 Understand Percent

Quick Review

A percent is a rate that compares a part to 100. The word *percent* means "of a hundred."

Example

Write the percent represented by the shaded part of the grid.

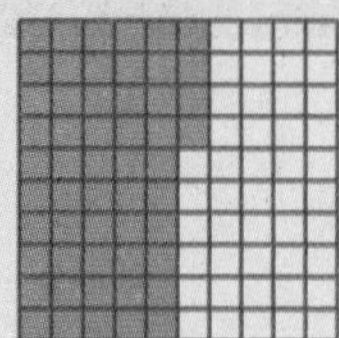

$\frac{54}{100}$ parts shaded = 54%

Practice

In 1 and 2, write the percent of each figure that is shaded.

1.

2. 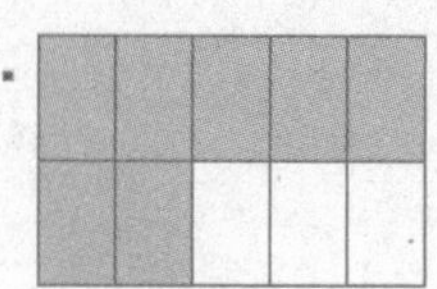

In 3 and 4, write each ratio as a percent.

3. 14 losses in 50 games

4. $\frac{4}{5}$ of the students ride a bus.

5. If $\overline{AB}$ represents 25%, what is the length of a line segment that is 100%?

A B
5 ft

LESSON 6-2 Relate Fractions, Decimals, and Percents

Quick Review

Fractions, decimals, and percents are three ways to show parts of a whole. You can write a percent as a fraction with 100 as the denominator. Then you can write that fraction as a decimal.

Example

Write 35% as a fraction and a decimal.

$35\% = \frac{35}{100}$ or $\frac{7}{20}$

$\frac{35}{100} = 0.35$

Practice

In 1–6, write each number using the two other forms of notation: fraction, decimal, or percent.

1. 0.16

2. $\frac{63}{100}$

3. 27%

4. $\frac{7}{8}$

5. 0.55

6. 7%

7. One piece of wheat bread contains 2 g of fiber, or 8% of the amount of fiber that most people need in a day. What is 8% as a decimal and as a fraction?

LESSON 6-3 Represent Percents Greater Than 100 or Less Than 1

Quick Review

Percents less than 1% are less than $\frac{1}{100}$, and percents greater than 100% are more than one whole. You can express percents greater than 100 or less than 1 in equivalent forms.

Example

Write 221% as a fraction and as a decimal.

Fraction: $\frac{221}{100}$

Decimal: $\frac{221}{100} = 221 \div 100 = 2.21$

Write $\frac{1}{4}$% as a fraction and as a decimal.

Fraction: $\frac{1}{4}\% = \frac{1}{4} \div 100$

$= \frac{1}{4} \times \frac{1}{100} = \frac{1}{400}$

Decimal: $\frac{1}{4}\% = 0.25\%$

$= \frac{0.25}{100}$

$= \frac{25}{10{,}000}$

$= 0.0025$

Practice

In 1–6, write each percent as a fraction and as a decimal.

1. 140%

2. $\frac{7}{10}$%

3. 375%

4. 0.33%

5. 0.5%

6. 250%

7. The radius of the planet Saturn is 945% of the radius of Earth. What is 945% expressed as a fraction and as a decimal?

LESSON 6-4 Estimate to Find Percent

Quick Review

Fraction equivalents, rounding, or compatible numbers can be used to estimate the percent of a number.

Example

Estimate 24% of 83.

$24\% \approx 25\%$ and $25\% = \frac{1}{4}$

83 rounds to 80.

$\frac{1}{4} \times 80 = 20$

24% of 83 is about 20.

Practice

In 1–6, estimate the percent of each number.

1. 22% of 96

2. 38% of 58

3. 9% of 89

4. 76% of 41

5. 48% of 71

6. 27% of 62

7. Joanna wants to buy a backpack that costs $37.98. The sales tax rate is 8.75%. Estimate the amount of sales tax that Joanna will pay.

LESSON 6-5 Find the Percent of a Number

Quick Review

Percent equations have a percent value, a whole, and a part.

Example

What is 16% of 73.5?

Let $x =$ the unknown part.

$x = 0.16 \cdot 73.5$ Write 16% as a decimal.

$x = 11.76$

16% of 73.5 is 11.76.

What percent of 22 is 9.35?

Let $p =$ the percent value.

$p \cdot 22 = 9.35$

$22p = 9.35$

$\frac{22p}{22} = \frac{9.35}{22}$

$p = 0.425 = 42.5\%$

42.5% of 22 is 9.35.

Practice

Find each part or percent.

1. 9% of 124

2. What percent of 20 is 3?

3. 24% of 35

4. What percent of 110 is 71.5?

5. 43% of 82

6. What percent of 30 is 24?

7. On Tuesday, 620 students attended a middle school. A survey showed that 341 students brought lunch to school that day. What percent of the students brought their lunches?

LESSON 6-6 Find the Whole Given a Part and the Percent

Quick Review

You can use an equation or a double number line diagram to find the whole when given the part and the percent.

Example

80% of what number is 96?

Let $n =$ the whole. Write an equation, rename the percent as a decimal, and solve for n.

$80\% \cdot n = 96$

$0.8n = 96$

$\frac{0.8n}{0.8} = \frac{96}{0.8}$

$n = 120$

80% of 120 is 96.

Practice

Find each whole.

1. 140% of what number is 308?

2. 62% of what number is 186?

3. 80% of what number is 120?

4. 40% of what number is 10?

5. Desmond paid 8.5% sales tax when he bought a new phone. The sales tax was $12.75. What was the total cost of the phone, including tax?

Fluency Practice

Crisscrossed

I can...
divide multidigit numbers.

6.NS.B.2

Find each quotient. Write your answers in the cross-number puzzle below. Each digit of your answer goes in its own box.

ACROSS

A 94,070 ÷ 46

C 3,828 ÷ 22

E 46,680 ÷ 15

F 61,065 ÷ 45

J 5,136 ÷ 214

K 9,840 ÷ 48

L 2,407 ÷ 29

N 67,870 ÷ 55

Q 9,114 ÷ 62

R 8,268 ÷ 12

T 80,120 ÷ 20

DOWN

A 7,644 ÷ 28

B 22,016 ÷ 43

D 49,980 ÷ 12

G 67,704 ÷ 13

H 10,582 ÷ 143

K 4,148 ÷ 17

M 10,062 ÷ 26

P 63,860 ÷ 31

Q 4,508 ÷ 23

S 7,238 ÷ 77

SOLVE AREA, SURFACE AREA, AND VOLUME PROBLEMS

? Topic Essential Question

How can the areas of certain shapes be found? What are the meanings of surface area and volume and how can surface area and volume be found?

Topic Overview

- 7-1 Find Areas of Parallelograms and Rhombuses
- 7-2 Solve Triangle Area Problems
- 7-3 Find Areas of Trapezoids and Kites
- 7-4 Find Areas of Polygons
- 7-5 Represent Solid Figures Using Nets
- 3-Act Mathematical Modeling: That's a Wrap
- 7-6 Find Surface Areas of Prisms
- 7-7 Find Surface Areas of Pyramids
- 7-8 Find Volume with Fractional Edge Lengths

Topic Vocabulary

- base
- edge
- face
- kite
- net
- polyhedron
- vertex

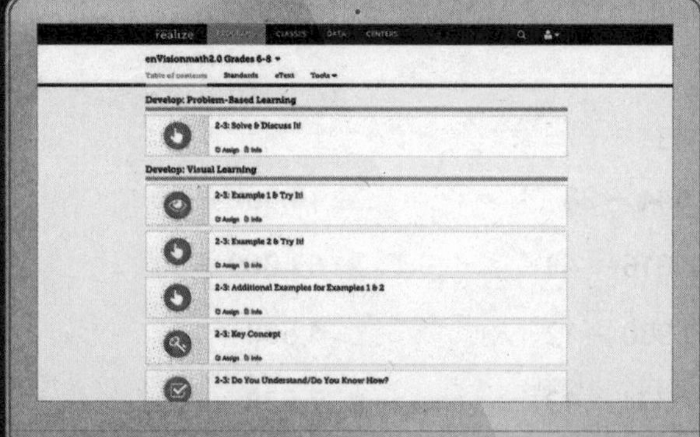

Go online | PearsonRealize.com

Lesson Digital Resources

INTERACTIVE ANIMATION Interact with visual learning animations.

ACTIVITY Use with *Solve & Discuss It*, *Explore I* and *Explain It* activities, and to explore Example

VIDEOS Watch clips to support *3-Act Mathema* *Modeling Lessons* and *STEM Projects*.

PRACTICE Practice what you've learned.

3-ACT MATH

That's a Wrap

That's a Wrap

How you wrap a gift can say a lot about you. Some people conserve resources by reusing paper bags instead of purchasing wrapping paper. It may not look as nice at first, but you can unleash your crafty side and decorate the gift yourself.

No matter what you use to wrap a gift, you always need to consider the size of the object and how much paper you'll need. Think about this during the 3-Act Mathematical Modeling lesson.

TUTORIALS Get help from ***Virtual Nerd***, right when you need it.

KEY CONCEPT Review important lesson content.

GLOSSARY Read and listen to English/Spanish definitions.

ASSESSMENT Show what you've learned.

Additional Digital Resources

MATH TOOLS Explore math with digital tools.

GAMES Play Math Games to help you learn.

ETEXT Interact with your Student's Edition online.

TOPIC 7

STEM Project

Did You Know?

Food packaging is designed to identify products and to attract customers. Packaging also ensures food remains fresh and free from damage and contamination.

Common types of material used for packaging are paper, cardboard, glass, steel, and aluminum. The best material to use for packaging depends on the contents—for example, soup in a paper bag could be rather messy!

Manufacturers consider several factors when designing packaging, such as cost, amount of material used, and potential environmental impact. Steel food cans are the most recycled food package in the United States.

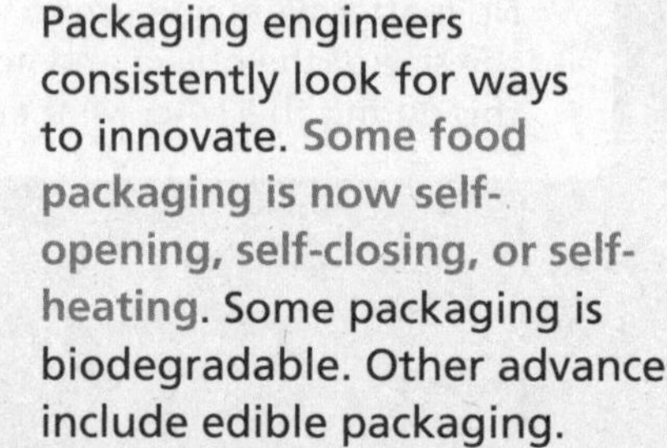

Packaging engineers consistently look for ways to innovate. Some food packaging is now self-opening, self-closing, or self-heating. Some packaging is biodegradable. Other advances include edible packaging.

Your Task: Pack It

Food packaging engineers consider many elements related to both form and function when designing packaging. How do engineers make decisions about package designs as they consider constraints, such as limited dimensions or materials? You and your classmates will use the engineering design process to explore and propose food packaging that satisfies certain criteria.

Review What You Know!

Vocabulary

Choose the best term from the box to complete each definition.

area
parallelogram
perpendicular
polygon
volume

1. A triangle is an example of a three-sided ___________.

2. ___________ lines form a right angle.

3. ___________ is the number of cubic units needed to fill a solid figure.

4. A ___________ has opposite sides that are parallel and the same length.

Evaluate Expressions

Find the value of each expression when $a = 12$, $b = 3$, $c = 4$, and $d = 9$.

5. ac
6. $\frac{1}{2}b$
7. abd
8. $0.5a$
9. $\frac{3}{4}(ad)$
10. $ab + cd$

Multiplication

Find each product.

11. 3.14×12
12. 45.8×5
13. 0.8×2.7
14. $14 \times 7.25 \times 2.5$
15. $1\frac{1}{2} \times \frac{1}{4}$
16. $2\frac{1}{3} \times 2\frac{1}{4} \times 1\frac{3}{8}$

Geometry

17. How are parallelograms and rectangles similar and how are they different?

18. How are the formulas for the area of a rectangle and the area of a triangle alike and different? Explain.

Build Vocabulary

Use the graphic organizer to help relate vocabulary terms that you studied before to the new vocabulary in this topic.

Types of Figures	Key Characteristics

Two-Dimensional Figures

Parts of Figures	Measures

Types of Figures	Key Characteristics

Three-Dimensional Figures

Parts of Figures	Measures

Lesson 7-1
Find Areas of Parallelograms and Rhombuses

Go Online | PearsonRealize.com

I can...
use what I know about areas of rectangles to find the areas of parallelograms and rhombuses.

Common Core Content Standards
6.G.A.1, 6.EE.A.2c

Mathematical Practices
MP.2, MP.3, MP.6, MP.7, MP.8

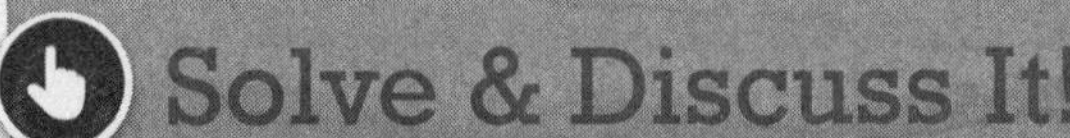

Solve & Discuss It!

Sofía drew the grid below and plotted the points *A*, *B*, *C*, and *D*. Connect point *A* to *B*, *B* to *C*, *C* to *D*, and *D* to *A*. Then find the area of the shape and explain how you found it. Using the same grid, move points *B* and *C* four units to the right. Connect the points to make a new parallelogram *ABCD*. What is the area of this shape?

Look for Relationships What relationships do you see between rectangles and parallelograms? MP.7

Focus on math practices

Generalize How can you find the area of any parallelogram? MP.8

Essential Question How can you use the area formula of a rectangle to find the area formula of a parallelogram?

EXAMPLE 1 Find the Area Formula of a Parallelogram

Scan for Multimedia

Look at the parallelogram below. If you move the triangle to the opposite side, you form a rectangle with the same area as the parallelogram. How can you find the area of a parallelogram?

Use Structure To compose a rectangle from a parallelogram, first decompose the parallelogram into a right triangle and a trapezoid. MP.7

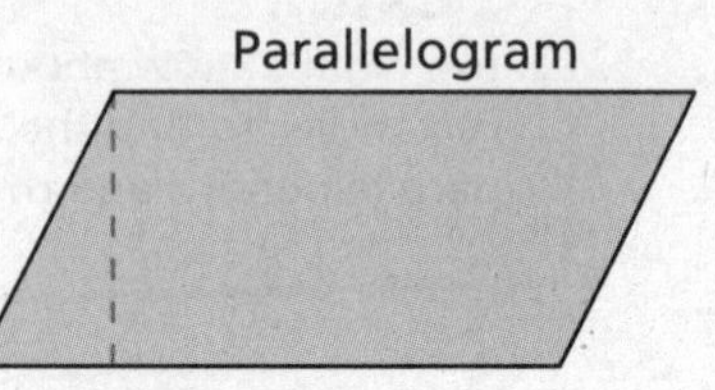

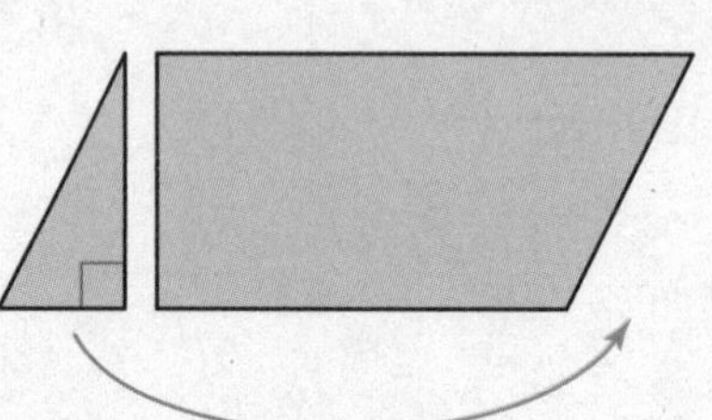

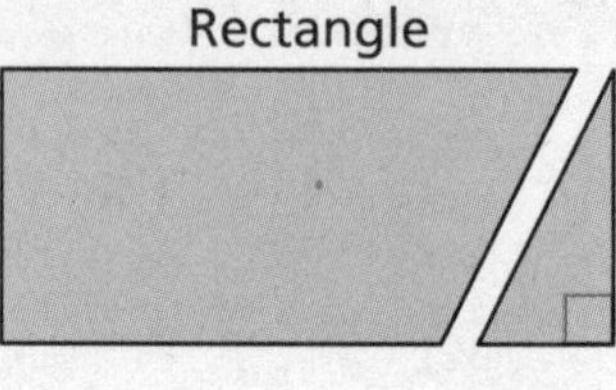

Create a rectangle.

The height of the parallelogram, h, which is perpendicular to the base, equals the width of the rectangle, w.

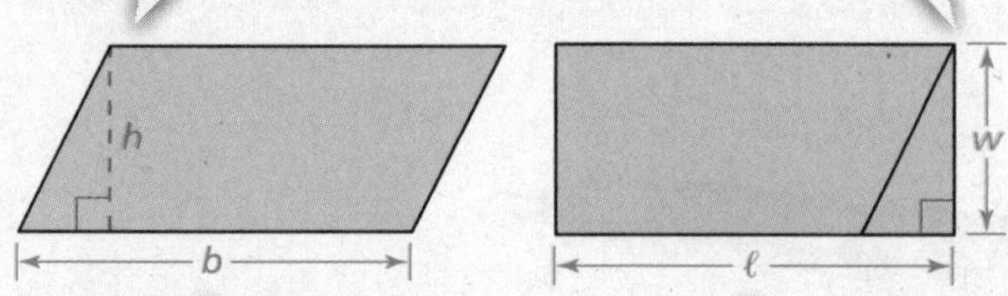

The base of the parallelogram, b, equals the length of the rectangle, ℓ.

The area of the parallelogram equals the area of the rectangle.

Area of a Rectangle $A = \ell \times w$

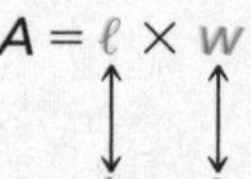

Area of a Parallelogram $A = b \times h$

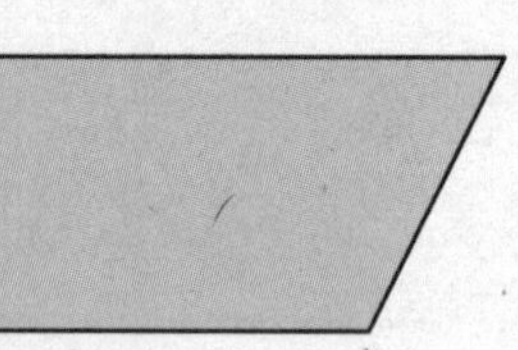

The formula for the area of a parallelogram is $A = bh$.

Try It!

Find the area of the parallelogram.

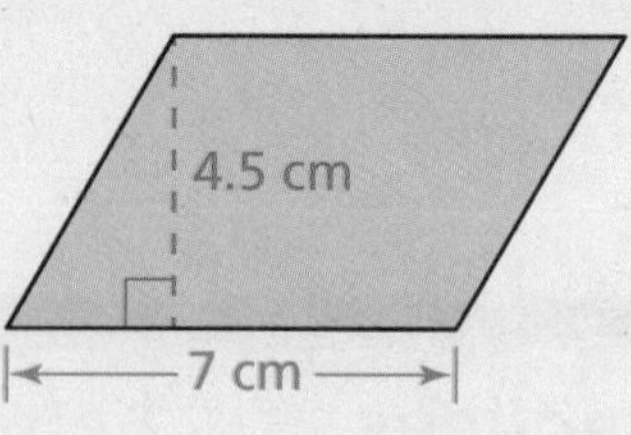

$A = \square \times h$

$A = \square \times \square$

$A = \square$

The area of the parallelogram is $\square$ cm^2.

Convince Me! Compare the area of this parallelogram to the area of a rectangle with a length of 7 cm and a width of 4.5 cm. Explain.

EXAMPLE 2  Find the Area of a Rhombus

  ACTIVITY  ASSESS

The pendant at the right is in the shape of a rhombus. A rhombus is a parallelogram with sides of equal length. What is the area of the pendant?

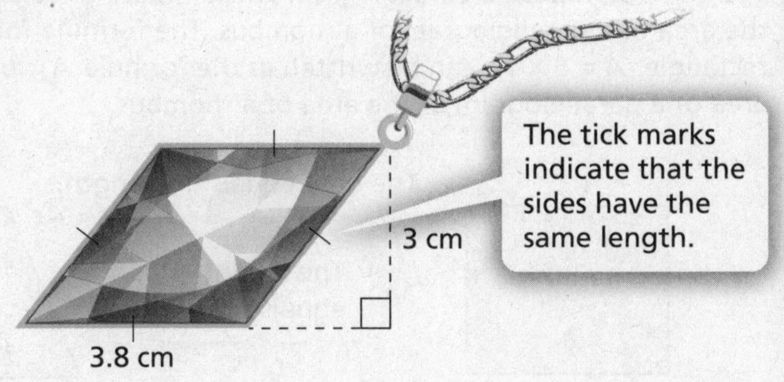

Be Precise You can use the formula for the area of a parallelogram to find the area of a rhombus. Remember to record area in square units. 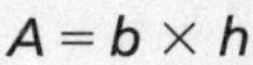

$A = b \times h$

$A = 3.8 \times 3$

$A = 11.4$

The area of the pendant is 11.4 cm^2.

EXAMPLE 3  Find the Base or Height of a Parallelogram

A. The area of the parallelogram is 72 m^2. What is the height of the parallelogram?

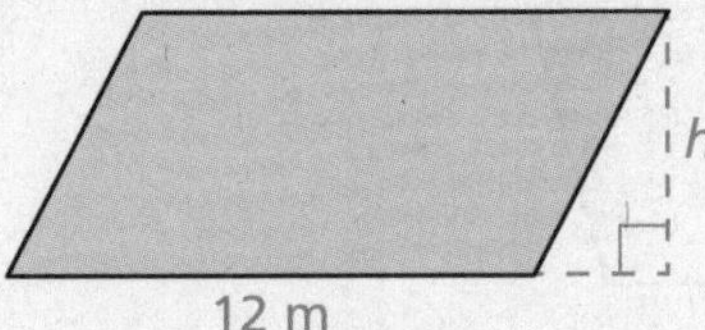

$A = b \times h$

$72 = 12 \times h$ — Substitute 72 for A and 12 for b.

$6 = h$

The height of the parallelogram is 6 m.

B. The area of the parallelogram is 135 $in.^2$. What is the base of the parallelogram?

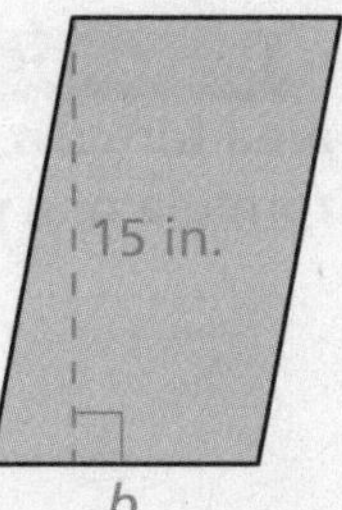

$A = b \times h$

$135 = b \times 15$ — Substitute 135 for A and 15 for h.

$9 = b$

The base of the parallelogram is 9 in.

Try It!

a. Find the area of the rhombus.

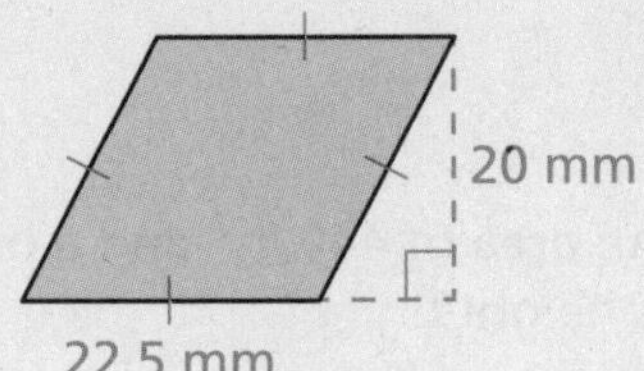

b. The area of the parallelogram is 65 ft^2. What is its height?

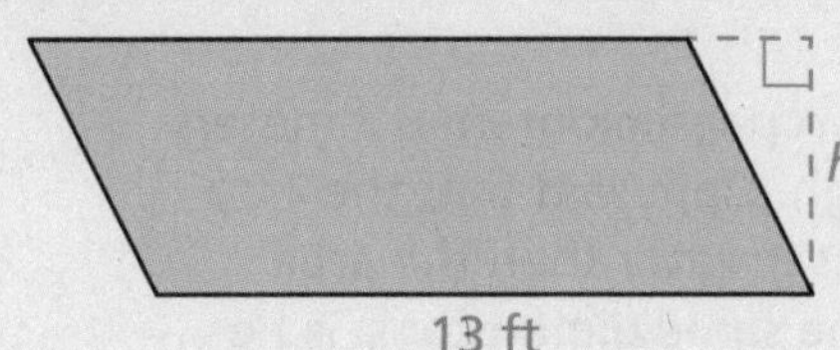

KEY CONCEPT

You can decompose a parallelogram and compose a rectangle to find the area of a parallelogram or a rhombus. The formula for the area of a rectangle, $A = \ell \times w$, can be written as the formula $A = b \times h$ to find the area of a parallelogram or the area of a rhombus.

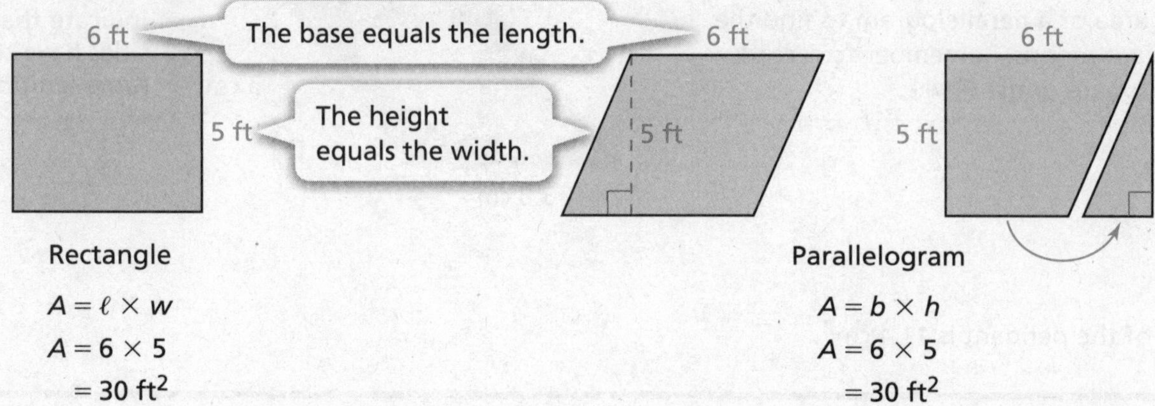

Rectangle

$A = \ell \times w$

$A = 6 \times 5$

$= 30\ ft^2$

Parallelogram

$A = b \times h$

$A = 6 \times 5$

$= 30\ ft^2$

Do You Understand?

1. **Essential Question** How can you use the area formula of a rectangle to find the area formula of a parallelogram?

2. Ken combined a triangle and a trapezoid to make a parallelogram. If the area of the triangle is 12 in.^{2} and the area of the trapezoid is 24 in.^{2}, what is the area of the parallelogram? Explain.

3. **Critique Reasoning** A parallelogram is 3 meters long and 7 meters high. Liam said that the parallelogram's area is greater than the area of a rectangle with the same dimensions. Is he correct? Explain. MP.3

Do You Know How?

In 4–6, use a formula to find the area.

4.

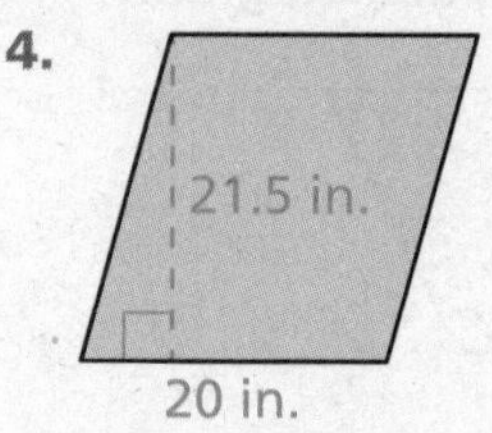

5.

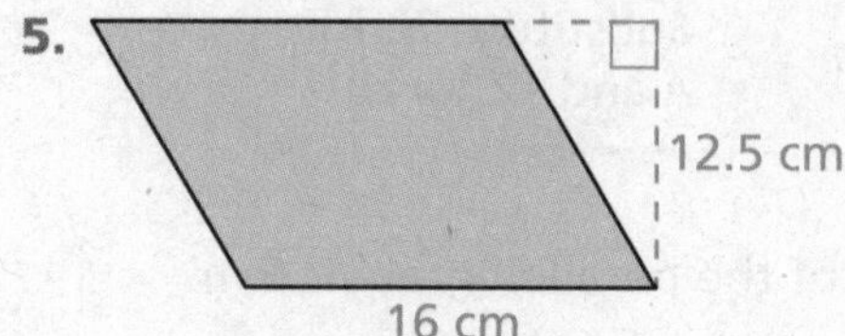

6.

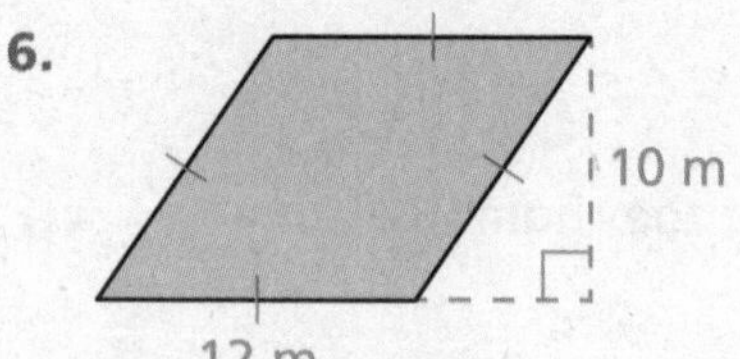

7. A rhombus has an area of 440 m^2 and a base of 22 m. What is its height?

Name: ______________________________

Practice & Problem Solving

Scan for Multimedia 

Leveled Practice **In 8–11, find the area of each parallelogram or rhombus.**

8.

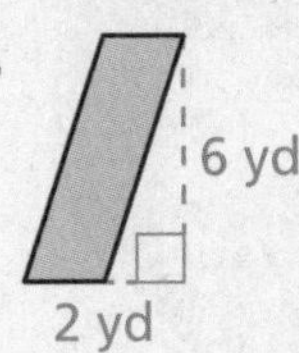

$A = b \cdot h$

$= \square \cdot 6$

$= \square$ yd^2

9.

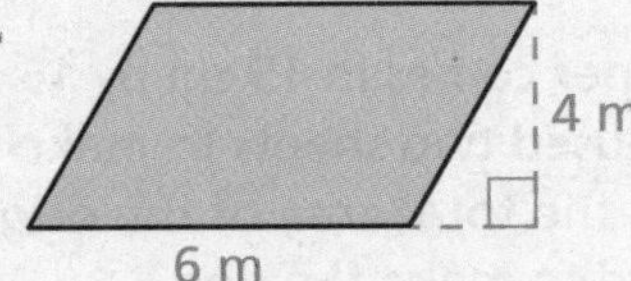

$A = b \cdot h$

$= \square \cdot \square$

$= \square$ m^2

10.

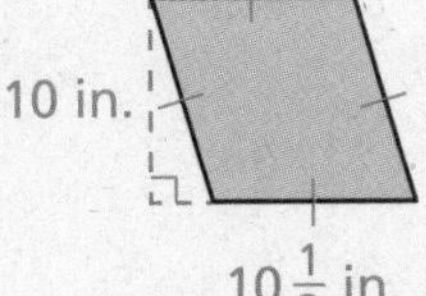

11.

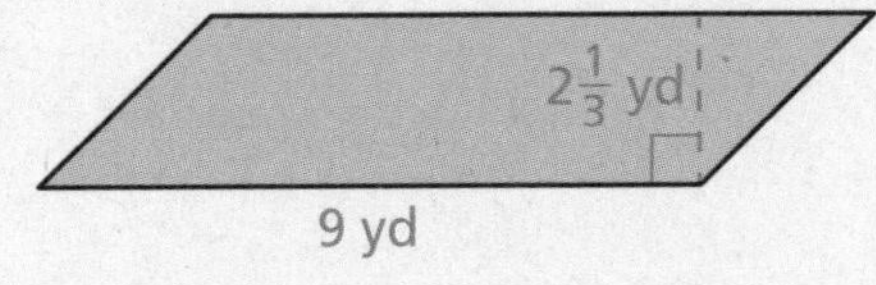

12. The area of the parallelogram is 132 in.^{2}. What is the height of the parallelogram?

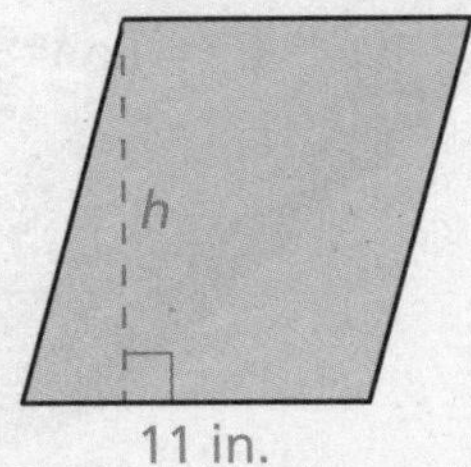

13. The area of the rhombus is 52 m^2. What is the base of the rhombus?

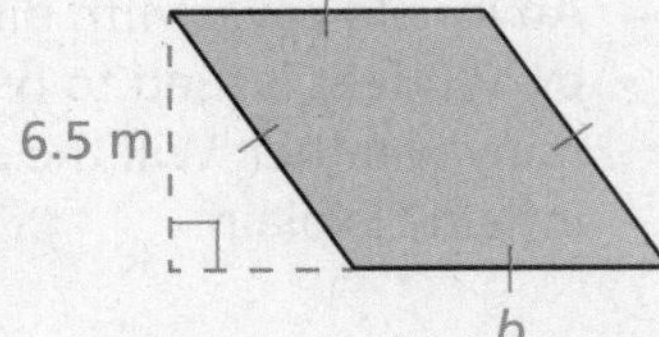

14. Micah and Jason made parallelogram-shaped stained glass windows with the same area. The height of Micah's window is 9 inches, and its base is 10 inches. The height of Jason's window is 6 inches. What is the base of Jason's window?

15. A rectangle has a length of 8 m and a width of 4.5 m. A parallelogram has a length of 6 m. The area of the parallelogram is twice the area of the rectangle. What is the height of the parallelogram?

In 16 and 17, use the picture at the right.

16. Hilary made an origami dog. What is the area of the parallelogram that is highlighted in the origami figure?

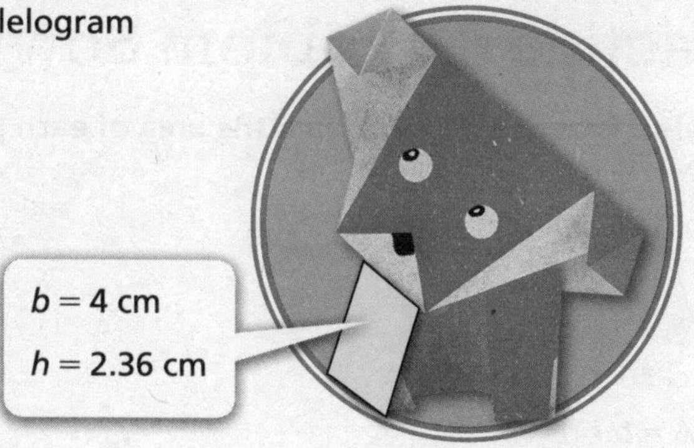

17. A type of origami paper comes in 15 cm by 15 cm square sheets. Hilary used two sheets to make the origami dog. What is the total area of the origami paper that Hilary used to make the dog?

18. Reasoning A rectangle and a parallelogram have the same base and the same height. How are their areas related? Provide an example to justify your answer. MP.2

19. Soshi's rhombus has a base of 12 in. and a height of 10 in. Jack's rhombus has base and height measures that are double those of Soshi's rhombus. Compare the area of Jack's rhombus to the area of Soshi's rhombus. Explain.

20. Higher Order Thinking The infield of a baseball diamond is in the shape of a rhombus. An infield cover with dimensions of 85 feet by 100 feet is used to protect the field during rainy weather. Will the cover protect the entire infield? Explain.

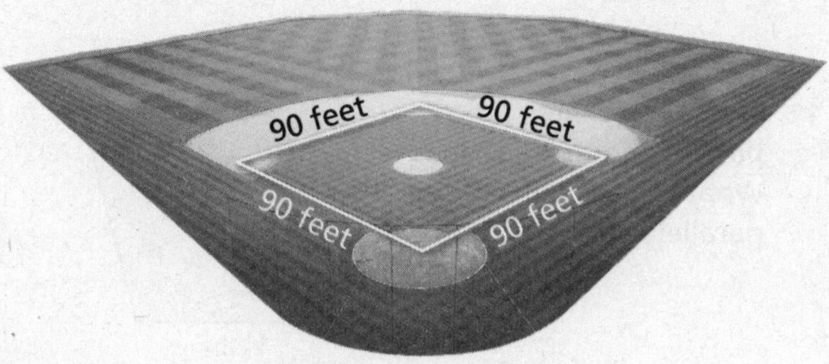

Assessment Practice

21. The parking space shown at the right has an area of 209 ft^2. A custom truck has rectangular dimensions of 13.5 ft by 8.5 ft. Can the truck fit in the parking space? Justify your answer.

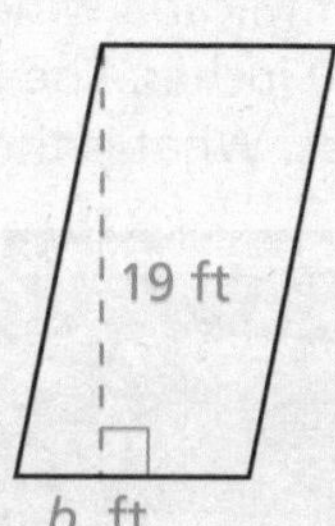

Lesson 7-2
Solve Triangle Area Problems

Go Online | PearsonRealize.com

I can...
find the areas of triangles.

Common Core Content Standards
6.G.A.1, 6.EE.A.2c

Mathematical Practices
MP.2, MP.3, MP.6, MP.7, MP.8

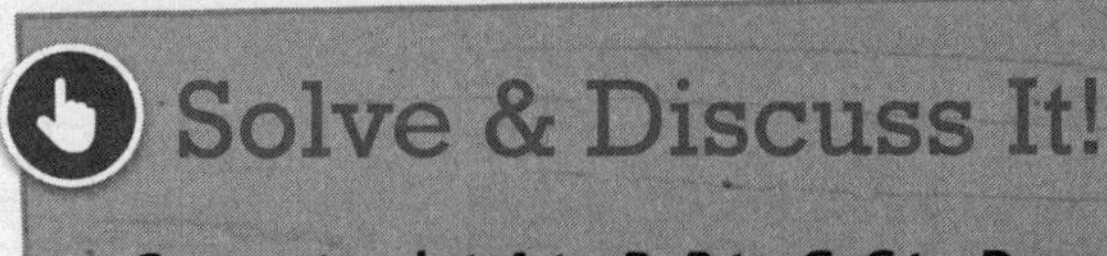

Connect point A to B, B to C, C to D, and D to A. Then draw a diagonal line connecting opposite vertices in the figure and find the area of each triangle formed.

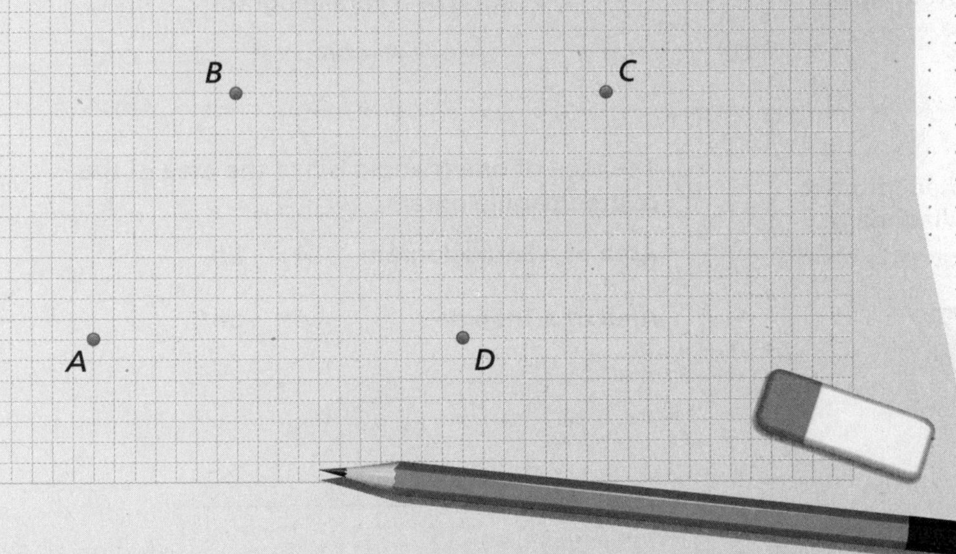

Use Structure What relationships do you see between the area of the parallelogram and the areas of the triangles? MP.7

Focus on math practices

Generalize What is a rule for finding the area of any triangle? MP.8

? Essential Question How can you find the area of a triangle?

EXAMPLE 1 Find the Area of a Triangle

Scan for Multimedia

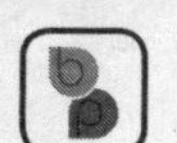

A parallelogram can be decomposed into two identical triangles. How can you use the formula for the area of a parallelogram to find the area of a triangle?

Reasoning How are the areas of parallelograms and triangles related? MP.2

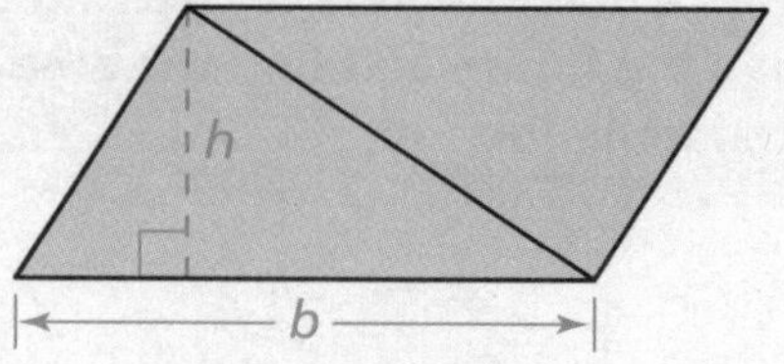

Area of a Parallelogram

$A = bh$

A parallelogram can be decomposed into two identical triangles when divided diagonally.

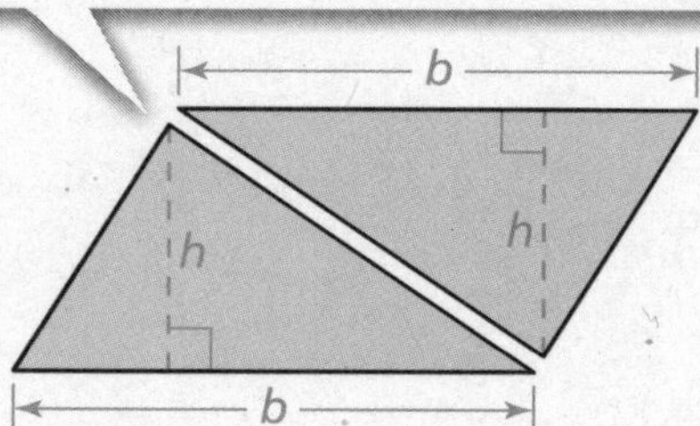

Identical triangles have the same base and height, so they also have the same area.

The area of one triangle is half the area of the related parallelogram.

Area of a Parallelogram $A = bh$

Area of a Triangle $A = \frac{1}{2}bh$

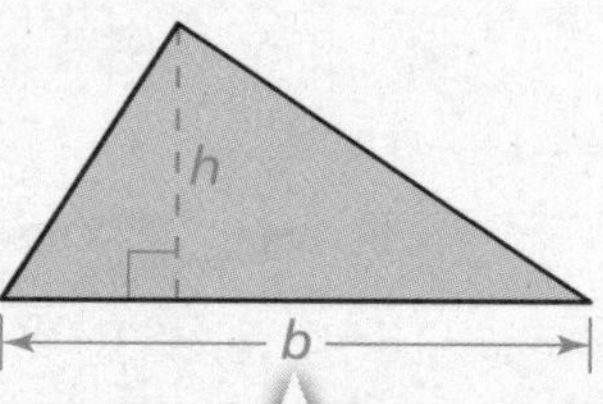

The formula for the area of a triangle is $A = \frac{1}{2}bh$.

Try It!

Use the formula $A = \frac{1}{2}bh$ to find the area of the triangle.

$A = \frac{1}{2} \times b \times h$

$A = \frac{1}{2} \times \square \times \square$

$A = \frac{1}{2} \times \square$

$A = \square$

5 cm

12 cm

The area of the triangle is $\square$ cm^2.

Convince Me! Two identical triangles form a parallelogram with a base of 8 inches and a height of 6 inches. What is the area of each triangle? Explain.

EXAMPLE 2  Find the Area of a Right Triangle

The side of a birdhouse is in the shape of a right triangle. What is the area of the side of the birdhouse?

Draw a triangle and compose a square.

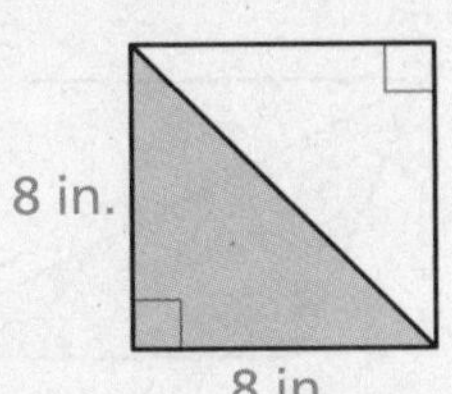

The two sides that form the right angle in a right triangle are its base and height.

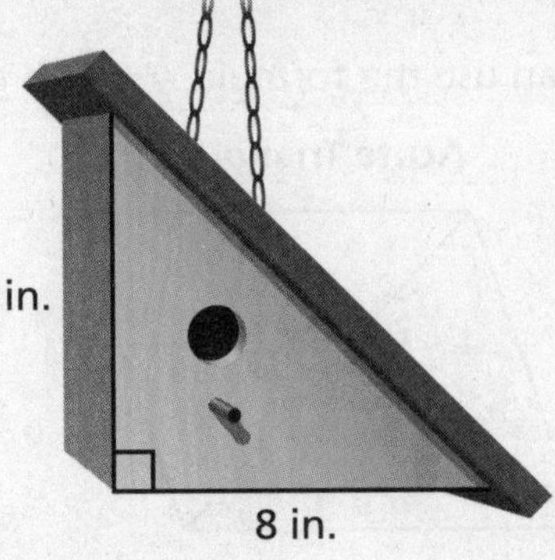

Generalize You can use the formula $A = \frac{1}{2}bh$ to find the area of *any* triangle when you know the base and height. MP.8

Find the area of the triangle.

$A = \frac{1}{2}bh$

$A = \frac{1}{2} \times 8 \times 8 = 32$

The area of the side of the birdhouse is 32 in.^{2}.

EXAMPLE 3  Identify the Corresponding Base and Height to Find the Area

Kaylan drew the triangle shown below. What is the area of the triangle?

Any side of a triangle can be its base. The height is the perpendicular distance from the base to the height of the opposite vertex.

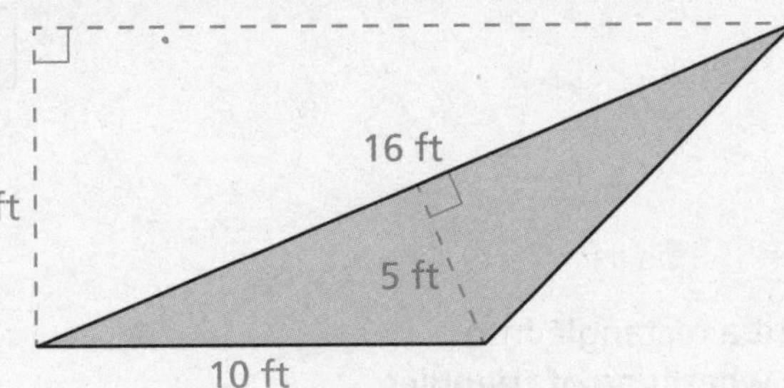

ONE WAY

$A = \frac{1}{2}bh$

$A = \frac{1}{2} \cdot 10 \cdot 8$

$A = 40$

Substitute a corresponding base of 10 ft and height of 8 ft.

The area is 40 ft^2.

ANOTHER WAY

$A = \frac{1}{2}bh$

$A = \frac{1}{2} \cdot 16 \cdot 5$

$A = 40$

Substitute a corresponding base and height.

The area is 40 ft^2.

Try It!

Find the area of each triangle.

a.

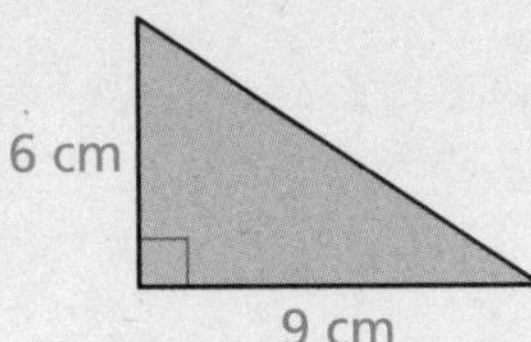

b.

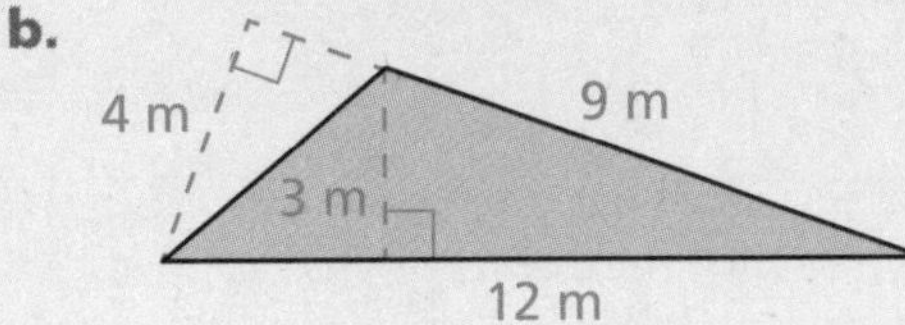

KEY CONCEPT 

KEY CONCEPT

You can use the formula $A = \frac{1}{2}bh$ to find the area of any triangle.

Acute Triangle

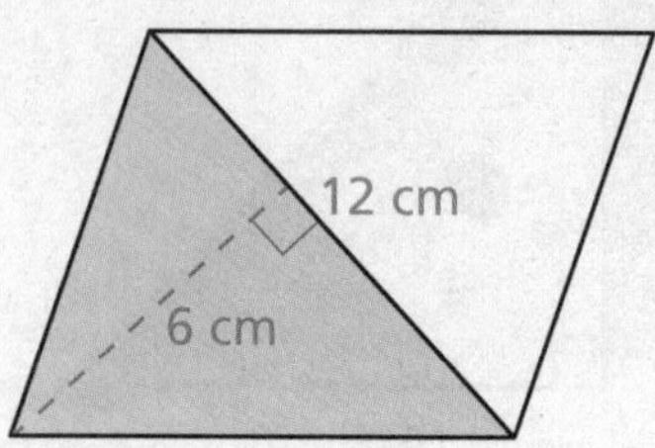

$A = \frac{1}{2}bh$

$A = \frac{1}{2} \times 12 \times 6$

$A = 36 \text{ cm}^2$

Right Triangle

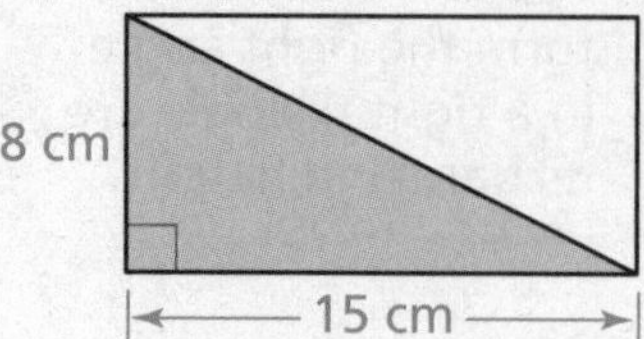

$A = \frac{1}{2}bh$

$A = \frac{1}{2} \times 15 \times 8$

$A = 60 \text{ cm}^2$

Obtuse Triangle

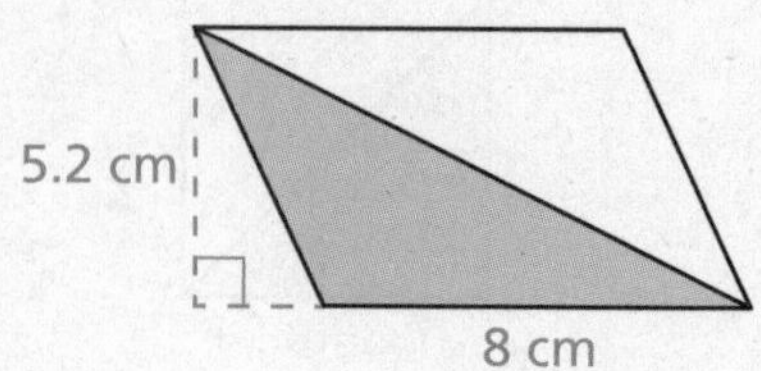

$A = \frac{1}{2}bh$

$A = \frac{1}{2} \times 8 \times 5.2$

$A = 20.8 \text{ cm}^2$

Do You Understand?

1. **Essential Question** How can you find the area of a triangle?

2. **Reasoning** If you cut a rectangle into 2 identical triangles, what type of triangles will they be? MP.2

3. **Construct Arguments** In Example 1, if the other diagonal were used to divide the parallelogram into two triangles, would the area of each of these triangles be half the area of the parallelogram? Explain. MP.3

Do You Know How?

In 4–6, find the area of each triangle.

4. 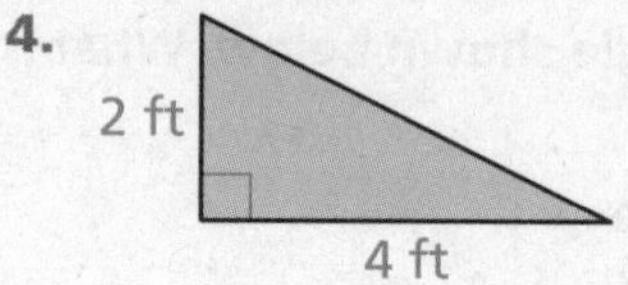

5.

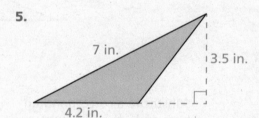

7 in.

3.5 in.

4.2 in.

6. 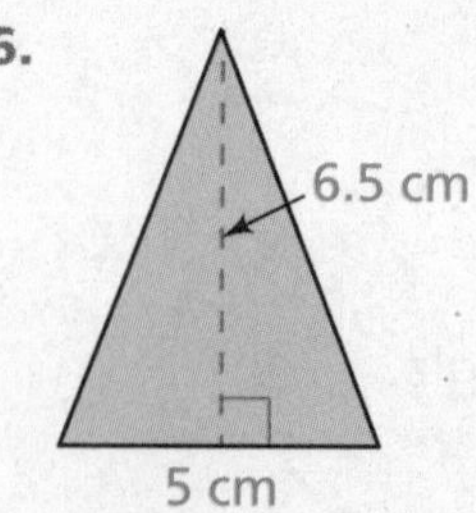

PRACTICE TUTORIAL

Name: ______________________________

Practice & Problem Solving  

Scan for Multimedia 

Leveled Practice In 7–12, find the area of each triangle.

7.

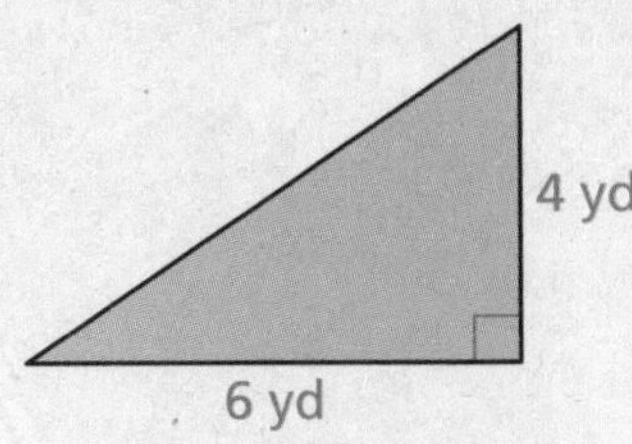

$A = \frac{1}{2}bh$

$= \frac{1}{2} \times$ ☐ $\times 4$

$=$ ☐ yd^2

8.

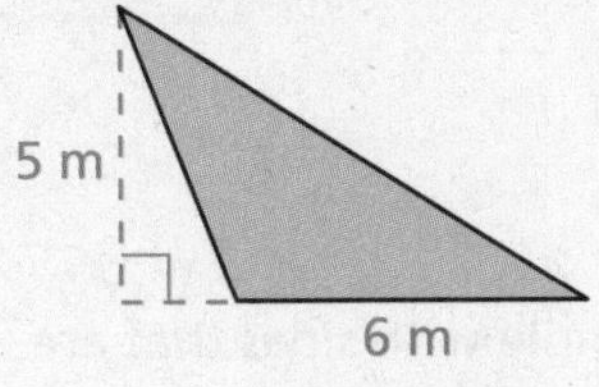

$A = \frac{1}{2}bh$

$= \frac{1}{2} \times$ ☐ $\times$ ☐

$=$ ☐ m^2

9.

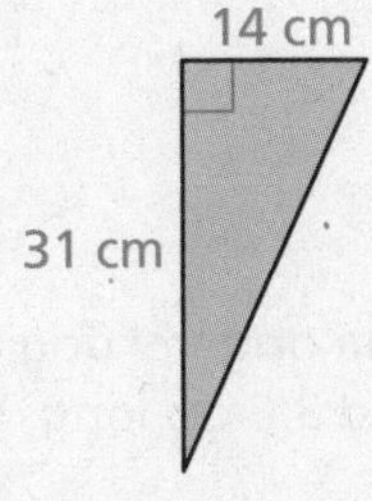

$A = \frac{1}{2}bh$

$= \frac{1}{2} \times$ ☐ $\times$ ☐

$=$ ☐ cm^2

10.

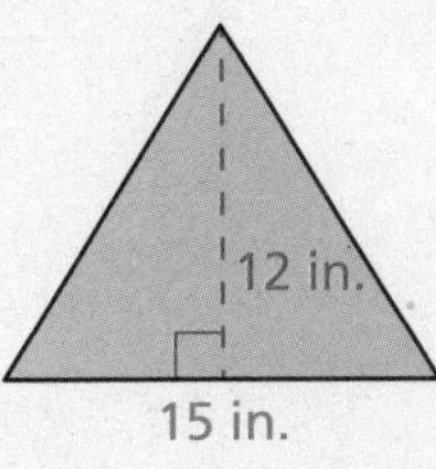

11.

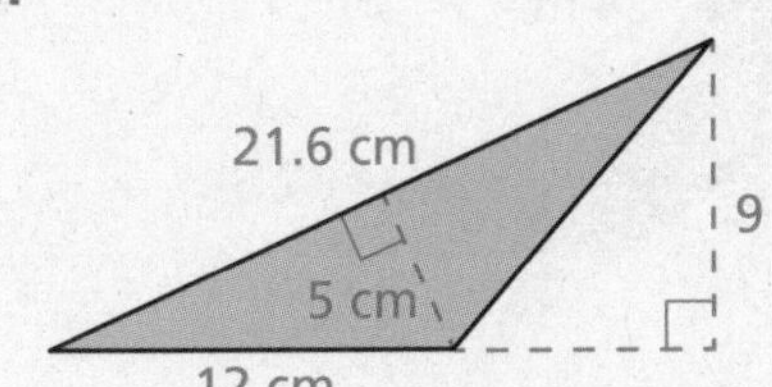

12.

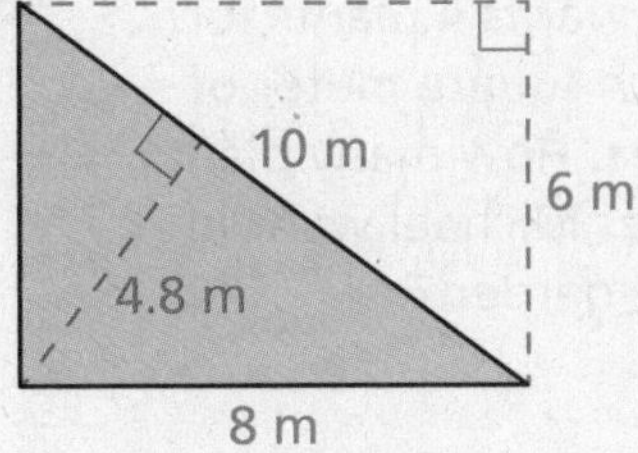

13. The vertices of a triangle are $A(0, 0)$, $B(3, 8)$, and $C(9, 0)$. What is the area of this triangle?

14. Be Precise The base of a triangle is 2 ft. The height of the triangle is 15 in. What is the area of the triangle in square inches? MP.6

15. Reasoning Ms. Lopez drew $\triangle ABC$, with a height of 6 inches and a base of 6 inches, and $\triangle RST$, with a height of 4 inches and a base of 8 inches. Which triangle has the greater area? Use an area formula to justify your answer. MP.2

16. The dimensions of the sail for Erica's sailboat are shown. Find the area of the sail.

15 ft

9 ft

In 17 and 18, use the picture at the right.

17. **Be Precise** What is the area in square millimeters of the yellow triangle outlined on the origami figure at the right? MP.6

$b = 3$ cm
$h = 1.76$ cm

18. The nose of the origami dog is a right triangle with sides that are 2 cm, 3 cm, and 3.6 cm long. What is the area of this triangle?

19. Michael is planting a garden in the shape of a right triangle. He wants 4 plants for each square meter of area. How many plants does Michael want in the garden?

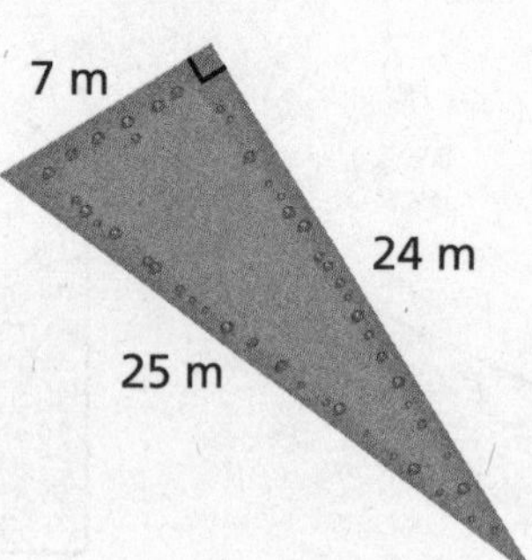

20. **Higher Order Thinking** If you know the area and the height of a triangle, how can you find the base?

Assessment Practice

21. Use each of the three corresponding base and height pairs to find the area of the triangle. Will the area be the same for each calculation? Explain.

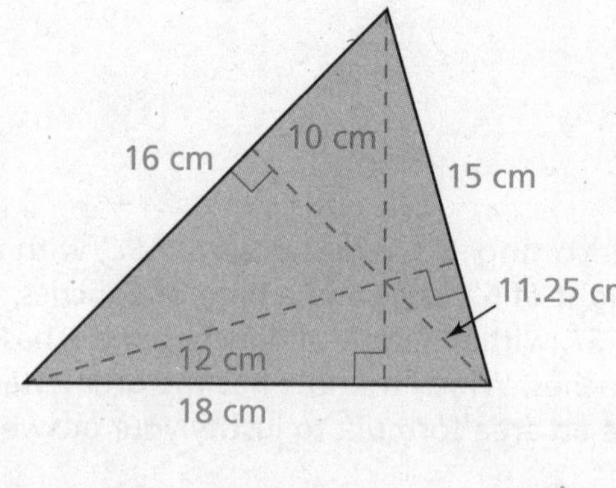

Lesson 7-3
Find Areas of Trapezoids and Kites

Go Online | PearsonRealize.com

I can...
find areas of trapezoids and kites.

Common Core Content Standards
6.G.A.1, 6.EE.A.2c

Mathematical Practices
MP.1, MP.3, MP.6, MP.7

Explain It!

The European basketball key was changed from a trapezoid shape to a rectangle in 2010. The diagram shows the shape of the key before 2010 outlined in blue.

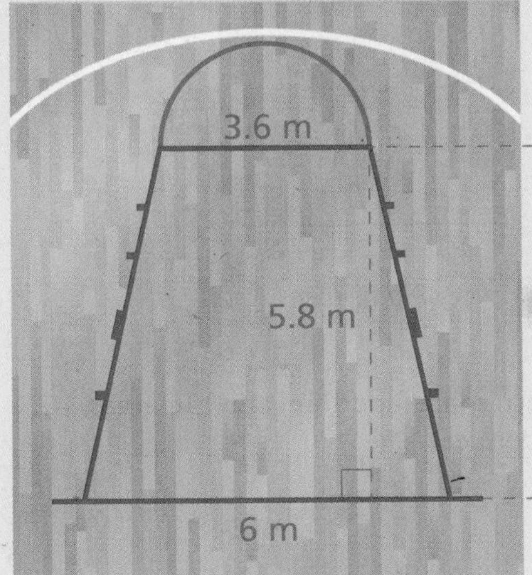

The key on a basketball court is the area between the foul line and the baseline.

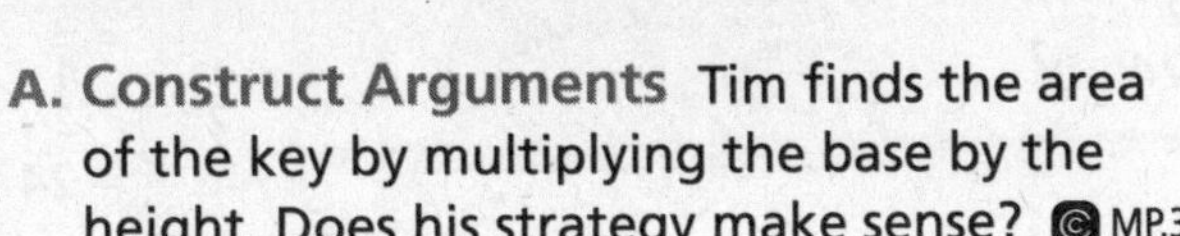

A. Construct Arguments Tim finds the area of the key by multiplying the base by the height. Does his strategy make sense? MP.3

B. Use Structure How could Tim find the area of the trapezoid by decomposing it into shapes he knows? What is the area of the key? MP.7

Focus on math practices

Use Structure How can you find the area of this kite? Explain. MP.7

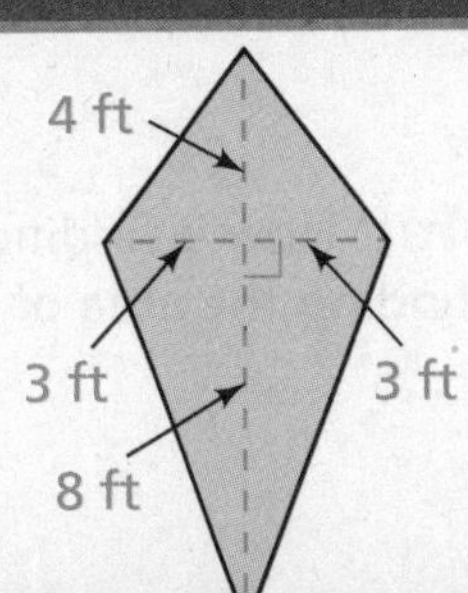

? **Essential Question** How can you find the areas of trapezoids and kites?

INTERACTIVE ANIMATION

ASSESS

EXAMPLE 1  Find the Area of a Trapezoid

Scan for Multimedia 

The pasture is in the shape of a trapezoid. What is the area of the pasture?

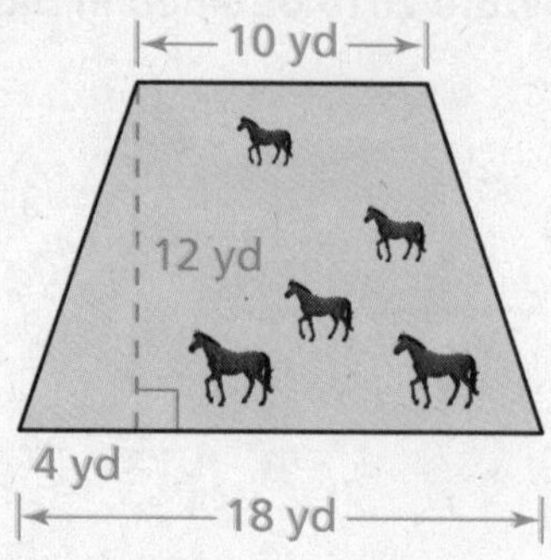

Be Precise What are the properties of a trapezoid and how can they help you to find the area of a trapezoid? MP.6

Decompose the trapezoid into a rectangle and two right triangles.

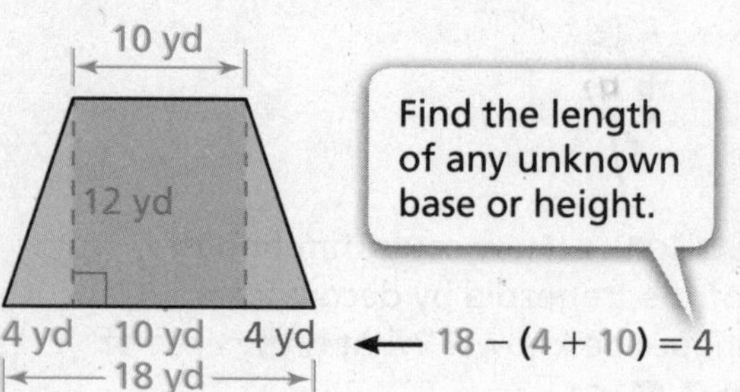

Find the area of each shape and then add the areas. The triangles are identical.

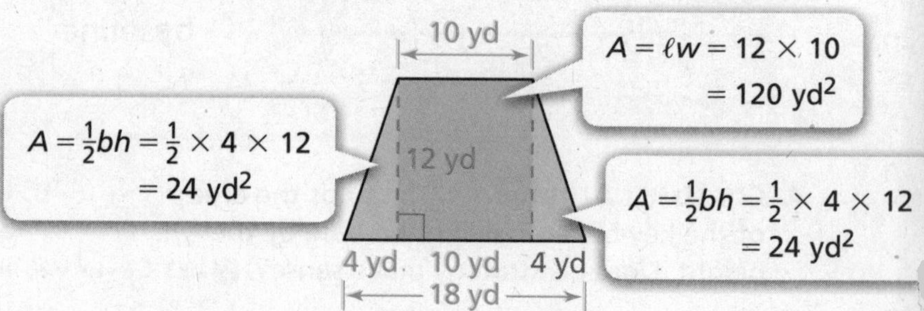

10 yd
$A = \ell w = 12 \times 10$
$= 120 \text{ yd}^2$
$A = \frac{1}{2}bh = \frac{1}{2} \times 4 \times 12$
$= 24 \text{ yd}^2$
12 yd
$A = \frac{1}{2}bh = \frac{1}{2} \times 4 \times 12$
$= 24 \text{ yd}^2$
4 yd 10 yd 4 yd
18 yd

Add the areas: $24 + 120 + 24 = 168$

The area of the pasture is 168 yd^2.

Try It!

How would you decompose this trapezoid to find its area? Find the area of the trapezoid.

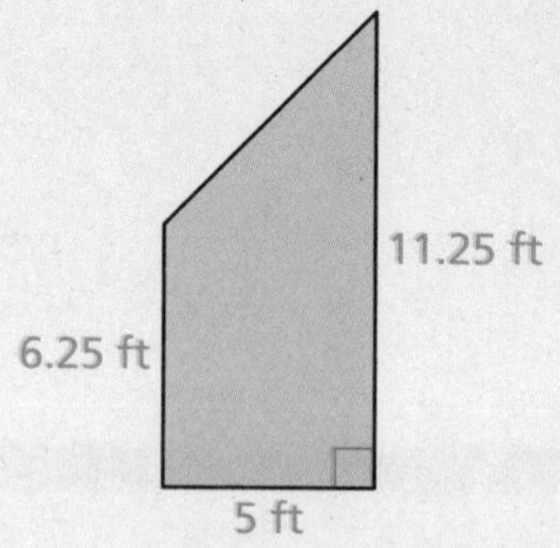

Convince Me! How is finding the area of the trapezoid in Example 1 different from finding the area of the trapezoid in the Try It!?

EXAMPLE 2 Find the Area of a Different Trapezoid

ACTIVITY

ASSESS

A builder needs to cut one stone in the shape of a trapezoid to fit in the space. What is the area of the front side of that stone?

Look for Relationships When you decompose a trapezoid into a rectangle and two triangles, the triangles are not always identical. MP.7

6 in.

5 in.

4 in.

12 in.

Draw lines to show the rectangle and the two triangles. Label needed measurements.

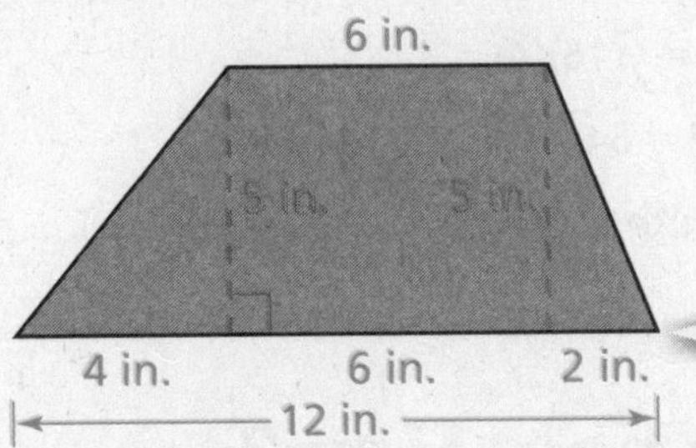

The triangles have different bases.

Find the areas:

Triangle: $A = \frac{1}{2}bh = \frac{1}{2}(4 \times 5) = 10$

Rectangle: $A = \ell w = 6 \times 5 = 30$

Triangle: $A = \frac{1}{2}bh = \frac{1}{2}(2 \times 5) = 5$

Add the areas:

$10 \text{ in.}^2 + 30 \text{ in.}^2 + 5 \text{ in.}^2 = 45 \text{ in.}^2$

The area of the side of the stone is 45 in.^2.

EXAMPLE 3 Find the Area of a Kite

Jackson has a rectangular piece of cloth that has an area of 298 cm^2. Does Jackson have enough cloth to make the kite shown?

A kite is a quadrilateral with two pairs of adjacent sides that are equal in length.

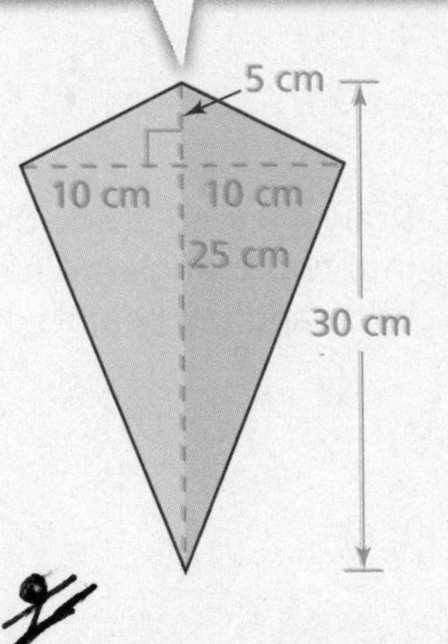

STEP 1 Decompose the kite into two identical triangles. Find the area of the triangles.

$A = \frac{1}{2}bh$

$A = \frac{1}{2} \cdot 30 \cdot 10$

$A = 150 \text{ cm}^2$

Each triangle has an area of 150 cm^2. The area of the kite is 300 cm^2.

STEP 2 Find the area of the kite. Compare the area of the kite to the area of the cloth.

$2 \times 150 \text{ cm}^2 = 300 \text{ cm}^2$

$300 \text{ cm}^2 > 298 \text{ cm}^2$

Jackson does not have enough cloth to make the kite.

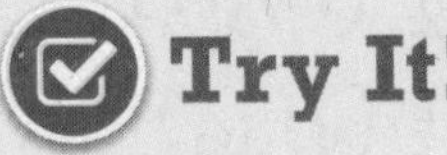

Try It!

Find the area of the trapezoid and the area of the kite.

a.

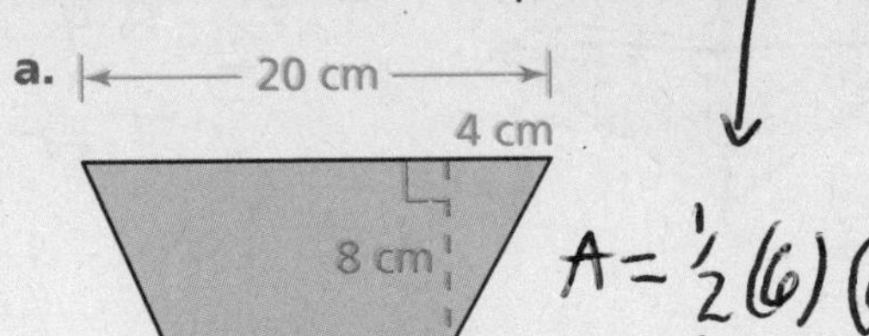

b.

10 in.

3 in.

4 in.

6 in.

3 in.

KEY CONCEPT

You can find the area of a trapezoid or a kite by decomposing the shapes into rectangles and triangles.

Trapezoid

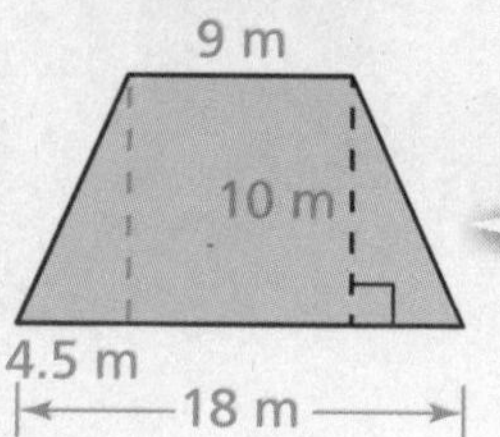

Decompose the trapezoid into two triangles and a rectangle. Find the length of the unknown triangle base.

Each triangle: $A = \frac{1}{2}(4.5)(10) = 22.5$

Rectangle: $A = 9(10) = 90$

Trapezoid: $A = 22.5 + 22.5 + 90 = 135$

The area of the trapezoid is 135 m^2.

Kite

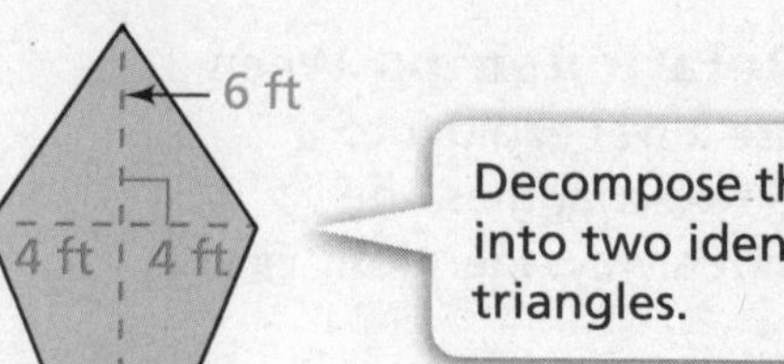

Decompose the kite into two identical triangles.

Each triangle: $A = \frac{1}{2}(16)(4) = 32$

Kite: $A = 32 + 32 = 64$

The area of the kite is 64 ft^2.

Do You Understand?

1. **Essential Question** How can you find the areas of trapezoids and kites?

2. Draw a line to divide the pasture in Example 1 into two triangles. What are the measures of the bases and the heights of the two triangles?

3. **Construct Arguments** In Example 3, how could you use 4 triangles to find the kite's area? MP.3

Do You Know How?

In 4–6, find the area of each trapezoid or kite.

4.

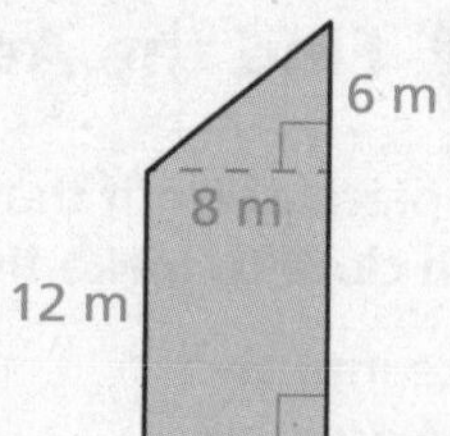

5.

6.

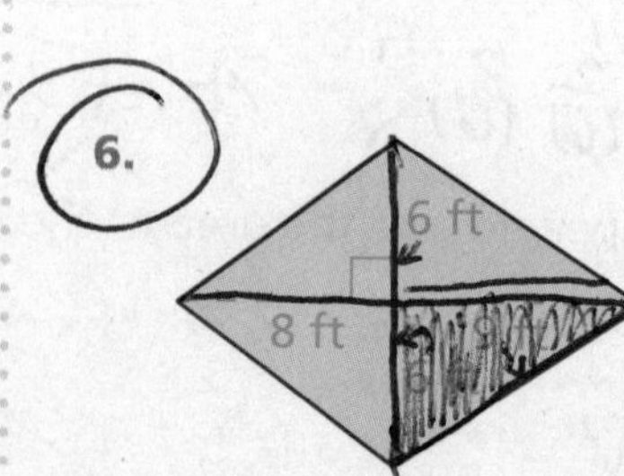

A = ½ (b)(h)
A = ½ (9)(6)
A = ½ 54
27 ft2

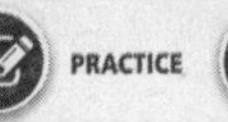

Name: ____________________

Practice & Problem Solving

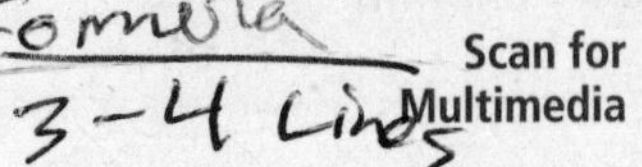

Leveled Practice In 7–12, find the area of each trapezoid or kite.

7. 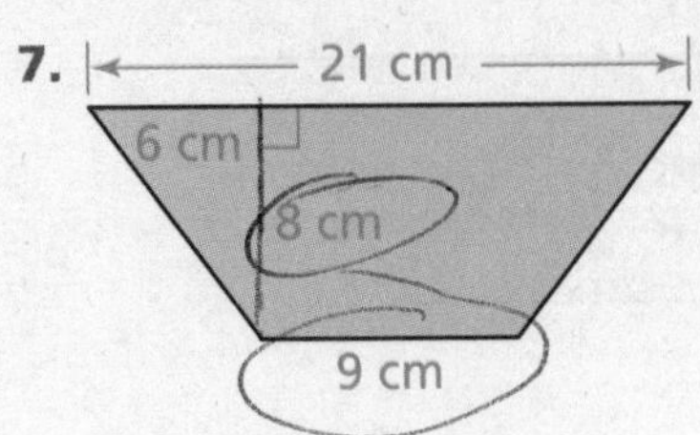

Each triangle:

$A = \frac{1}{2}bh$

$= \frac{1}{2} \times \square \times 8$

$= \square \text{ cm}^2$

Rectangle:

$A = \ell w$

$= \square \times 8$

$= \square \text{ cm}^2$

Trapezoid:

$A = \square + \square + \square = \square \text{ cm}^2$

8. 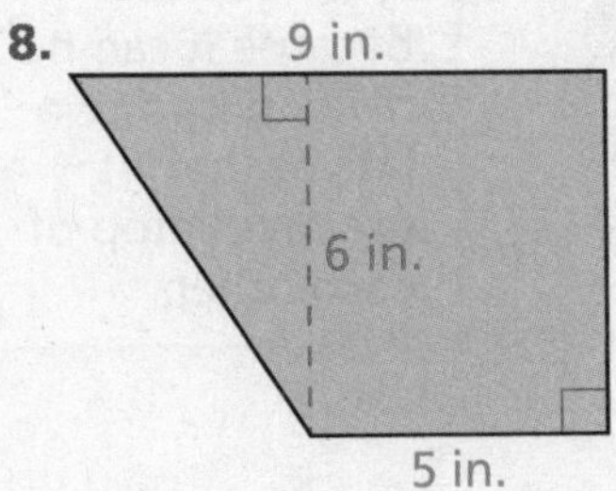

9. 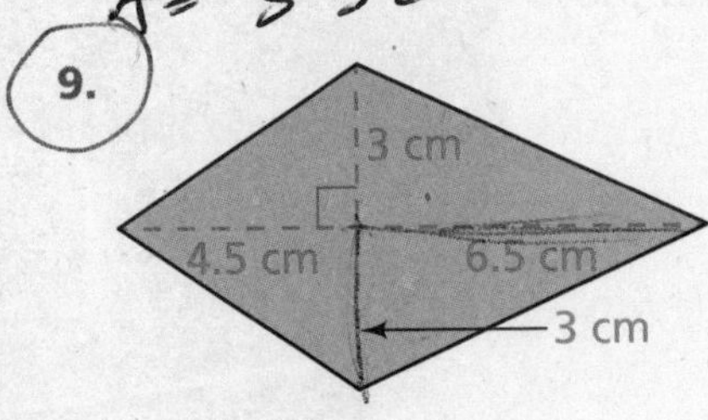

10. 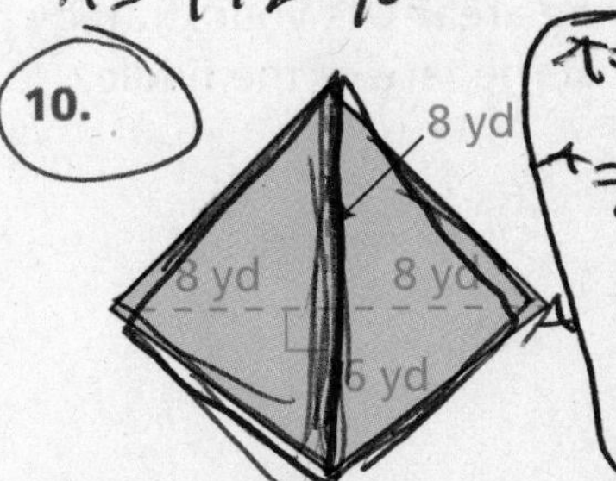

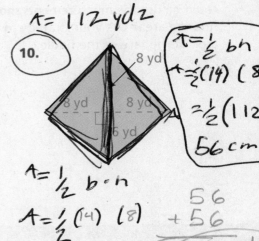

11. A sidewall of a building is shown below. What is the area of the wall?

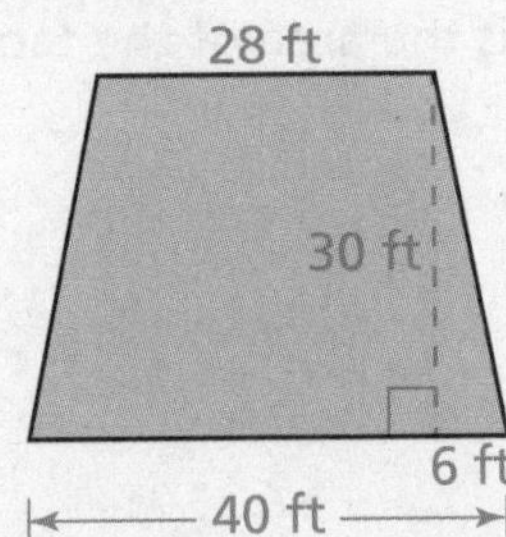

12. **Be Precise** The window has the shape of a kite. How many square meters of glass were used to make the window? MP.6

13. The area of the kite is 30 m^2. What is the value of x? Explain.

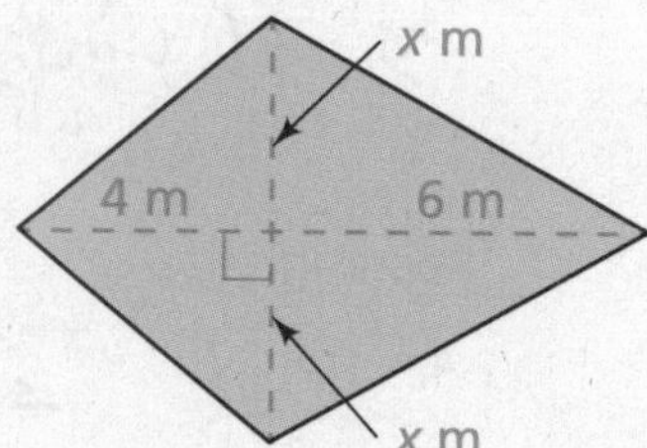

14. **Make Sense and Persevere** Hunter drew two identical trapezoids and composed them to form a parallelogram. Use the area of the parallelogram to find the area of one trapezoid. Explain. MP.1

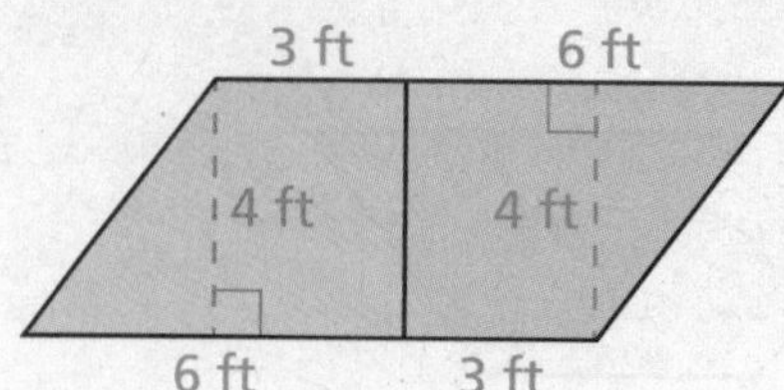

15. **Higher Order Thinking** A craftsman wants to build this symmetrical fiddle. He needs to know the area of the face of the fiddle. How could he use the measurements shown to find the area? Use your strategy to find the area of the face of the fiddle.

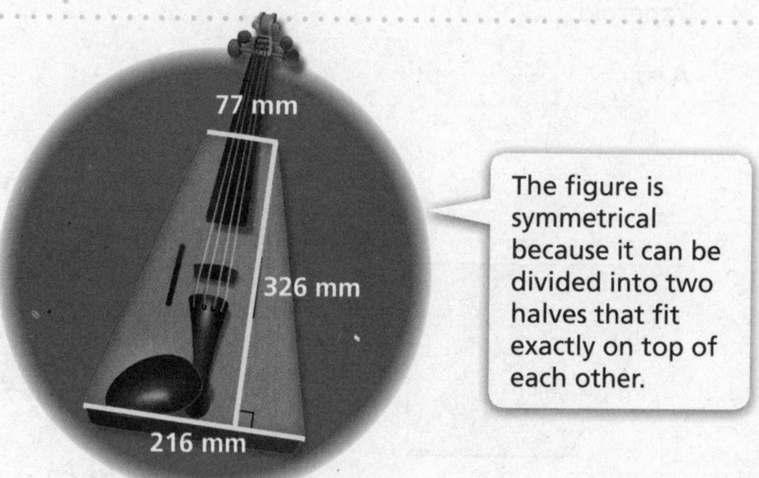

Assessment Practice

16. Marique is making a large table in the shape of a trapezoid. She needs to calculate the area of the table. The longest side of the table is twice as long as the table's width.

PART A

Write numbers in the boxes to show the missing dimensions.

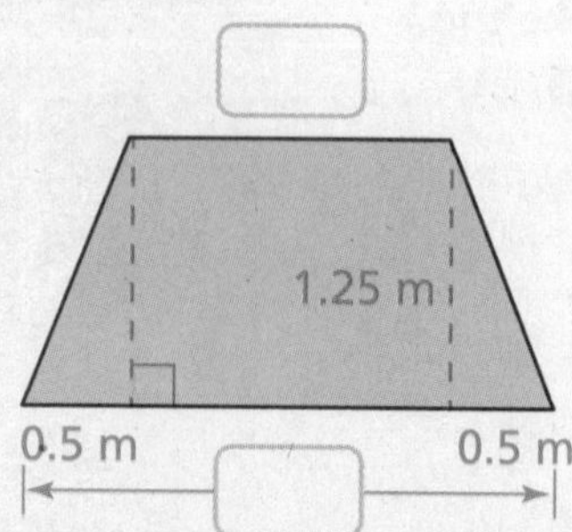

PART B

What is the area of the table?

Lesson 7-4
Find Areas of Polygons

Go Online | PearsonRealize.com

I can...
find the areas of polygons.

Common Core Content Standards
6.G.A.1, 6.EE.A.2c, 6.G.A.3, 6.NS.C.6c, 6.NS.C.8

Mathematical Practices
MP.1, MP.4, MP.6, MP.7

Solve & Discuss It!

ACTIVITY

Gabrielle wants to cover the floors of a room and a hallway in her dollhouse. She measured the room and hallway and sketched the floor plan below. How much felt does Gabrielle need?

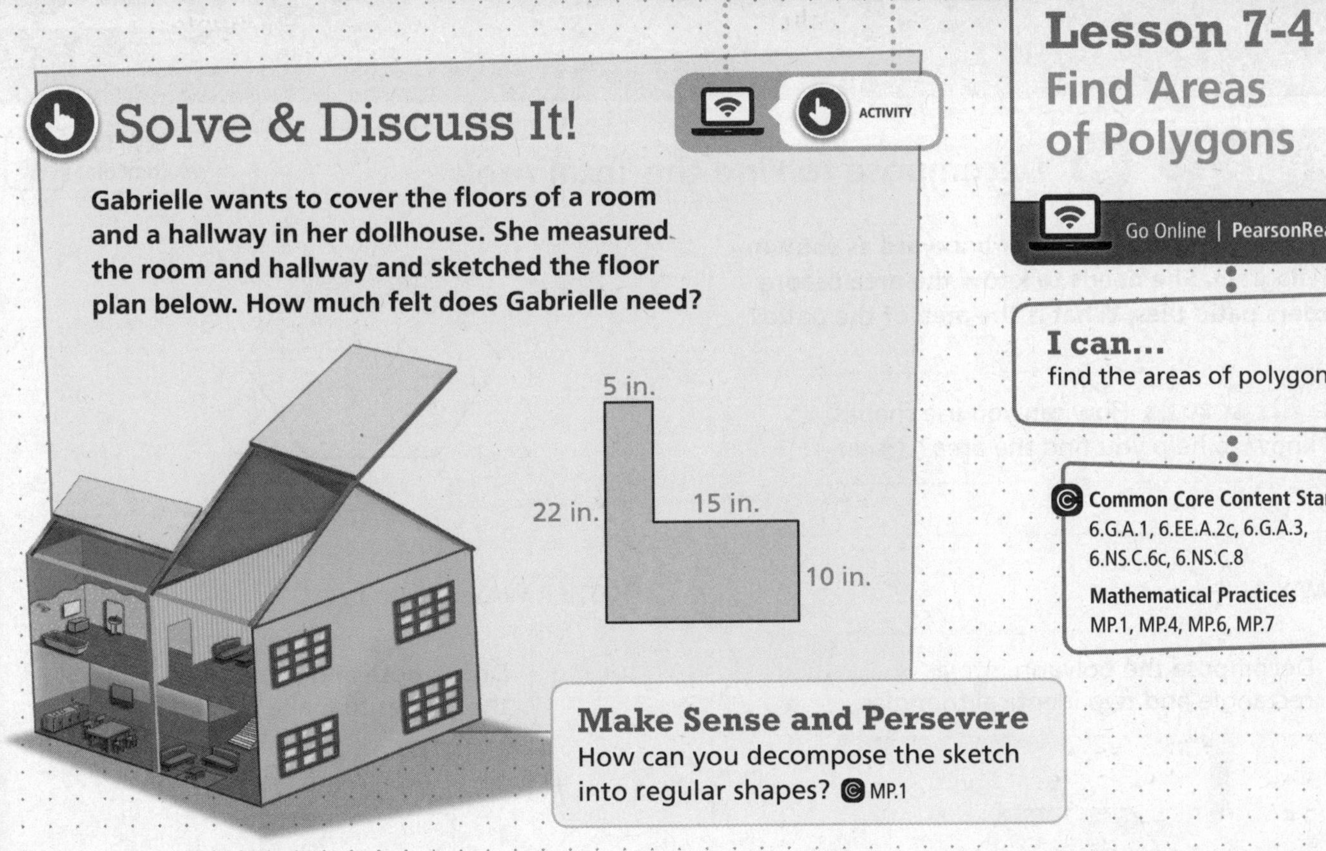

Make Sense and Persevere
How can you decompose the sketch into regular shapes? MP.1

Focus on math practices

Make Sense and Persevere Show another way to find the area of the sketch. MP.7

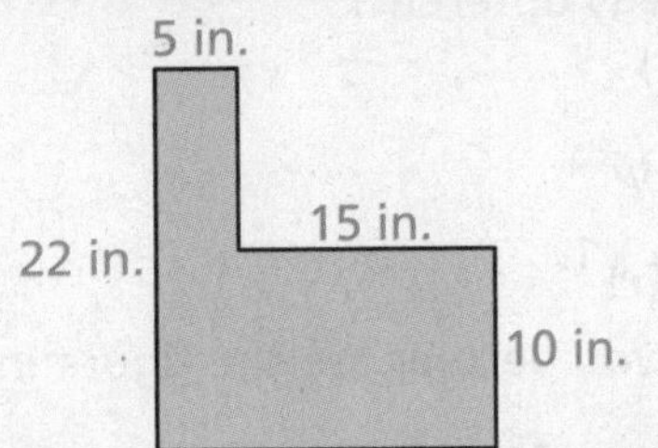

? Essential Question How can you find the areas of polygons?

EXAMPLE 1  Decompose to Find the Total Area

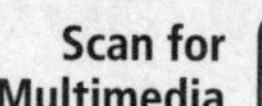

Denise is building a patio in her backyard as shown in the diagram. She needs to know the area before she orders patio tiles. What is the area of the patio?

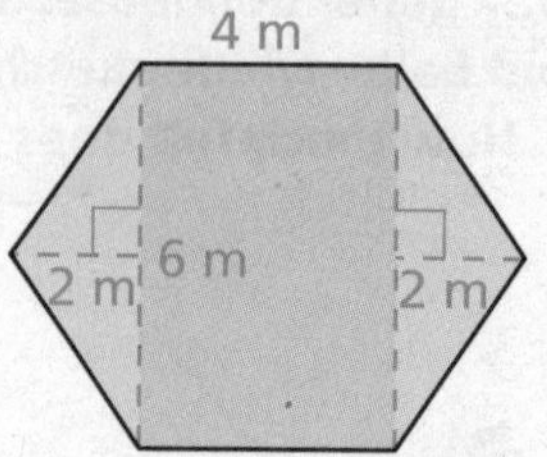

Use Structure How can you use shapes you know to help you find the area? MP.7

ONE WAY

Decompose the polygon into a rectangle and two identical triangles.

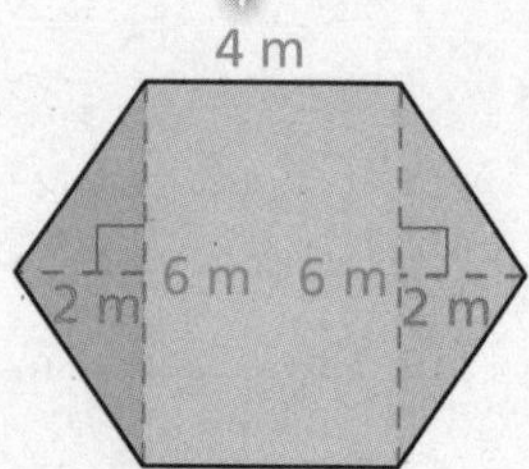

Find the area of each shape.

Each Triangle

$A = \frac{1}{2}bh$

$= \frac{1}{2}(6 \cdot 2)$

$= 6$

Rectangle

$A = \ell w$

$= 6 \cdot 4$

$= 24$

Add the areas: $6 + 6 + 24 = 36$.

The area of the patio is 36 m^2.

ANOTHER WAY

Decompose and recompose the shapes to make a square.

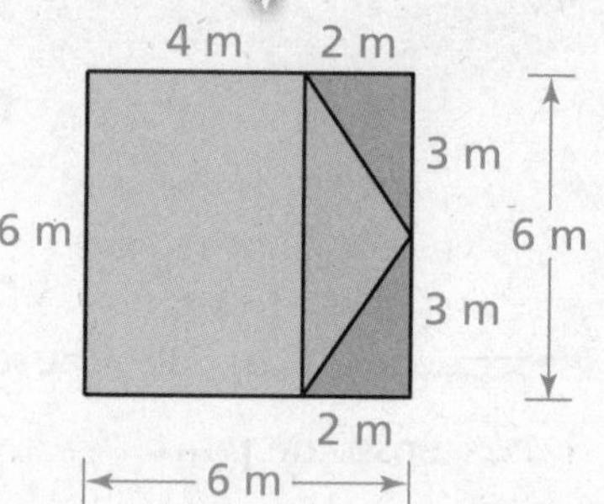

Find the area of the square.

$A = \ell w$

$= 6 \cdot 6$

$= 36$

The area of the patio is 36 m^2.

Try It!

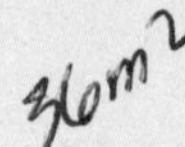

Shari found the area of the patio by composing the shapes as shown at the right. How is Shari's strategy different?

A= b·h A= b·h A= b·h
A=2·3 A=4·6
A= 6m² A= 24m²

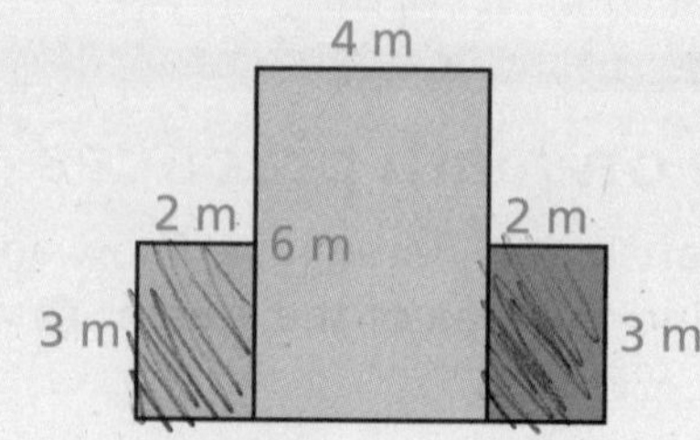

Convince Me! How could you decompose the figure in the Try It! into two rectangles?

EXAMPLE 2 Subtract to Find the Total Area

The Robinsons are planning to resurface the path that surrounds their garden, as shown. What is the area of the path?

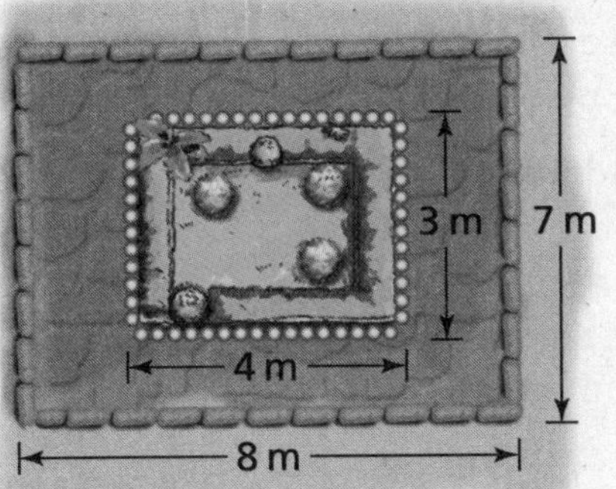

Make Sense and Persevere The area of the path can be found by subtracting the area of the garden from the total area of the garden and the path. MP.1

STEP 1 Find the total area of the garden and the path.

$A = \ell w$

$= 8 \times 7$

$= 56 \text{ m}^2$

STEP 2 Find the area of the garden.

$A = \ell w$

$= 4 \times 3$

$= 12 \text{ m}^2$

STEP 3 Subtract the area of the garden from the total area of the garden and the path.

$56 - 12 = 44$

The area of the path is 44 m^2.

EXAMPLE 3 Find the Area of a Polygon on the Coordinate Plane

The floor plan for a new stage at a school is sketched on a coordinate plane. A flooring expert recommends bamboo flooring for the stage floor. How much bamboo flooring, in square meters, does the school need?

Each square represents 1 square meter.

STEP 1 Decompose the polygon. Find the needed dimensions.

STEP 2 Find the area of each part.

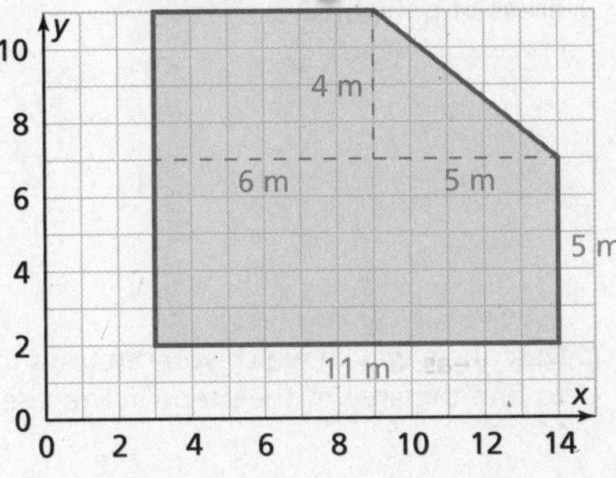

Right Triangle

$A = \frac{1}{2}bh$

$= \frac{1}{2} \cdot 5 \cdot 4$

$= 10$

Rectangles

$A = \ell w$

$= 6 \cdot 4$

$= 24$

$A = \ell w$

$= 11 \cdot 5$

$= 55$

Add the areas: $10 + 24 + 55 = 89$

The school needs 89 m^2 of bamboo flooring.

Try It!

Find the area of the shaded region in square units.

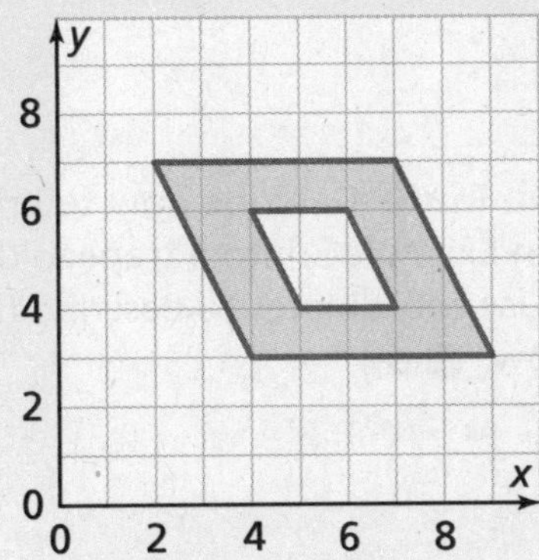

KEY CONCEPT

There are many ways to find the area of a polygon. You can decompose or compose shapes, or you can use addition or subtraction, to calculate the area.

Use Addition

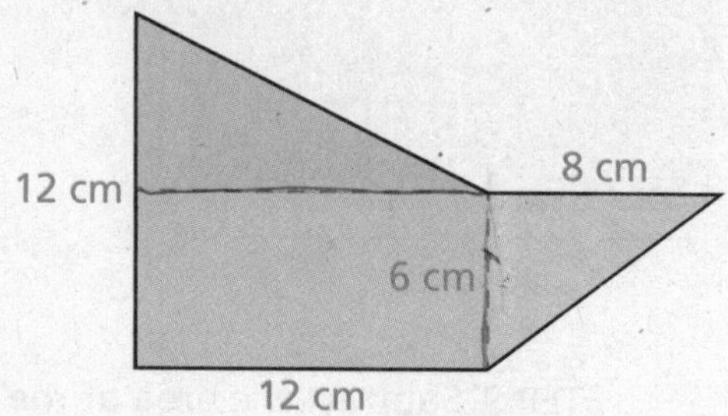

Blue triangle: $A = \frac{1}{2}(12)(6) = 36$

Green triangle: $A = \frac{1}{2}(8)(6) = 24$

Rectangle: $A = (12)(6) = 72$

$36 + 24 + 72 = 132$

The area of the polygon is 132 cm^2.

Use Subtraction

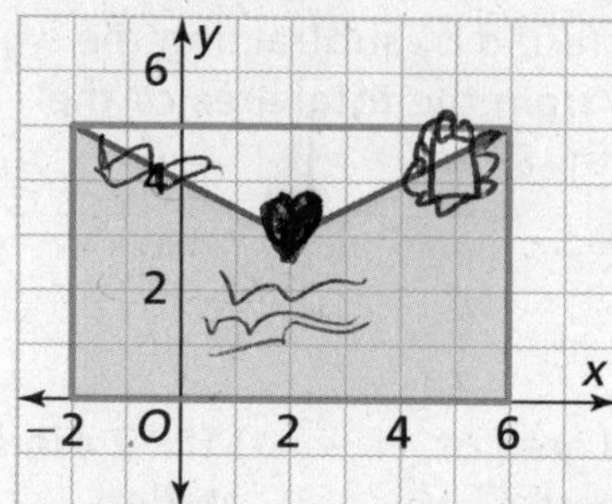

Draw a rectangle around the polygon.

Rectangle: $A = 8 \times 5 = 40$

Triangle: $A = \frac{1}{2} \times 8 \times 2 = 8$

$40 - 8 = 32$

The area of the polygon is 32 square units.

Do You Understand?

1. **Essential Question** How can you find the areas of polygons?

2. Describe a way in which you can use subtraction to find the area of the shape in Exercise 4.

3. **Model with Math** Describe how to break the floor plan in Example 3 into a trapezoid and a rectangle. Use coordinates to describe the line you can draw. MP.4

Do You Know How?

In 4 and 5, find the area of each polygon.

4.

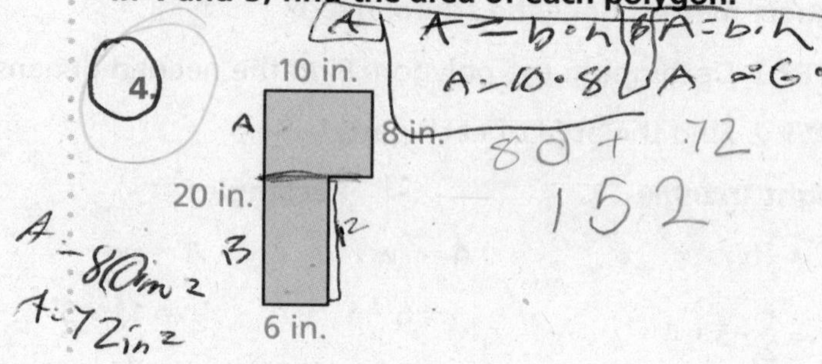

5. A polygon with vertices at (6, 2), (9, 5), (12, 2), (12, −4), and (6, −4)

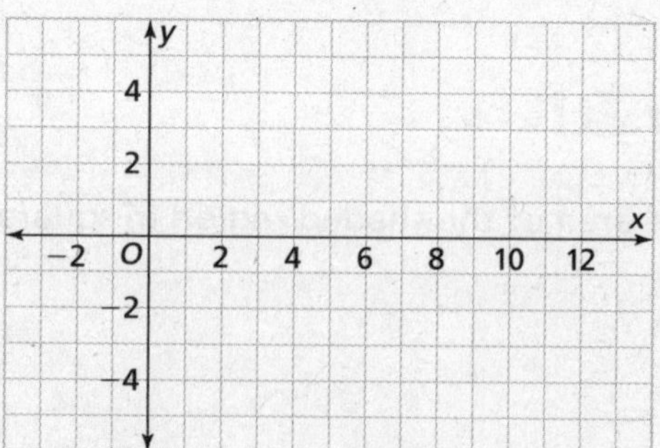

Name: ______________________________

Practice & Problem Solving

In 6–9, find the area of each polygon or shaded region.

6.

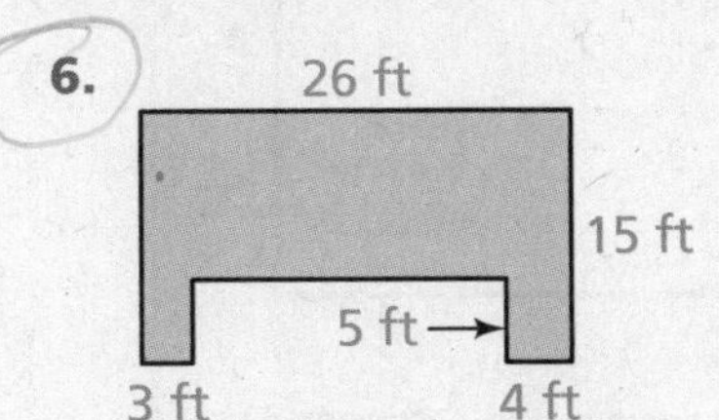

7.

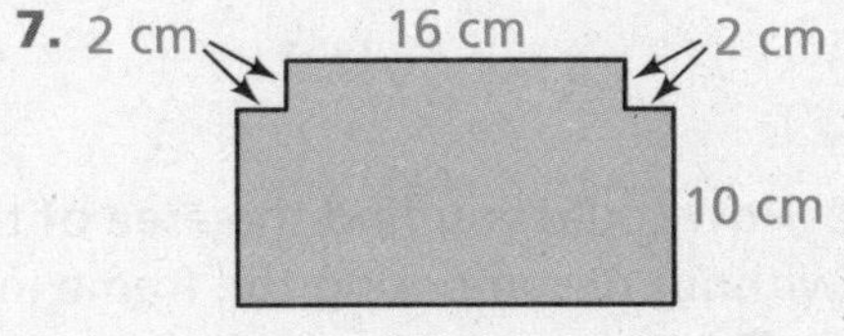

8.

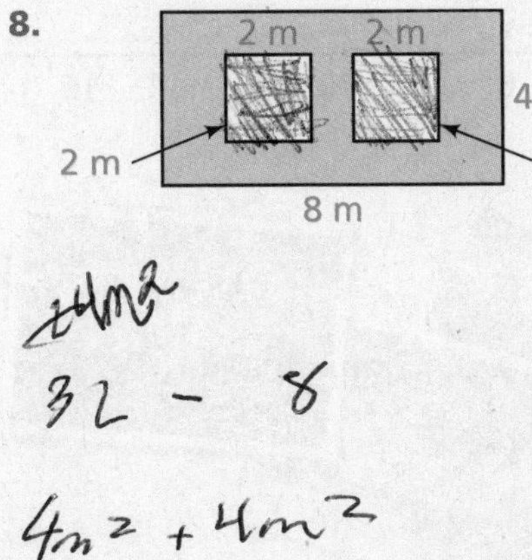

9.

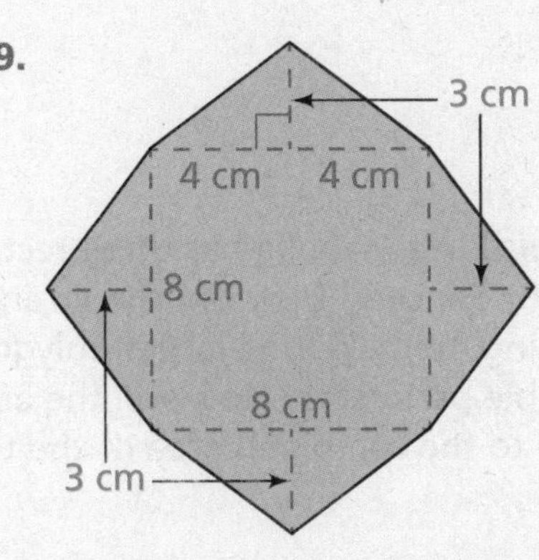

In 10 and 11, find the area in square units of each polygon.

10.

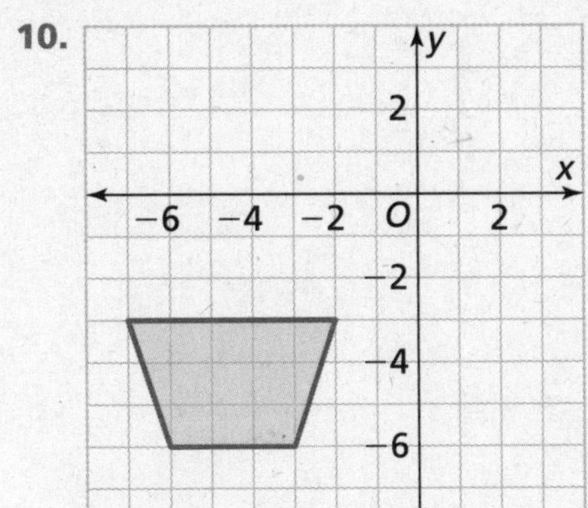

11.

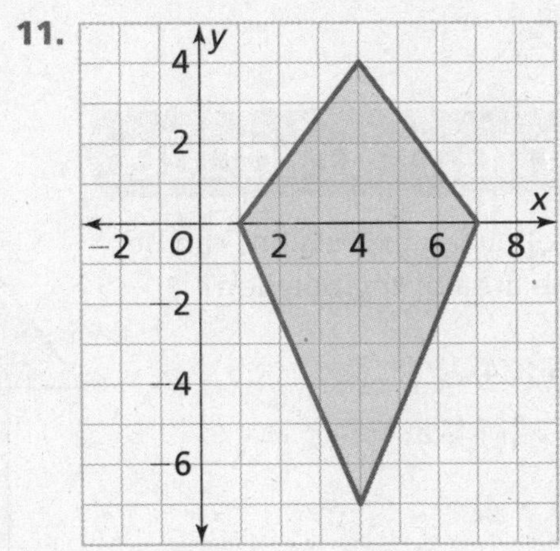

12. Be Precise Diego is designing an exercise room. How many square feet of rubber flooring will he need to cover the floor? The product is sold in whole square yards. How many square yards should Diego buy? Explain. MP.6

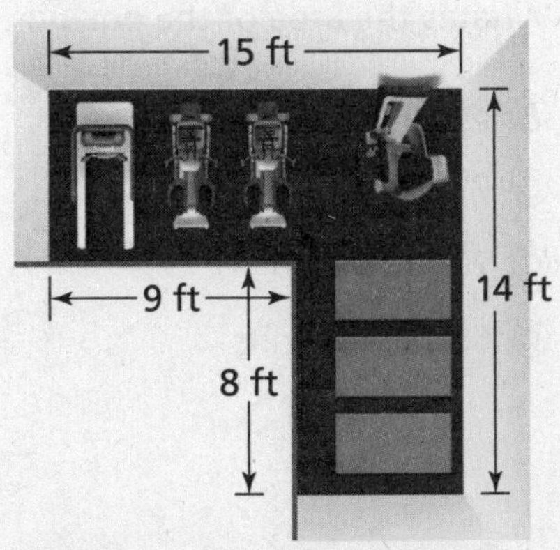

In 13 and 14, use the diagram at the right.

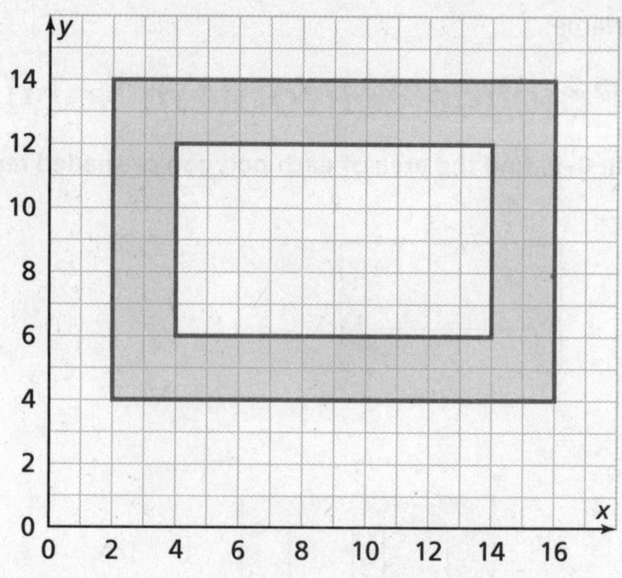

13. David drew this diagram of a picture frame that he is going to make. Each square represents 1 square inch. What is the area of the picture frame?

14. Use Structure How could you find the area of the picture frame without decomposing the frame into smaller shapes? MP.7

15. Higher Order Thinking Isabella has three rectangular cards that are 4 inches by 5 inches. How can she arrange the cards, without overlapping, to make one larger polygon with the smallest possible perimeter? How will the area of the polygon compare to the combined area of the three cards?

Assessment Practice

16. Which of the following expressions can be used to find the area of the polygon?

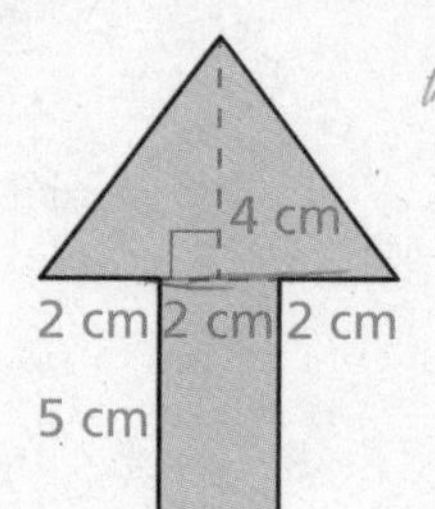

Ⓐ $(2 \times 5) + (6 \times 4)$

Ⓑ $(5 \times 2) + 2 \cdot \frac{1}{2}(3 \times 4)$

Ⓒ $(6 \times 5) - (3 \times 4)$

Ⓓ $(6 \times 9) - (3 \times 4)$

17. What is the area of the polygon at the right?

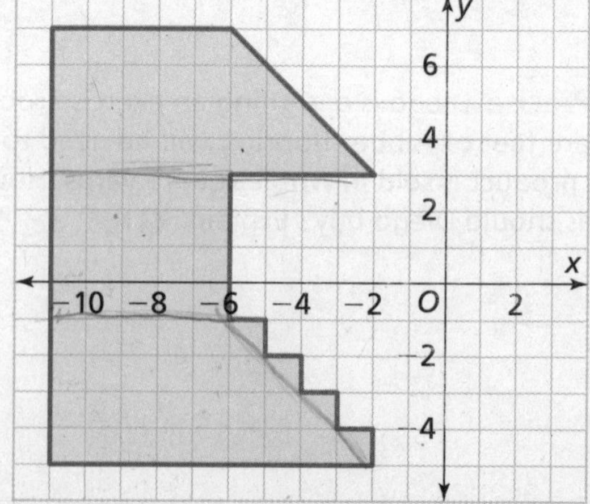

Ⓐ 86 square units

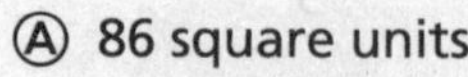

Ⓑ 78 square units

Ⓒ 70 square units

Ⓓ 68 square units

Name: madelyn zinck 03/21/2021

MID-TOPIC CHECKPOINT

TOPIC 7

1. **Vocabulary** How many pairs of opposite sides are parallel in a trapezoid? How is this different from a parallelogram? *Lesson 7-3*

In 2–4, select *True* or *False* for each statement. Use the figures at the right. *Lessons 7-1, 7-2, and 7-3*

	True	False
2. The area of the triangle is 180 cm^2.	☐	☑
3. The area of the parallelogram is 11 ft^2.	☑	☐
4. The area of the trapezoid is 36 m^2.	☑	☐

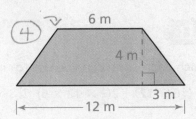

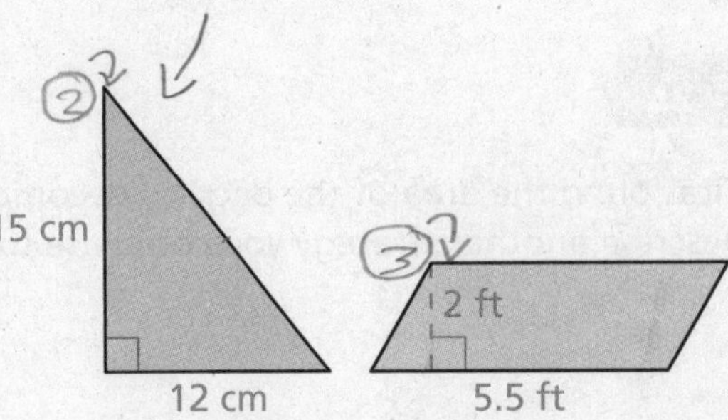

6 m
4 m
3 m
12 m

5. An earring has the shape of a rhombus. The height is 5.2 mm and the length of each side is 6 mm. What is the area of the earring? *Lesson 7-1*

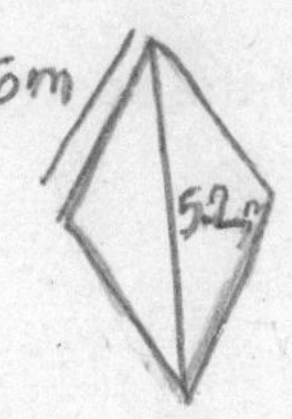

6. Shane covered the front of the kite at the right with paper. How many square inches of paper did Shane use? *Lesson 7-3*

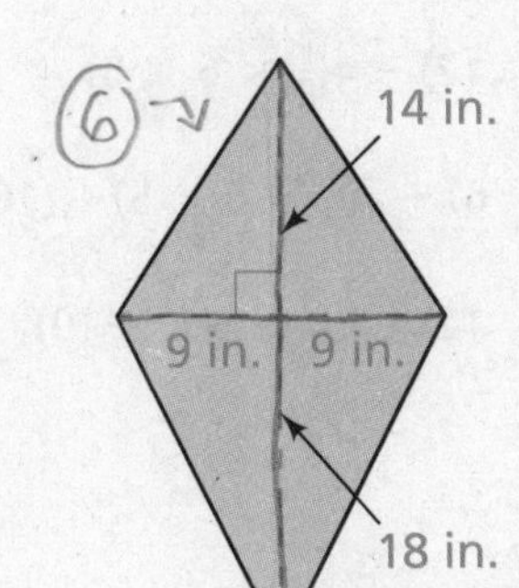

7. Explain one way to find the area of the polygon at the right. Then find the area in square units. *Lesson 7-4*

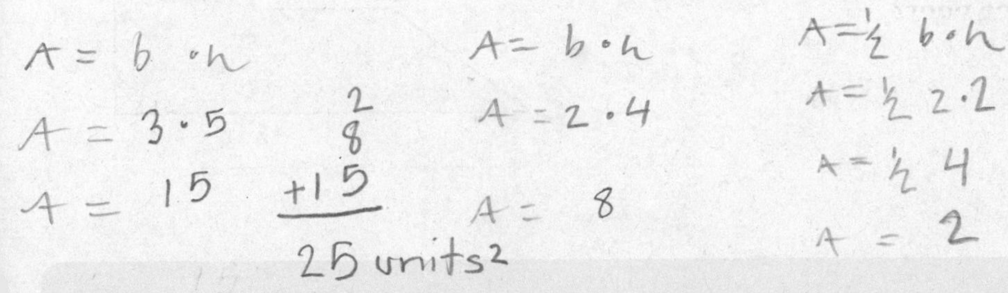

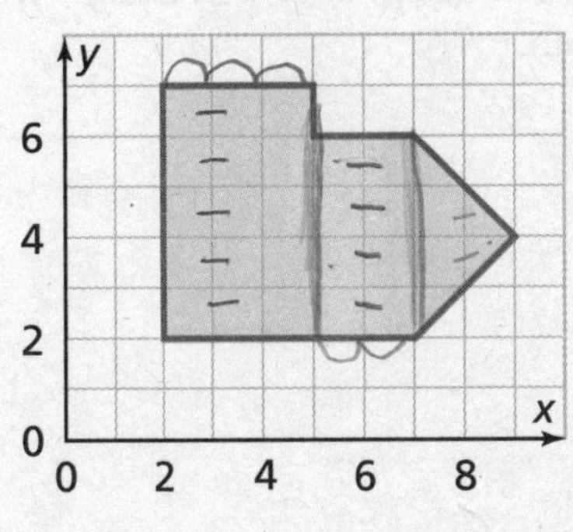

How well did you do on the mid-topic checkpoint? Fill in the stars.

☆ ☆ ☆

MID-TOPIC PERFORMANCE TASK

Kira hires a contractor to build a new deck in her backyard. A design for the deck is shown.

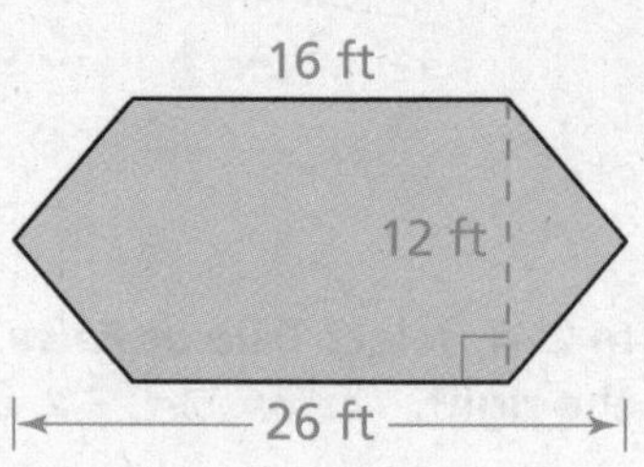

PART A

Kira found the area of the deck by decomposing it into two identical trapezoids. Describe another strategy you could use to find the area of the deck.

PART B

Which expression can you use to find the area of the deck? Select all that apply.

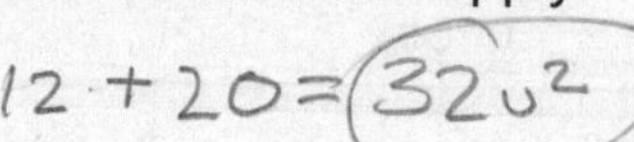
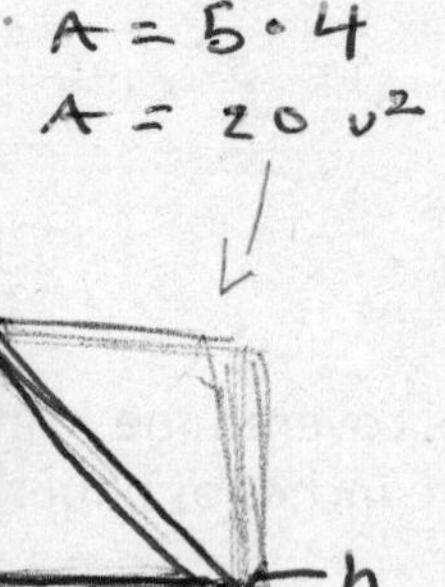

- ☐ $(16 \times 12) + 2(\frac{1}{2} \times 12 \times 5)$
- ☐ $(26 \times 12) + 2(\frac{1}{2} \times 12 \times 5)$
- ☐ $(26 \times 12) - 4(\frac{1}{2} \times 6 \times 5)$
- ☐ $(16 \times 6) + 2(\frac{1}{2} \times 6 \times 5) + (16 \times 6) + 2(\frac{1}{2} \times 6 \times 5)$
- ☐ $(16 \times 12) + 2(\frac{1}{2} \times 12 \times 10)$

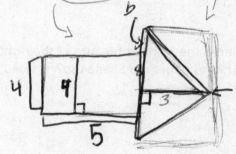

PART C

A second design for Kira's deck is shown at the right. Find the areas of the two deck designs. Which design will give Kira the deck with the greater area? Explain.

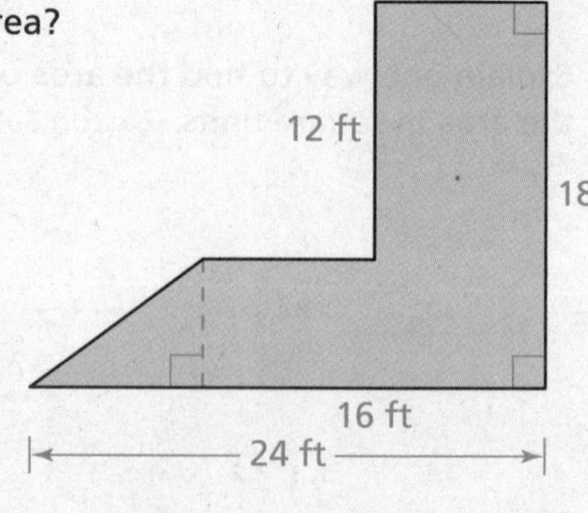

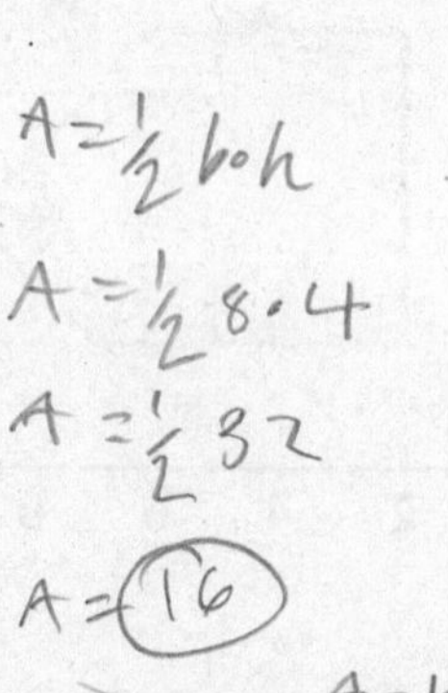
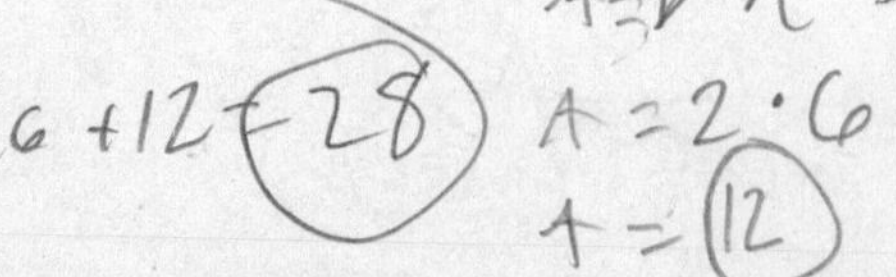

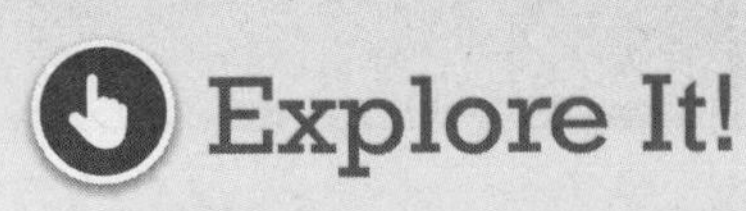

Explore It!

Jamal is breaking down items for recycling and wonders what this box will look like when it is unfolded and flat.

Lesson 7-5
Represent Solid Figures Using Nets

Go Online | PearsonRealize.com

I can...
represent solid figures using nets.

Common Core Content Standards
6.G.A.4

Mathematical Practices
MP.1, MP.2, MP.3, MP.6, MP.7

A. How do the sides of the box help you think about what the unfolded box will look like?

B. How can you use the grid to represent the unfolded box?

□ = 1 square inch.

Focus on math practices

Reasoning Is there another way to represent the unfolded box on the grid? Explain. MP.2

? Essential Question How do you classify and represent solid figures?

EXAMPLE 1  Classify Solids

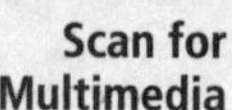 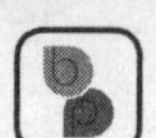

Scan for Multimedia

How can you classify a polyhedron?

A polyhedron is a three-dimensional solid figure made of flat polygon-shaped surfaces called faces. The line segment where two faces intersect is called an edge. The point where several edges meet is called a vertex.

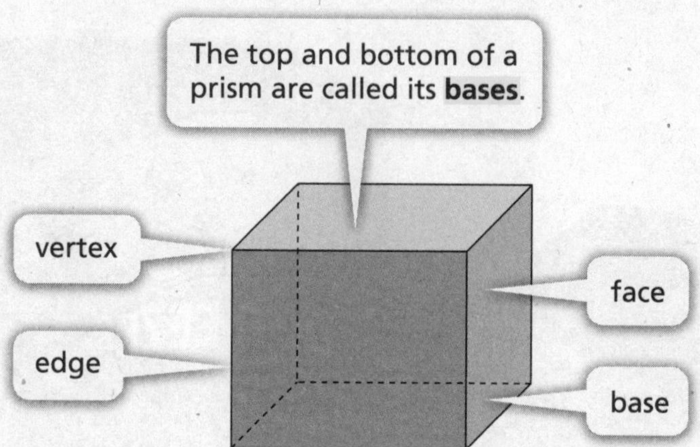

Prisms

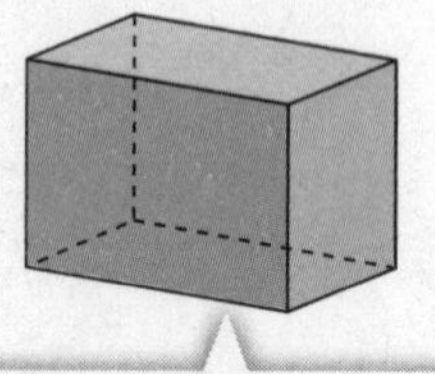

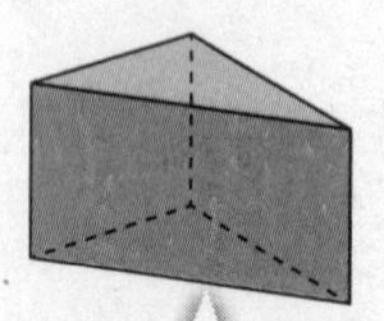

- Prisms have polygonal faces.
- Prisms have two identical, parallel, polygon-shaped bases.
- Prisms are named by the shape of their bases.

Pyramids

The base of a pyramid is the face opposite the vertex where the triangular faces meet.

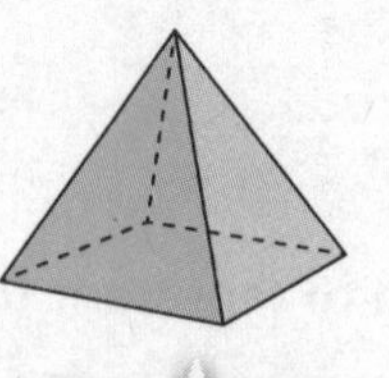

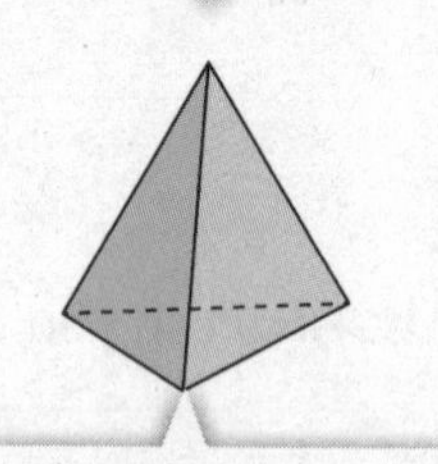

- Pyramids have one base.
- Pyramids are named by the shape of their bases.
- All other faces of pyramids are triangular.

Try It!

Classify this solid figure.

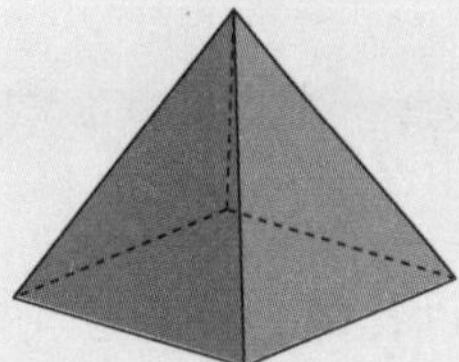

Convince Me! What attributes of a solid figure should you identify to classify it as a polyhedron?

EXAMPLE 2  Identify a Solid Figure from a Net

  ACTIVITY  ASSESS

What solid is represented by the net?

To identify a solid figure, determine the number and types of faces in the net.

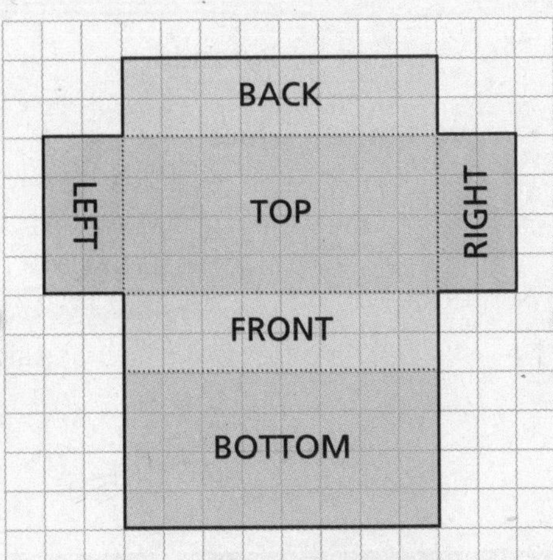

Use Structure How can you use the structure of the net to identify the solid figure? MP.7

A net is a plane figure pattern which, when folded, makes a solid.

The net shows three pairs of identical rectangular faces.

This is a net of a rectangular prism.

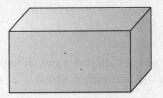

EXAMPLE 3  Draw a Net of a Solid Figure

How can you draw a net of a rectangular prism that has a height of 2 units and bases that are 4 units long and 2 units wide?

STEP 1 Draw one base of the prism.

STEP 2 Above and below the base, draw a rectangle with the same width as the base and a height of 2 units.

STEP 3 Draw three additional rectangles, in line with the base, that have the same length as the base and a width of 2 units.

Be Precise How can you determine whether the dimensions in the net match the dimensions of the rectangular prism? MP.6

Try It!

Identify the solid from its net.

Shape of polygonal faces: ______

Shape of base(s): ______

This is a net of a ______.

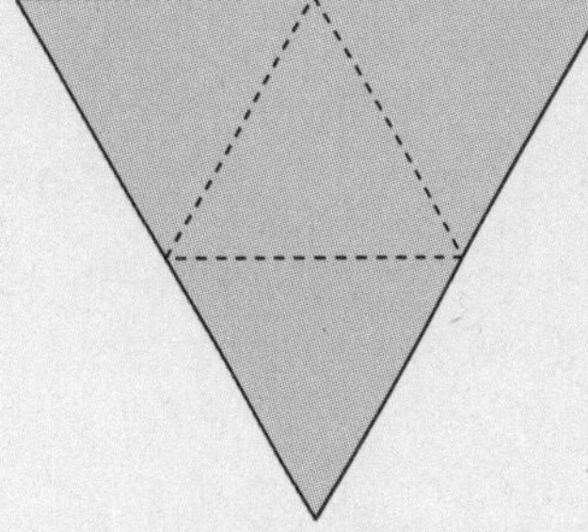

You can use nets to represent solid figures.

Prism

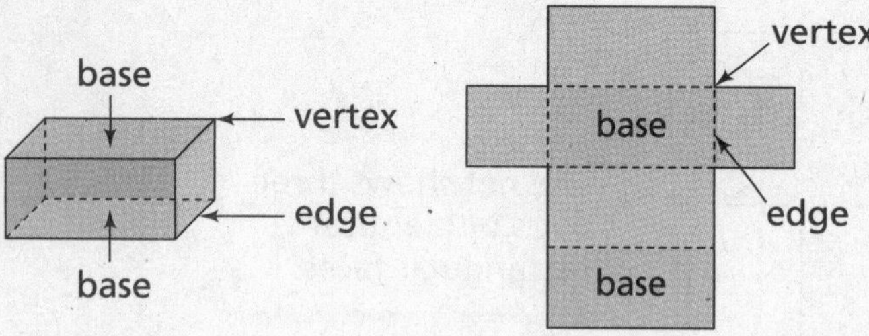

Pyramid

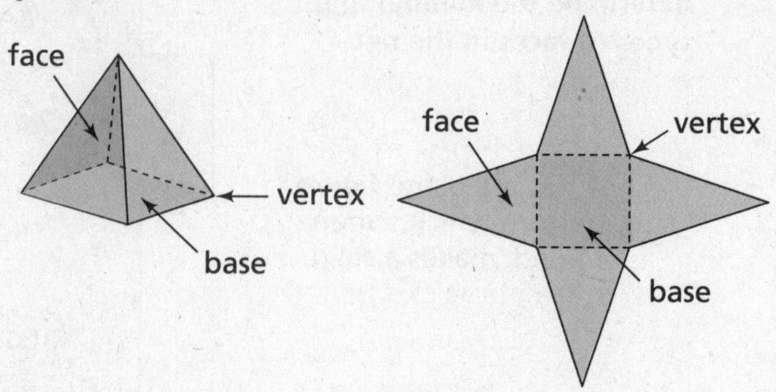

Do You Understand?

1. **Essential Question** How do you classify and represent solid figures?

2. **Use Structure** Explain the difference between a vertex and an edge. MP.7

3. **Be Precise** Explain the difference between a pyramid and a prism. MP.6

4. Describe the net of a triangular prism.

Do You Know How?

In 5 and 6, classify the solid figures.

5.

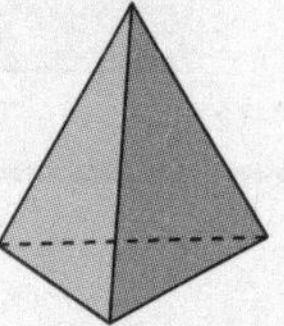

6.

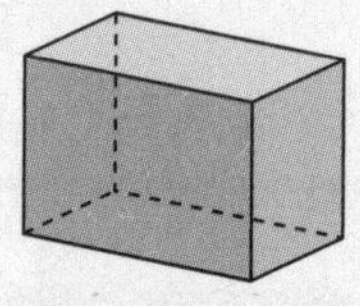

In 7 and 8, identify each solid from its net.

7.

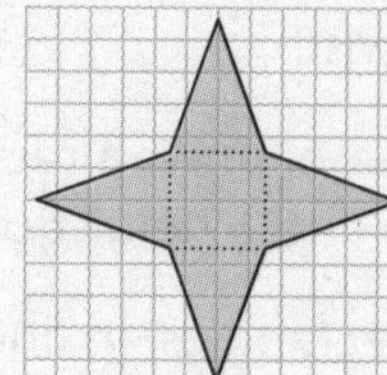

8.

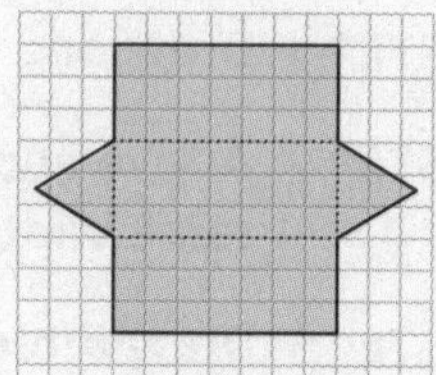

9. Draw a net of a rectangular prism that has a height of 2 units and bases that are 3 units long and 1 unit wide.

Name: ____________________

Practice & Problem Solving

Scan for Multimedia

In 10–12, classify the solid figures.

10.

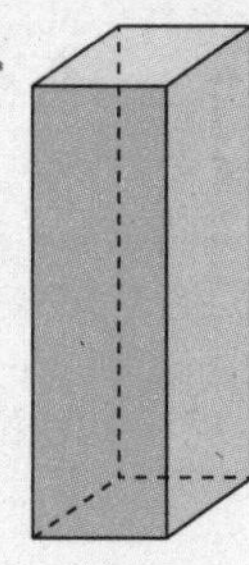

11.

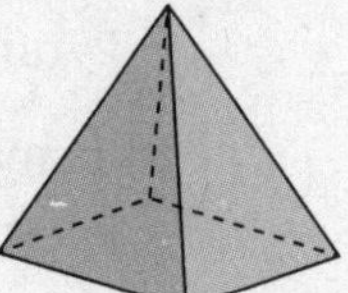

12.

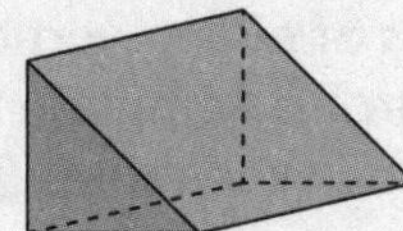

In 13–15, identify each solid from its net.

13.

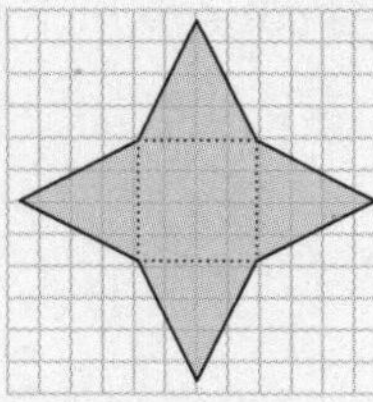

14.

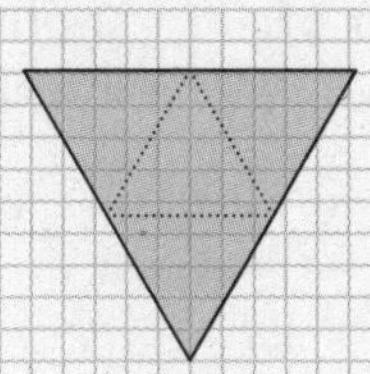

15.

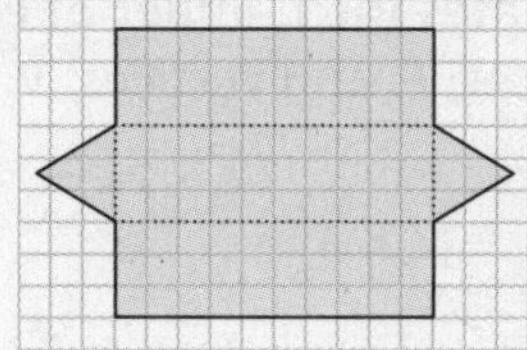

16. Ryan is going to draw a net of a rectangular prism. How many rectangles should there be in his drawing?

17. Kayla is going to draw a net of a square pyramid. How many triangles should there be in her drawing?

18. **Make Sense and Persevere** Zari folds the net below into a model of a solid figure. How many edges, faces, and vertices does the model have? MP.1

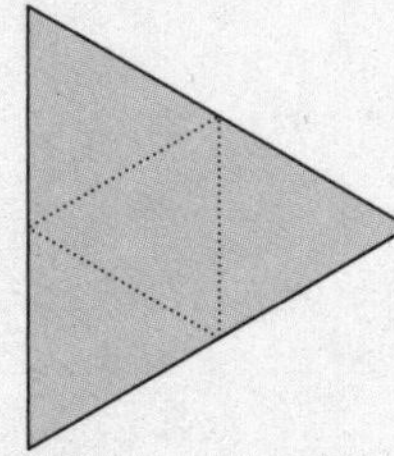

19. **Critique Reasoning** Tomas says that the net below can be folded to make a rectangular prism. Do you agree with Tomas? Explain. MP.3

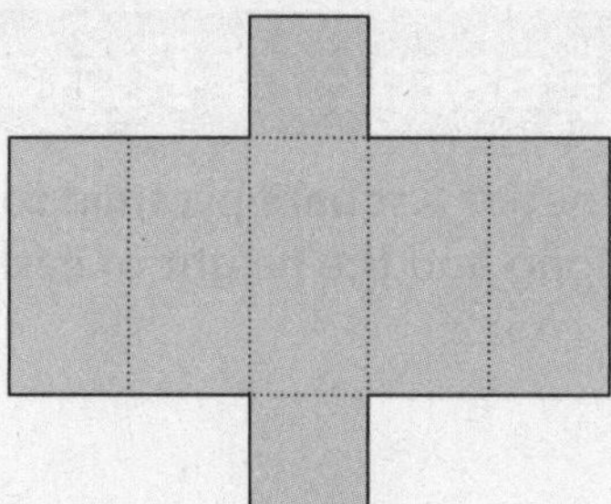

In 20–22, use the table at the right.

20. Look for Relationships The Swiss mathematician Leonhard Euler (OY-ler) and the French mathematician René Descartes (dã KART) both discovered a pattern in the numbers of edges, vertices, and faces of polyhedrons. Complete the table. Describe a pattern in the table. MP.7

Polyhedron	Faces (F)	Vertices (V)	$F + V$	Edges (E)
Triangular Pyramid				
Rectangular Pyramid				
Triangular Prism				
Rectangular Prism				

21. Higher Order Thinking Write an equation that relates the number of edges, E, to the number of faces, F, and vertices, V.

22. Use the equation that you wrote in Exercise 21 to find the number of vertices of a cube, which has 12 edges and 6 faces.

23. Corey bought the mailing tube shown at the right to mail a poster.

a. The mailing tube has the shape of which polyhedron?

b. How many faces does the mailing tube have?

c. When Corey bought the mailing tube, it was unfolded and looked like a net. What polygons would Corey have seen in the unfolded mailing tube?

Assessment Practice

24. Draw a net of a square pyramid for which the base is 2 units long and the height of each triangular face is 5 units.

3-Act Mathematical Modeling: That's a Wrap

Go Online | PearsonRealize.com

Common Core Content Standards
6.G.A.4, 6.EE.A.2c

Mathematical Practices
MP.4

ACT 1

1. After watching the video, what is the first question that comes to mind?

2. Write the Main Question you will answer.

3. Construct Arguments Predict an answer to this Main Question. Explain your prediction. MP.3

4. On the number line below, write a number that is too small to be the answer. Write a number that is too large.

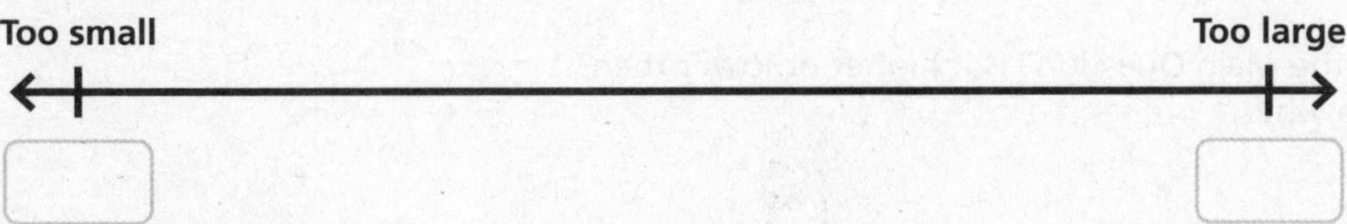

5. Plot your prediction on the same number line.

ACT 2

6. What information in this situation would be helpful to know? How would you use that information?

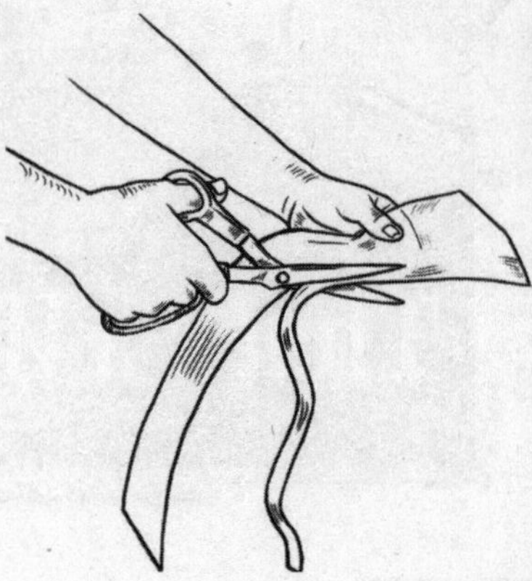

7. **Use Appropriate Tools** What tools can you use to get the information you need? Record the information as you find it. MP.5

8. **Model with Math** Represent the situation using the mathematical content, concepts, and skills from this topic. Use your representation to answer the Main Question. MP.4

9. What is your answer to the Main Question? Is it higher or lower than your prediction? Explain why.

ACT 3

10. Write the answer you saw in the video.

11. Reasoning Does your answer match the answer in the video? If not, what are some reasons that would explain the difference? MP.2

12. Make Sense and Persevere Would you change your model now that you know the answer? Explain. MP.1

ACT 3 Extension

Reflect

13. Model with Math Explain how you used a mathematical model to represent the situation. How did the model help you answer the Main Question? MP.4

14. Look for Relationships Explain how the dimensions of the gift are related to the area of its net. MP.7

SEQUEL

15. Critique Reasoning A classmate says that if all dimensions of the gift were doubled, you would need twice as many squares. Do you agree? Justify his reasoning or explain his error. MP.3

Lesson 7-6
Find Surface Areas of Prisms

Go Online | PearsonRealize.com

I can...
draw a net of a prism and use it to find the prism's surface area

Common Core Content Standards
6.G.A.4, 6.EE.A.2a, 6.EE.A.2c, 6.EE.B.6

Mathematical Practices
MP.1, MP.3, MP.5, MP.6

Solve & Discuss It!

ACTIVITY

Marianne orders boxes to pack gifts. When they arrive, she finds flat pieces of cardboard as shown below. Marianne needs to cover each face of the boxes with green paper. What is the least amount of paper needed to cover each box? Explain.

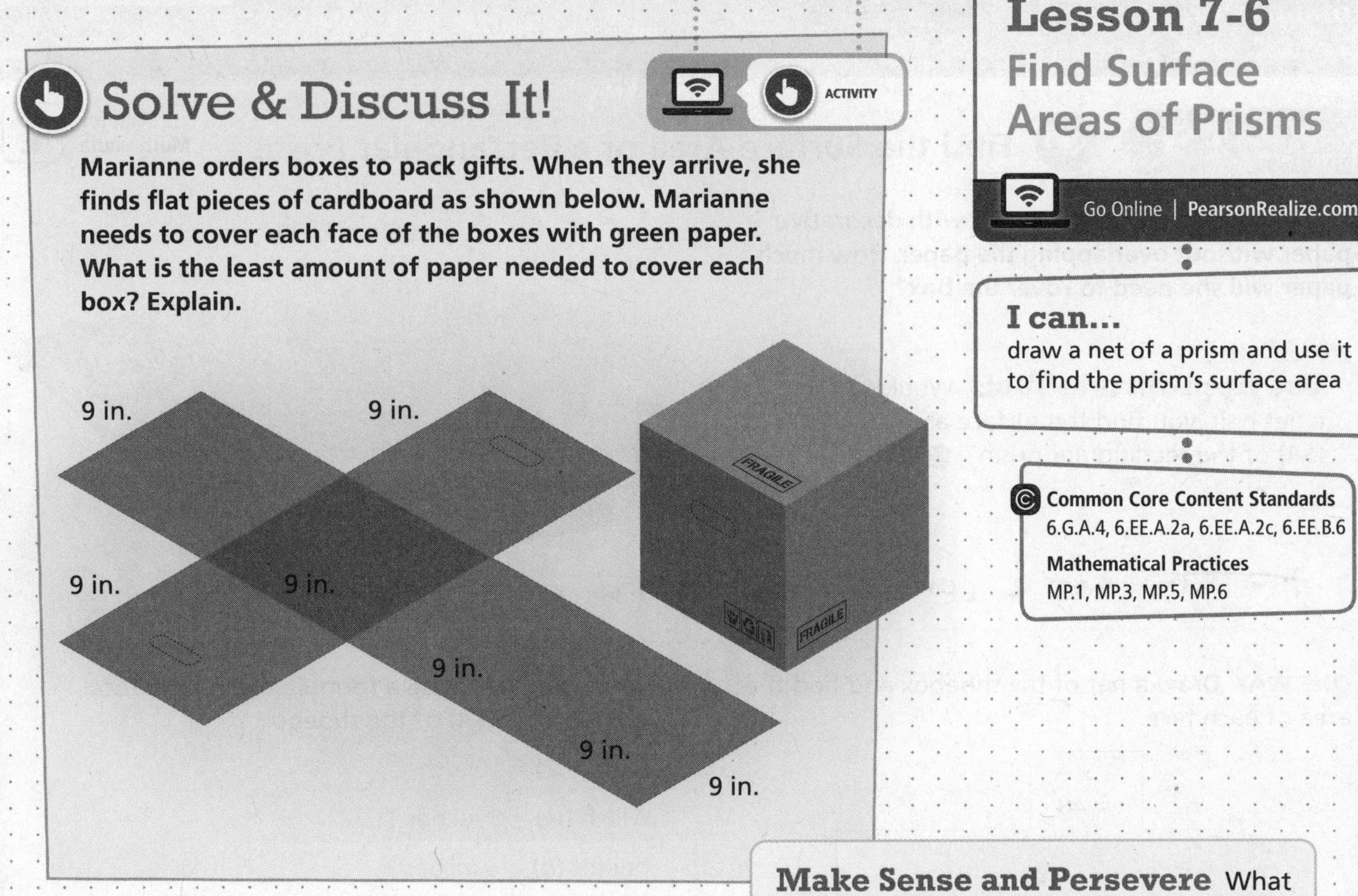

Make Sense and Persevere What solid figure does this net represent? MP.1

Focus on math practices

Make Sense and Persevere Suppose Marianne has only one large sheet of green paper that is 15 inches by 30 inches. Is the area of this sheet of paper great enough to cover all of the faces of one box? Explain. MP.1

? **Essential Question** How can you find the surface area of a prism?

INTERACTIVE ANIMATION | ASSESS

EXAMPLE 1 Find the Surface Area of a Rectangular Prism

Scan for Multimedia

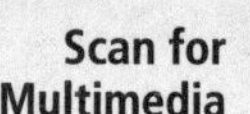

Kelly wants to cover a shoebox with decorative paper without overlapping the paper. How much paper will she need to cover the box?

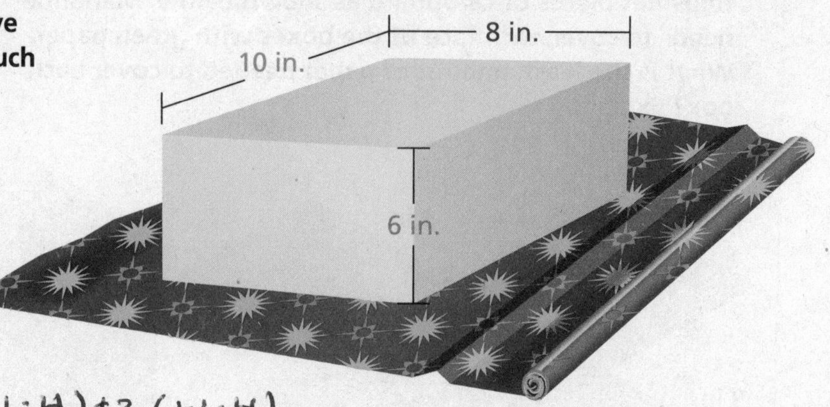

Use Appropriate Tools Would a net help you find the surface area (*SA*) of the rectangular prism? MP.5

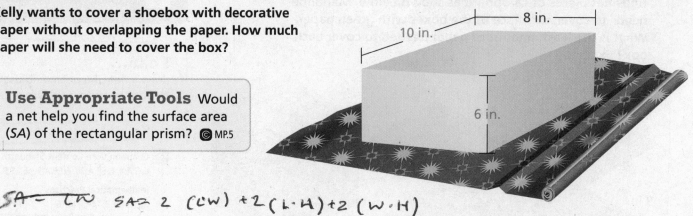

ONE WAY Draw a net of the shoebox and find the area of each face.

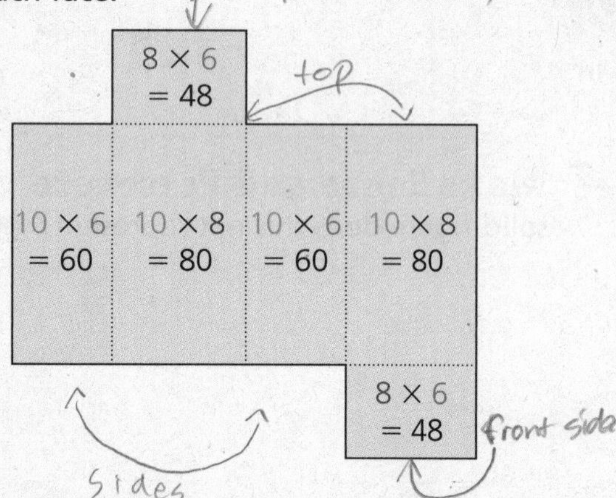

Add the areas. Kelly needs 376 square inches of paper to cover the box.

ANOTHER WAY Use a formula to find the total surface area (*SA*) of the shoebox.

length (ℓ) = 10 inches

width (w) = 8 inches

height (h) = 6 inches

$SA = 2(\ell w) + 2(wh) + 2(\ell h)$

$= 2(10 \cdot 8) + 2(8 \cdot 6) + 2(10 \cdot 6)$

$= 2(80) + 2(48) + 2(60)$

$= 376$

The area of each face in the net is calculated in the formula.

Kelly needs 376 square inches of paper to cover the box.

Try It!

Use the net and the formula to find the surface area of the prism.

$SA = 2(\ell w) + 2(wh) + 2(\ell h)$

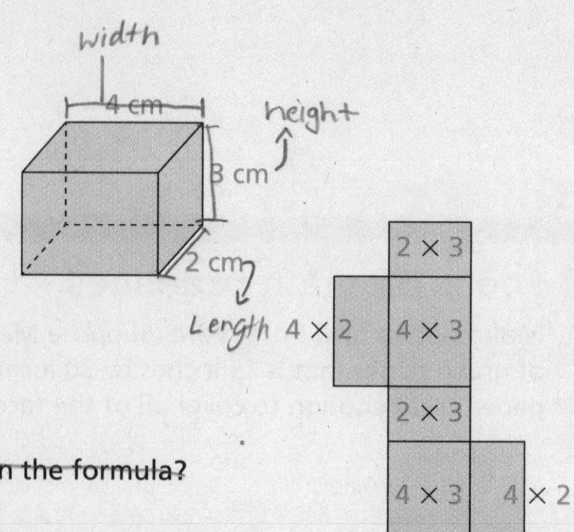

Convince Me! Why are ℓw, wh, and ℓh each multiplied by 2 in the formula?

EXAMPLE 2  Find the Surface Area of a Cube

Sam built a storage cube out of plywood. How many square meters of plywood did Sam use for the cube?

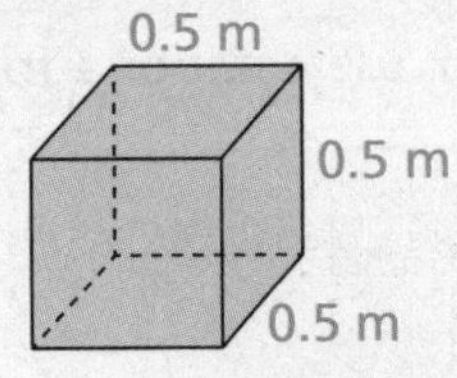

Be Precise Remember to express surface area in square units. MP.6

Draw a net of the cube.

The formula for the area of one square is $A = s^2$. Because there are 6 equal squares in the net, the formula for the surface area of a cube is $SA = 6s^2$. Use the formula to find the surface area.

$SA = 6(0.5)^2$

$SA = 6(0.25)$

$SA = 1.5$

Sam used 1.5 m^2 of plywood to build the cube.

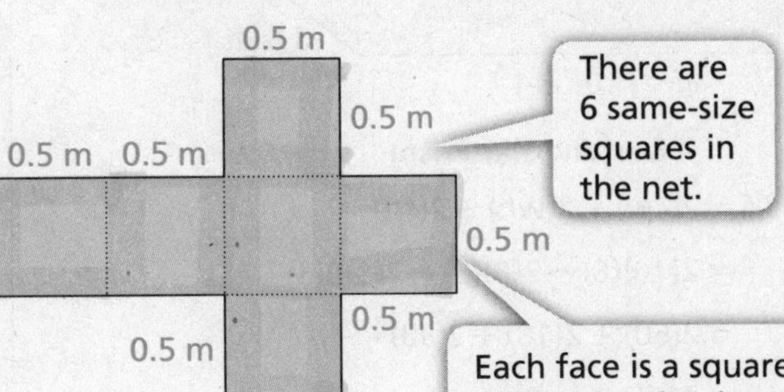

EXAMPLE 3  Find the Surface Area of a Triangular Prism

Find the surface area of the triangular prism.

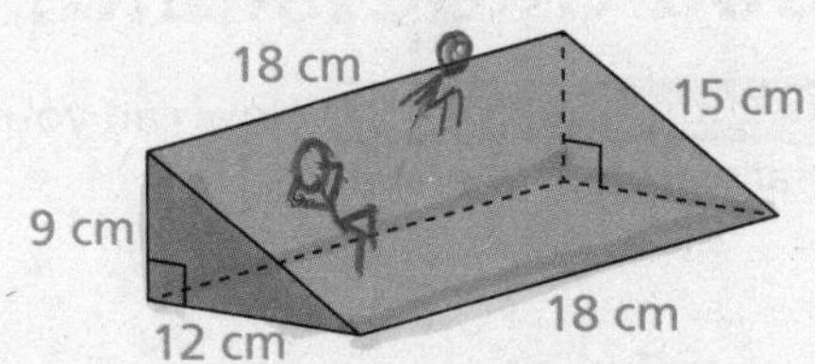

Use the net to find the area of each face of the prism. Then add the areas.

Area of triangular bases: $A = \frac{1}{2}bh = \frac{1}{2}(12)(9) = 54$

There are 2 triangular bases.

Area of bottom: $A = \ell w = 12(18) = 216$

Area of back: $A = \ell w = 9(18) = 162$

Area of sloped face: $A = \ell w = 18(15) = 270$

$SA = 2(54) + 216 + 162 + 270 = 756$

The surface area of the triangular prism is 756 cm^2.

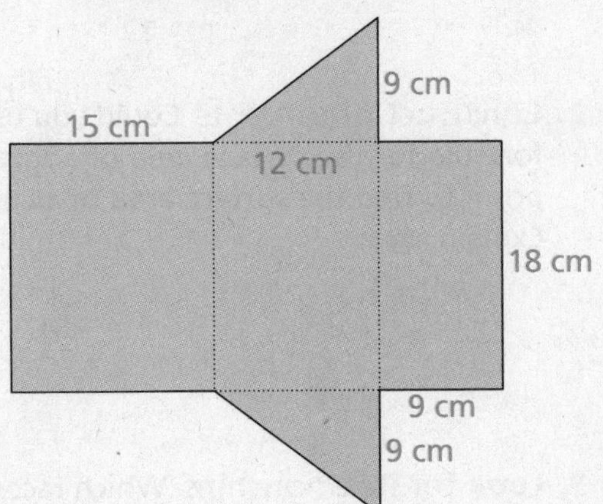

Try It!

Find the surface area of each prism.

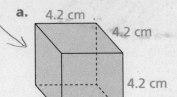

a. 4.2 cm, 4.2 cm, 4.2 cm

b.

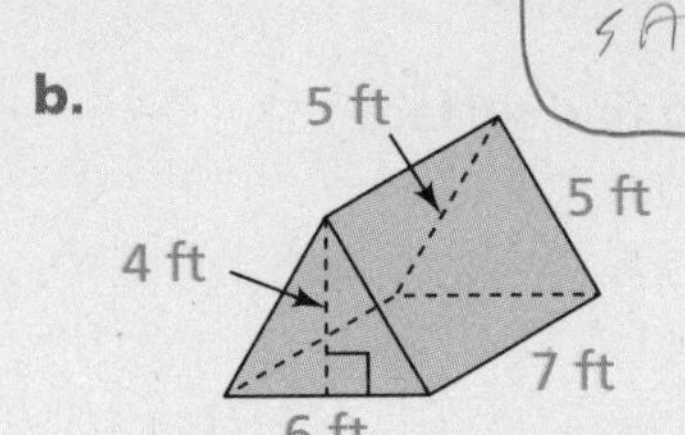

KEY CONCEPT

To find the surface area of a prism, use a net or a formula.

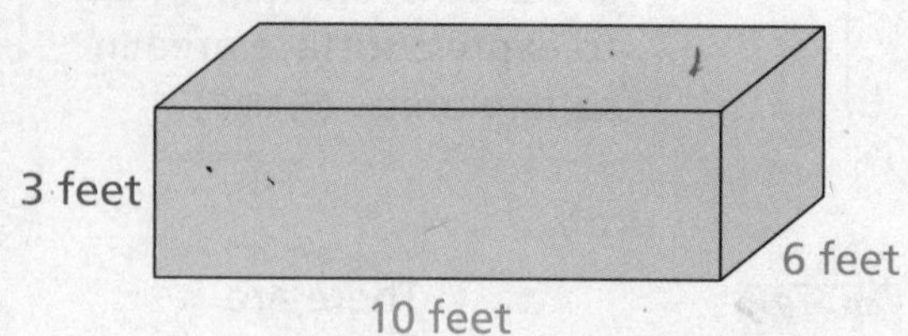

Rectangular Prism

$SA = 2(\ell w) + 2(wh) + 2(\ell h)$

$= 2(10)(6) + 2(6)(3) + 2(10)(3)$

$= 2(60) + 2(18) + 2(30)$

$= 216$

The surface area is 216 ft^2.

$6 \times 3 = 18$

$10 \times 3 = 30$ | $10 \times 6 = 60$ | $10 \times 3 = 30$ | $10 \times 6 = 60$

$6 \times 3 = 18$

Do You Understand?

1. **Essential Question** How can you find the surface area of a prism?

SA = 2(L·W) + 2(W·h) + 2(L·h)
SA = 2(10·5) + 2(5·2) + 2(10·2)
160 ft²

2. **Construct Arguments** Could you use the formula for the surface area of a rectangular prism to find the surface area of a cube? Explain. MP.3

SA = 6(s)²
SA = 6(7)²
SA = 6(49)
294 cm²

3. **Look for Relationships** Which faces of a rectangular prism always have the same area? MP.7

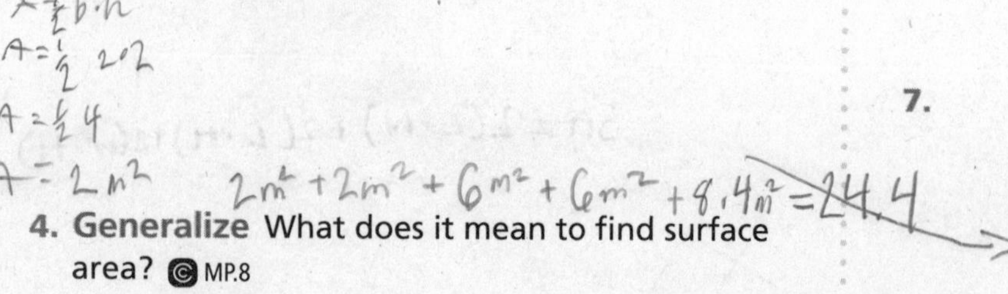

4. **Generalize** What does it mean to find surface area? MP.8

Do You Know How?

In 5–7, find the surface area of each prism.

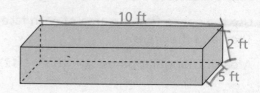

5. 10 ft, 2 ft, 5 ft

6.

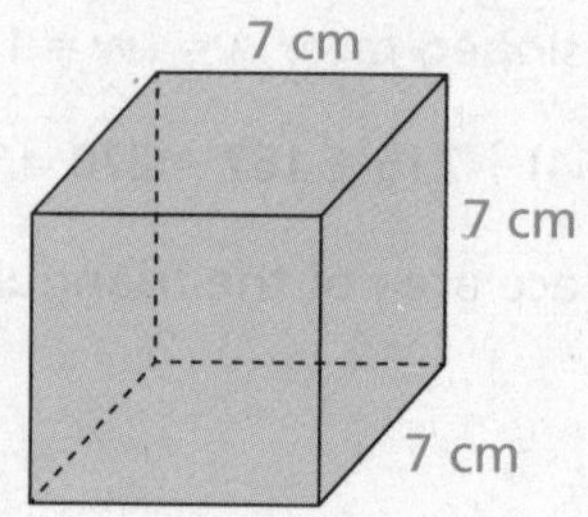

7.

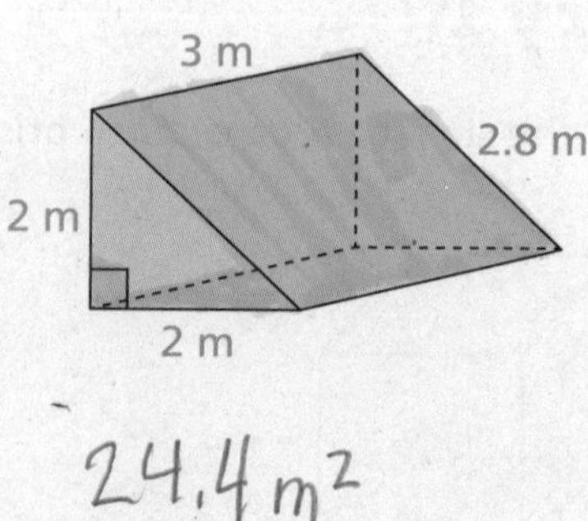

24.4 m²

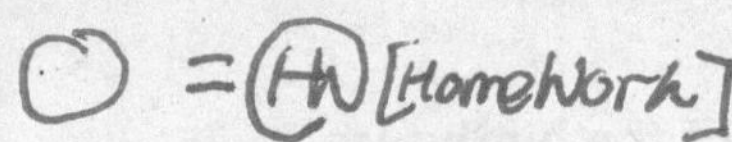

Name: Madelyn Zinck

Practice & Problem Solving

In 8–13, find the surface area of each prism.

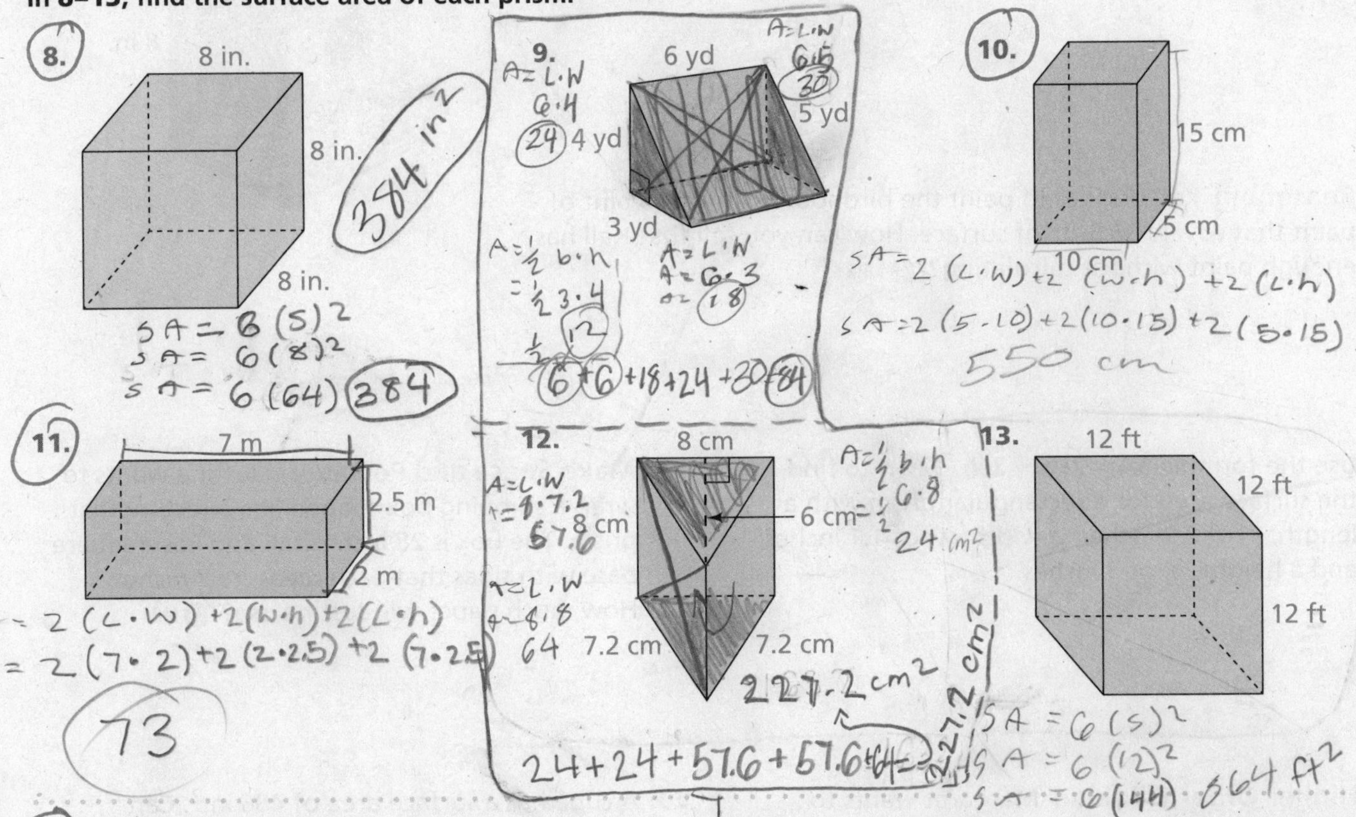

14. Critique Reasoning Jacob says that the surface area of the cube is less than 1,000 cm². Do you agree with Jacob? Explain. MP.3

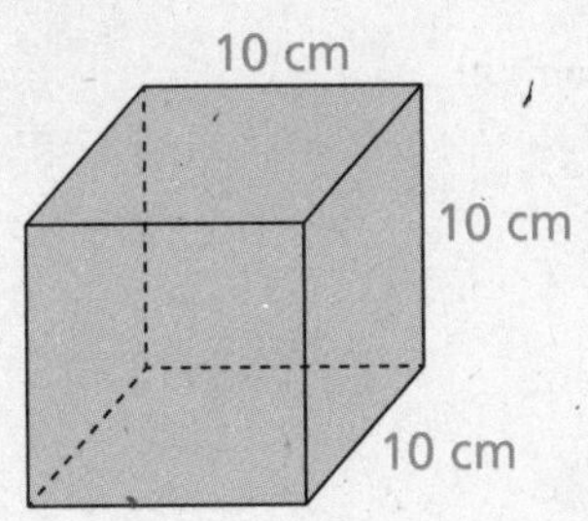

15. You want to wrap a paperweight shaped like the triangular prism shown. How many square inches of wrapping paper do you need to completely cover the prism?

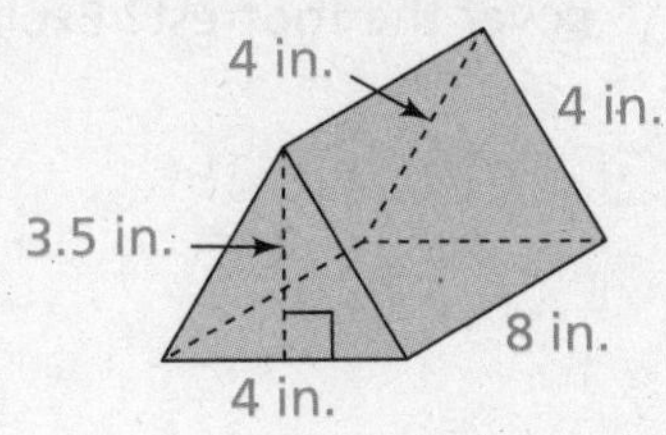

16. Sasha has 2 blocks of clay shaped like the rectangular prism below. She joins them to form a rectangular prism with a length of 12 inches. What is the surface area of the larger prism?

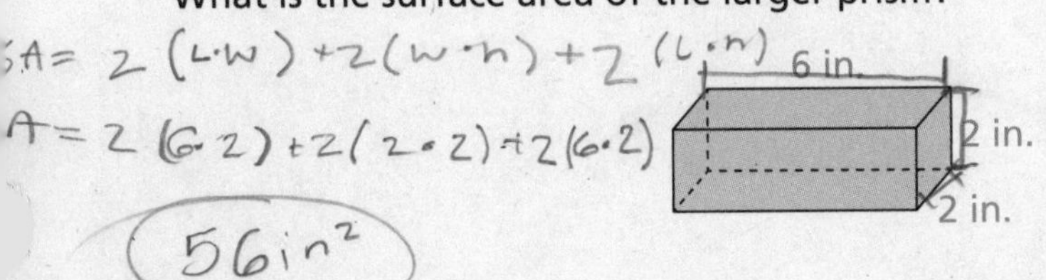

17. A rectangular prism has a length of 12 cm, a height of 6 cm, and a width of 4 cm. Use the formula $SA = 2(\ell w) + 2(wh) + 2(\ell h)$ to find the surface area of the rectangular prism.

In 18 and 19, use the diagram of the birdhouse.

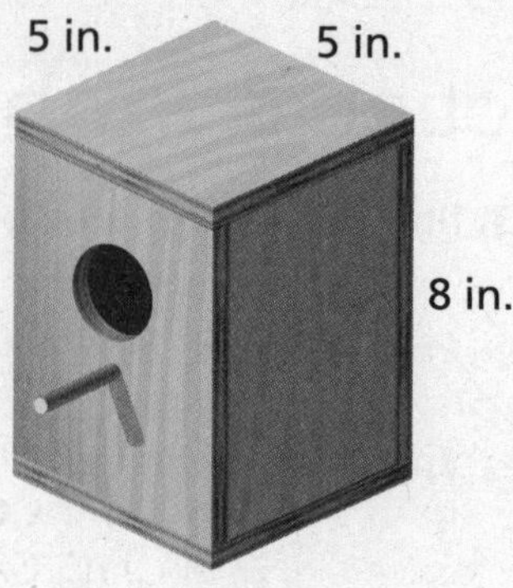

18. Kali wants to build this birdhouse. She bought a 24-inch by 48-inch sheet of plywood. Does Kali have enough wood to make the birdhouse? Explain.

19. Reasoning Kali decides to paint the birdhouse. She has a pint of paint that covers 32.5 ft^2 of surface. How can you tell that Kali has enough paint without calculating? MP.2

20. Use the formula $SA = 2\ell w + 2\ell h + 2wh$ to find the surface area for a rectangular prism with a length, ℓ, of 2.3 inches; a width, w, of 1.1 inches; and a height, h, of 3 inches.

21. Make Sense and Persevere Justine wants to wrap a shipping box shaped like a rectangular prism. The box is 28 inches tall and has a square base with sides that each measure 2 inches. How much paper will Justine use? MP.1

22. Higher Order Thinking Margaret wants to cover a footrest in the shape of a rectangular prism with cotton fabric. The footrest is 18 inches by 12 inches by 10 inches. Margaret has 1 square yard of fabric. Can she completely cover the footrest? Explain.

23. A cube has a surface area of 486 in.^{2}. Can the length of each side of the cube be 11 in.? Explain.

Assessment Practice

24. What is the surface area of a rectangular prism with a height of 2 feet, a length of 4.2 feet, and a width of 2.5 feet?

25. What is the surface area of a cube where each side has a length of 6.75 feet?

Lesson 7-7
Find Surface Areas of Pyramids

Go Online | PearsonRealize.com

I can...
draw a net of a pyramid and use it to find the pyramid's surface area.

Common Core Content Standards
6.G.A.4, 6.EE.A.2a, 6.EE.A.2c, 6.EE.B.6

Mathematical Practices
MP.2, MP.3, MP.5, MP.7

Solve & Discuss It!

ACTIVITY

The fence in Marci's front yard has decorative tops, in the shape of square pyramids, every 6 feet. Marci paints each face of each top a different color before attaching the tops to the fence. What is the total surface area that she paints on each decorative top?

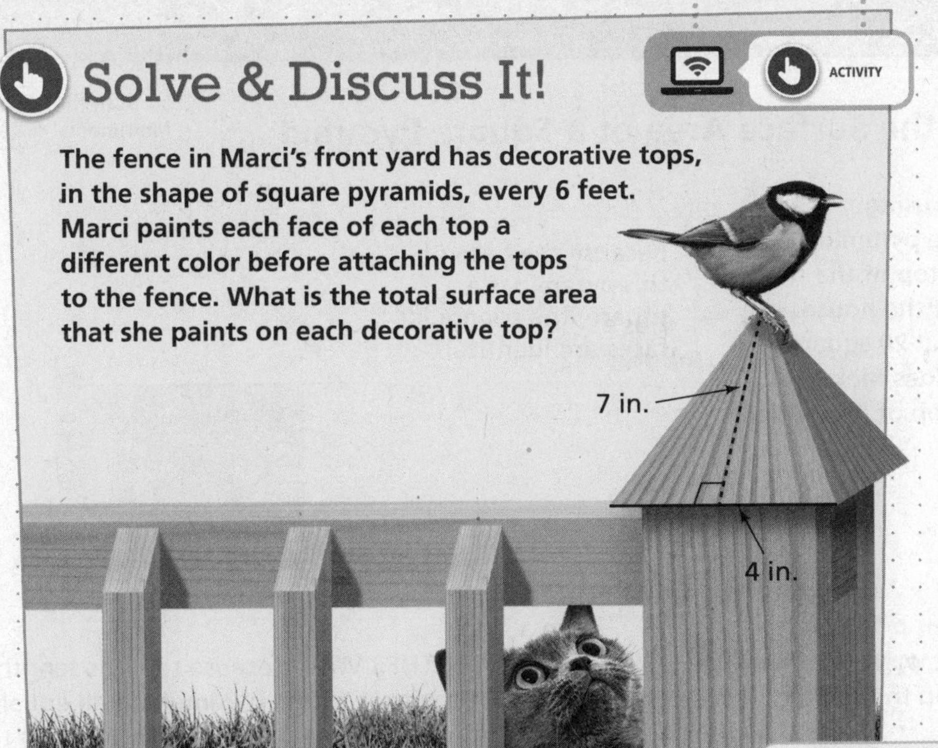

Use Appropriate Tools
What tools can you use to help solve this problem? MP.5

Focus on math practices

Use Structure Suppose the side lengths of the square base of each decorative top are increased by 2 inches. What is the total surface area of each top? MP.7

? Essential Question How can you find the surface area of a pyramid?

EXAMPLE 1  Find the Surface Area of a Square Pyramid

Scan for Multimedia 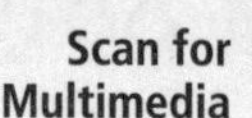

Maxwell made a model of a house using a cube for the bottom and a square pyramid for the top. He wants to paint the top of the house blue to match the bottom of the house. One tube of craft paint covers about 20 square inches. How many tubes of paint does Maxwell need to cover all the faces of the top of his model?

Because the base of this pyramid is a square, the triangular faces are identical.

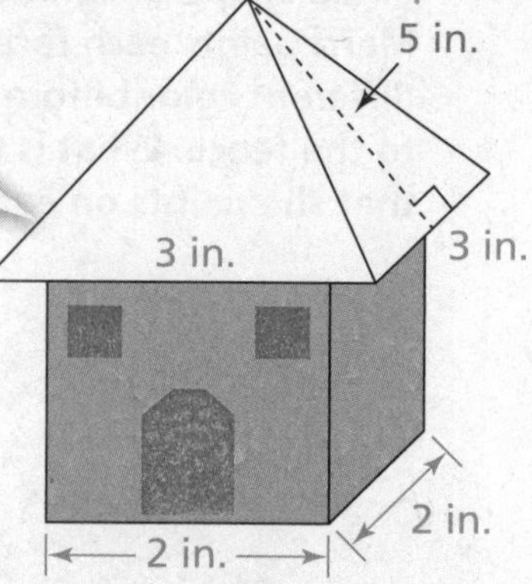

ONE WAY Draw a net of the square pyramid. Then find the sum of the areas of the base and the faces.

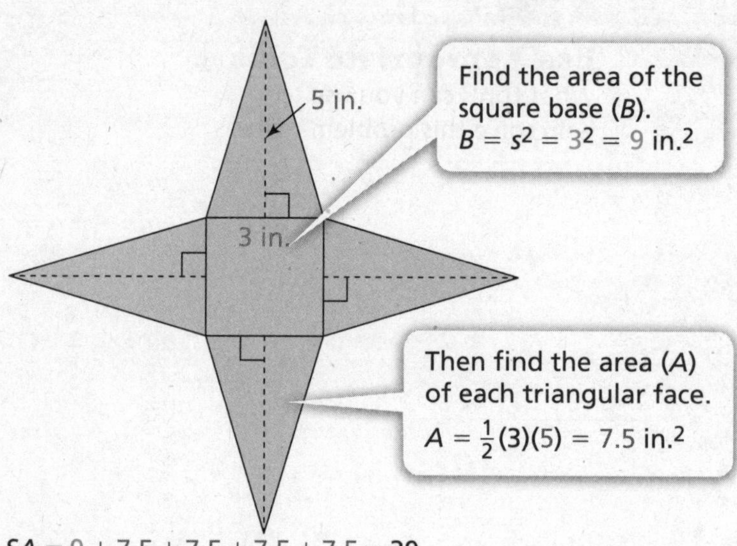

Find the area of the square base (B).
$B = s^2 = 3^2 = 9$ in.^{2}

Then find the area (A) of each triangular face.
$A = \frac{1}{2}(3)(5) = 7.5$ in.^{2}

$SA = 9 + 7.5 + 7.5 + 7.5 + 7.5 = 39$

The surface area is 39 in.^{2}, so Maxwell needs 2 tubes of craft paint.

ANOTHER WAY Because the side lengths of the base of the pyramid are all equal, you can use the formula $SA = B + (nA)$ to find the surface area (SA).

B = area of the base of the pyramid, 9

n = number of faces, 4

A = area of each triangular face, 7.5

$SA = B + (n \times A)$

$SA = 9 + (4 \times 7.5)$

$SA = 39$

The formula finds the sum of the areas of the base and each face in the net.

The surface area is 39 in.^{2}, so Maxwell needs 2 tubes of craft paint.

Try It!

Find the surface area of the square pyramid. Draw a net to find the areas of the base and each face of the pyramid.

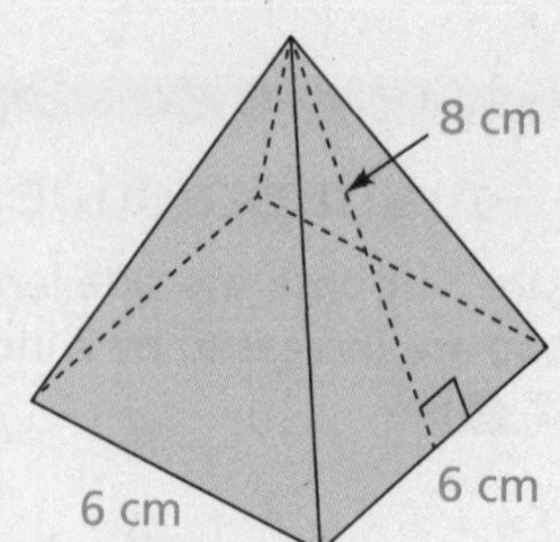

Convince Me! For the pyramid in the Try It!, what values would you use for B, n, and A in the formula $SA = B + (nA)$?

EXAMPLE 2

Find the Surface Area of a Triangular Pyramid

Tamara made a small gift box that has the shape of a triangular pyramid. The faces of the box are identical equilateral triangles. How many square centimeters of cardboard did Tamara use for the box?

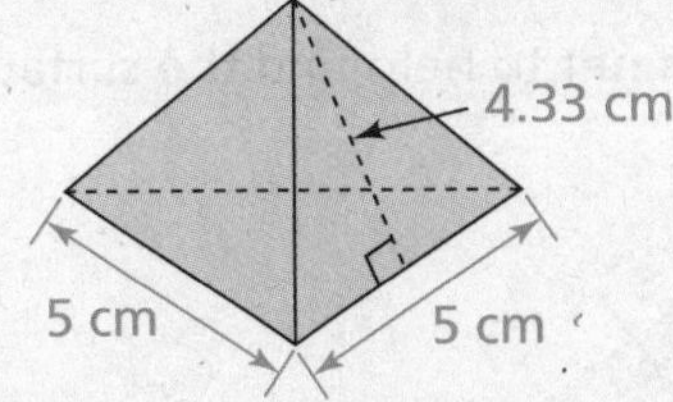

STEP 1 Draw a net.

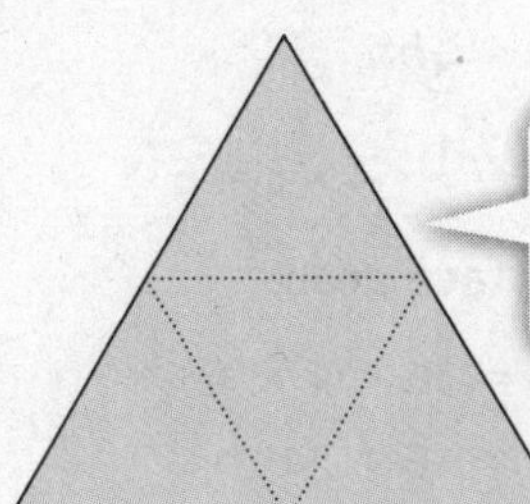

The faces of the triangular pyramid are 4 identical equilateral triangles.

STEP 2 Find the area (T) of each equilateral triangle.

$T = \frac{1}{2}bh$

$T = \frac{1}{2}(5)(4.33)$

$= 10.825 \text{ cm}^2$

STEP 3 Find the surface area (SA) of the triangular pyramid.

$SA = 4T$

$SA = 4 \times 10.825$

$= 43.3 \text{ cm}^2$

Tamara used 43.3 cm^2 of cardboard for the box.

Reasoning If you know the faces are identical equilateral triangles, then you just find the area of one triangle and multiply by 4. MP.2

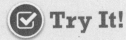

Try It!

Draw a net and find the surface area of the triangular pyramid.

Find the area (T) of each equilateral triangle.

$T = \frac{1}{2}bh$

$T = \frac{1}{2} \times \square \times \square$

$= \square$

The area of each equilateral triangle is $\square$ m^2.

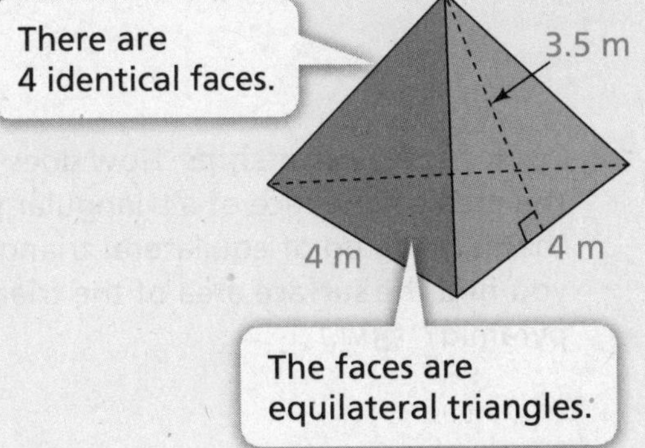

Find the surface area (SA) of the triangular pyramid.

$SA = 4T$

$SA = \square \times T$

$SA = 4 \times \square$

$= \square$

The surface area of the triangular pyramid is $\square$ m^2.

KEY CONCEPT

You can use a net to help find the surface area of a pyramid.

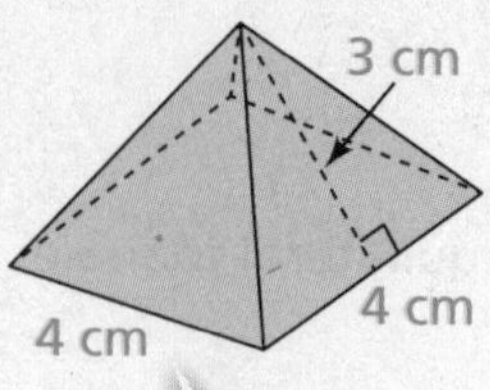

Use the dimensions shown on the pyramid to draw an accurate net.

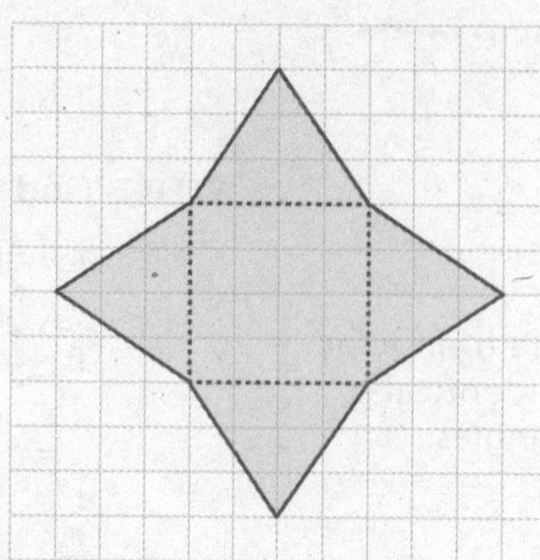

Square base:

$B = s^2$

$= 4 \cdot 4 = 16$

Each triangular face:

$A = \frac{1}{2}bh$

$= \frac{1}{2} \cdot 4 \cdot 3 = 6$

Surface area:

$SA = 16 + 4 \times 6$

$= 16 + 24$

$= 40$

The surface area is 40 cm^2.

Do You Understand?

1. **Essential Question** How can you find the surface area of a pyramid?

2. **Look for Relationships** How does finding the area of one face of a triangular pyramid that is made up of equilateral triangles help you find the surface area of the triangular pyramid? MP.7

3. **Make Sense and Persevere** In the formula $SA = 4T$, for the surface area of a triangular pyramid in which the faces are equilateral triangles, what does the variable T represent? MP.1

Do You Know How?

4. Each side of the base of a square pyramid is 4 inches and the height of each triangular face is 3 inches. Draw a net for this pyramid and find its surface area.

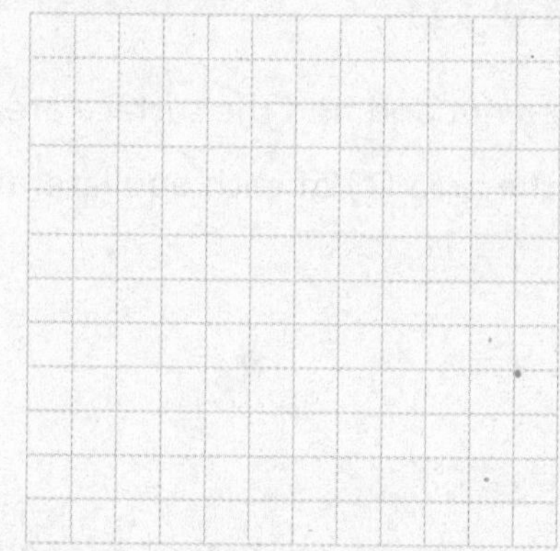

5. The faces of this triangular pyramid are equilateral triangles. Draw a net of the pyramid and use it to find the surface area.

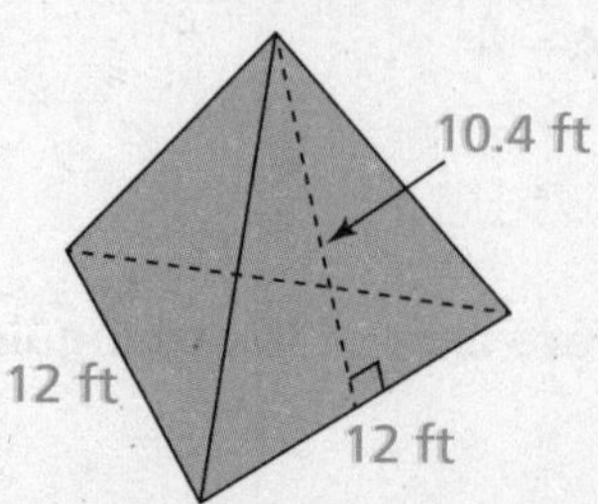

PRACTICE TUTORIAL

Name: ____________________

Practice & Problem Solving

Scan for Multimedia

Leveled Practice **In 6 and 7, find the surface area of each pyramid. The faces of each triangular pyramid are equilateral triangles.**

6.

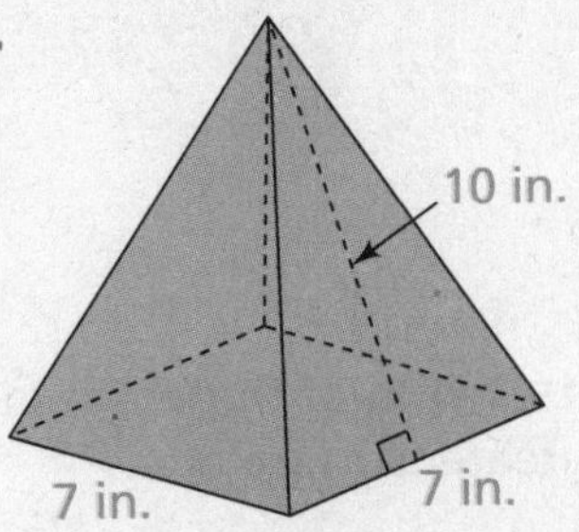

Area of base, B: $7 \times 7 = \square$

Area of each triangular face, A:

$\frac{1}{2} \times 7 \times \square = \square$

Number of triangular faces, n: $\square$

$SA = B + (n \times A)$

$SA = \square + (\square \times \square) = \square$

The surface area is $\square$ in.^{2}.

7.

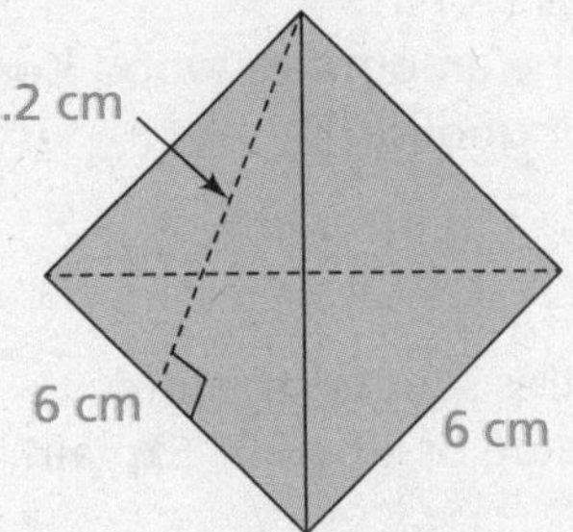

Area of each triangular face, T:

$\frac{1}{2} \times \square \times \square = \square$

$SA = 4T$

$SA = 4 \times \square$

$SA = \square$

The surface area is $\square$ cm^2.

8. Complete the net at the right to find the surface area of this triangular pyramid. The faces of the pyramid are equilateral triangles.

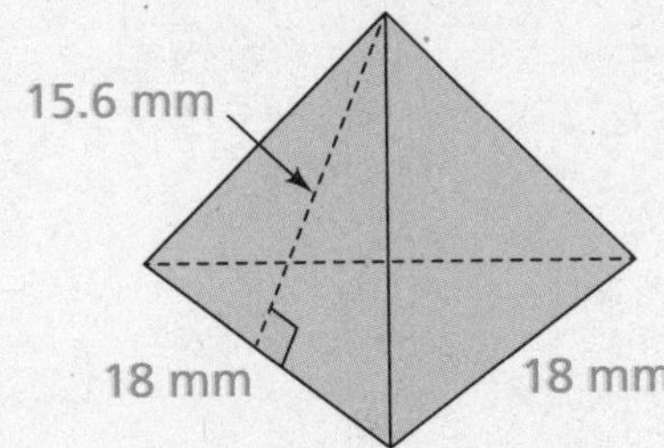

$\square$ mm^2

$\square$ mm^2

$\square$ mm^2

$\square$ mm^2

9. Simone is designing a piece of artwork in the shape of a square pyramid for a hotel. She wants to cover the pyramid with decorative glass. How many square feet of glass does Simone need to cover the entire pyramid?

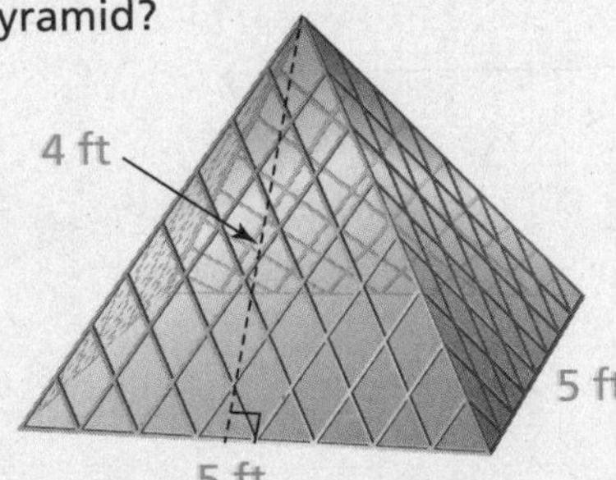

10. Critique Reasoning Kurt says that the surface area of this triangular pyramid with faces that are equilateral triangles is 173 cm^2. Do you agree with Kurt? Explain. MP.3

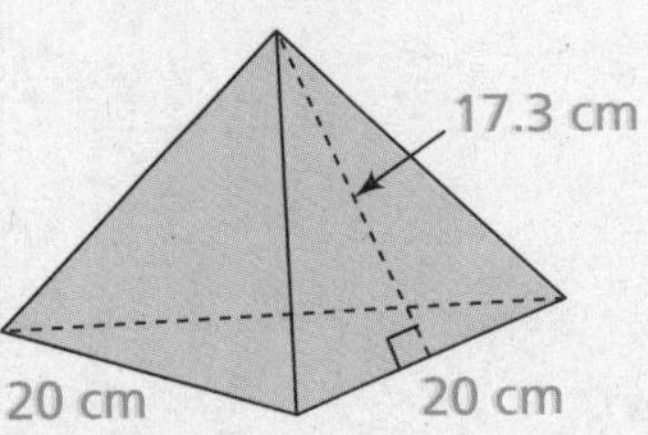

In 11 and 12, use the pyramid and net shown.

11. Model with Math Ken drew a square pyramid and its net to represent a doghouse that he is building. Complete the net by filling in the missing measures. MP.4

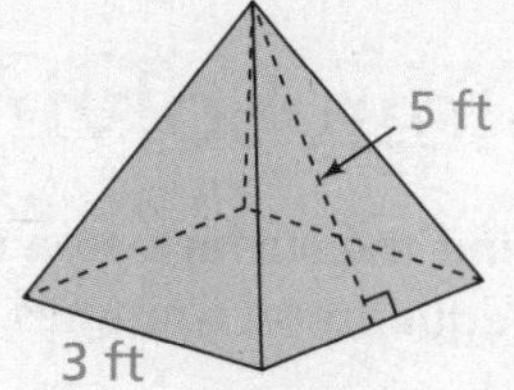

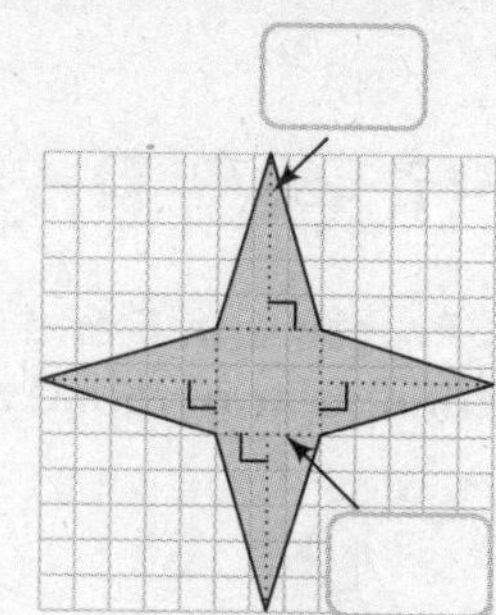

12. Use the net to find the amount of wood Ken needs to make the doghouse.

13. The surface area of this square pyramid is 644 ft^2. Can the value of x be 20? Explain.

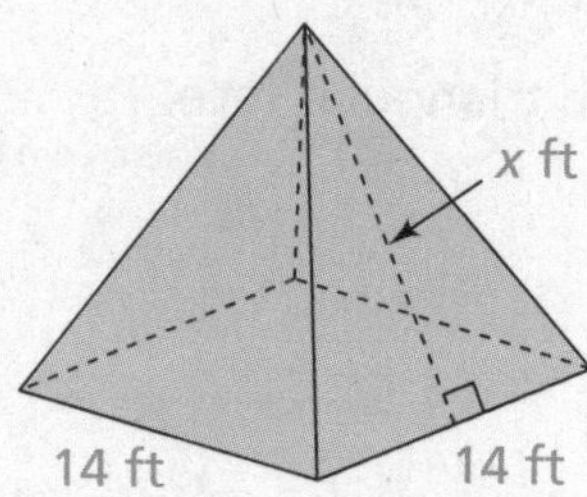

14. Construct Arguments Which of these pyramids do you think has the greater surface area? Explain. MP.3

- Square pyramid: The base is 10 cm by 10 cm and the triangular faces have a height of 8.66 cm.
- Triangular pyramid: All the faces are equilateral triangles with a base of 10 cm and a height of 8.66 cm.

15. Higher Order Thinking The base of a pyramid can be any polygon. How many faces does a pentagonal pyramid have? Describe the shapes of the faces.

16. Vocabulary What is the term used to describe a point where three or more edges of a solid figure meet?

Assessment Practice

17. Which net represents the pyramid with the greatest surface area?

Ⓐ

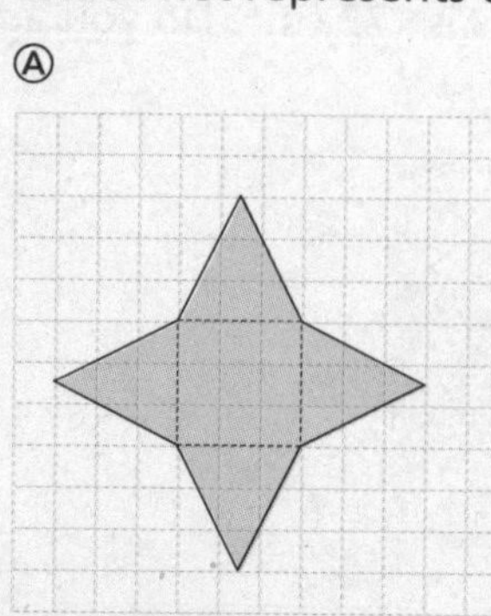

Ⓑ

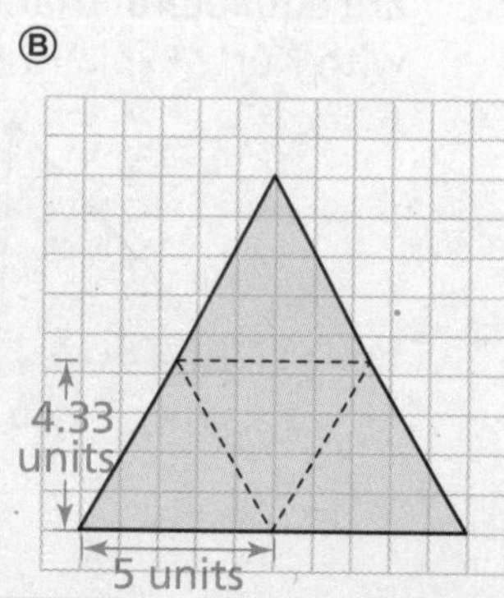

Ⓒ

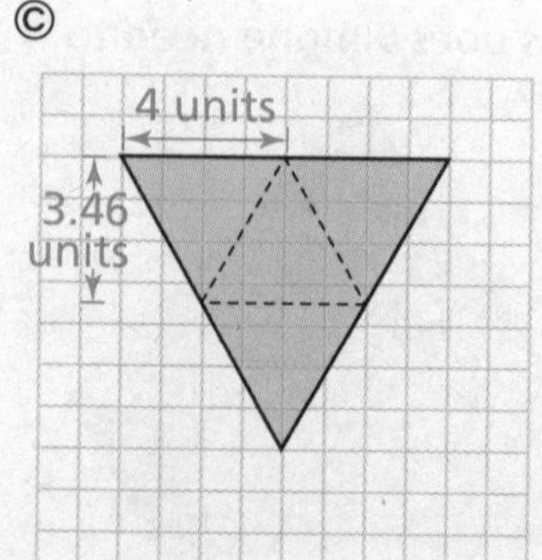

Ⓓ

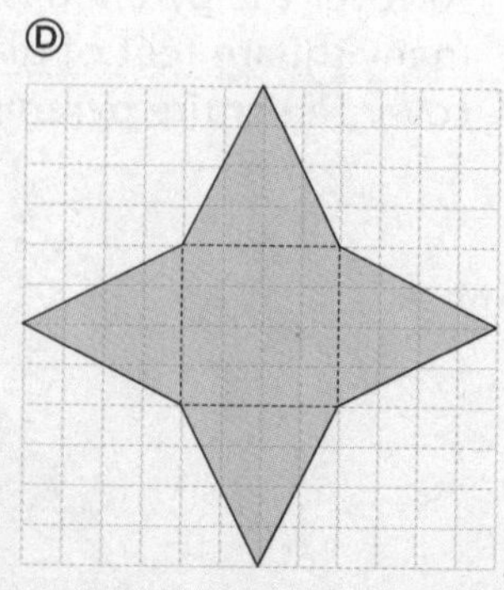

Lesson 7-8
Find Volume with Fractional Edge Lengths

Go Online | PearsonRealize.com

I can...
find the volume of a rectangular prism with fractional edge lengths.

Common Core Content Standards
6.G.A.2, 6.EE.A.2a, 6.EE.A.2c, 6.EE.B.6

Mathematical Practices
MP.1, MP.3, MP.6, MP.7

Solve & Discuss It!

ACTIVITY

A rectangular prism has the dimensions shown. What is the volume of this rectangular prism?

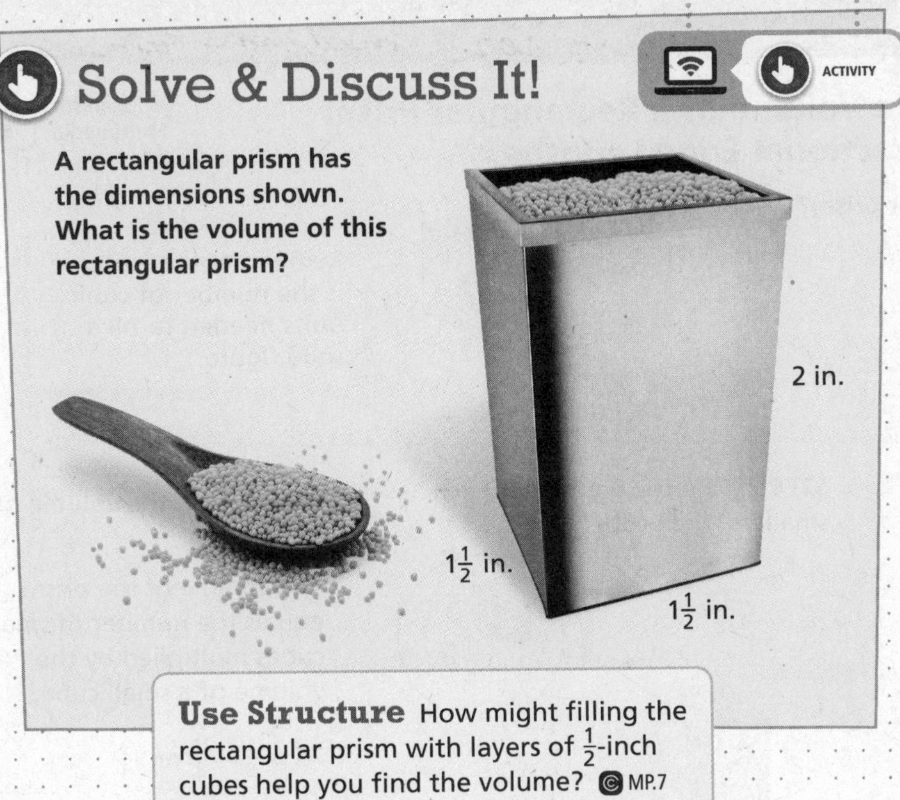

Use Structure How might filling the rectangular prism with layers of $\frac{1}{2}$-inch cubes help you find the volume? MP.7

Focus on math practices

Look for Relationships You know how to use the formula $V = \ell wh$ to find the volume of a rectangular prism. How might you use the formula to find the volume of the prism above? MP.7

? Essential Question How can you find the volume of a rectangular prism with fractional edge lengths?

04/05/2021 madelyn zinck

EXAMPLE 1 Find the Volume of a Rectangular Prism with Fractional Edge Lengths

Scan for Multimedia

What is the volume of the rectangular prism?

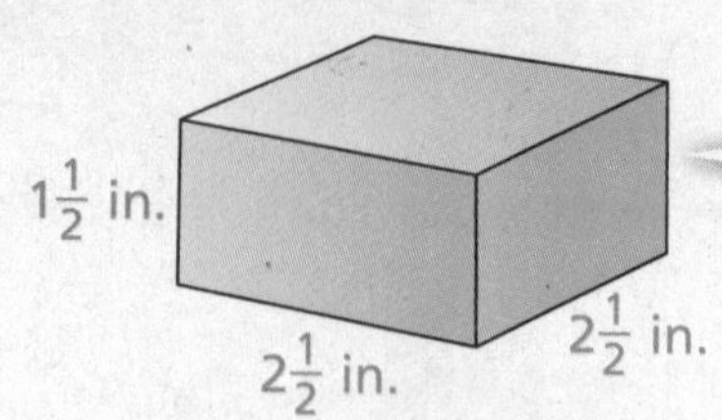

Remember that volume is the number of cubic units needed to fill a solid figure.

STEP 1 Find the number of $\frac{1}{2}$-inch cubes that will fill the prism.

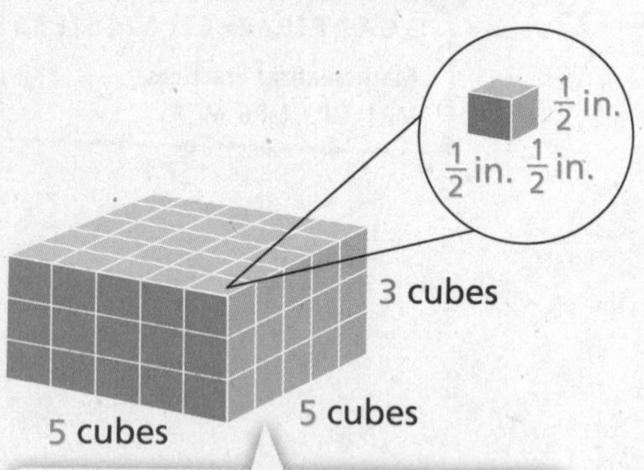

Five $\frac{1}{2}$-inch cubes fit along each $2\frac{1}{2}$-inch edge of the prism.

The bottom layer has 5×5, or 25 cubes.

The prism is 3 cubes high, so there are 25×3, or 75, cubes in the prism.

STEP 2 Find the volume of each smaller $\frac{1}{2}$-inch cube.

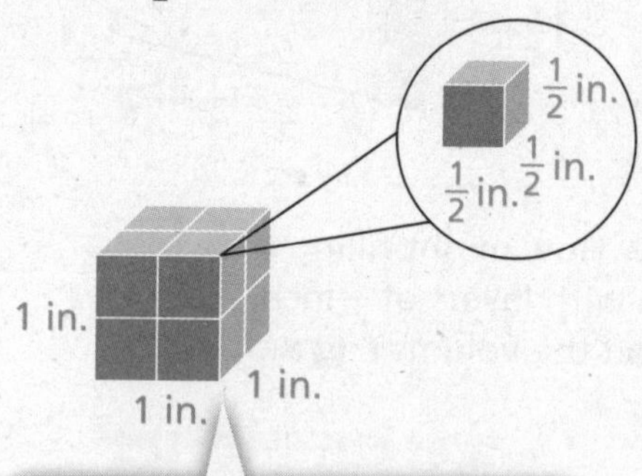

There are 4 smaller cubes on the bottom layer of the unit cube, and the unit cube is 2 smaller cubes high.

There are 4×2, or 8, smaller cubes in the unit cube. So each $\frac{1}{2}$-inch cube has $\frac{1}{8}$ the volume of a unit cube, or $\frac{1}{8} \times 1 \text{ in.}^3 = \frac{1}{8} \text{ in.}^3$.

STEP 3 Find the volume of the prism.

The volume of the prism equals the number of small cubes multiplied by the volume of a small cube.

$75 \times \frac{1}{8} = \frac{75}{8}$ or $9\frac{3}{8}$

Number of small cubes

Volume of small cube

Be Precise Use the correct units to describe area and volume. MP.6

The volume of the prism is $9\frac{3}{8}$ in.^{3}.

Try It!

Find the volume of the rectangular prism built from $\frac{1}{2}$-inch cubes.

The bottom layer has ☐ cubes. The prism is ☐ cubes high. There are a total of ☐ cubes in the prism. Each cube has a volume of ☐ in.^{3}.

Volume of prism = ☐ × ☐ = ☐ in.^{3}.

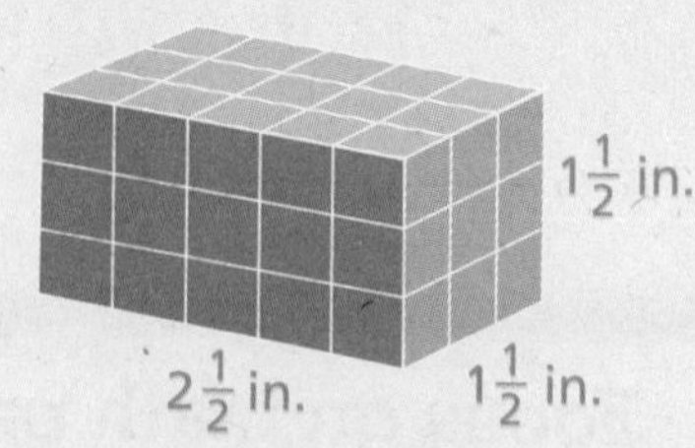

Convince Me! Suppose that the length of the rectangular prism in the Try It! were $3\frac{1}{2}$ inches instead of $2\frac{1}{2}$ inches. How many cubes would there be in the prism? What would be the volume of the prism?

  ACTIVITY  ASSESS

EXAMPLE 2  Use a Formula to Find the Volume of a Rectangular Prism

Sean bought the fish tank shown. What is the volume of Sean's fish tank?

> **Look for Relationships** The volume V of any prism equals the area of the base, B, times the height of the prism, h. $V = Bh$. In a rectangular prism, $B = \ell \times w$. 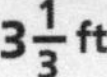 MP.7

Use the formula $V = \ell wh$ to find the volume of the fish tank.

$V = 3\frac{1}{3} \times 1 \times 1\frac{1}{3}$

$V = \frac{10}{3} \times \frac{1}{1} \times \frac{4}{3}$

Substitute the values for the length, width, and height. Rename mixed numbers as fractions to solve.

$V = \frac{40}{9}$ or $4\frac{4}{9}$

The volume of the fish tank is $4\frac{4}{9}$ ft^3.

EXAMPLE 3  Use a Formula to Find the Volume of a Cube

Adah has a ring box in the shape of a cube. What is the volume of Adah's ring box?

The length, width, and height of a cube are the same.

Because a cube is a rectangular prism, its volume is also the product of its length, width, and height. Since the length, width, and height of a cube are equivalent, let s represent the length of each edge.

Volume $= s \times s \times s = s^3$

$V = \left(2\frac{1}{2}\right)^3 = 2\frac{1}{2} \times 2\frac{1}{2} \times 2\frac{1}{2}$

Rename mixed numbers as fractions to solve.

$V = \frac{5}{2} \times \frac{5}{2} \times \frac{5}{2}$

$V = \frac{125}{8}$ or $15\frac{5}{8}$

The volume of the ring box is $15\frac{5}{8}$ in.^{3}.

Try It!

Find the volume of each rectangular prism.

a.

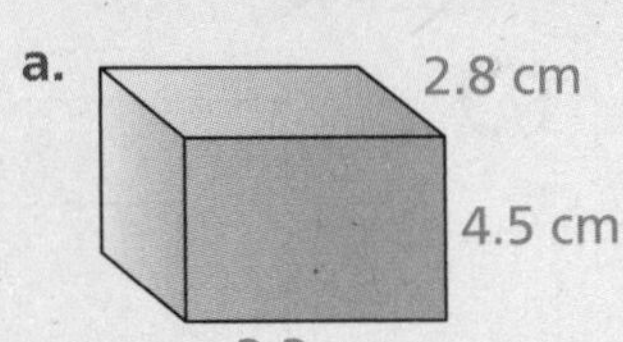

b.

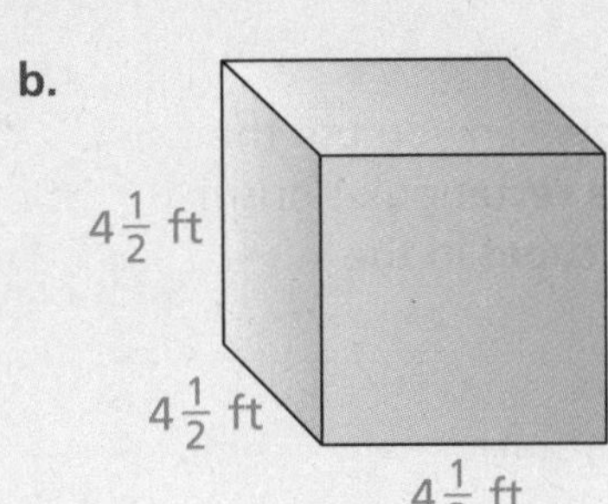

KEY CONCEPT

You can find the volume of a rectangular prism with fractional edge lengths by determining the number of same-sized cubes with unit fraction edge lengths needed to completely fill the prism, then multiplying that number of cubes by the volume of each cube. You can also apply a formula.

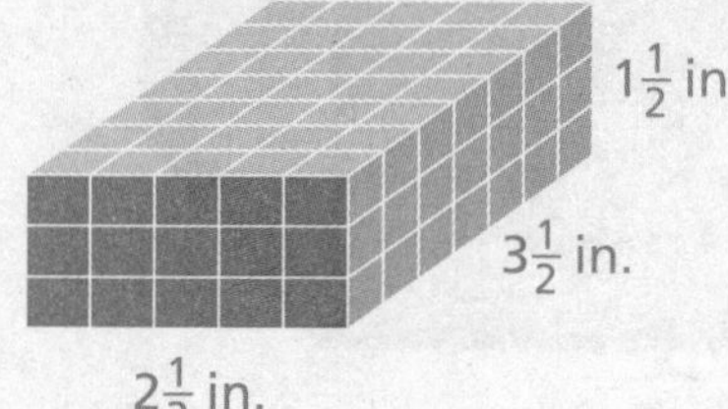

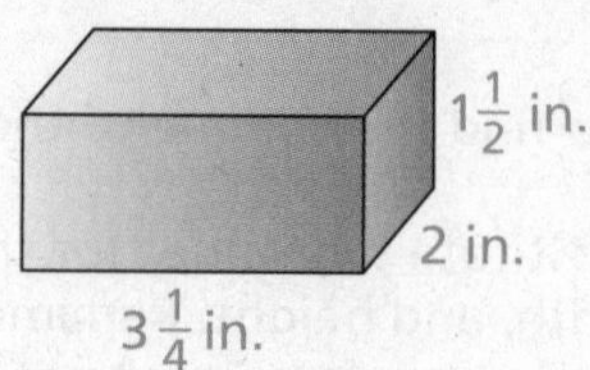

Each $\frac{1}{2}$-inch cube has a volume of $\frac{1}{8}$ in.^{3}.

Prism Dimensions:

Five $\frac{1}{2}$-inch cubes wide

Seven $\frac{1}{2}$-inch cubes long

Three $\frac{1}{2}$-inch cubes tall

$5 \times 7 \times 3 =$ One hundred five $\frac{1}{2}$-inch cubes

$V = 105 \times \frac{1}{8} = 13\frac{1}{8}$

The volume of the prism is $13\frac{1}{8}$ in.^{3}.

$V = \ell wh$

$V = 3\frac{1}{4} \times 2 \times 1\frac{1}{2}$

$V = \frac{13}{4} \times \frac{2}{1} \times \frac{3}{2}$

$V = \frac{78}{8}$ or $9\frac{3}{4}$

The volume of the prism is $9\frac{3}{4}$ in.^{3}.

Do You Understand?

1. **Essential Question** How can you find the volume of a rectangular prism with fractional edge lengths?

2. How is finding the volume of a rectangular prism with fractional edge lengths similar to finding the volume of a rectangular prism with whole number edge lengths?

3. **Construct Arguments** How can you use the number of $\frac{1}{2}$-inch cubes in a rectangular prism to find the number of unit cubes in the rectangular prism? MP.3

Do You Know How?

In 4 and 5, tell how many of each size of cube can fill a 1-inch cube.

4. Edge = $\frac{1}{3}$ inch

5. Edge = $\frac{1}{4}$ inch

V = l · w · h

In 6–9, find the volume of each rectangular prism.

6.

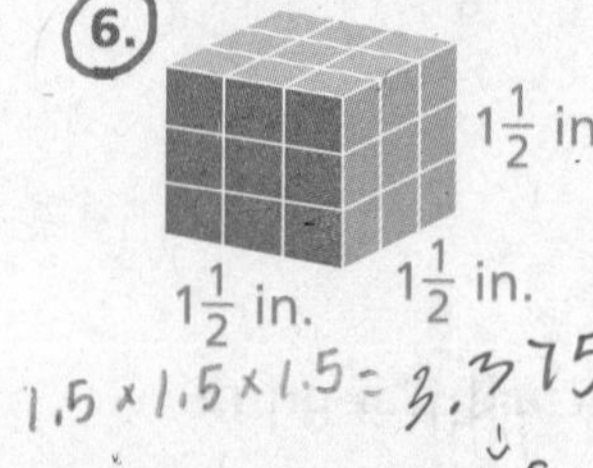

1.5 × 1.5 × 1.5 = 3.375

7.

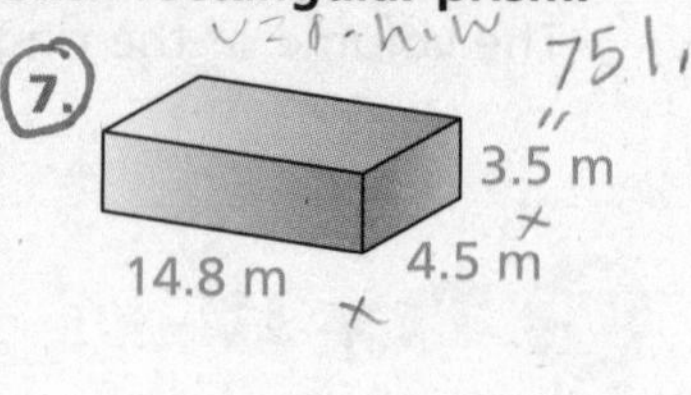

8.

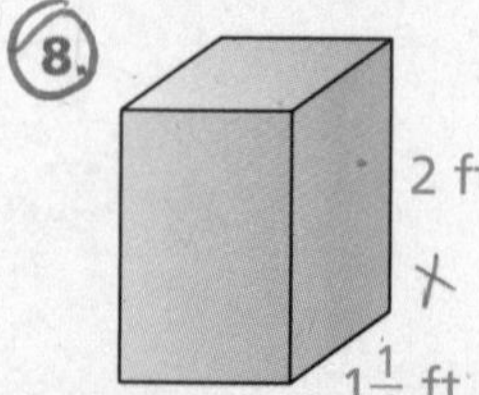

9.

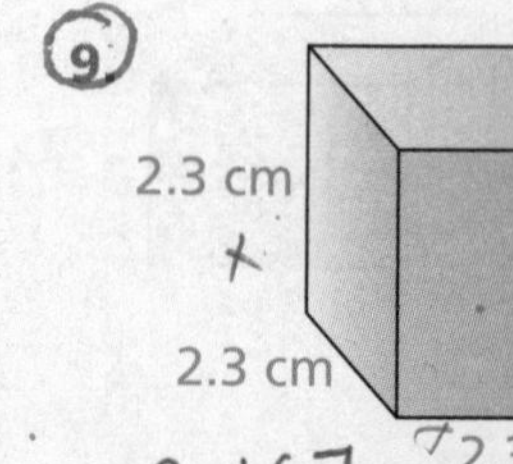

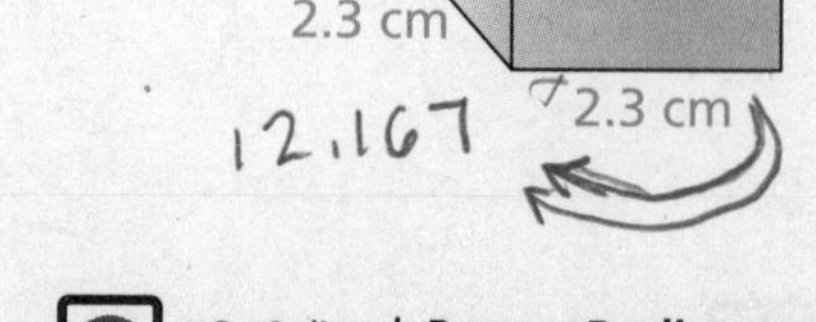

Name: ______________________________

Practice & Problem Solving  

Scan for Multimedia 

In 10–13, find the volume of each rectangular prism.

10.

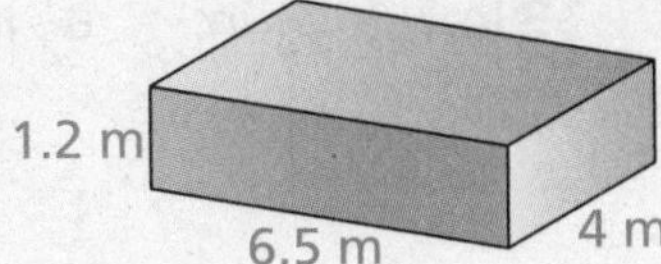

11.

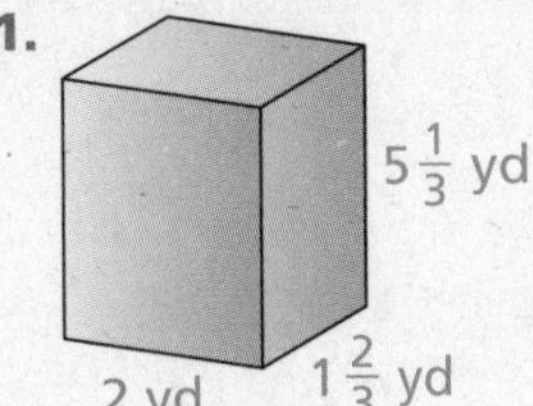

12.

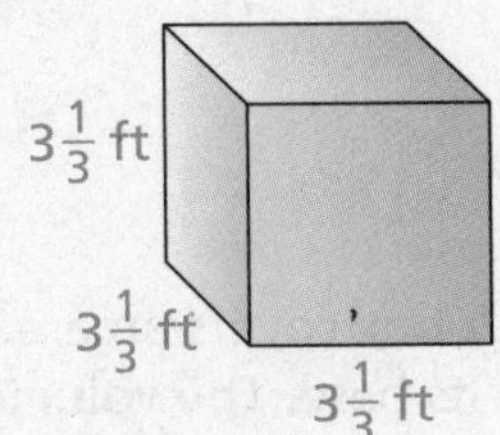

13.

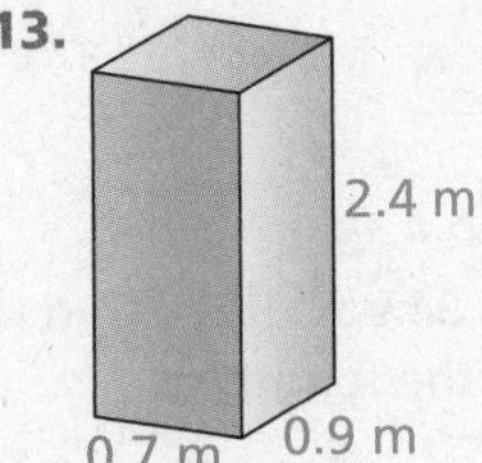

14. A clear box has the shape of a rectangular prism and is filled with sand. Find the volume of the box.

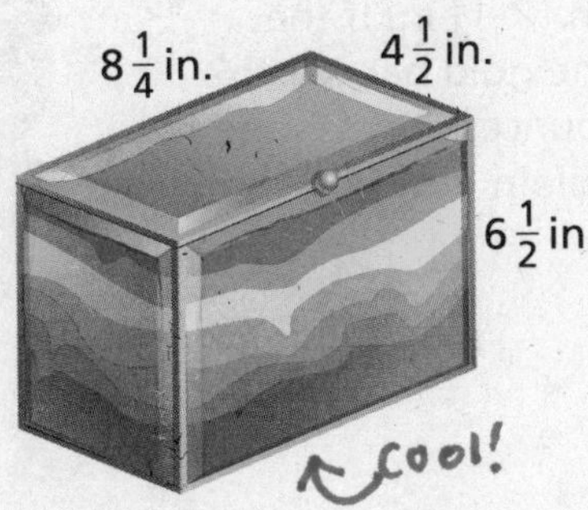

15. Use Structure A rectangular prism has a length of $2\frac{1}{2}$ yd, a width of $1\frac{1}{2}$ yd, and a height of $1\frac{1}{2}$ yd. You use cubes with fractional edge lengths of $\frac{1}{2}$ yd to find the volume. How many cubes are there for each of the length, width, and height of the prism? What is the volume of the prism? MP.7

16. A gift box has the shape of a cube. The length of each side is 10.5 cm. What is the volume of the gift box?

17. A school locker has a length of 1 ft, a width of 18 in., and a height of $2\frac{1}{2}$ ft. What is the volume of the locker in cubic feet?

In 18 and 19, use the table.

18. Use Structure Sandy has two boxes with the dimensions shown. She wants to use the box with the greater volume to ship a gift to her friend. Which box should Sandy use? Explain. MP.7

	Length	Width	Height
Box A	$7\frac{1}{2}$ in.	2 in.	$11\frac{1}{2}$ in.
Box B	9 in.	$2\frac{1}{4}$ in.	$8\frac{1}{2}$ in.

19. Sandy finds a third box, box C, that has a length of 8 inches, a width of $2\frac{3}{4}$ inches, and a height of $10\frac{1}{2}$ inches. If Sandy wants to use the box with the greatest volume, should she use box C? Explain.

20. The volume of a large crate is 84 yd^3. It is $2\frac{2}{3}$ yd wide and $4\frac{2}{3}$ yd high. What is the length of the crate?

21. Higher Order Thinking A box covers an area of $8\frac{3}{4}$ in.^{2} when resting on its base. The volume of the box is $74\frac{3}{8}$ in.^{3}. Can you find the surface area of the box? Explain.

22. Make Sense and Persevere A gold bar is similar in shape to a rectangular prism. A standard mint bar is approximately 7 in. $\times$ $3\frac{5}{8}$ in. $\times$ $1\frac{3}{4}$ in. If the value of gold is $1,313 per ounce, about how much is one gold bar worth? Use the formula $w \approx 11.15n$, where w is the weight in ounces and n is the volume in cubic inches, to find the weight in ounces. Explain how you found your answer. MP.1

Assessment Practice

23. Find the volume of the prism.

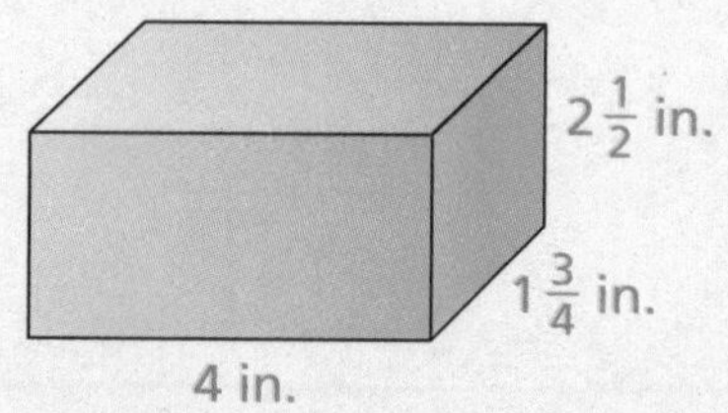

REVIEW TOPIC 7

? Topic Essential Question

How can the areas of certain shapes be found? What are the meanings of surface area and volume and how can surface area and volume be found?

Vocabulary Review

Write the vocabulary term that best represents each item.

Vocabulary	net	rhombus	trapezoid	vertex	volume

1. The measure of the space this solid figure occupies.

______

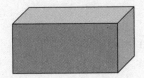

2.

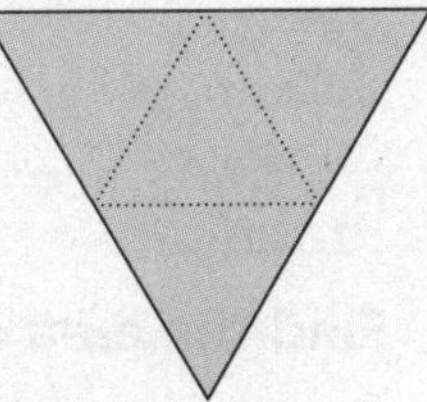

______

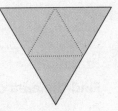

3.

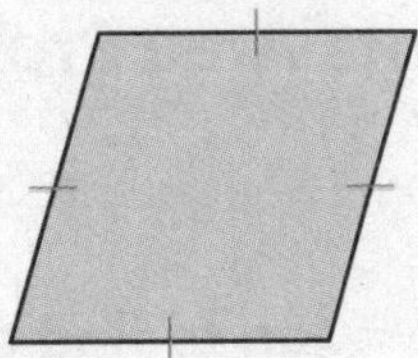

______

4. Point A

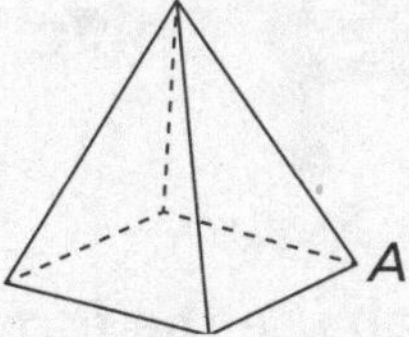

______

Use Vocabulary in Writing

Describe how to find the area of the quadrilateral. Use vocabulary words in your explanation.

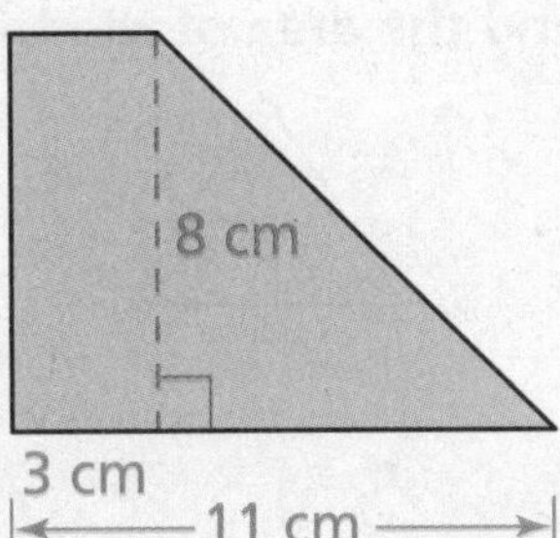

Concepts and Skills Review

LESSON 7-1 Find Areas of Parallelograms and Rhombuses

Quick Review

You can use the formula $A = bh$ to find the area of a parallelogram or a rhombus.

Example

Find the area of the parallelogram.

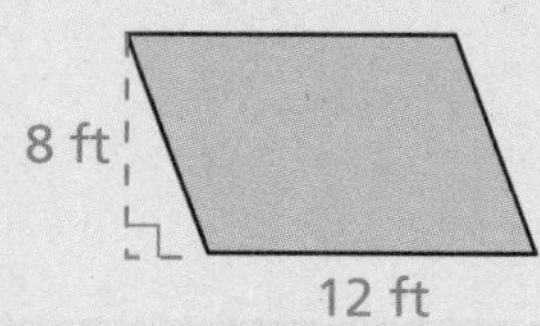

$A = bh$

$A = 12 \times 8$

$A = 96$

The area of the parallelogram is 96 ft^2.

Practice

In 1–4, find the area of each parallelogram or rhombus.

1. 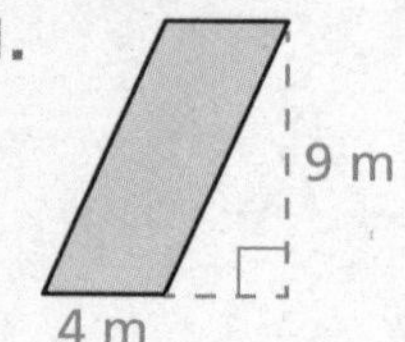

2. 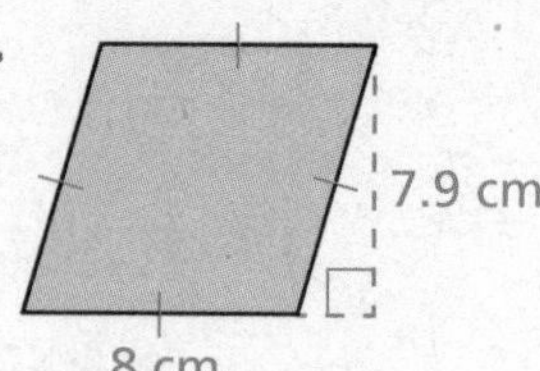

3. Rhombus
$b = 14$ in.
$h = 9$ in.

4. Parallelogram
$b = 12$ ft
$h = 8.5$ ft

5. A rhombus has an area of 375 mm^2 and a base of 25 mm. What is its height?

LESSON 7-2 Solve Triangle Area Problems

Quick Review

You can use the formula $A = \frac{1}{2}bh$ to find the area of any triangle.

Example

Find the area of the triangle.

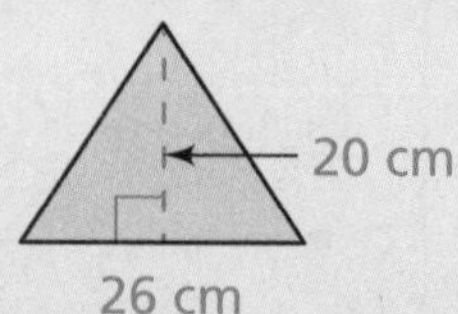

$A = \frac{1}{2} \times (26 \times 20)$

$A = 260$ cm^2

Practice

Find the area of each triangle.

1. 5 yd, 2 yd

2. 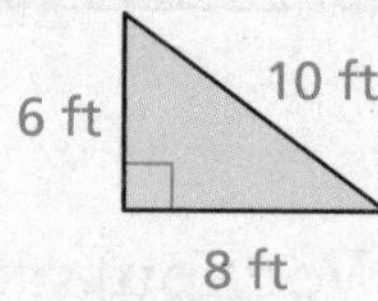

3. $b = 12.4$ cm
$h = 18$ cm

4. $b = 3.5$ m
$h = 6$ m

LESSON 7-3 Find Areas of Trapezoids and Kites

Quick Review

You can find the area of a trapezoid by decomposing it into a rectangle and one or more triangles. You can find the area of a kite by decomposing it into triangles.

Example

Find the area of the trapezoid and the kite.

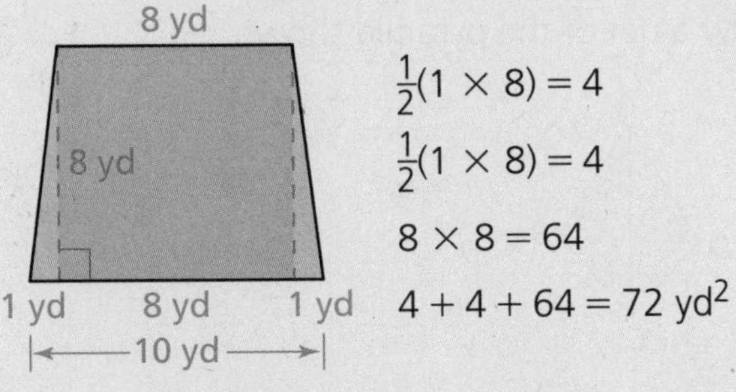

$\frac{1}{2}(1 \times 8) = 4$

$\frac{1}{2}(1 \times 8) = 4$

$8 \times 8 = 64$

$4 + 4 + 64 = 72 \text{ yd}^2$

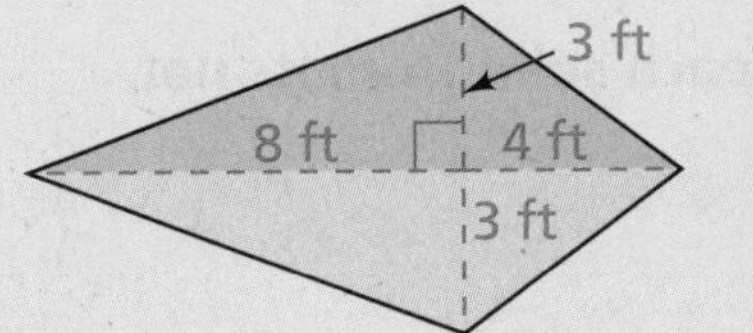

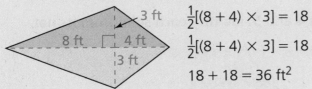

$\frac{1}{2}[(8 + 4) \times 3] = 18$

$\frac{1}{2}[(8 + 4) \times 3] = 18$

$18 + 18 = 36 \text{ ft}^2$

Practice

Find the area of each trapezoid or kite.

1. 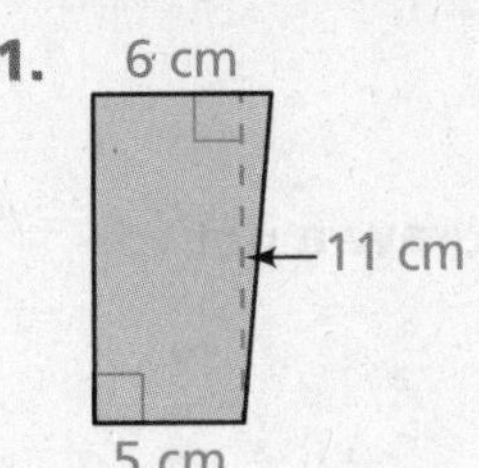

2. 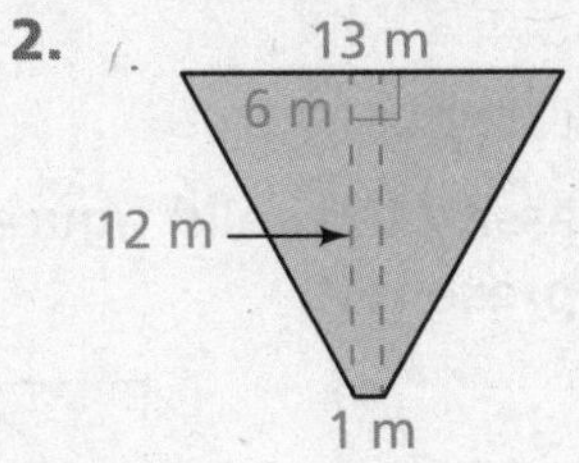

3. 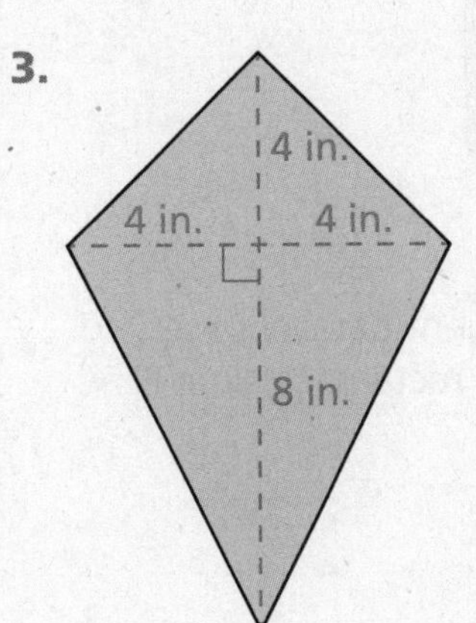

4. 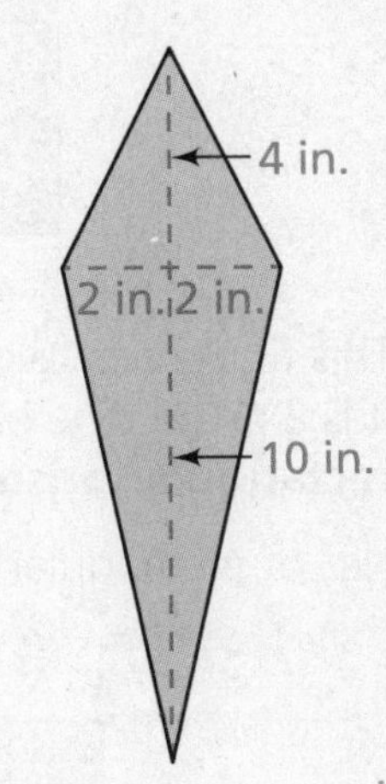

LESSON 7-4 Find Areas of Polygons

Quick Review

To find the area of a polygon, you can decompose or compose shapes, then use addition or subtraction to calculate the area.

Example

Find the area of the polygon.

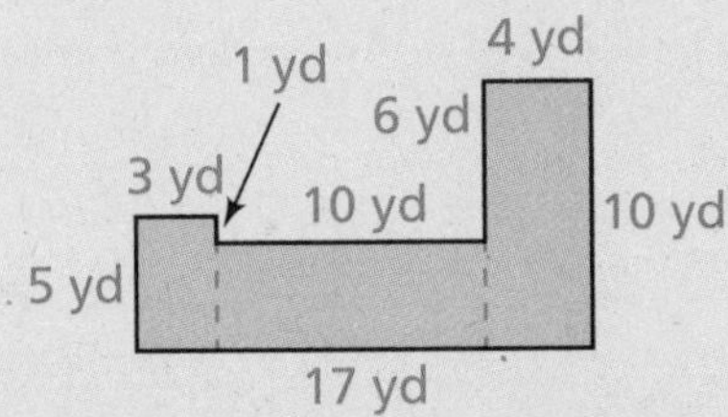

Area = $(3 \times 5) + (10 \times 4) + (4 \times 10)$

$= 15 + 40 + 40 = 95$

The area of the polygon is 95 yd^2.

Practice

1. Find the area of the polygon.

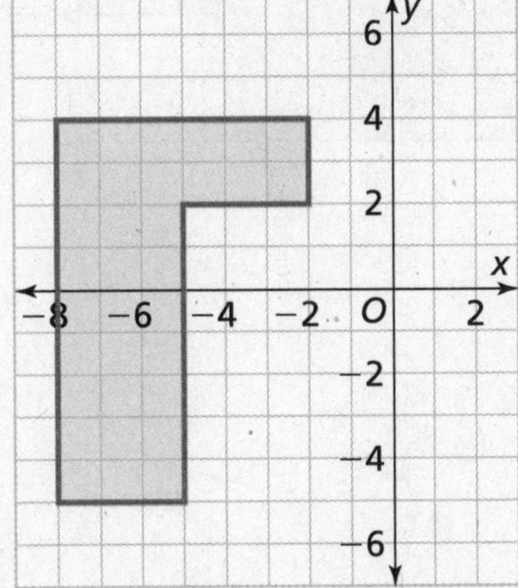

LESSON **7-5** Represent Solid Figures Using Nets

Quick Review

You can use nets to represent solid figures.

Example

Classify the solid figure and draw a net to represent it.

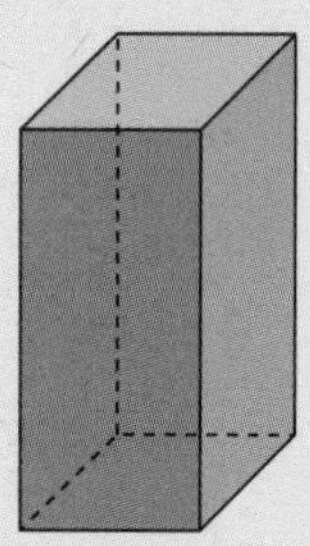

This figure has two congruent parallel bases, so it is a prism. The bases are rectangles, so it is a **rectangular prism**.

Net of rectangular prism:

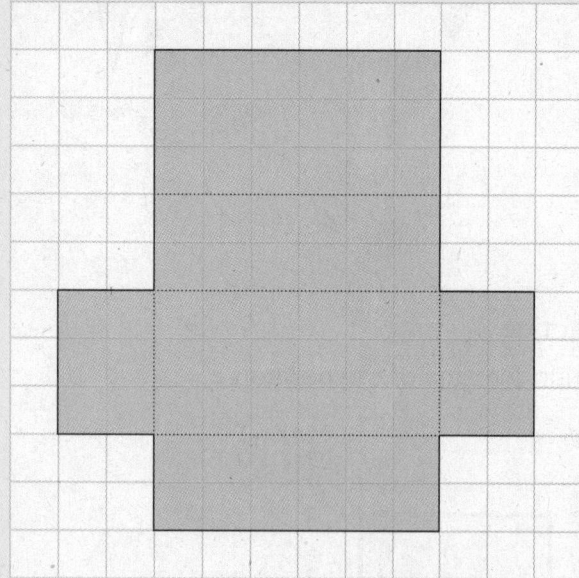

Practice

In 1 and 2, classify the solid figures.

1.

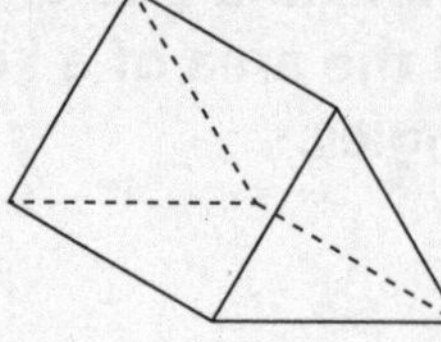

2.

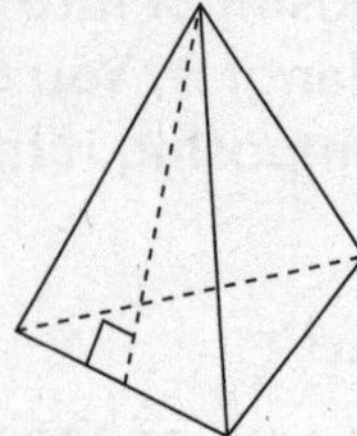

3. Draw a net of the pyramid shown.

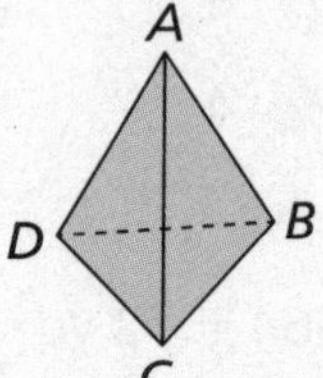

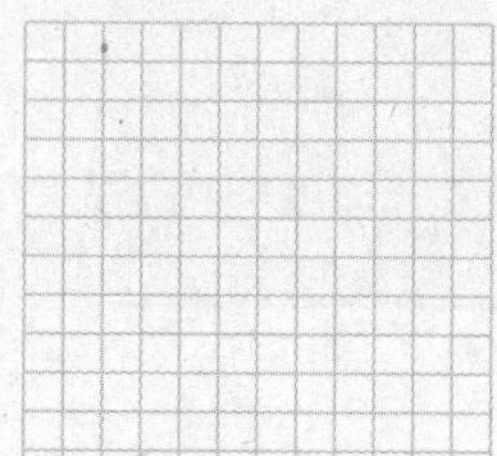

In 4 and 5, identify each solid from its net.

4.

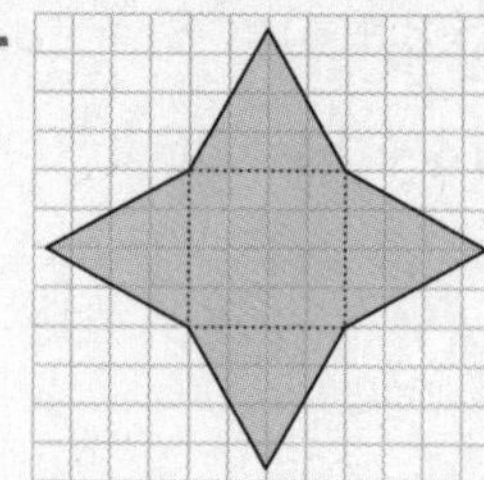

5.

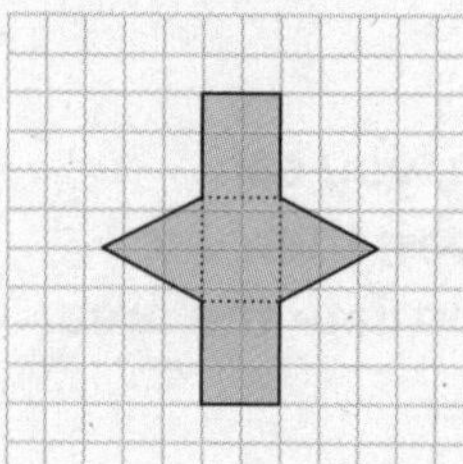

LESSON 7-6 Find Surface Areas of Prisms

Quick Review

You can use a net or a formula to find the surface area of a prism.

Example

Find the surface area.

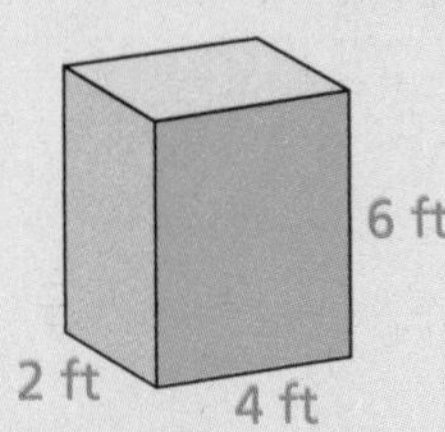

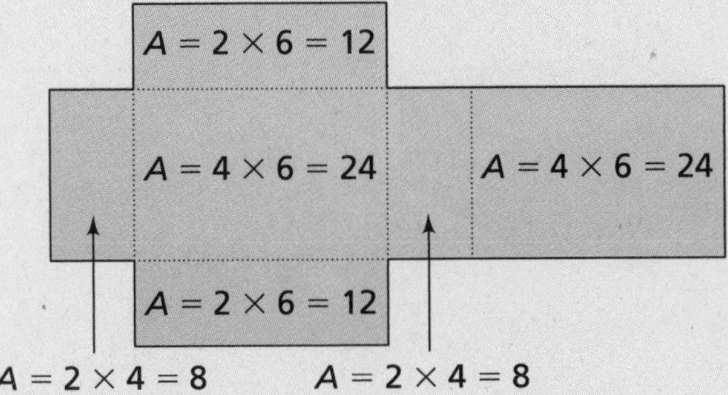

$SA = 2(8) + 2(12) + 2(24) = 88 \text{ ft}^2$

Practice

Find the surface area of each prism.

1.

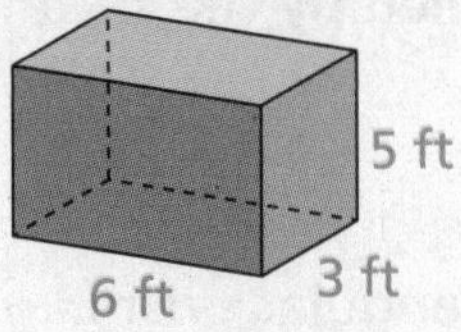

2.

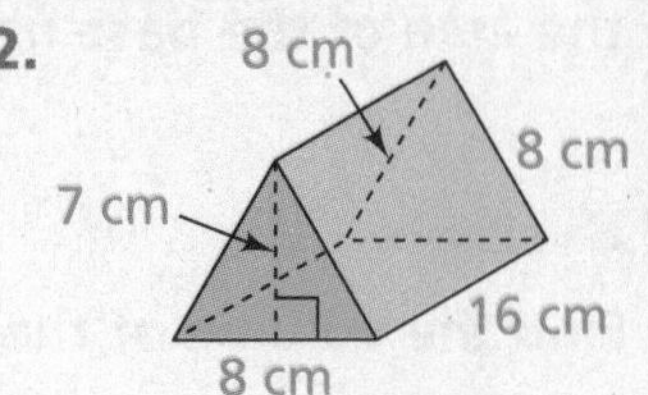

3. Cube
$s = 9.4$ m

4. Cube
$s = 7$ cm

5. Rectangular prism
$\ell = 12$ in.
$w = 7$ in.
$h = 3$ in.

6. Rectangular prism
$\ell = 5$ cm
$w = 6$ cm
$h = 7$ cm

LESSON 7-7 Find Surface Areas of Pyramids

Quick Review

You can use a net or a formula to find the surface area of a pyramid.

Example

Find the surface area.

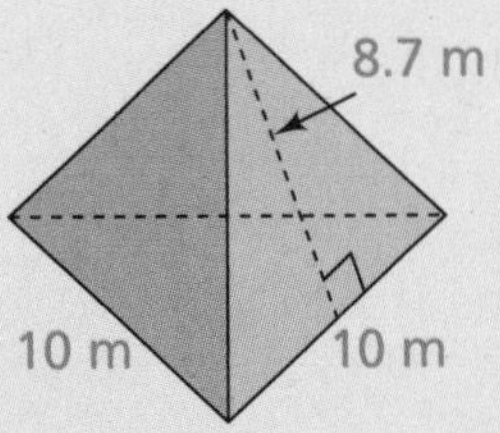

Area of one triangle:

$T = \frac{1}{2} \times 10 \times 8.7 = 43.5$

$SA = 4T$

$= 4 \times 43.5$

$= 174$

The surface area of the pyramid is 174 m^2.

Practice

In 1 and 2, find the surface area of each pyramid.

1.

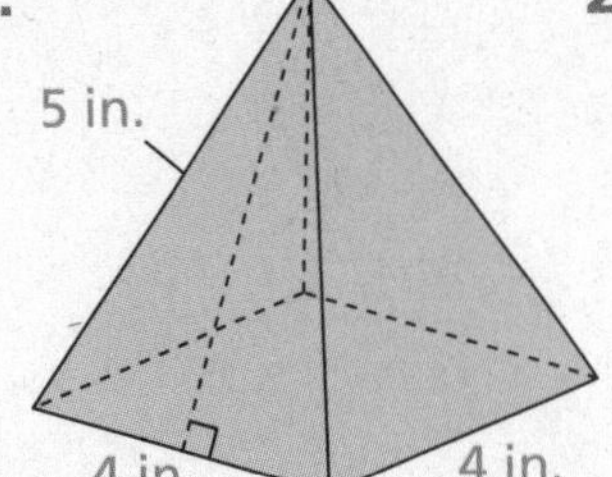

2.

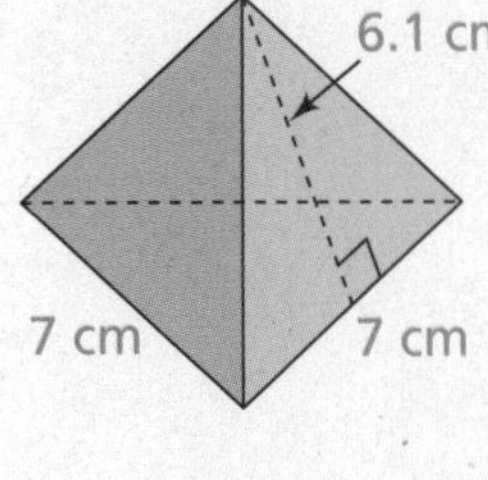

3. Each side of the base of a square pyramid is 10 ft and the height of each triangular face is 7 ft. Find the surface area of the pyramid.

LESSON 7-8 Find Volume with Fractional Edge Lengths

Quick Review

The volume of a rectangular prism is equal to the area of the base multiplied by the height.

Example

Find the volume of the rectangular prism.

STEP 1 Find the number of small $\frac{1}{4}$-in. cubes that will fill the prism.

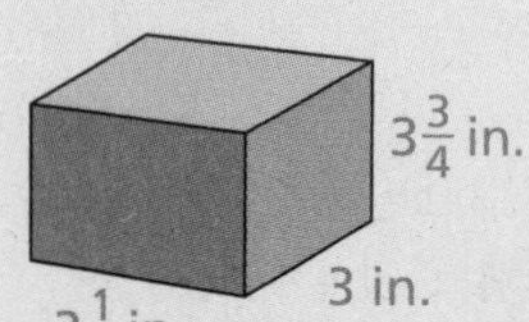

14 small $\frac{1}{4}$-in. cubes fit along the $3\frac{1}{2}$ in. side.

12 small $\frac{1}{4}$-in. cubes fit along the 3 in. side.

15 small $\frac{1}{4}$-in. cubes fit along the $3\frac{3}{4}$ in. side.

$14 \cdot 12 \cdot 15 = 2{,}520$ small $\frac{1}{4}$-in. cubes fill the prism.

STEP 2 Find the volume of each small $\frac{1}{4}$-in. cube.

$V = \ell wh = \frac{1}{4}\text{ in.} \cdot \frac{1}{4}\text{ in.} \cdot \frac{1}{4}\text{ in.} = \frac{1}{64}\text{ in.}^3$

STEP 3 Find the volume of the prism.

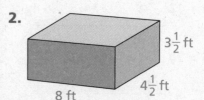

$2{,}520 \cdot \frac{1}{64}\text{ in.}^3 = 39\frac{3}{8}\text{ in.}^3$

You can also use a formula.

$V = \ell wh = 3\frac{1}{2}\text{ in.} \times 3\text{ in.} \times 3\frac{3}{4}\text{ in.} = 39\frac{3}{8}\text{ in.}^3$

Practice

Find the volume of each rectangular prism.

1.

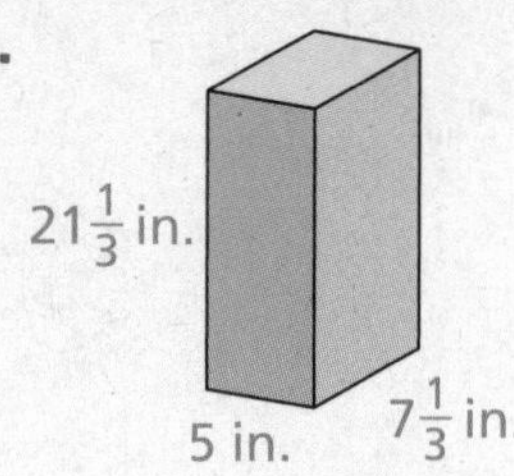

2.

$3\frac{1}{2}$ ft

$4\frac{1}{2}$ ft

8 ft

3.

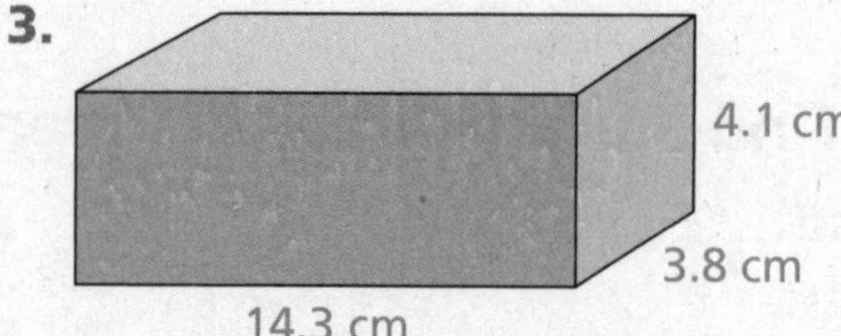

Hidden Clue

For each ordered pair, simplify the two coordinates. Then locate and label the corresponding point on the graph. Draw line segments to connect the points in alphabetical order. Connect *L* to *E* to complete the picture, then use the completed picture to help answer the riddle below.

I can...
multiply and divide multidigit decimals.
6.NS.B.3

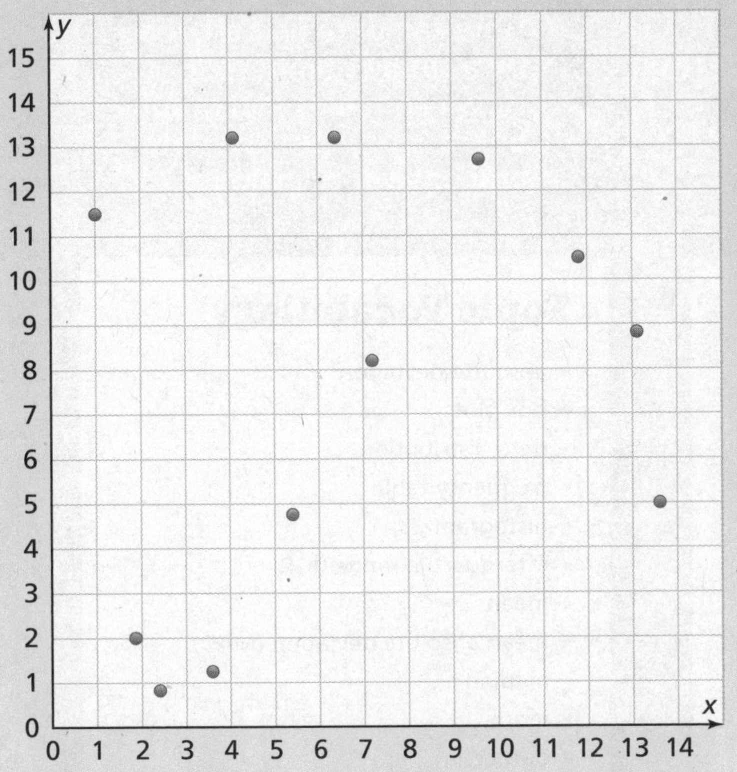

What goes up when rain comes down?

A (1.2 × 1.55, 2.7 ÷ 1.35) ___ , ___

B (1.25 × 1.92, 0.48 ÷ 0.6) ___ , ___

C (5.04 ÷ 1.4, 0.5 × 2.5) ___ , ___

D (2.16 × 2.5, 11.9 ÷ 2.5) ___ , ___

E (16.56 ÷ 2.3, 5.125 × 1.6) ___ , ___

F (6.12 ÷ 0.45, 6.25 × 0.8) ___ , ___

G (2.62 × 5, 12.32 ÷ 1.4) ___ , ___

H (29.5 × 0.4, 3.675 ÷ 0.35) ___ , ___

I (12.48 ÷ 1.3, 10.16 × 1.25) ___ , ___

J (20 × 0.32, 59.4 ÷ 4.5) ___ , ___

K (7.79 ÷ 1.9, 40 × 0.33) ___ , ___

L (25 × 0.04, 48.3 ÷ 4.2) ___ , ___

DISPLAY, DESCRIBE, AND SUMMARIZE DATA

? Topic Essential Question

How can data be described by a single number?
How can tables and graphs be used to represent data and answer questions?

Topic Overview

Topic Vocabulary

- absolute deviation
- box plot
- data distribution
- frequency table
- histogram
- interquartile range (IQR)
- mean
- mean absolute deviation (MAD)
- median
- mode
- outlier
- quartile
- range
- statistical question

Go online | **PearsonRealize.com**

Lesson Digital Resources

INTERACTIVE ANIMATION Interact with visual learning animations.

ACTIVITY Use with ***Solve & Discuss It***, ***Explore*** and ***Explain It*** activities, and to explore Example

VIDEOS Watch clips to support ***3-Act Mathema Modeling Lessons*** and ***STEM Projects***.

PRACTICE Practice what you've learned.

3-ACT MATH

Vocal Range

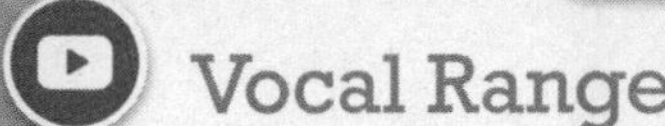

Vocal Range

Have you ever disagreed with the judge on a reality TV show? Reality TV competitions rely on the different opinions of the judges to make the show more exciting. There are lots of factors to consider when comparing two contestants on a show. Think about this during the 3-Act Mathematical Modeling lesson.

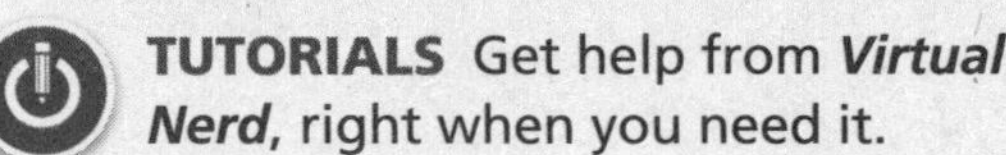

TUTORIALS Get help from ***Virtual Nerd***, right when you need it.

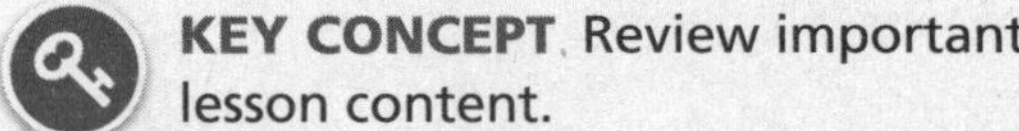

KEY CONCEPT Review important lesson content.

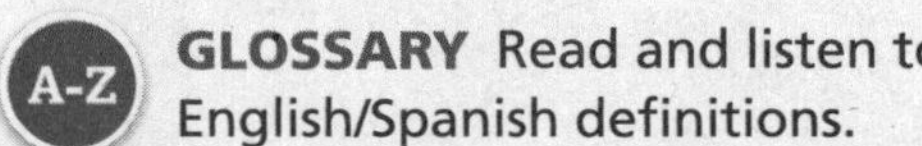

GLOSSARY Read and listen to English/Spanish definitions.

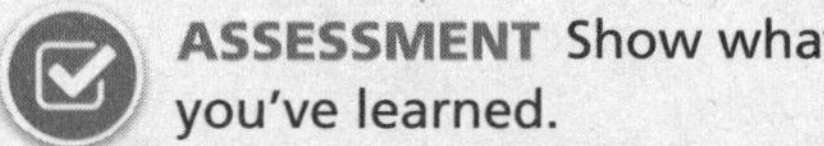

ASSESSMENT Show what you've learned.

Additional Digital Resources

MATH TOOLS Explore math with digital tools.

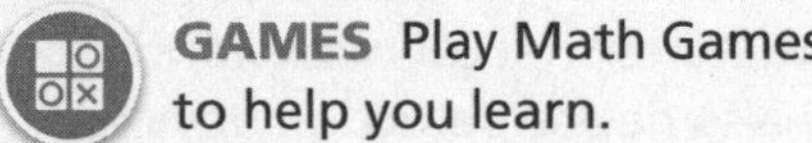

GAMES Play Math Games to help you learn.

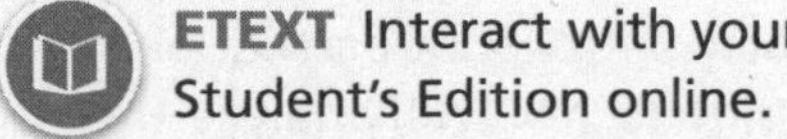

ETEXT Interact with your Student's Edition online.

TOPIC 8

STEM Project

Did You Know?

Earthquakes are caused by the sudden release of energy in the Earth's crust when friction between tectonic plates causes rocks to break along fault lines.

RING OF FIRE

PACIFIC OCEAN

Nearly 80% of Earth's largest earthquakes occur along the "Ring of Fire." Many tectonic plates meet in this horseshoe-shaped region around the Pacific Ocean.

The 1964 Alaskan earthquake magnitude of 9.2 was the strongest recorded in North America. It sent tsunamis as far away as Peru, New Zealand, and Japan.

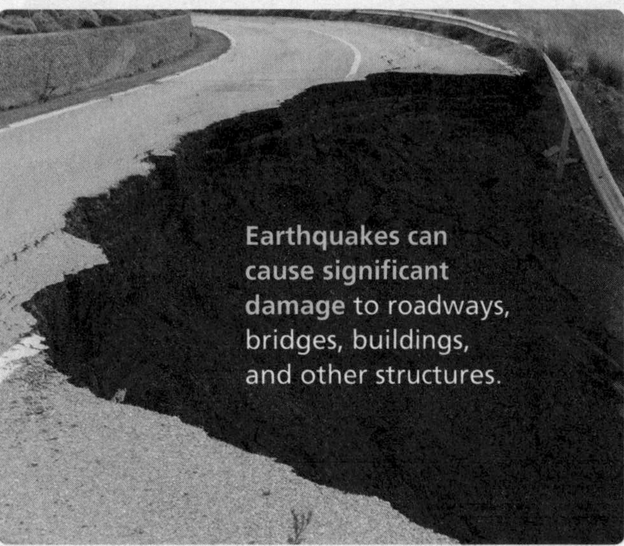

Earthquakes can cause significant damage to roadways, bridges, buildings, and other structures.

The shape of a pagoda is known for resisting damage from earthquakes.

Your Task: Shake It Up

Engineers design sturdy bridges, buildings, dams and other structures that can withstand earthquakes. They also devise detection devices to predict earthquakes. You and your classmates will gather and display data about earthquake frequency and magnitude. You will analyze the data and determine what constraints engineers must consider when designing roadways, bridges, homes, and other structures.

Review What You Know!

GET READY!

TOPIC 8

Vocabulary

Choose the best term from the box to complete each sentence.

bar graph
data
dot plot
tally chart

1. __________ are pieces of gathered information.
2. Display data as marks above a number line in a __________.
3. Use the lengths of bars to show and compare data in a __________.

Summarize Data

Use the number of text messages Henry sent each day: 6, 12, 2, 6, 3, 4, 2, 5, 6.

4. What is the least value?
5. What is the greatest value?
6. What numbers are repeated?
7. How many text messages did Henry send in all?

Display Data

8. The table shows the time students spend doing chores each day. Draw a dot plot to show the data.

Minutes Doing Chores Each Day
20, 25, 45, 20, 30, 40, 30, 25, 20, 15, 35, 40

Analyze Data

Use the graph to answer the questions about a student's test performance.

9. How many more points were earned on Test 3 than on Test 1?
10. Which two tests have the least difference in score? What is the difference?
11. What is the greatest difference between two scores? How do you know?

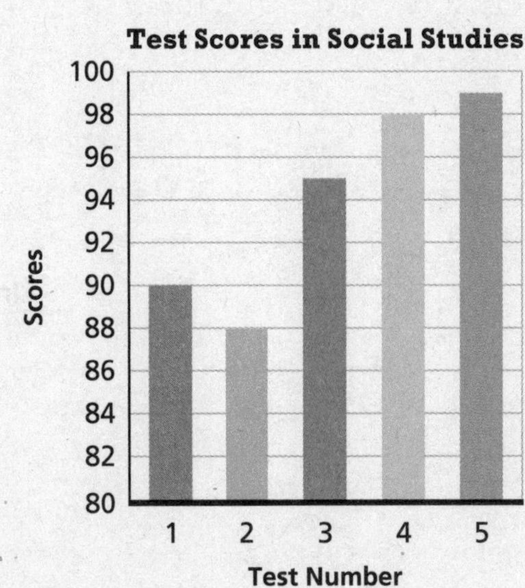

Build Vocabulary

Complete the graphic organizer by writing the definition of each measure.

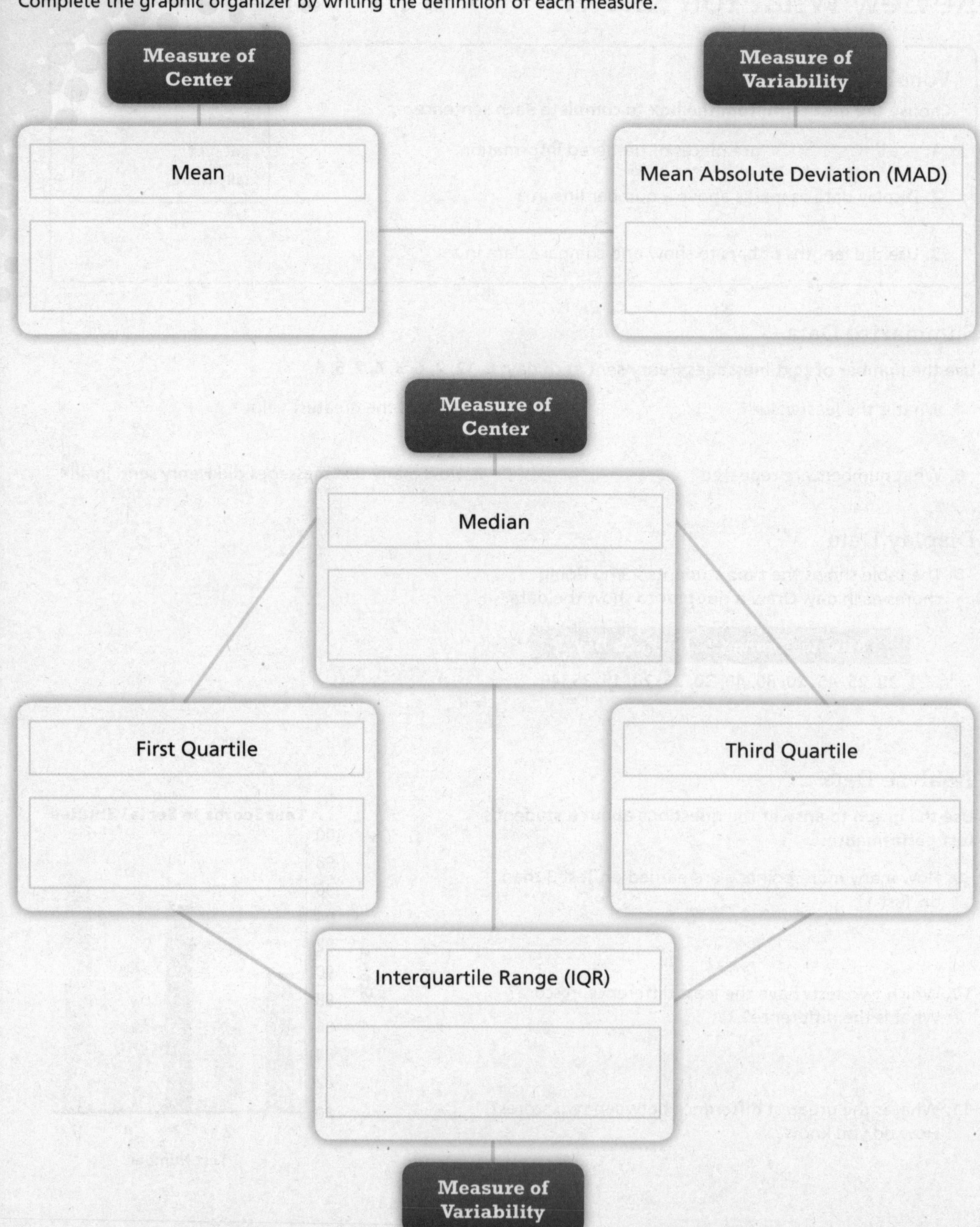

Lesson 8-1

Recognize Statistical Questions

Go Online | PearsonRealize.com

I can...
identify and write statistical questions.

Common Core Content Standards
6.SP.A.1, 6.SP.B.4

Mathematical Practices
MP.1, MP.2, MP.4, MP.8

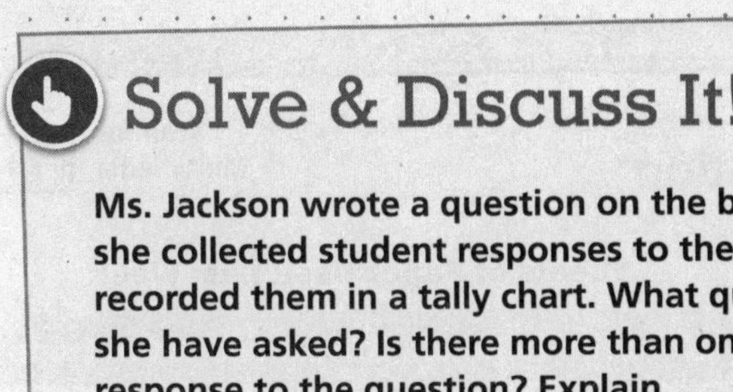

Solve & Discuss It!

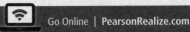

Ms. Jackson wrote a question on the board. Then she collected student responses to the question and recorded them in a tally chart. What question could she have asked? Is there more than one possible response to the question? Explain.

Make Sense and Persevere
What other questions could you ask that would result in a variety of numerical answers? MP.1

Focus on math practices

Reasoning Suppose Ms. Jackson wants to know the amount of time her students spent outdoors the previous afternoon. What question might she ask each student to gather the data? MP.2

Essential Question How are statistical questions different from other questions?

EXAMPLE 1  Recognize a Statistical Question

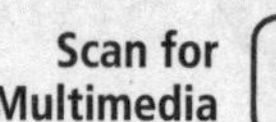

Scan for Multimedia

Mr. Borden asked his students a question and recorded the data in a table. What question did Mr. Borden ask?

- What is the area of an $8\frac{1}{2}$" × 11" sheet of notebook paper?
- How many sheets of paper did you use last week?
- Did Bill use notebook paper to write his book report?

Make Sense and Persevere How does thinking about possible answers to the questions help you determine which questions are statistical? MP.1

Sheets of Paper Used Last Week

Number of Sheets	Number of Students
5	I
10	I
15	II
20	IIII
25	𝍸 I
30	𝍸

A **statistical question** always has variability in the responses. This is, it has a range of responses.

The question *How many sheets of paper did you use last week?* can have a range of answers so it is a statistical question.

The questions *What is the area of an $8\frac{1}{2}$" × 11" sheet of notebook paper?* and *Did Bill use notebook paper to write his book report?* have only one answer, so they are not statistical questions.

Mr. Borden asked, *How many sheets of paper did you use last week?*

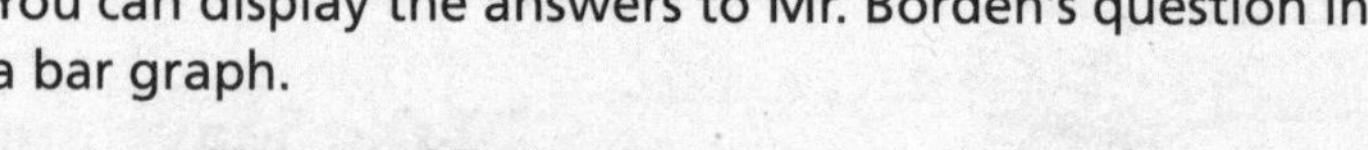

You can display the answers to Mr. Borden's question in a bar graph.

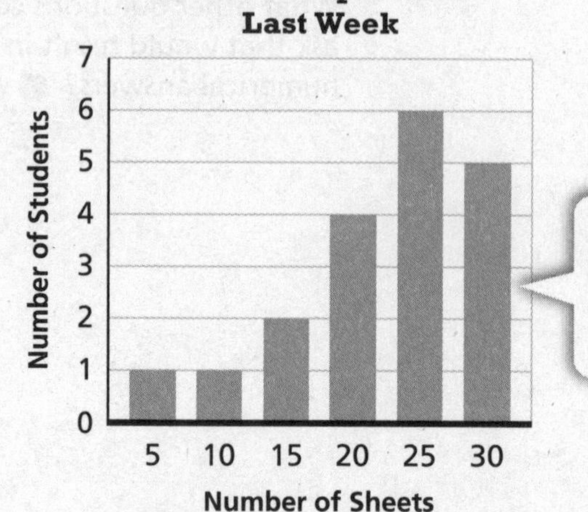

The bar graph shows that there is a range of possible answers to Mr. Borden's question.

Mr. Borden's question is a statistical question.

Try It!

Is the question *What was the high temperature on March 8 of last year?* a statistical question? Explain.

Convince Me! How could you change the question above to make it a statistical question?

EXAMPLE 2  Use Data to Identify a Statistical Question with Multiple Answers

Lucia surveyed the students in her class and made a dot plot of the results. What question could Lucia have asked?

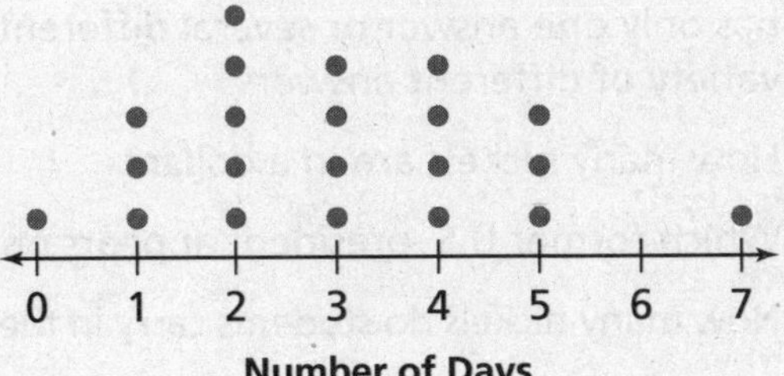

Look at the title and labels on the dot plot.

> **Model with Math** A dot plot can be used to display the answers to a statistical question. MP.4

The dot plot shows the number of days different students exercise each week. The statistical question Lucia could have asked is *How many days do you exercise each week?*

Try It!

What is another statistical question Lucia might ask about the exercise the students in her class do each week?

EXAMPLE 3  Use Data to Identify a Statistical Question with Two Answers

Dante surveyed students to see how they feel about a proposal to choose a new school mascot. The frequency table shows the results. What question did Dante likely ask? Is this a statistical question?

Dante likely asked a question such as *Do you want a new mascot?* There are only two answers, Yes or No. Because there is more than one possible answer, this is a statistical question.

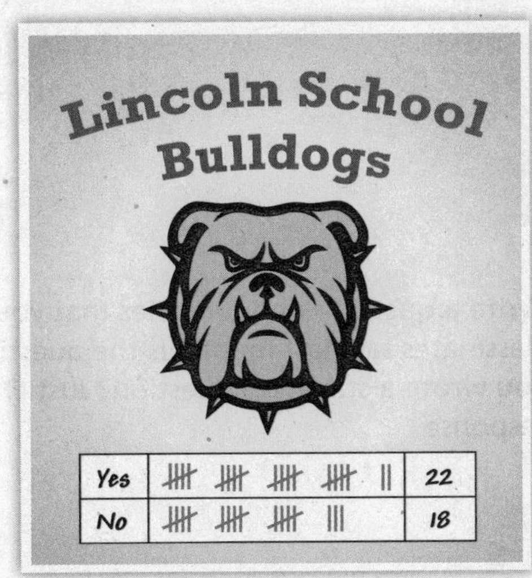

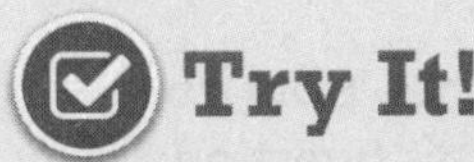

How could Dante change his statistical question so that there would be more than two possible answers?

KEY CONCEPT 

To recognize and write statistical questions, determine whether the question has only one answer or several different answers. Statistical questions have a variety of different answers.

How many nickels are in a dollar?	Not statistical
Which former U.S. president appears on a nickel?	Not statistical
How many nickels do students carry in their backpacks?	Statistical

Do You Understand?

1. **Essential Question** How are statistical questions different from other questions?

2. **Generalize** How does examining the answers to a question help you determine if the question is a statistical question? MP.8

3. Write a question about movies that your classmates saw last month. Is the question you wrote a statistical question? Justify your response.

4. Choose which is a statistical question: *What are the ages of the students in this class?* or *How many pennies equal 1 dollar?* Explain.

Do You Know How?

5. Determine which of the questions below are statistical questions.
   a. In which months are the birthdays of everyone in your class?
   b. Does Sue wear glasses?
   c. Who is the current president of the United States?
   d. How tall are the students in Grade 6?
   e. What is the least populated state?
   f. How many fish are in the pond?

6. Mr. Borden asked his students, *How far from school do students live?* Is his question a statistical question? Explain.

7. Mr. Borden also asked his students, *How do you get to school each day?* Is this question statistical? Explain.

Name: ____________________

Practice & Problem Solving

Scan for Multimedia

In 8 and 9, write a statistical question that you could ask to gather data on each topic.

8. Number of pets classmates own

9. Heights of different household plants

10. Kim asked her classmates, *How many siblings do you have?* She collected the following responses: 0, 1, 2, 1, 2, 0, 3, 1, 0, 5, 5, 1, 3, 1, 0, 2, 4, 1, 3, 0. Make a dot plot to display the data.

11. Sergei asked his classmates, *Will you take Spanish or French next year?* He collected these responses: 15 classmates chose Spanish and 13 chose French. Make a frequency table to display the data.

12. Is the following a statistical question? Explain. *How many plays do students see in a year?*

13. Is the following a statistical question? Explain. *How do shoppers in a town pay for groceries?*

In 14 and 15, use the dot plot at the right.

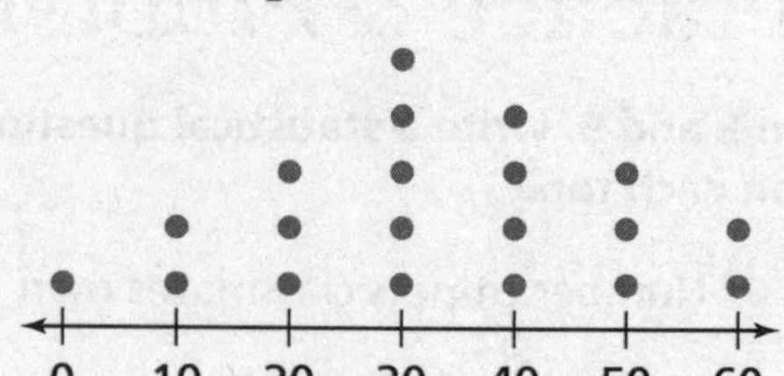

14. Make Sense and Persevere What statistical question could have been asked to collect the data shown in the dot plot? MP.1

15. Higher Order Thinking If the data in the dot plot show how many minutes students spent on homework the previous night, how many hours in all did these students spend doing homework? Did a typical student from this group spend more or fewer than 20 minutes on homework?

16. Vocabulary Wyatt says that a *statistical question* must have a numerical answer. Do you agree with Wyatt? Explain.

17. Reasoning Ms. Miller asks parents, *Do you support switching to a new lunch vendor for our school program?* How many different responses could she get? Is this a statistical question? MP.2

Assessment Practice

18. Ms. Williams asked each student in her class these two questions:

- *How many digits are in a phone number, including the area code?*
- *In a typical week, on how many days do you spend some time watching television?*

PART A

Which of the questions that Ms. Williams asked is a statistical question? Explain.

PART B

The results of the statistical question that Ms. Williams asked are shown below. Make a bar graph to display the data.

2 3 0 5 4 1 2 3 7 2
1 6 0 2 2 1 3 4 3 4

Solve & Discuss It!

ACTIVITY

Eight students were surveyed about the number of hours they spend each week reading for fun. Order their responses from least to greatest values. What do you notice about the number of hours these students spent reading each week?

Lesson 8-2
Summarize Data Using Mean, Median, Mode, and Range

Go Online | PearsonRealize.com

I can...
identify the mean, median, mode, and range of a data set.

Common Core Content Standards
6.SP.A.3, 6.SP.B.5c

Mathematical Practices
MP.2, MP.3, MP.7, MP.8

Look for Relationships
How does ordering the responses from least to greatest help you analyze the data set? MP.7

Focus on math practices

Critique Reasoning Jamal says that the middle value in a data set is the number that occurs most often. Evan disagrees. Why does Jamal say what he says and why does Evan disagree? Explain. MP.3

Essential Question How can you use a single measure to describe a data set?

EXAMPLE 1 Use the Mean to Describe a Data Set

Scan for Multimedia

Carla is in a bowling league. The league is ranking the teams by average score. What is the mean, or average, final score of the five bowlers on Carla's team?

The **mean**, or average, is the sum of all the values in a data set divided by the total number of data values in the set.

Generalize You can summarize a data set by using a mean. MP.8

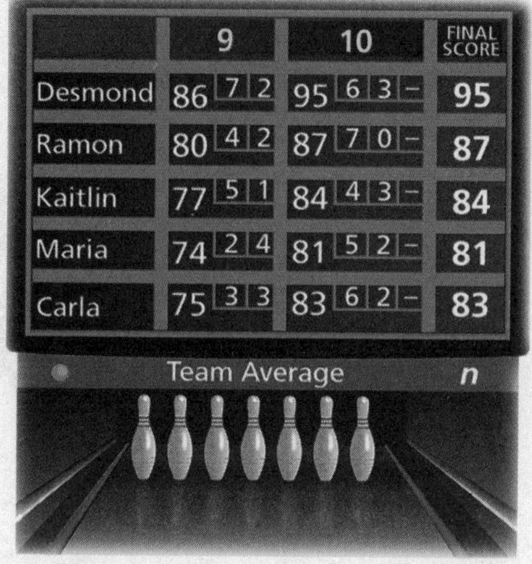

9
10
FINAL SCORE
Desmond 86 7 2 95 6 3 – 95
Ramon 80 4 2 87 7 0 – 87
Kaitlin 77 5 1 84 4 3 – 84
Maria 74 2 4 81 5 2 – 81
Carla 75 3 3 83 6 2 – 83
Team Average n

To find the mean, equally share the final scores among the five bowlers.

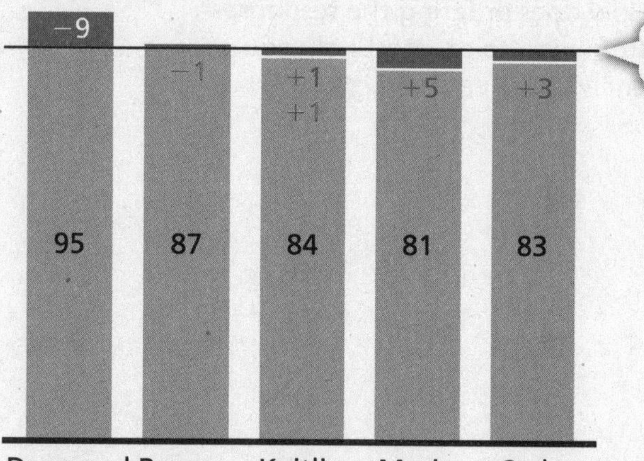

A mean is a measure of center. A measure of center summarizes a data set with a single value.

To calculate the mean, add the scores in the data set. Then divide the sum by the number of values in the data set.

$$\begin{array}{r} \overset{2}{9}5 \\ 87 \\ 84 \\ 81 \\ +\,83 \\ \hline 430 \end{array} \qquad \begin{array}{r} 86 \\ 5\overline{)430} \\ -\,40 \\ \hline 30 \\ -\,30 \\ \hline 0 \end{array}$$

The mean, or average, final score is 86.

Try It!

The next week, Maria bowls a 151-point game. The other bowlers match their scores. What is the new mean final score for the team? Explain.

Convince Me! How did the mean final score change from the Example to the Try It!?

EXAMPLE 2  Use the Median to Describe a Data Set

Trey and Sarah each download songs to their music libraries. Their players list each type of music and the total playing time in minutes for each type. How can Trey and Sarah each summarize their data sets using the median?

The **median** is a measure of center. It is the middle data value. To find the median, order the values from least to greatest, then find the middle value.

Trey's Music Library

Music Type	Minutes
Blues	62
Classical	72
Country	61
Gospel	67
Jazz	67
Movie Soundtrack	63
Popular	59

Sarah's Music Library

Music Type	Minutes
Rock	37
Rap	42
Hip Hop	38
Bluegrass	46
New Age	51
Opera	35

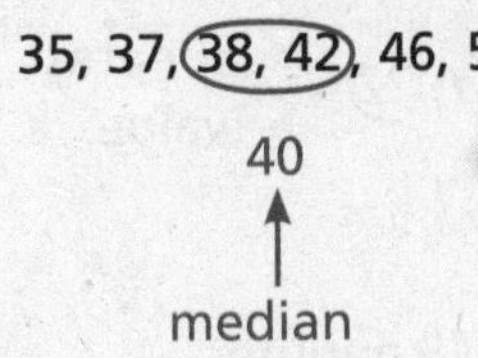

Find the median for Trey's data set.

59, 61, 62, (63), 67, 67, 72

↑ median

Trey's median playing time is 63 minutes.

Find the median for Sarah's data set.

35, 37, (38, 42), 46, 51

40

↑ median

The median is the average of the two middle values.

Sarah's median playing time is 40 minutes.

EXAMPLE 3  Use the Mode to Describe a Data Set

Look at Trey's and Sarah's music libraries. How can Trey and Sarah each summarize their data sets using the mode?

The **mode** is a measure of center. It is the value that occurs most often. A data set can have one mode, no mode, or more than one mode.

Find the mode for Trey's data set.

59, 61, 62, 63, (67), (67), 72

mode

The value 67 appears twice. Every other value only appears once.

Trey's mode playing time is 67 minutes.

Find the mode for Sarah's data set.

35, 37, 38, 42, 46, 51

No values repeat in Sarah's data set.

There is no mode playing time in Sarah's data set.

Try It!

Nadia's grades on four quizzes were 95, 75, 85, and 95. Find the mean, median, and mode for Nadia's grades.

EXAMPLE 4  Use the Range to Describe a Data Set

Look at Trey's and Sarah's music libraries. What is the range of the playing times in each of their data sets?

The **range** is a measure of variability. A measure of variability describes how the values in a data set vary with a single number. The range is the difference of the greatest value and the least value.

Trey's Music Library

Music Type	Minutes
Blues	62
Classical	72
Country	61
Gospel	67
Jazz	67
Movie Soundtrack	63
Popular	59

Sarah's Music Library

Music Type	Minutes
Rock	37
Rap	42
Hip Hop	38
Bluegrass	46
New Age	51
Opera	35

Find the range for Trey's data set.

least value → (59), 61, 62, 63, 67, 67, (72) ← greatest value

72 − 59 = (13) ← range

The range of playing times is 13 minutes.

Find the range for Sarah's data set.

least value → (35), 37, 38, 42, 46, (51) ← greatest value

51 − 35 = (16) ← range

The range of playing times is 16 minutes.

EXAMPLE 5  Use the Mean, Median, Mode, and Range to Describe a Data Set

Seven people waited in line for the "Whirl and Twirl" carnival ride. Find the mean, median, mode, and range of the wait times for the carnival ride. What do the mean, median, and mode tell you about the wait times? What does the range, as a measure of variability, tell you about the wait times?

Carnival Ride Wait Times

Person	Wait time (min.)
A	12
B	12
C	15
D	10
E	14
F	15
G	13

Mean: 13

Median: 13

Modes: 12 and 15

Range: 5

The mean, median, and mode each give a measure of the typical wait time for the ride. The mean and median wait times were 13 minutes. Two pairs each waited 12 or 15 minutes. The range uses a single number to describe how the wait times vary. The wait times vary by 5 minutes.

Try It!

Find the mean, median, mode, and range for the following set of data.

4, 6, 8, 3, 2, 1, 0, 12, 9

KEY CONCEPT

You can summarize a set of data using a measure of center, such as the mean, median, or mode, or a measure of variability, such as the range.

Number of Hours of TV Watched in a Week	
Juan	7
Tyrone	10
Abigail	16
Lateisha	9
Helen	12
Albert	21
Tim	14
Josh	8
Anita	13
Henry	15

Mean

$(7 + 10 + 16 + 9 + 12 + 21 + 14 + 8 + 13 + 15) \div 10 = 12.5$

Median

7, 8, 9, 10, 12, 13, 14, 15, 16, 21

$(12 + 13) \div 2 = 12.5$

Mode

7, 8, 9, 10, 12, 13, 14, 15, 16, 21

There is no mode.

Range

7, 8, 9, 10, 12, 13, 14, 15, 16, 21

$21 - 7 = 14$

The average number of hours of TV watched each week is 12.5 hours. The range of hours watched is 14 hours.

Do You Understand?

1. **Essential Question** How can you use a single measure to describe a data set?

2. Maddie scored 3 goals, 2 goals, and 4 goals during her last three soccer games. How can you find the mean, or average, number of goals Maddie scored?

3. **Use Structure** Why is it important to order the data when finding the median? MP.7

Do You Know How?

The table shows data about the students in three classes.

Teacher	Boys	Girls
Ms. Green	15	14
Mr. Nesbit	12	12
Ms. Jackson	12	16

4. What is the mean number of boys in the three classes? What is the mean number of girls in the three classes?

5. What is the mode of the number of girls in the three classes?

6. What is the median number of students in the three classes?

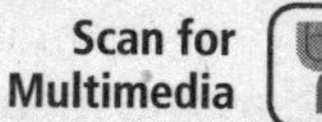

PRACTICE TUTORIAL

Name: ______________________________

Practice & Problem Solving

Scan for Multimedia

In 7–10, use the data shown in the table to find each mean.

7. Technical marks from judges

8. Presentation marks from judges

9. Find the combined marks, or total score, awarded by each of the 7 judges. Record your answers in the table.

10. What is the mean total score awarded by the judges?

A U.S. Figure Skater's Scores

Judge	Technical Marks	Presentation Marks	Total Score
A	5.9	5.4	
B	5.8	5.7	
C	5.8	5.6	
D	5.6	5.3	
E	5.9	5.5	
F	5.6	5.3	
G	6.0	5.7	

In 11–14, use the data in the table.

States Traveled To or Lived In
1, 3, 5, 2, 5, 2, 10, 7, 1, 2, 4, 1, 2, 7, 12

11. Order the data from least to greatest.

12. What are the median, mode, and range of the data?

13. Use Structure The student who traveled to 3 states visited 3 new states during a vacation. Does increasing the 3 to 6 change the median? If so, how? MP.7

14. Look for Relationships Does increasing the 3 to 6 change the mode? If so, how? MP.7

In 15–17, use the data table.

Forecasted Temperatures

Day	Low (°F)	High (°F)
Monday	42	55
Tuesday	44	57
Wednesday	45	60
Thursday	34	45
Friday	40	50

15. What is the average low temperature forecasted for the five days?

16. What is the average high temperature forecasted for the five days?

17. The forecast for Wednesday is later changed to a high of 70°F. Without calculating the new mean, describe how this changes the mean high temperature for the 5 days.

18. **Vocabulary** What term is used to describe the difference between the greatest and the least values of a data set?

19. **Critique Reasoning** Lewis thinks that since the data 5, 0, 4, 0, 0 has a mode of 0, the data has no mode. Critique Lewis's reasoning. MP.3

20. Chester scored 84, 88, and 80 on his first 3 math tests. How can you find Chester's mean, or average, score on these tests?

21. **Reasoning** Use the information in Exercise 20. Suppose Chester scores a 90 on his next test. Without doing any calculations, will Chester's mean score increase, decrease, or stay the same? Explain. MP.2

22. On Monday, Jeremiah collects data on the number of cars that pass through an intersection each hour from 6 A.M. to 10 A.M. He records the following data: 15, 27, 37, 29, and 12. If Jeremiah removes the 12 from his data set, will the mean change? Explain.

23. On Tuesday, Jeremiah finds the mean number of cars that pass through the same intersection from 6 A.M. to 10 A.M. was 22. Using the data from Exercise 22, how many fewer cars passed through the intersection on Tuesday?

In 24–26, use the data table.

Known Number of Moons of the Planets	
Mercury	0
Venus	0
Earth	1
Mars	2
Jupiter	50
Saturn	53
Uranus	27
Neptune	13

24. What are the median, mode, and range of these data?

25. What is the mean number of moons for the 8 planets, rounded to the nearest whole number?

26. If you include Pluto's moons in the data, the median is 5.

a. How many moons does Pluto have? Explain.

b. Would including Pluto affect the range of the data? Explain.

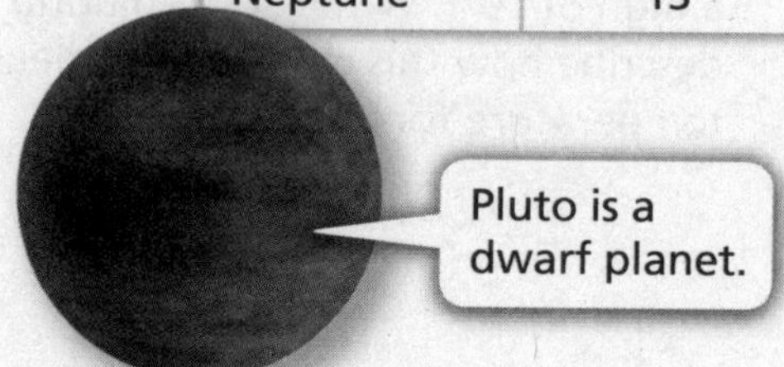

Pluto is a dwarf planet.

27. Higher Order Thinking Is the median always, sometimes, or never one of the data values? Explain.

28. Critique Reasoning Maria says the mean of the scores 7, 8, 3, 0, 2 is 5, because she added the scores and divided by 4. Is she correct? Explain why or why not. MP.3

Assessment Practice

29. Use the data table to find the statistical measures. Draw a line to match each measure on the left to its value on the right.

mean	$257
median	$265
mode	$269
range	$299

Cost of Snowboards ($) at Ski Shop
265
237
325
281
265
252
494
273

Solve & Discuss It!

To track how many raisins are needed for packaging, a quality control inspector at a food processing plant collected data for the number of raisins in small boxes. Describe the data, including minimum value, maximum value, and median. Then describe what you notice about the values between the minimum and the median, and between the median and maximum.

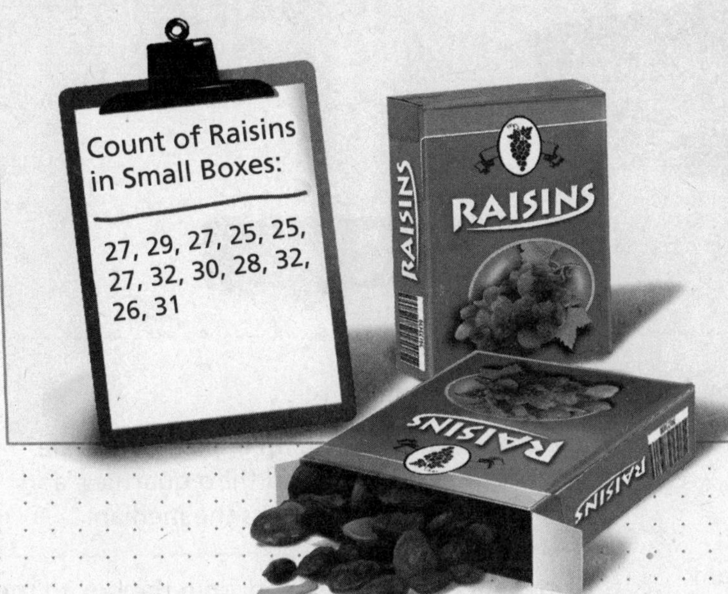

Lesson 8-3

Display Data in Box Plots

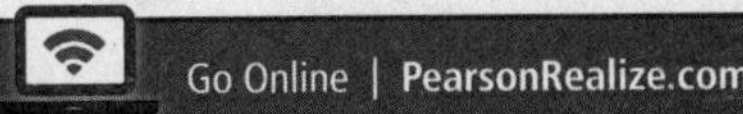

I can...
make and interpret box plots.

Common Core Content Standards
6.SP.B.4

Mathematical Practices
MP.1, MP.2, MP.3, MP.4

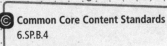

Reasoning How can ordering the numbers of raisins in small boxes from least to greatest help you find the median? MP.2

Focus on math practices

Construct Arguments The median of the first half of the data is 26.5, and the median of the second half of the data is 30.5. Why would this information be helpful and what do those medians show? Explain. MP.3

Essential Question Why is a box plot useful for representing certain types of data?

EXAMPLE 1  Make a Box Plot

Scan for Multimedia 

Helen wants to display the lengths of 15 fish she caught this year to compare to the lengths of fish she caught last year. How can she use the data to make a box plot?

Length of Fish (in.)		
7	9	10
7	13	13
10	15	15
18	11	13
22	14	17

A box plot is a diagram that shows the distribution of data values using the median, quartiles, minimum value, and maximum value on a number line.

Find the minimum, median, and maximum values of the data.

(7) 7, 9, 10, 10, 11, 13, (13) 13, 14, 15, 15, 17, 18, (22)

Minimum — Median — Maximum

Find the median for each half.

7, 7, 9, (10) 10, 11, 13, (13) 13, 14, 15, (15) 17, 18, 22

First Quartile (Median of 1st Half) — Second Quartile (Median) — Third Quartile (Median of 2nd Half)

Quartiles are values that divide a data set into four equal parts.

Draw the box plot.

Show a number line with an appropriate scale, a box between the first and third quartiles, and a vertical segment that shows the median.

Draw segments that extend from the box to the minimum value and to the maximum value.

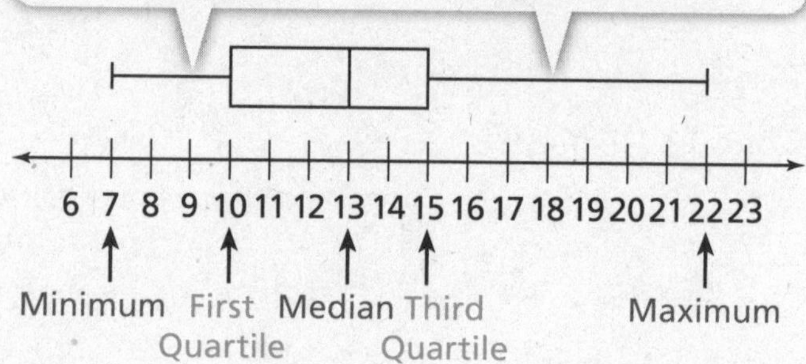

Try It!

The lengths in inches of 11 fish that Helen caught last year are listed below.

7, 8, 12, 12, 12, 13, 14, 15, 16, 17, 22

Circle the first quartile, median, and third quartile.

Convince Me! How is the distribution of Helen's data this year different from Helen's data last year? Draw a box plot of last year's data and use it to support your answer.

6 7 8 9 10 11 12 13 14 15 16 17 18 19 20 21 22 23

ACTIVITY

ASSESS

EXAMPLE 2  Make a Box Plot When the Number of Values Is Even

The Earth Club collected enough donations online to build compost bins. How can the club record the donation information in a box plot?

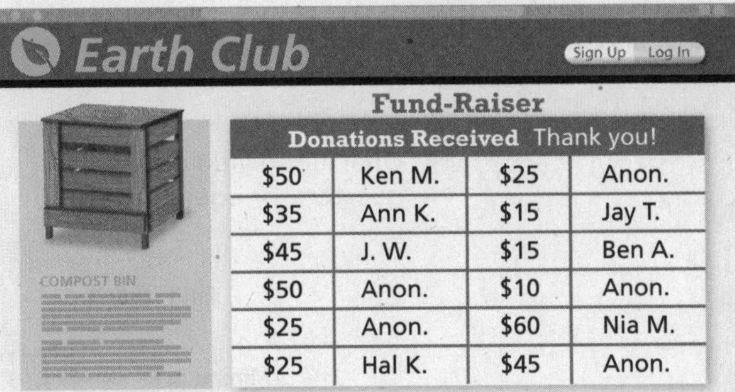

Fund-Raiser

Donations Received	Thank you!		
$50	Ken M.	$25	Anon.
$35	Ann K.	$15	Jay T.
$45	J. W.	$15	Ben A.
$50	Anon.	$10	Anon.
$25	Anon.	$60	Nia M.
$25	Hal K.	$45	Anon.

Model with Math A box plot is helpful when analyzing a data set because it visually represents the data set by dividing it into four equal parts. A data table does not visually show the division of data. MP.4

STEP 1 Find the minimum, median, and maximum values as well as the first and third quartiles.

There are 12 values. So, the median is the average of the two middle numbers.

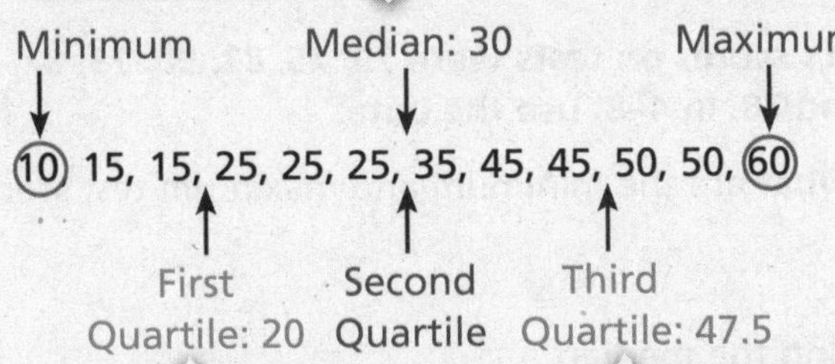

There are 6 values in each half. The quartiles are the averages of the two middle numbers in each half.

STEP 2 Draw a box plot.

The donation values range from $10 to $60, in $5 increments. So, a good scale for the number line is $5 to $65, numbered by 5s.

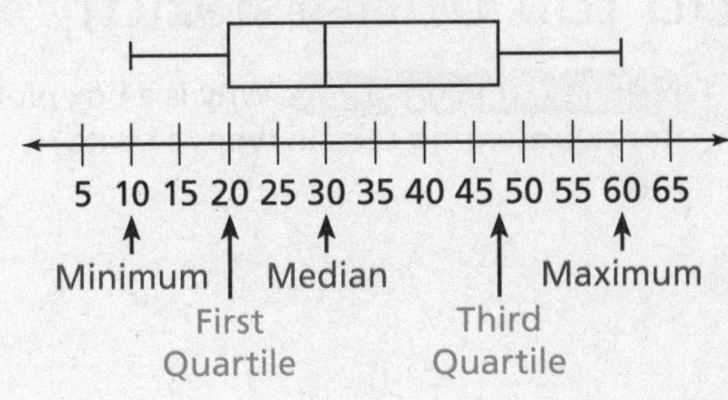

EXAMPLE 3  Interpret a Box Plot

The box plot shows the distribution of the weights, in pounds, of bags of donated clothing. What information do you know from the box plot?

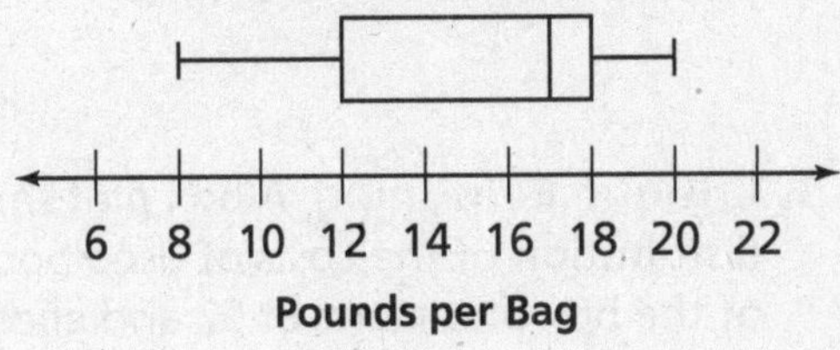

The minimum is 8, so the lightest bag weighs 8 pounds.

The maximum is 20, so the heaviest bag weighs 20 pounds.

The median weight for the bags is about 17 pounds.

The first quartile weight is 12 pounds, and the third quartile weight is 18 pounds.

Try It!

The ages of 12 volunteers participating in a beach clean-up are shown:

15, 27, 9, 15, 21, 9, 21, 9, 15, 21, 21, 24

Record the ages in a box plot.

KEY CONCEPT

A box plot shows a distribution of data values on a number line. A box plot visually represents a data set divided into four equal parts.

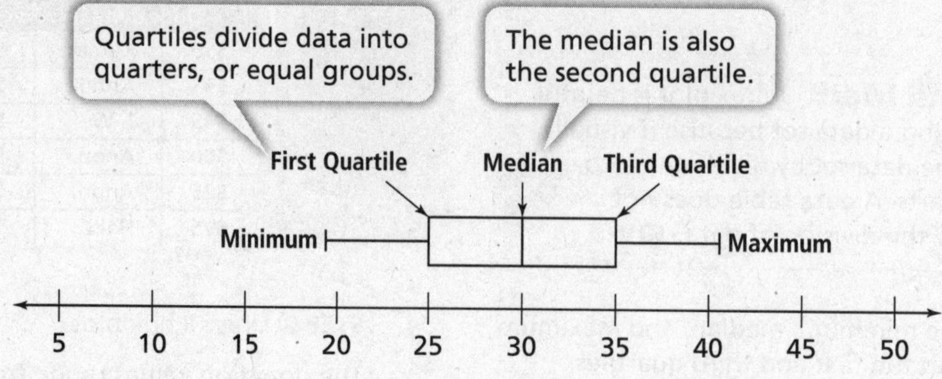

Do You Understand?

1. **Essential Question** Why is a box plot useful for representing certain types of data?

2. What values are included inside the box of a box plot?

3. **Critique Reasoning** A box plot shows the distribution of the costs of used books. The box of the box plot starts at $2 and ends at $5. Alex says this means that about one-quarter of the books cost between $2 and $5. Is Alex correct? Explain. MP.3

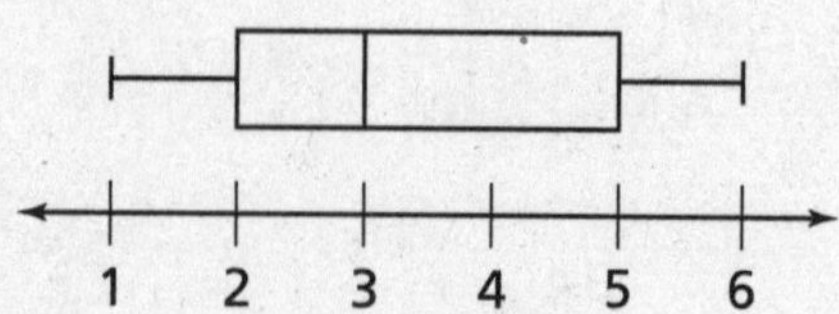

Do You Know How?

Sarah's scores on tests were 79, 75, 82, 90, 73, 82, 78, 85, and 78. In 4–8, use the data.

4. What are the minimum and maximum test scores?

5. Find the median.

6. Find the first and the third quartiles.

7. Draw a box plot that shows the distribution of Sarah's test scores.

8. Eric is in Sarah's class. This box plot shows his scores on the same nine tests. How do Eric's scores compare to Sarah's?

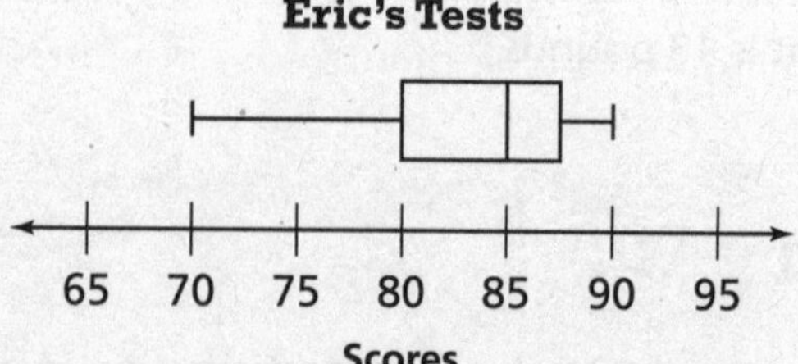

PRACTICE TUTORIAL

Name: ______________________________

Practice & Problem Solving

Scan for Multimedia

Leveled Practice In 9 and 10, use this data set, which shows how many minutes Enzo practiced violin each day for 10 days.

40, 25, 45, 55, 30, 25, 30, 50, 30, 40

9. Find the statistical measures that you need to make a box plot of Enzo's practice times.

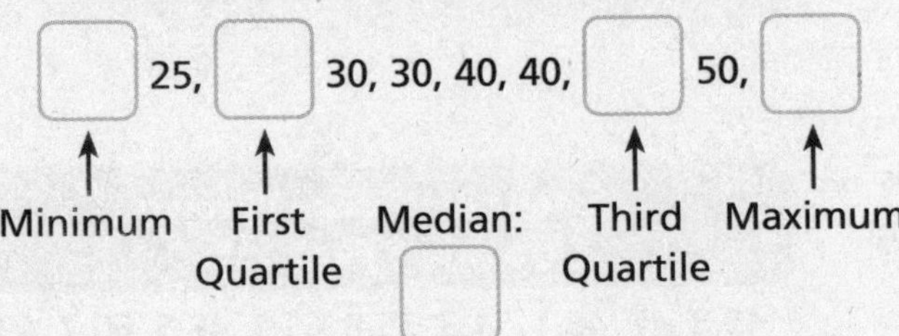

10. Complete the box plot to represent Enzo's practice times.

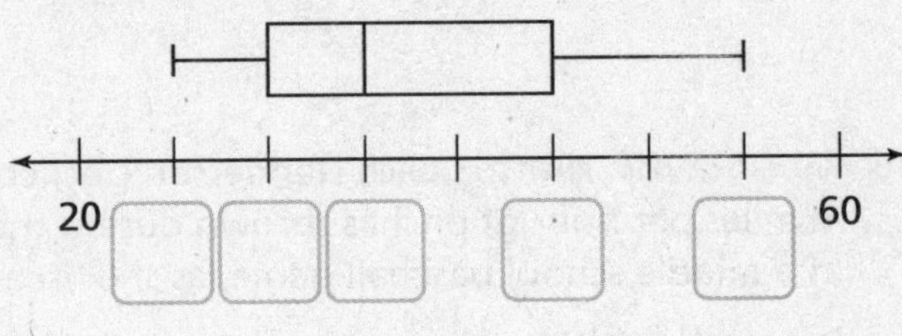

In 11 and 12, use this data set, which shows the prices, in dollars, of tickets to 10 plays at the community theater.

14, 22, 8, 14, 16, 8, 20, 14, 10, 18

11. Find the minimum, maximum, median, and quartile ticket prices.

Minimum: ☐ First Quartile: ☐

Median: ☐ Third Quartile: ☐

Maximum: ☐

12. Make a box plot to display the ticket prices.

In 13 and 14, draw box plots using the data provided.

13. The sprint times, in seconds, of students who tried out for the track team:

44, 40, 40, 42, 49, 43, 41, 47, 54, 48, 42, 52, 48

14. Scores earned on science tests:

73, 78, 66, 61, 85, 90, 99, 76, 64, 70, 72, 72, 93, 81

In 15 and 16, use the box plot to answer the question.

15. How many words per minute does the fastest keyboarder type?

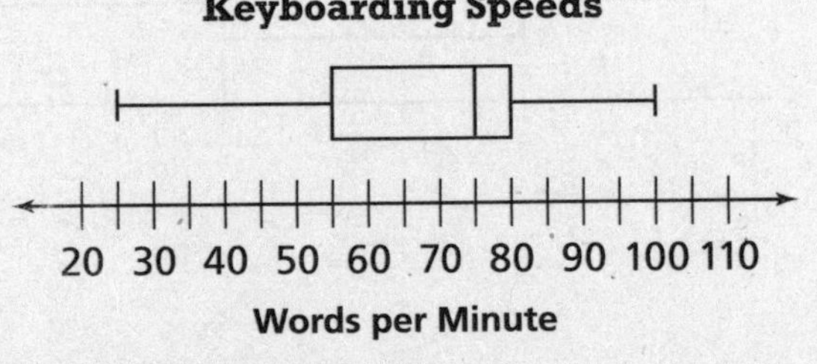

16. How many words per minute do the fastest 50% of keyboarders type?

Keyboarding Speeds

10 20 30 40 50 60 70 80 90 100

Words per Minute

17. Reasoning The price per share of Electric Company's stock during 9 days, rounded to the nearest dollar, was as follows: \$16, \$17, \$16, \$16, \$18, \$18, \$21, \$22, \$19.

Use a box plot to determine how much greater the third quartile's price per share was than the first quartile's price per share. MP.2

18. Make Sense and Persevere The temperature forecast for Topeka, Kansas, for the next 8 days is shown. Use a box plot to determine the range for the lower half of the temperatures. MP.1

DAILY HIGH TEMPERATURES

SUN	MON	TUE	WED	THU	FRI	SAT	SUN
29°	31°	24°	26°	29°	35°	27°	32°

19. Model with Math Coach Henderson clocked the speeds in miles per hour of pitches thrown during the first inning of a middle school baseball game, as shown at the right.

Draw a box plot to display the data and write two conclusions about the data shown in the box plot. MP.4

Speeds of Pitches Thrown (in miles per hour)								
45.3	47	48.1	51.3	55.8	61.1	48.5	60.7	49

20. Critique Reasoning Tanya recorded the ages of 10 local babysitters: 20, 16, 18, 13, 14, 13, 12, 16, 22, 18. She says that the box plot below shows the distribution of ages. What error did she make? MP.3

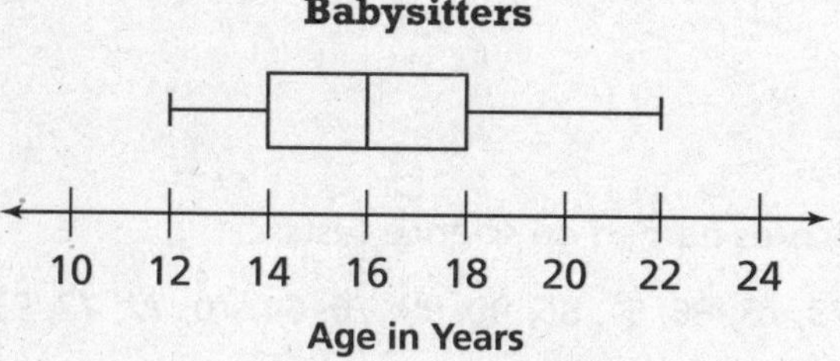

21. Higher Order Thinking Alana made this box plot to represent classroom attendance last month. Without seeing the values, what conclusions can you make about whether attendance was mostly high or low last month? Explain.

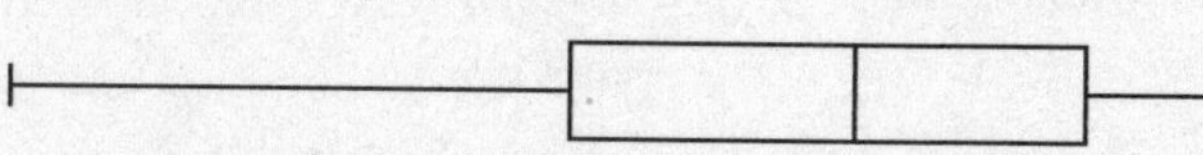

Assessment Practice

22. Use the data given to complete the box plot.

The ages in years of the students in Caryn's gymnastics class are shown in the table.

Ages of Students in Years										
12	11	9	18	10	11	7	16	14	11	6

Complete the box plot to show the distribution of the students' ages.

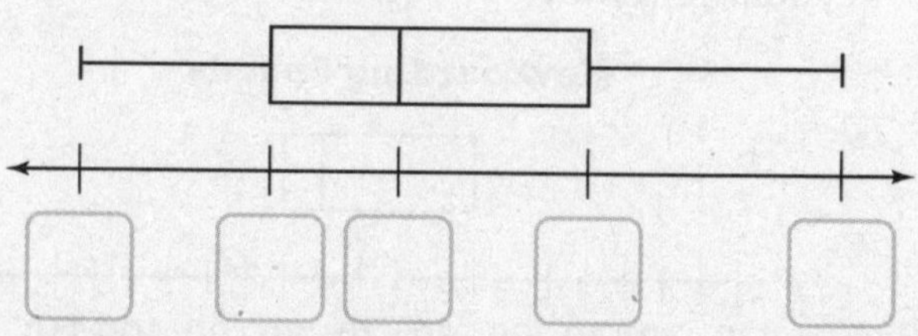

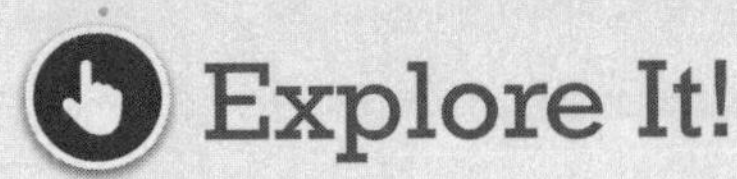

Explore It!

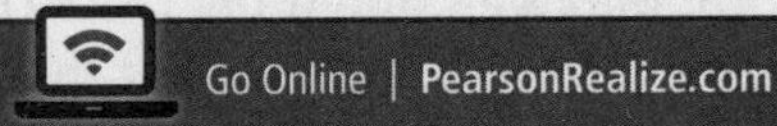

Lesson 8-4
Display Data in Frequency Tables and Histograms

I can...
make and analyze frequency tables and histograms.

Common Core Content Standards
6.SP.B.4, 6.SP.B.5a
Mathematical Practices
MP.2, MP.4, MP.6, MP.7, MP.8

The students in a sixth-grade class recorded the number of letters in their first and last names combined.

HELLO
my name is
Justine Marcello (15)
Number of Letters in
Sixth-Grade Students' Names
15, 11, 14, 8, 10, 15, 17, 16, 19, 12,
13, 12, 14, 15, 11, 16, 9, 12, 13, 10

A. How can the data be organized? Describe one way to organize the data.

B. Describe another way to organize the data.

C. Compare the two ways. What do you notice about the data in each way?

Focus on math practices

Generalize What generalization can you make about the data set? MP.8

Essential Question How can a frequency table or histogram help you organize and analyze data?

EXAMPLE 1  Make a Frequency Table and a Histogram

Scan for Multimedia 

Mr. Maxwell timed the cross-country team in a 2-mile run and recorded the times in the table shown. He wants to analyze the runners' times. What is one way that Mr. Maxwell can organize the data?

Team Times					
16:45	14:25	18:40	16:03	15:12	19:15
17:14	14:02	16:52	15:18	17:49	17:55

A **frequency table** shows the number of times a value occurs in each category or interval.

Mr. Maxwell can set up time intervals for the data, and then count the number, or frequency, of times for each interval.

Running Times	Tally	Frequency
14:00–15:59	||||	4
16:00–17:59	~~||||~~ |	6
18:00–19:59	||	2

Then he can use the frequency table to make a histogram.

Display the data by drawing a bar for each interval.

Look for Relationships How is a histogram similar to and different from a bar graph? MP.7

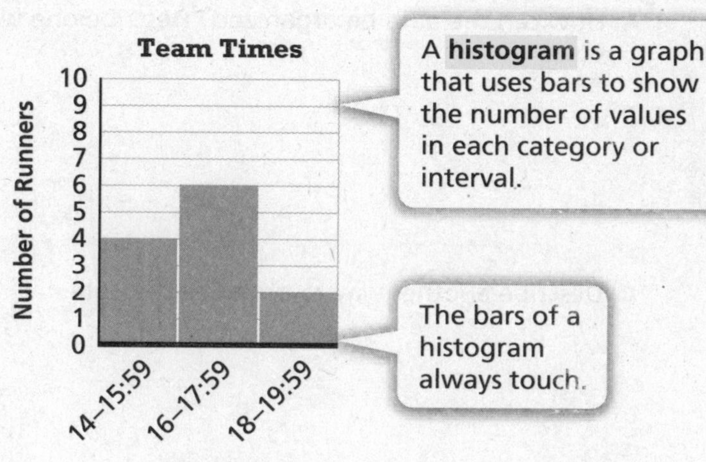

Try It!

This histogram shows a different way to represent Mr. Maxwell's data. Fill in the boxes with appropriate times and shade the bars for the last three intervals. How have the intervals changed?

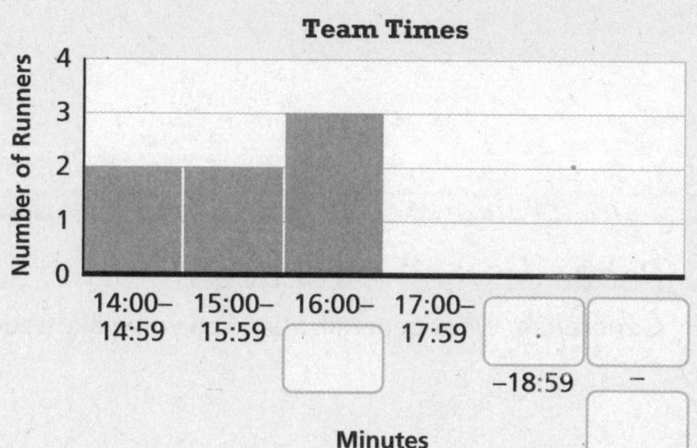

Convince Me! How is the analysis of the information displayed different between the two histograms?

EXAMPLE 2  Use a Frequency Table to Solve Problems

Zack surveys a group of middle school students and asks them how many texts they sent yesterday. The table shows the results.

Number of Texts	Tally	Frequency
0–19	卌	5
20–39	||||	4
40–59	卌 卌	10
60–79	卌 卌 |	11
80–99	卌 |||	8

a. Is the greatest number of texts sent between 60 and 79?

The greatest frequency is 11, which corresponds to students who sent 60–79 texts. However, the greatest number of texts sent is between 80 and 99.

b. Is the lowest number of texts sent between 20 and 39?

The lowest frequency is 4, which corresponds to students who sent 20–39 texts. However, the lowest number of texts sent is between 0 and 19.

Try It!

How many students sent between 20 and 59 texts?

EXAMPLE 3  Use a Histogram to Solve Problems

The histogram shows the number of points that Kendra scored during each basketball game she played last season.

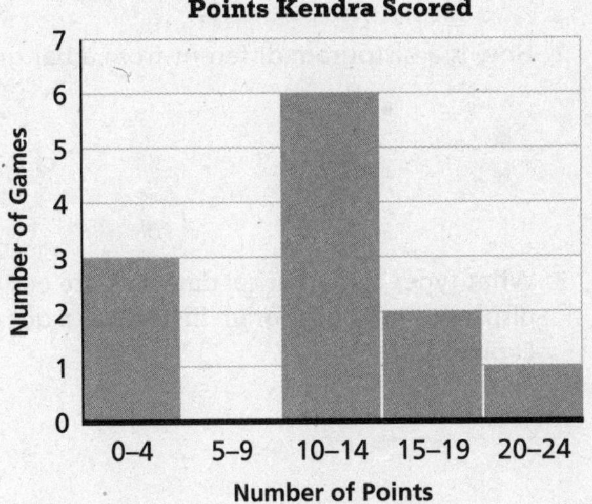

a. How many games did Kendra play last season?

The total number of games can be found by adding the number of games shown by each bar.

$3 + 0 + 6 + 2 + 1 = 12$

Kendra played 12 games.

b. In how many games did Kendra score from 5 to 9 points?

There is no bar on the histogram for 5–9 points. Kendra did not score 5–9 points in any games last season.

Try It!

Does the histogram show the mode of the number of points Kendra scored in the games? Explain.

KEY CONCEPT

Data displays can be used to help make sense of data.

Bags of Popcorn Sold Each Day
62, 65, 58, 31, 64, 58, 66, 68, 56, 67, 68, 51

You can organize data in a frequency table.

Bags	Tally	Frequency
30–39	|	1
40–49		0
50–59	||||	4
60–69	~~||||~~ ||	7

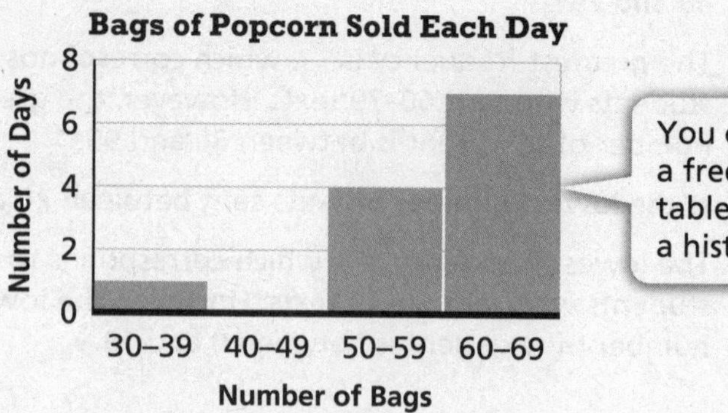

You can use a frequency table to make a histogram.

Do You Understand?

1. **Essential Question** How can a frequency table or histogram help you organize and analyze data?

2. How is a histogram different from a bar graph?

3. What types of numerical data sets are easier to display using a histogram instead of a dot plot? Explain.

4. **Reasoning** How are frequency tables and histograms alike and how are they different? MP.2

Do You Know How?

5. A data set contains ages ranging from 6 to 27.

6, 11, 9, 13, 18, 15, 21, 15, 17, 24, 27, 12

Complete the frequency table and histogram.

Ages	Tally	Frequency
6–10		
11–15		
16–20		
21–25		
26–30		

Name: ____________________

Practice & Problem Solving

Scan for Multimedia 

Leveled Practice **In 6–11, use the data in the chart.**

Number of Songs on Phones
125, 289, 115, 203, 192, 178, 256, 248, 165, 233, 147, 209, 225, 184, 156, 201, 143, 125, 263, 210

6. Complete the frequency table below for the number of songs stored on phones.

Song Range	Tally	Frequency
100–149		
150–199		
200–		
–		

7. Use your frequency table to complete the histogram.

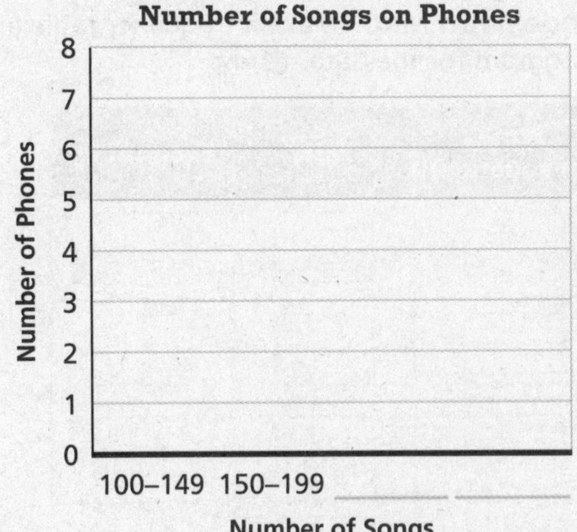

8. How many people have between 150 and 199 songs stored on their phones?

9. Do more than half of the phones have fewer than 149 songs stored on them?

10. Is the greatest number of songs stored on phones between 200 and 249 songs?

11. Are there more phones that have between 200 and 249 songs stored on them than have between 150 and 199 songs?

In 12–14, use the data in the histogram.

12. How many students in Ms. Gioia's class took the science test?

13. How many more students had scores that were 80 or lower than had scores that were higher than 90?

14. Be Precise Can you tell from the histogram how many students scored 83 on the test? Explain. MP.6

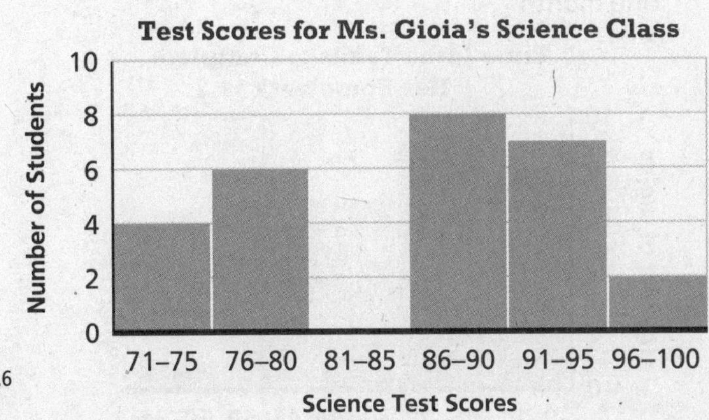

In 15–17, use the data in the chart.

Bicycle Stopping Times (in seconds)
15, 25, 11, 8, 10, 21, 18, 23, 19, 9, 14, 16, 24, 18, 10, 16, 24, 18, 9, 14

15. Reasoning Todd wants to know how many people took 20 seconds or more to stop a bike safely. Would a frequency table or a histogram be the better way to show this? Explain. MP.2

16. Higher Order Thinking When organizing the data, what interval should Todd use? Explain.

17. Model with Math Make a frequency table and histogram for the data. MP.4

Time (in seconds)	Tally	Frequency

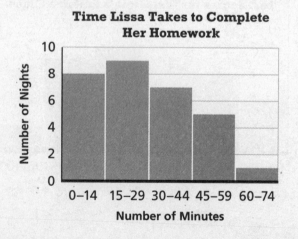

Assessment Practice

18. Lissa recorded the time it took her to complete her homework each night for one month.

Time Lissa Takes to Complete Her Homework

10
8
6
4
2
0
Number of Nights
0–14 15–29 30–44 45–59 60–74
Number of Minutes

According to the histogram, which statements accurately describe Lissa's data? Select all that apply.

- ☐ Lissa worked on her homework for at least an hour one time.
- ☐ On more than half of the nights in the month, Lissa spent less than 30 minutes on her homework.
- ☐ The most time spent on homework each night was between 15 and 29 minutes.
- ☐ It took between 15 and 29 minutes more often than it took between 30 and 59 minutes.
- ☐ There were 31 days in that month.

Name: ______________________

TOPIC 8

MID-TOPIC CHECKPOINT

1. **Vocabulary** Describe how the mean and the mode are alike and how they are different. *Lesson 8-2*

2. A P.E. teacher recorded how many sit-ups the students in her class did in one minute. Which statements describe the data? Select all that apply. *Lesson 8-4*

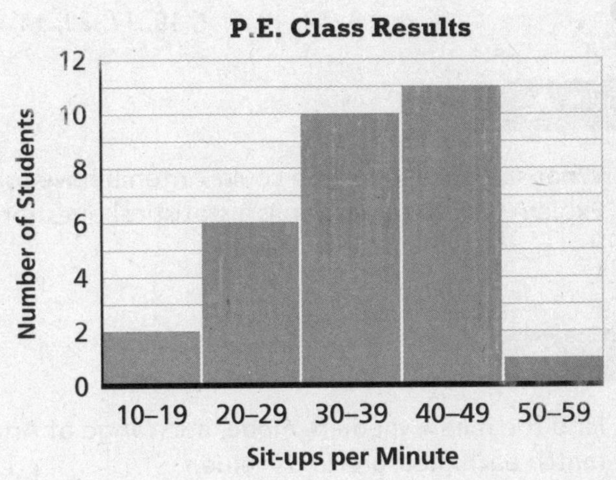

- ☐ Every student did at least 10 sit-ups in one minute.
- ☐ Two students did 50 or more sit-ups in one minute.
- ☐ Eight more students did 30 to 39 sit-ups than did 10 to 19 sit-ups.
- ☐ More than half of the students did 40 or more sit-ups in one minute.
- ☐ There are 30 students in the class.

In 3 and 4, determine whether each question is *statistical* or *not statistical*. Explain.

3. How many pages did Liz read yesterday? *Lesson 8-1*

4. How many books did each of the students in grade 6 read last year? *Lesson 8-1*

In 5 and 6, use the table of cousins' ages at a family reunion.

Cousins' Ages (years)
10, 9, 10, 14, 21, 11, 16, 10, 16

5. Make a box plot of the ages. *Lesson 8-3*

6. Which measure of the ages has the greatest value? *Lesson 8-2*

Ⓐ mean Ⓑ median Ⓒ mode Ⓓ range

How well did you do on the mid-topic checkpoint? Fill in the stars. ☆☆☆

TOPIC 8

MID-TOPIC PERFORMANCE TASK

Antonia surveys a group of students entered in a school science fair. Her results are shown.

Hours Spent on Project
8, 12, 10, 5, 2, 10, 17, 20, 14, 22

PART A

What statistical question could Antonia have asked to gather these data? Explain why the question is a statistical question.

PART B

Find the mean, median, mode, and range of Antonia's data. Draw lines to match each measure to its value.

mean	10 hours
median	11 hours
mode	12 hours
range	20 hours

PART C

Choose reasonable intervals and then make a frequency table and a histogram to show Antonia's data.

Hours	Tally	Frequency

Hours Spent on Project

Number of Students

Total Number of Hours

Lesson 8-5
Summarize Data Using Measures of Variability

Go Online | PearsonRealize.com

I can...
use measures of variability to describe a data set.

Common Core Content Standards
6.SP.B.5c, 6.SP.B.4

Mathematical Practices
MP.2, MP.3, MP.4

Solve & Discuss It!

ACTIVITY

Suppose you collected data from 11 people about the number of pieces of fruit they have eaten in the past week. The median number is 6 pieces of fruit.

Make two possible dot plots that could be used to display the data—one in which the data vary a little and one in which the data vary a lot. Explain how you created your dot plots.

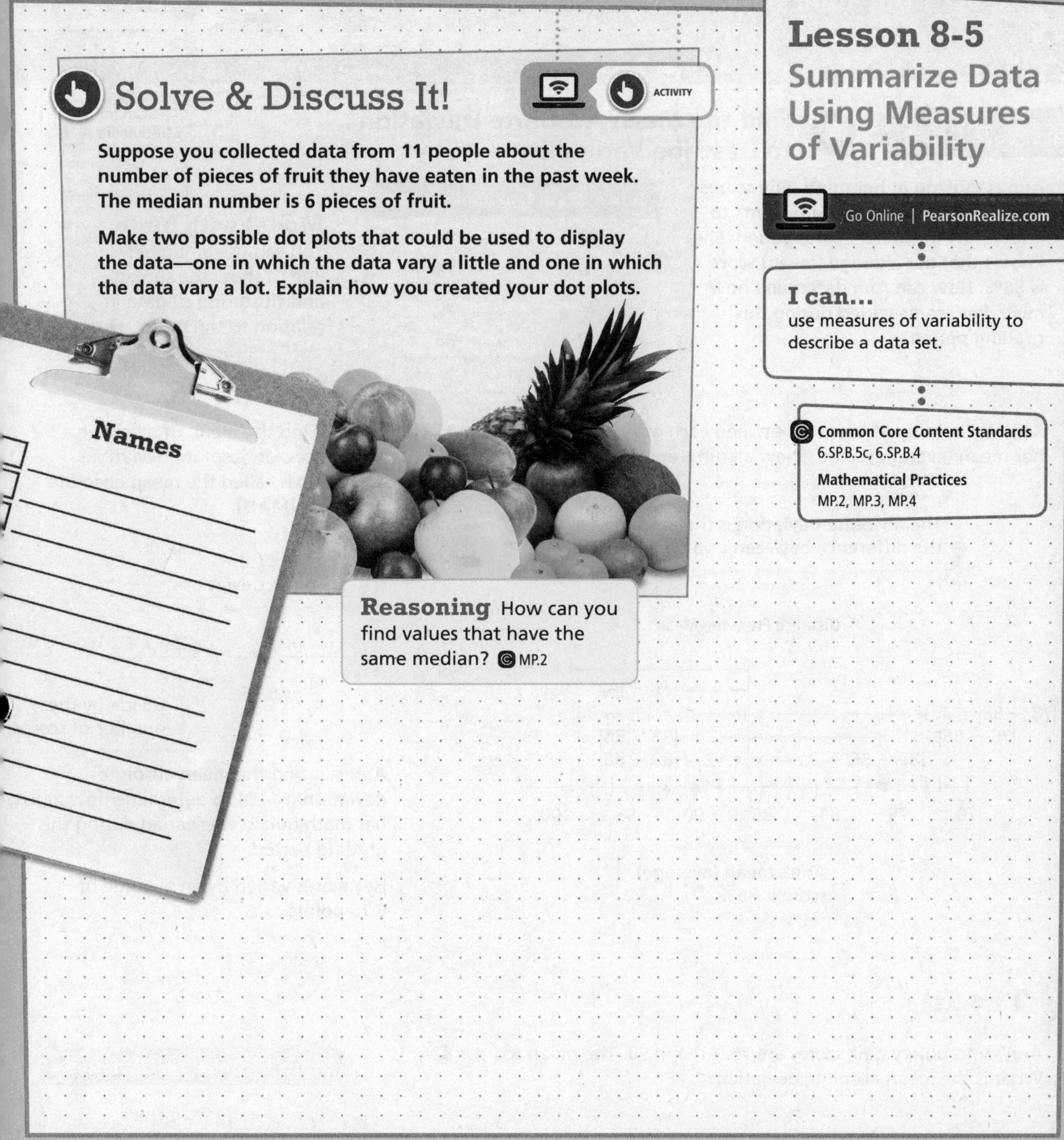

Reasoning How can you find values that have the same median? MP.2

Focus on math practices

Critique Reasoning Jackline says that only 3 people surveyed ate more than six pieces of fruit in the past week. Do you agree? Explain why or why not. MP.3

 **Essential Question** How can the variability of data be described using a single number?

EXAMPLE 1  Find the Mean Absolute Deviation to Describe Variability

Ann is looking at her math quiz scores for one grading period. She wants to know how much her scores varied. She knows that her average (mean) score is 86%. How can Ann determine how much her scores varied during this grading period?

Ann's Math Quiz Scores (%)	
82	99
76	73
92	90
88	88

Model with Math
You can use a number line to show the spread and clustering of data in relation to the mean. MP.4

STEP 1 Find the differences between each of Ann's quiz scores and her mean (average) score. Show all differences as positive integers.

The **absolute deviation** is the absolute value of the difference between a value and the mean.

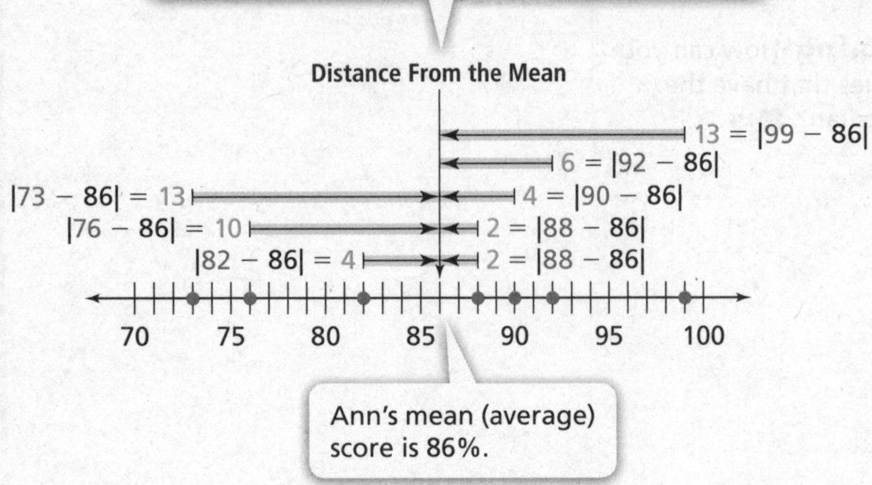

Ann's mean (average) score is 86%.

STEP 2 Find the mean of all of the differences, or absolute deviations. This value is called the **mean absolute deviation (MAD)**.

Add all of the absolute deviations.

$$\frac{13 + 10 + 4 + 2 + 2 + 4 + 6 + 13}{8}$$

$$= \frac{54}{8} \text{ or } 6.75$$

Divide by the number of scores.

Ann can find the mean absolute deviation (MAD) to determine how much her math quiz scores varied during this grading period.

Her scores varied by an average of 6.75 points.

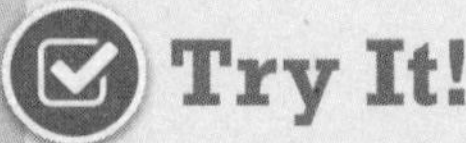 Try It!

Ann's vocabulary quiz scores are 75, 81, and 90. The mean score is 82. What is the mean absolute deviation?

Score	Absolute Deviation
75	|82 − 75| = ☐
81	|☐ − ☐| = ☐
90	|☐ − ☐| = ☐

Convince Me! Can the mean absolute deviation ever have a negative value? Explain.

EXAMPLE 2  Find the Interquartile Range (IQR) to Describe Variability

  ACTIVITY  ASSESS

The dot plot shows Ann's science quiz scores. How can Ann determine the variability in her science quiz scores?

78 79 80 81 82 83 84

Ann's Science Quiz Scores (%)

Draw a box plot to determine the interquartile range.

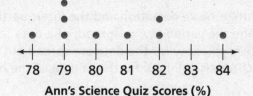

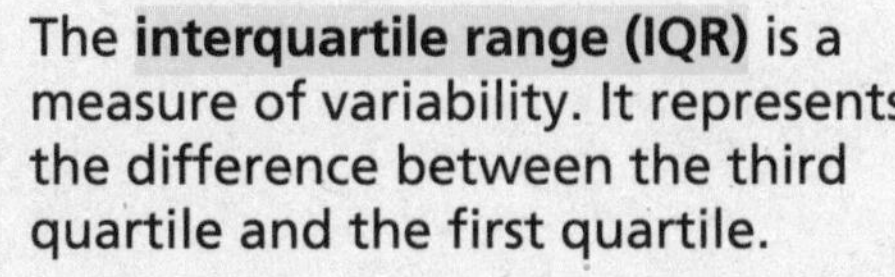
The **interquartile range (IQR)** is a measure of variability. It represents the difference between the third quartile and the first quartile.

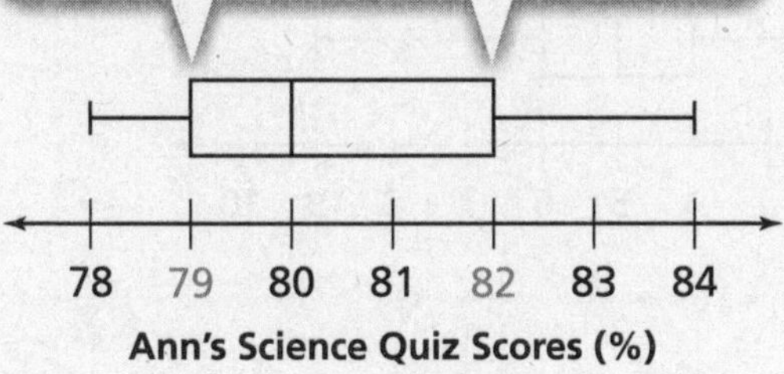

The interquartile range is 82 − 79 = 3.
So, at least half of Ann's science quiz scores were within 3 points.

 Try It!

The dot plot shows the distribution of Ann's health quiz scores. How can the IQR describe her scores?

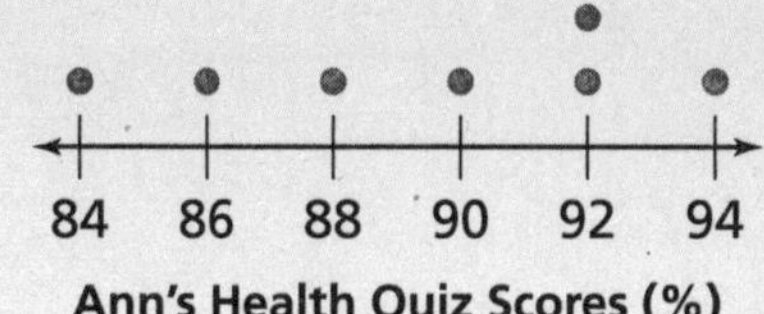

EXAMPLE 3  Use the Mean Absolute Deviation (MAD) to Find the Variability of a Data Set

Jonah recorded the points his team scored during its last nine basketball games. The mean number of points scored was 42 and the MAD was $4.\overline{4}$. How can Jonah use these measures to describe the variability of the points his team scored during the last nine games?

The MAD shows that the scores generally varied greatly from the mean. The scores were mostly less than 38 (42 − 4.4 = 37.6) or greater than 46 (42 + 4.4 = 46.4).

 Try It!

Jonah's team scored 36, 37, 38, 38, 41, 46, 47, 47, and 48 points in the last nine games. Find the IQR and range of the points Jonah's team scored in its last nine games. Are these good measures for describing the points scored?

KEY CONCEPT

The mean absolute deviation and the interquartile range each use a single number to describe the variability, or spread, of a data set. The **mean absolute deviation (MAD)** tells you how far the data are spread out from the mean. The **interquartile range (IQR)** tells you how far the middle of the data is spread out from the median.

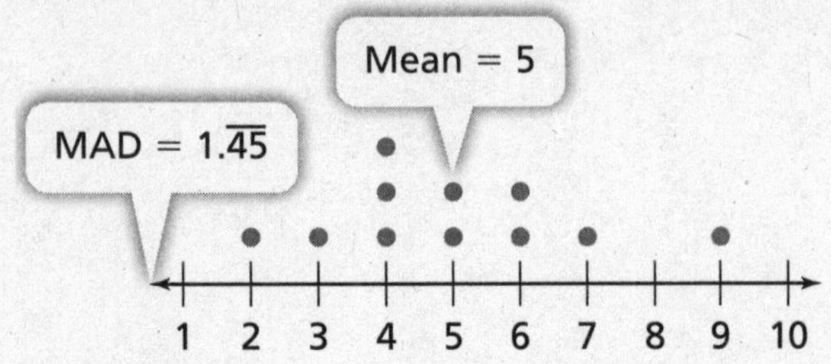

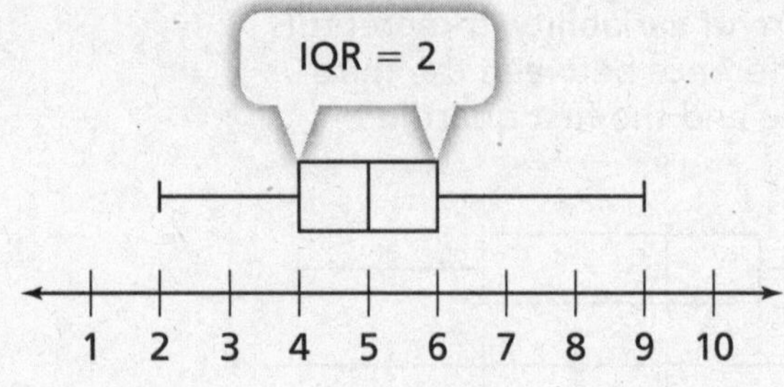

Do You Understand?

1. **Essential Question** How can the variability of data be described using a single number?

2. What does the IQR show that the range does not show?

3. **Reasoning** Two data sets have the same mean, 8. However, the MAD of Data Set A is 2 and the MAD of Data Set B is 4. What does this indicate about the variability of the data sets? MP.2

Do You Know How?

In 4–7, use these data.

Davita works at a shoe store. She measured the feet of nine customers and found that their shoe sizes were 4, 5, 5, 6, 7, 8, 8, 10, and 10.

4. Find the mean.

5. Find the sum of the absolute deviations from the mean.

6. Find the mean absolute deviation. Explain how you found the MAD.

7. Find the range and IQR. How is each calculated?

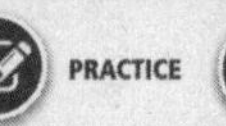

Name: ________________

Practice & Problem Solving

Scan for Multimedia

8. Leveled Practice The mean of the data set is 3. Find the absolute deviation of each of the green values.

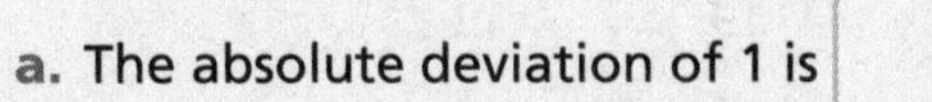

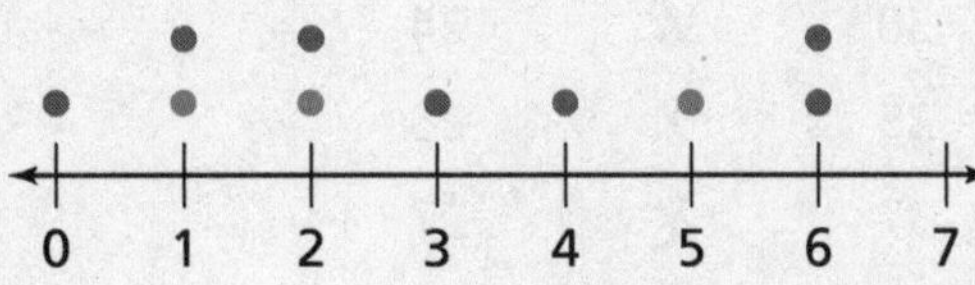

a. The absolute deviation of 1 is ☐.

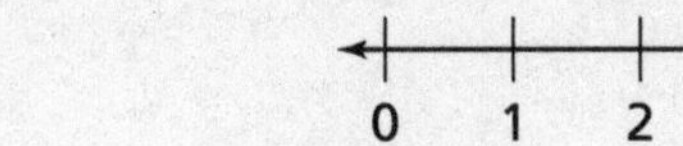

b. The absolute deviation of 2 is ☐.

c. The absolute deviation of 5 is ☐.

In 9 and 10, use the data table showing the number of miles that Jill biked on 9 days.

9. Find the mean.

Miles Biked		
5	9	11
10	8	6
7	12	4

10. Find the MAD of this data set. What does this tell you about the number of miles that Jill biked?

In 11 and 12, use the data shown in the dot plot.

11. What are the mean and the MAD?

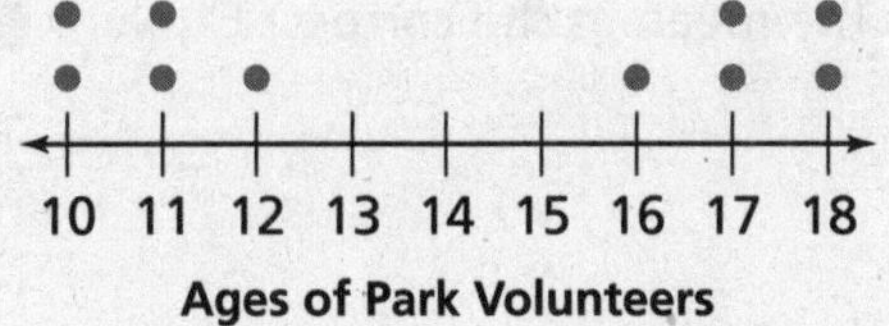

Ages of Park Volunteers

12. Describe the variability of the data.

In 13 and 14, use the data shown in the box plot.

13. What are the range and the IQR?

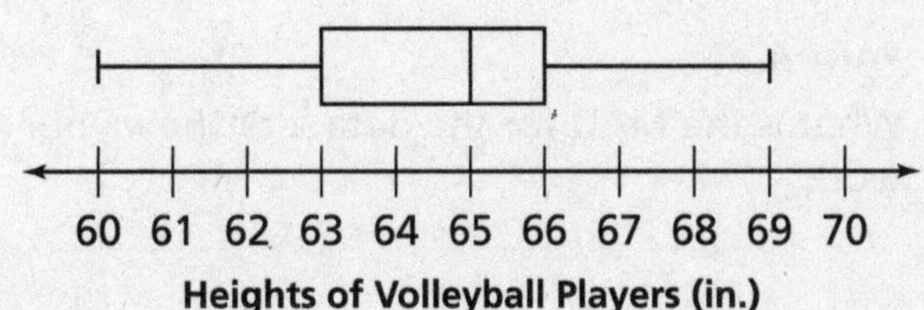

Heights of Volleyball Players (in.)

14. Describe the variability of the data.

15. The data set shows prices for concert tickets in 10 major cities.

City	Price ($)	City	Price ($)
Q	45	V	36
R	50	W	24
S	35	X	25
T	37	Y	27
U	29	Z	43

a. Find the IQR of the data set.

b. How do prices vary within the middle 50%?

16. **Reasoning** The MAD of the data set in the table is about 6.7. Does the value 4 deviate more or less than most of the values in the table? Explain. MP.2

4	28	25
19	7	13
16	22	10

In 17–19, use the data set shown in the table.

Temperatures (°F)			
11	17	20	16
19	16	15	22

17. **Vocabulary** What is the term used to describe the range of the middle half of the data set? Find that value for this data.

18. **Critique Reasoning** Dina said that the greatest absolute deviation will be found from the highest temperature because it has to be the farthest from the mean. Is she correct? Explain. MP.3

19. **Higher Order Thinking** What is the MAD for the data and what does it tell you about the temperatures?

Assessment Practice

20. Harlo recorded the tide, in feet, every hour during an 8-hour period as shown in the table.

Tide (ft)
3, 7, 11, 15, 20, 31, 39, 42

PART A

What is the MAD for the data set? Show your work.

PART B

Is the IQR greater or less than the MAD? What does this tell you about the variability of the data?

Lesson 8-6

Choose Appropriate Statistical Measures

Go Online | PearsonRealize.com

I can...
select and use appropriate statistical measures.

Common Core Content Standards
6.SP.B.5d, 6.SP.B.5c

Mathematical Practices
MP.1, MP.2, MP.3, MP.7

Solve & Discuss It!

The prices in dollars of athletic shoes in one store are shown below. Does the mean, median, or mode best describe the typical price for shoes at this store?

Look for Relationships
How can you use the spread and clustering of data to help decide which statistical measures to use? MP.7

Focus on math practices

Construct Arguments Which measure would the store most likely use in its advertising? Explain why this measure should be used. MP.3

 **Essential Question** Why is one statistical measure more useful than another to describe a given situation?

EXAMPLE 1  Choose the Best Measure of Center to Describe a Data Set

Scan for Multimedia 

Gary reviews the scores on his weekly quizzes. What measure should Gary use to get the best sense of how well he is doing on his weekly quizzes?

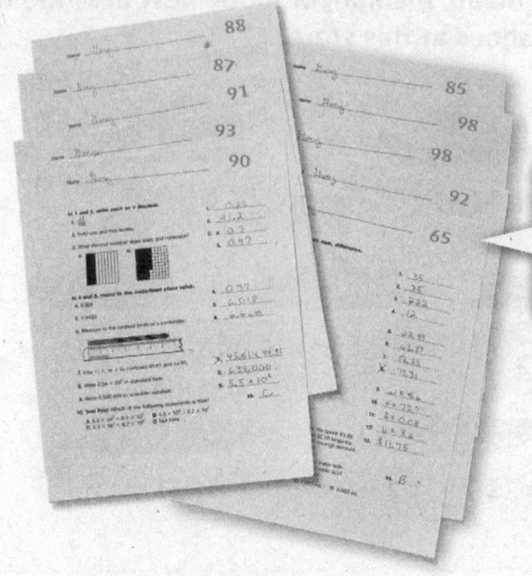

An **outlier** is a data value that is very different from the other values.

Make Sense and Persevere
What does the distribution of the data in a dot plot tell you about the shape of the data? MP.1

Display Gary's scores on a dot plot. Describe the shape of the data. Then find the mean, median, and mode of the data set.

65 is an outlier. It "lies outside" most of the other values in the data set.

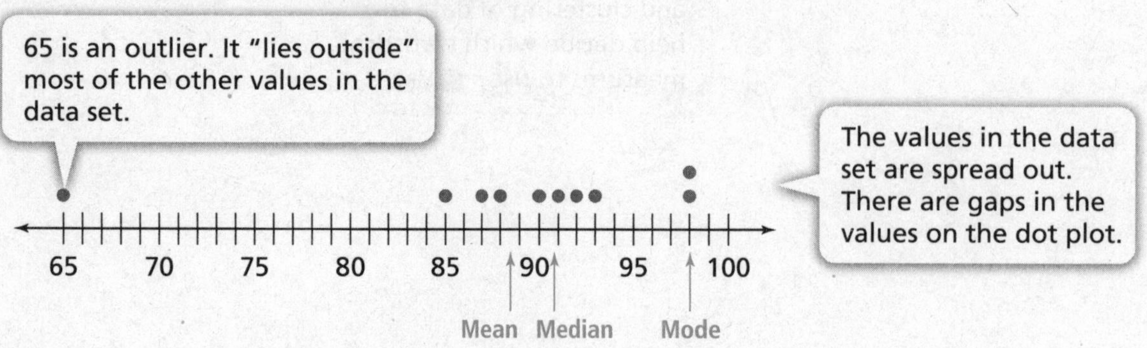

The values in the data set are spread out. There are gaps in the values on the dot plot.

The outlier causes the mean to be less than the values of largest group of data. The best measure to use is the median because the outlier does not affect the median.

Try It!

If Gary scored a 70 on his next weekly quiz, how would that affect his mean score?

Convince Me! Gary says that he usually scores 98 on his weekly quiz. What measure of center did Gary use? Explain.

EXAMPLE 2 

Choose the Best Measure of Variability to Describe a Data Set

John and Yoshi are computer lab partners. During a spreadsheet project, they decide to enter their French quiz scores on their shared tablet.

	A John	B Yoshi
1	65	80
2	87	80
3	87	82
4	88	82
5	90	84
6	91	84
7	92	86
8	93	86
9	93	88
10	93	88

Quiz Scores

A. Choose a measure of variability and use it to describe John's quiz scores.

John's scores contain an outlier, 65, so the median is a better measure of center for his data than the mean.

Use the IQR when the median is the appropriate measure of center.

First Quartile = 87 Third Quartile = 93

IQR = 93 − 87 = 6

At least half of John's quiz scores are between 87 and 93. This accurately describes how his scores are clustered.

B. Choose a measure of variability and use it to describe Yoshi's quiz scores.

Yoshi's scores range from 80 to 88, so there is no outlier. The mean, 84, is a good measure of center for her data.

Use the MAD when the mean is the appropriate measure of center.

$$\text{MAD} = \frac{4+4+2+2+0+0+2+2+4+4}{10} = \frac{24}{10} = 2.4$$

Yoshi's scores are typically within 2.4 points of her mean score of 84.

Try It!

Suppose the French teacher says that she will drop each student's lowest quiz score. Would the MAD now be a good measure of variability for John's quiz scores? Calculate the MAD without John's lowest score and use it to justify your answer.

John's lowest score is ☐.

Without the lowest score, John's mean score is ☐.

$$\text{MAD} = \frac{\square + \square + \square + \square + \square + \square + \square + \square + \square}{9}$$

$$= \frac{\square}{9} = \square$$

The statistical measure that is most appropriate to describe the center and variability of a data set should be chosen based on an analysis of the spread, clustering, and outliers in the data set.

The **mean** is a good choice to describe the center of a data set when the data are clustered together.

When the mean is used, the **mean absolute deviation (MAD)** is a good choice to describe the variability.

The **median** is a good choice to describe the center of a data set when the data contain an outlier.

When the median is used, the **interquartile range (IQR)** is a good choice to describe the variability.

The **mode** is sometimes a good choice to describe the center of a data set if the data is not numeric or does not fall in intervals.

The median and mode are the same, 30. Both describe the center of the data set.

The outlier will increase the mean. The mean and MAD are *not* the best choices.

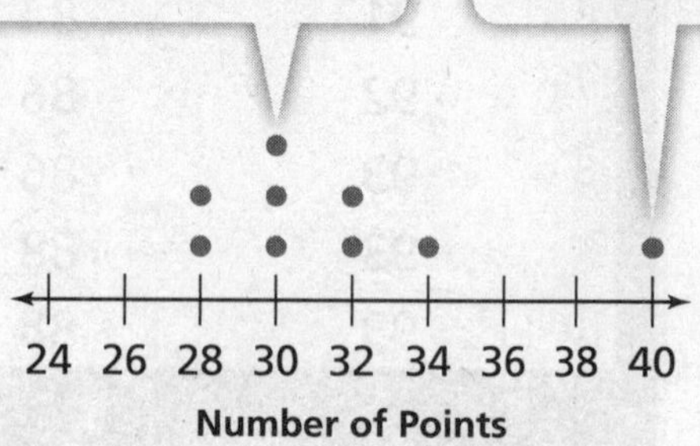

The middle half of the data is clustered together. The IQR is a good measure of the variability of the data set because it uses the median.

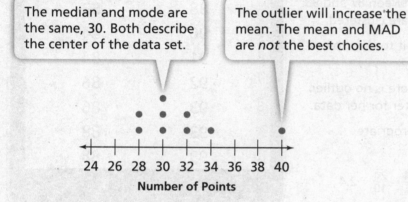

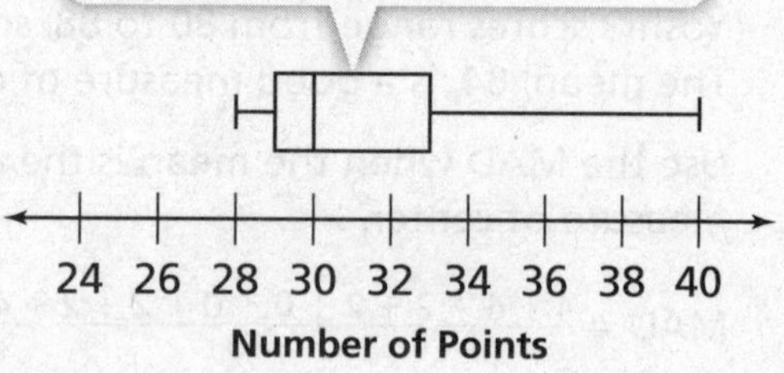

Do You Understand?

1. **Essential Question** Why is one statistical measure more useful than another to describe a given situation?

2. **Reasoning** You cannot find a good measure of center for a data set. What is probably true of the data set? MP.2

Do You Know How?

In 3–5, use the basketball team's scores for one season: 44, 43, 42, 40, 42, 45, 39, 38, 18.

3. Find the mean, median, and mode of the scores.

4. Is the median or mean the best measure of center for these data? Explain.

5. Find the measure of variability that best describes the data set.

Name: ______________________________

Practice & Problem Solving

Scan for Multimedia

In 6–8, use the data to answer the questions.

Each of five different stores sell a quart of milk for one of the following prices: $1.50, $1.55, $1.80, $1.70, $1.50.

6. What are the mean, median, and mode of the data?

7. Which measure of center best describes these data? Which measure of variability?

8. Find the best measure of variability for these data. Describe the variability.

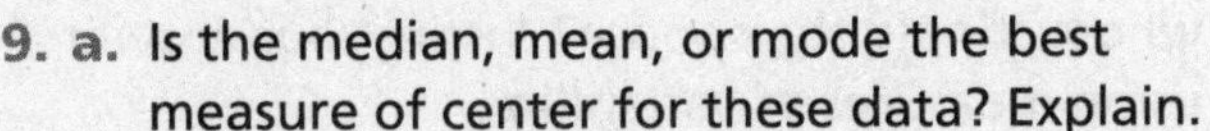

In 9–11, use the dot plot at the right.

The dot plot shows the hourly wages of cashiers at a supermarket.

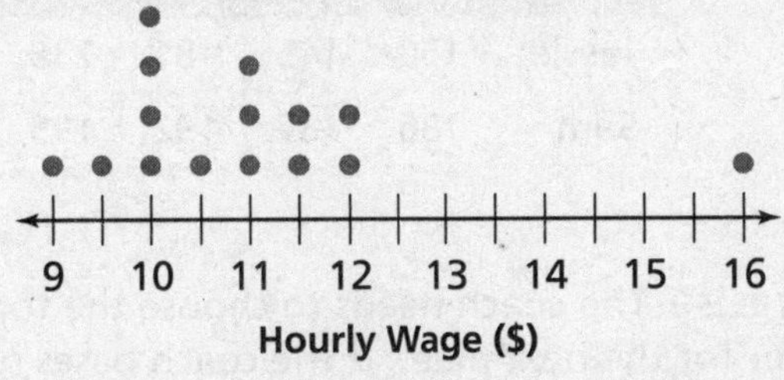

9. a. Is the median, mean, or mode the best measure of center for these data? Explain.

b. Find that measure of center.

10. Identify a good measure of variability for these data. Find the value.

11. Write a sentence describing the variability of the wages.

12. Critique Reasoning Hayden looks at the dot plot. He believes that the data set contains outliers and argues that the best measure of variability is the IQR because the median is a good measure to describe a data set that contains outliers. Is Hayden correct? Explain. MP.3

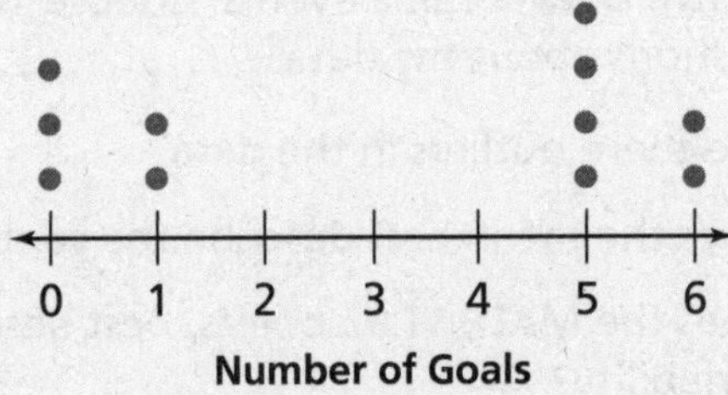

In 13–16, use the table at the right.

The table shows measures of center based on 5 data points for attendance at a national ice skating competition.

Mean	Median	Mode
14,000	13,000	12,500

13. Vocabulary What is the term and the value of the middle number of the data set?

14. Make Sense and Persevere Which value in the data set occurs at least twice? Can it occur 3 times? Explain. MP.1

15. Reasoning Why must the other two numbers in the data set be greater than or equal to 13,000? MP.2

16. Model with Math What must be the sum of the two remaining numbers, x and y? Write an equation to show how to find this sum. MP.4

In 17 and 18, use the table.

Game Scores for the Bravo Bowling Team									
Jessie	150	145	181	235	196	211	204	221	185
Sam	186	187	192	195	194	157	157	162	200

17. Be Precise The coach needs to choose the top bowler for the next meet. If the coach bases her decision on the player with the best average, whom should she choose? Justify your answer using measures of center. MP.6

18. Higher Order Thinking If the coach bases her decision on the player who is most consistent, whom should she choose? Justify your answer using measures of variability.

Assessment Practice

19. The table at the right shows the winning bowling scores during the last five bowl-a-rama events. Choose Yes or No to answer the questions about the data.

Winning Scores				
121	159	146	132	149

19a. Are there outliers in the data? ○ Yes ○ No

19b. Does the mean best describe the center? ○ Yes ○ No

19c. Does the MAD, 11.92 points, best describe the variability? ○ Yes ○ No

19d. Does the IQR, 27.5 points, best describe the spread? ○ Yes ○ No

Lesson 8-7
Summarize Data Distributions

Go Online | PearsonRealize.com

I can...
summarize numerical data sets.

Common Core Content Standards
6.SP.A.2, 6.SP.B.5b, 6.SP.B.4, 6.SP.B.5c

Mathematical Practices
MP.3, MP.4, MP.8

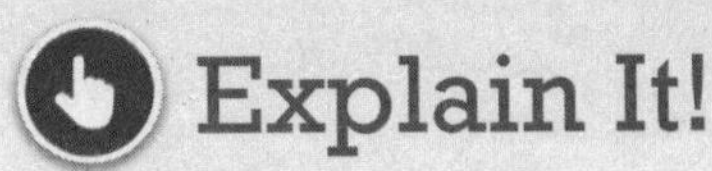

Explain It!

George tosses two six-sided number cubes 20 times. He records his results in a dot plot.

George's Cube Tosses

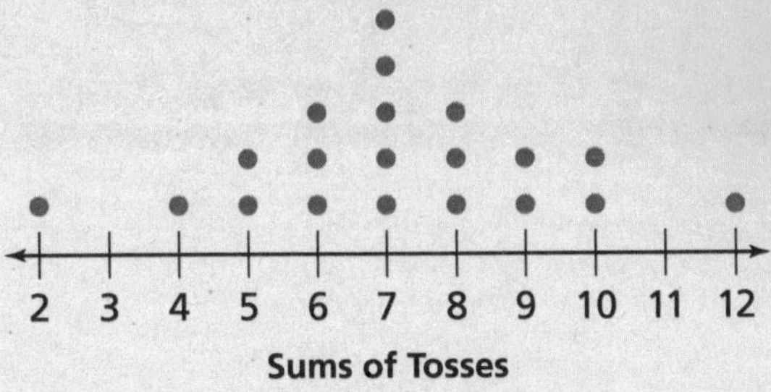

A. Describe the shape of the data distribution.

B. Critique Reasoning George says that he expects to roll a sum of 11 on his next roll. Do you agree? Justify your reasoning. MP.3

Focus on math practices

Construct Arguments Suppose George tossed the number cubes 20 more times and added the data to his dot plot. Would you expect the shape of the distribution to be different? Construct an argument that supports your reasoning. MP.3

? Essential Question How can you summarize a data distribution?

INTERACTIVE ANIMATION

ASSESS

EXAMPLE 1 Summarize a Distribution That Is Symmetric

Scan for Multimedia

A science class is testing how different types of fertilizer affect the growth of plants. The dot plot shows the heights of the plants being grown in the science lab. How can you describe the data?

STEP 1 To describe a **data distribution**, or how the data values are arranged, look at the overall shape.

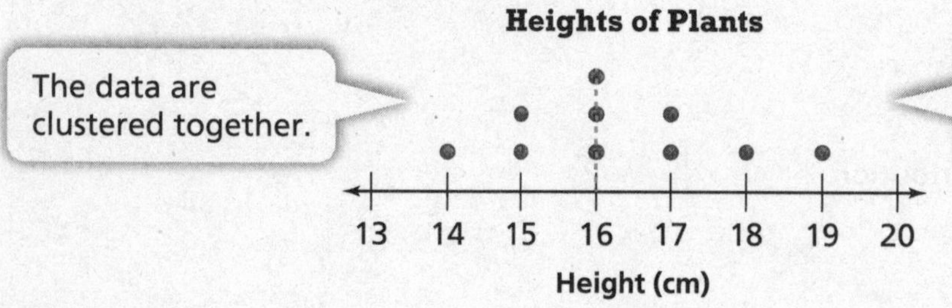
Heights of Plants
The data are clustered together.
The dotted red line shows that the data are roughly symmetric.
13 14 15 16 17 18 19 20
Height (cm)

STEP 2 Since the data are roughly symmetric, the mean is the best measure of center.

$$\frac{14 + 15 + 15 + 16 + 16 + 16 + 17 + 17 + 18 + 19}{10} = 16.3$$

The mean height is 16.3 cm.

Find the mean absolute deviation (MAD).

$$\frac{2.3 + 1.3 + 1.3 + 0.3 + 0.3 + 0.3 + 0.7 + 0.7 + 1.7 + 2.7}{10} = 1.16$$

The mean absolute deviation is 1.16 cm, so a typical height is about 1.16 cm from the mean.

Generalize Since the mean is the best measure of center, the MAD is the best measure of variability. MP.8

Try It!

Does the shape of the distribution match what you found when you used measures of center and variability? Explain.

Convince Me! What are some factors that might explain why some plants grew more or less than others in the science lab?

EXAMPLE 2  Summarize a Distribution Shown in a Dot Plot

The fat content, in grams, was measured for one slice ($\frac{1}{8}$ pizza) of 24 different 12-inch pizzas. The data are displayed in the dot plot. How can the data be used to describe the fat content of a slice of pizza?

STEP 1 Look at the distribution of the data in the dot plot.

There are gaps between 6 and 8, and between 16 and 19.

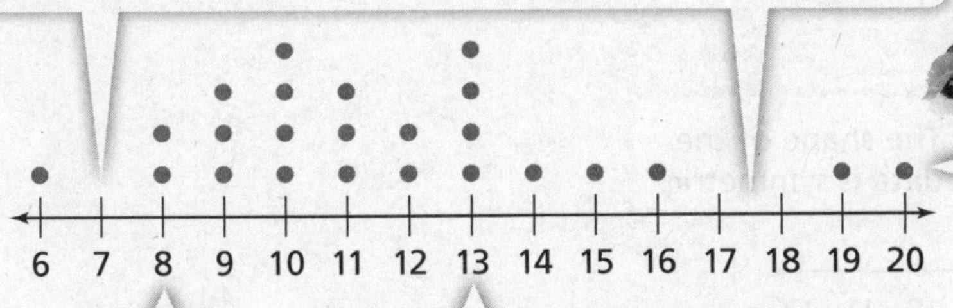

The data are not symmetric. They are more spread out to the right.

Most data points are grouped between 8 and 13.

STEP 2 Because the data are not symmetric, the mean is not the best measure of center. Use the median and the IQR to describe the data distribution.

Median = 11 IQR = 13 − 9.5 = 3.5

The fat content of at least half of the slices is between 9.5 g and 13 g. The typical slice of pizza has a fat content of 11 g.

EXAMPLE 3  Summarize a Distribution Shown in a Box Plot

The box plot displays data for the number of days the temperature was above 80°F for the month of July. The data were collected over a ten-year period. How can you summarize these data?

Days above 80°F in July

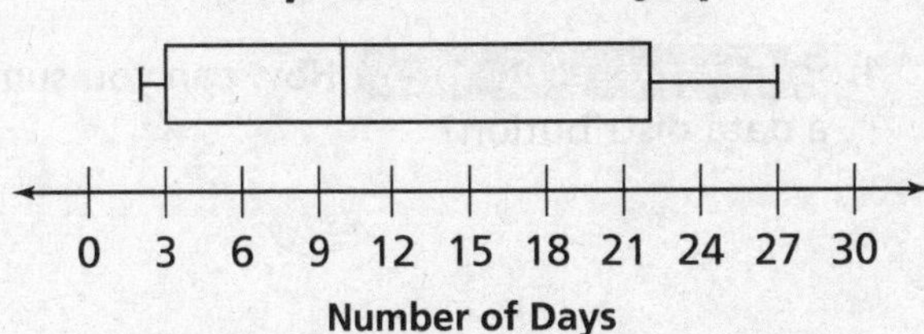

First, look at the overall shape. Then find measures of center and variability.

- The data are spread out to the right.
- The median is the center of the data.
- The first quartile is 3 and the third quartile is 22. At least half of the data fall between 3 days and 22 days. The interquartile range is 19 days.
- 25% of the years, the number of days with temperatures above 80°F in July was 3 days or less.

Model with Math You can select a box plot, dot plot, or other method to display data. You can use that display to help describe the data set. MP.4

Try It!

Why does it make sense to look at the overall shape before deciding which measures to use?

KEY CONCEPT

To describe a set of data, look at the shape and observe how the data are clustered or spread out.

A distribution can be symmetric and clustered in the center. When the data are symmetric, use the mean and mean absolute deviation (MAD) to describe the data.

Weights of Fruit

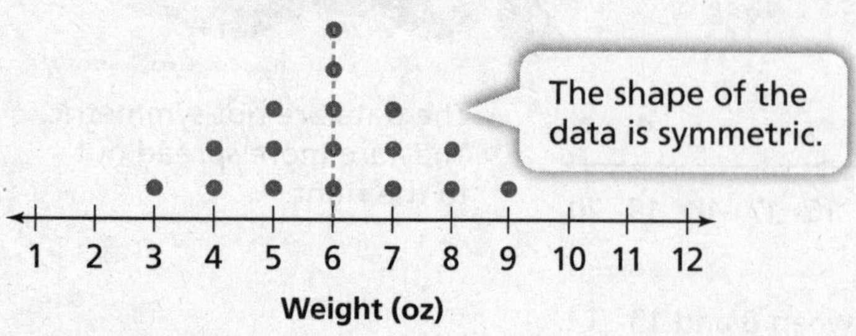

The shape of the data is symmetric.

A distribution can show gaps, clusters, or outliers. It may spread out more to one side. When the data are not symmetric, use the median and interquartile range (IQR) to describe the data.

Weights of Fruit

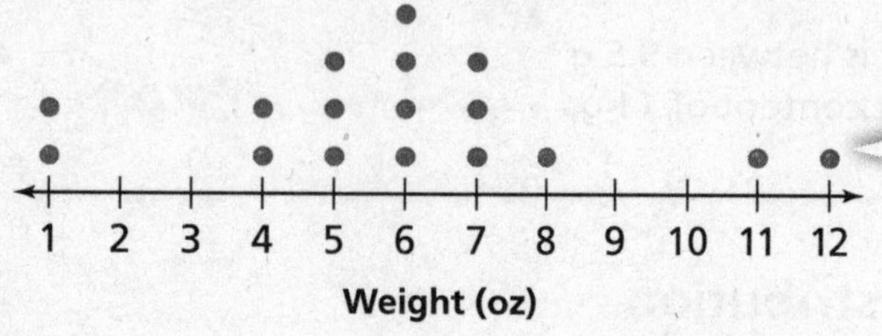

There are gaps between 1 and 4, and between 8 and 11. Most data points are grouped between 4 and 8.

Do You Understand?

1. **Essential Question** How can you summarize a data distribution?

2. Reasoning This data set has an outlier.

0, 40, 50, 60, 60, 70, 80, 80

How would the median and the mean be affected if the outlier was removed? MP.2

Do You Know How?

3. Five different students measured the length of a shadow in inches as follows: 38, $38\frac{1}{2}$, $37\frac{3}{4}$, 38, $38\frac{1}{4}$. Make a generalization about the data distribution of the shadow measurements.

4. What are the mean, the median, and the interquartile range of the data set in Exercise 3?

PRACTICE TUTORIAL

Name: ______________________

Practice & Problem Solving

Scan for Multimedia

In 5–8, use the data table.

Number of Home Runs Hit by Players on My Team									
Player Number	1	2	3	4	5	6	7	8	9
Home Runs	21	9	12	20	7	11	9	10	9

5. What are the mean and the median?

6. Draw a box plot of the data.

7. Describe the overall shape of the data.

8. Make a generalization about the data distribution.

9. Be Precise A doctor asked 15 people how many hours they spend exercising each week. The dot plot displays the data.

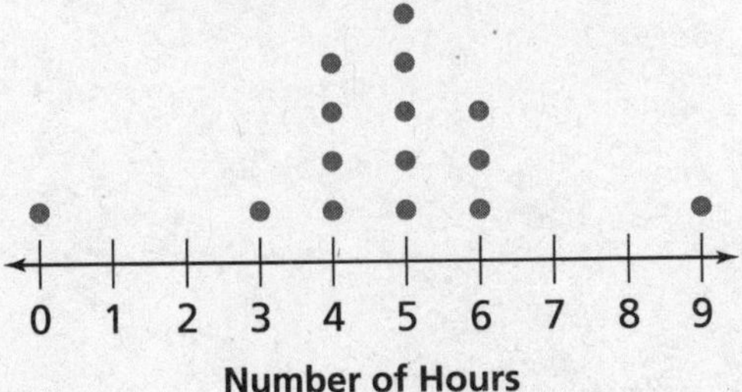

What do any clusters and gaps in the dot plot tell you about the exercise habits of these people? MP.6

10. Look for Relationships Describe the pattern in the dot plot. Then write about a situation that this data could represent. Explain why your situation has this pattern. MP.7

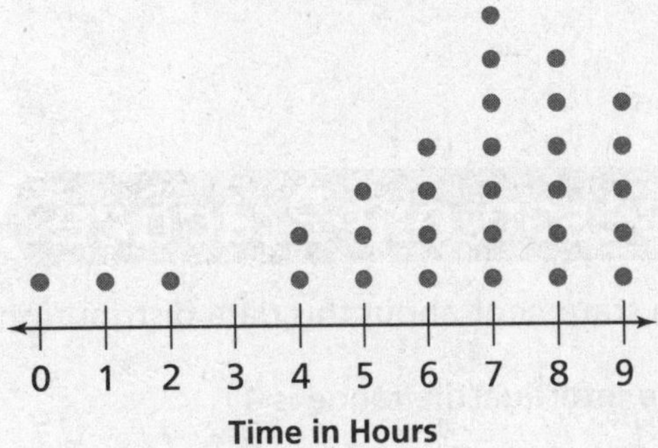

In **11** and **12**, use the data in the table.

Adult	1	2	3	4	5
Salary	$35,000	$46,000	$38,000	$34,000	$52,000
Adult	6	7	8	9	10
Salary	$99,000	$64,000	$435,000	$22,000	$88,000

11. Model with Math Make a box plot for the data. What are the median, first quartile, third quartile, and interquartile range? MP.4

12. Higher Order Thinking Which data value most affects your choice of a measure of center to describe the data? Explain.

In **13–15**, use the data in the dot plot.

13. Describe the shape of the data.

Spanish Quiz Scores

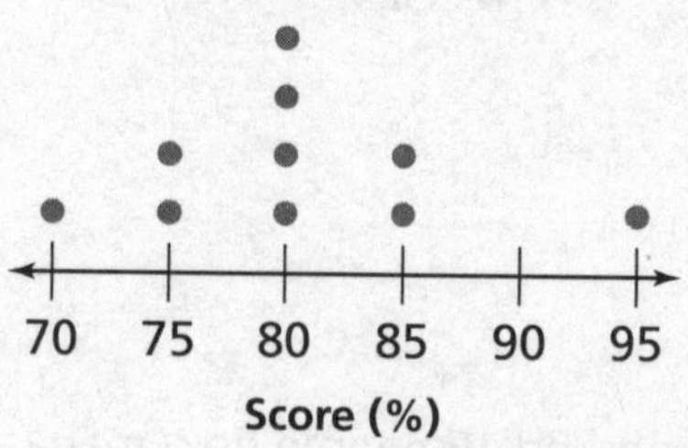

14. Describe the typical quiz scores of the students. Explain your choice of measure.

15. Describe the variability of the quiz scores.

Assessment Practice

16. Which statement about this data distribution is **NOT** true?

Ⓐ The interquartile range is 4.

Ⓑ The median is the preferable measure of center.

Ⓒ The data cluster from 2 to 7.

Ⓓ The distribution is symmetrical.

Number of Miles Students Ran in a Week

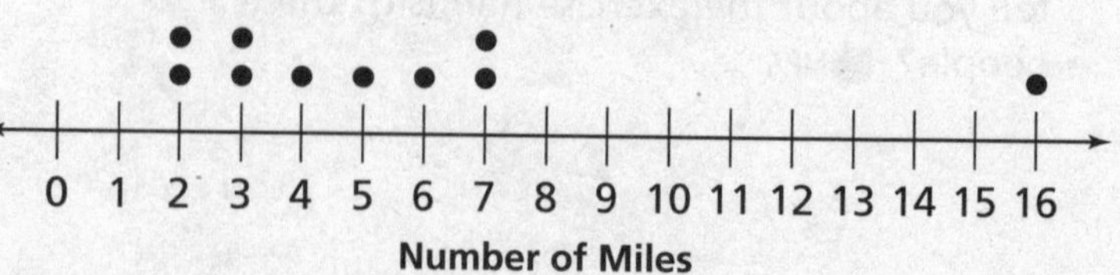

3-Act Mathematical Modeling: Vocal Range

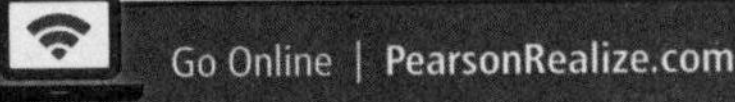

Common Core Content Standards
6.SP.A.2, 6.SP.A.3, 6.SP.B.5

Mathematical Practices
MP.4

ACT 1

1. After watching the video, what is the first question that comes to mind?

2. Write the Main Question you will answer.

3. Make a prediction to answer this Main Question.

The person who should win the competition is ______.

4. Construct Arguments Explain how you arrived at your prediction. MP.3

5. What information in this situation would be helpful to know? How would you use that information?

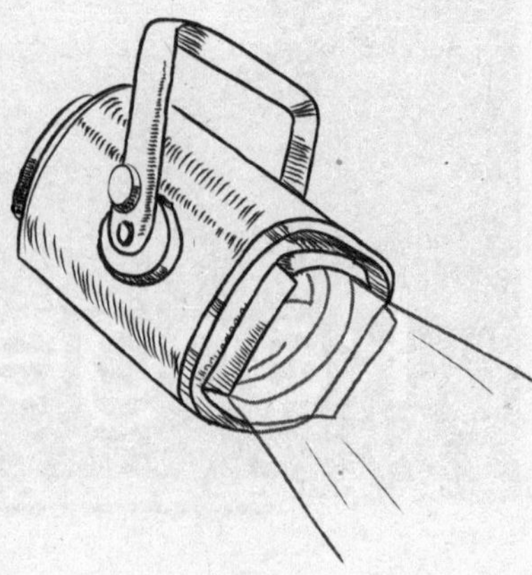

6. **Use Appropriate Tools** What tools can you use to get the information you need? Record the information as you find it. MP.5

7. **Model with Math** Represent the situation using the mathematical content, concepts, and skills from this topic. Use your representation to answer the Main Question. MP.4

8. What is your answer to the Main Question? Does it differ from your prediction? Explain.

9. Write the answer you saw in the video.

10. **Reasoning** Does your answer match the answer in the video? If not, what are some reasons that would explain the difference? MP.2

11. **Make Sense and Persevere** Would you change your model now that you know the answer? Explain. MP.1

ACT 3 Extension

Reflect

12. Model with Math Explain how you used a mathematical model to represent the situation. How did the model help you answer the Main Question? MP.4

13. Use Appropriate Tools What tools or technology did you use to answer the Main Question? What other tools did your classmates use? MP.5

SEQUEL

14. Be Precise Design your own singing competition. Explain how you would score each performance and how you would use those scores to choose a winner. Use a different method than you did to answer the Main Question. MP.6

TOPIC 8 REVIEW

? Topic Essential Question

How can data be described by a single number? How can tables and graphs be used to represent data and answer questions?

Vocabulary Review

Write *always, sometimes,* or *never* for each statement.

1. Intervals in a *frequency table* go beyond the values in a data set. ______________
2. You can calculate the *IQR* from a *box plot*. ______________
3. You can calculate the *mean* from a *histogram*. ______________
4. The *MAD* is a negative value. ______________
5. The *range* is a measure of variability. ______________
6. The *mean, median,* and *mode* are the same value. ______________

Use Vocabulary in Writing

Describe measures of variability and when you would use them to summarize a data set. Use vocabulary words in your explanation.

Concepts and Skills Review

LESSON 8-1 Recognize Statistical Questions

Quick Review

A statistical question anticipates that there will be a variety of answers.

Example

Ramon surveyed his classmates to determine the answer to the statistical question "How many hours do my classmates spend online each week?" The question yielded a variety of numerical answers. Ramon made this dot plot to display the data.

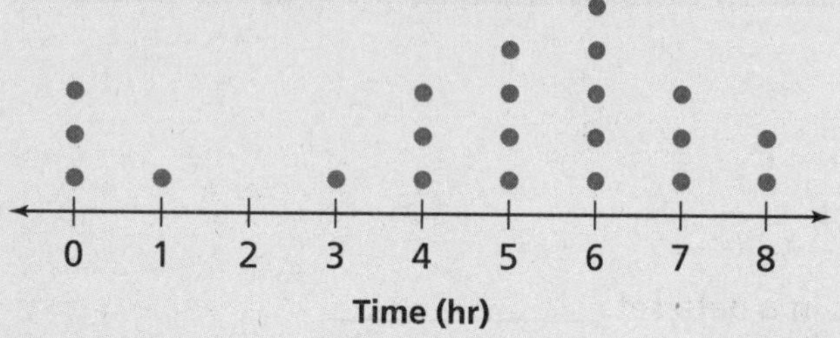

Practice

In 1–4, tell whether each question is statistical.

1. How many stations are there in a subway system?

2. How would passengers of a subway system rate the quality of service on a scale of 1 to 10?

3. How many passengers travel on each of the Green, Blue, Red, and Orange Lines of the subway system each day?

4. How much does it cost for a ticket to ride the subway from Station A to Station B?

LESSON 8-2 Summarize Data Using Mean, Median, Mode, and Range

Quick Review

The mean is the sum of all the values in a data set divided by the total number of values in the set. The median is the middle data value in a set arranged in numerical order. The mode is the value that occurs most often in a set. The range is the difference between the highest and lowest values in a set.

Example

Find the mean, median, mode, and range of the following set of data.

Total Game Points				
129	124	128	120	124

Mean: 125 Median: 124

Mode: 124 Range: 9

Practice

In 1–6, find the mean, median, mode, and range of each data set.

1. 2, 5, 5

2. 11, 13, 13, 11, 13

3. 27, 26, 25, 20

4. 100, 200, 500, 300, 500

5. 1.4, 1.3, 1.1, 1.4, 1.9, 1.8, 1.7, 1.4

6. 450, 0, 500, 750, 0

ESSON 8-3 Display Data in Box Plots

Quick Review

Quartiles divide a data set into four equal groups. A box plot uses the minimum, first quartile, median, third quartile, and maximum values in a data set to show how the data are distributed.

Example

Make a box plot of the distances, in feet, that seven paper airplanes flew: 60, 75, 45, 55, 70, 40, 65.

40 (45) 55 (60) 65 (70) 75

First Quartile Median Third Quartile

Paper Airplane Distances

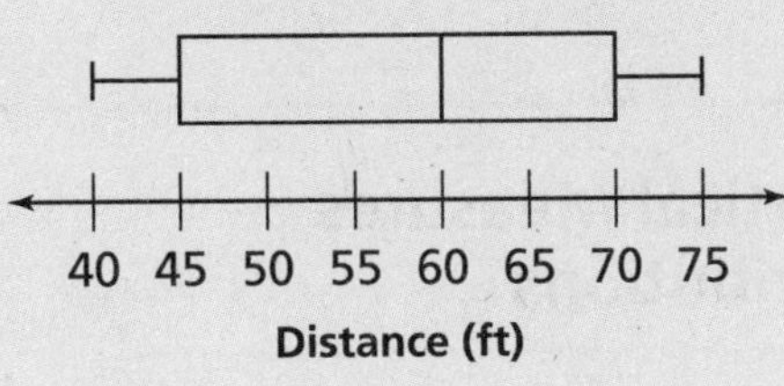

Practice

In 1 and 2, use the data to create a box plot.

1. 27, 31, 30, 33, 29, 25, 28

2. 3, 1, 3, 7, 5, 2, 3, 6, 3

LESSON 8-4 Display Data in Frequency Tables and Histograms

Quick Review

A frequency table shows the number of times a data value or a range of data values occurs in a data set. A histogram is a graph that uses bars to show the frequency of equal ranges or groups of data.

Example

Organize the ages of the campers listed below in a frequency table.

12, 14, 12, 14, 10, 11, 15, 13, 13, 11, 12, 12, 7, 14, 12

Divide the data into equal intervals and mark the frequency of the data using tally marks. Then write the frequency.

Ages of Campers	6–8	9–11	12–14	15–17
Tally	I	III	~~IIII~~ ~~IIII~~	I
Frequency	1	3	10	1

Practice

1. Represent the data in the frequency table on the left in a histogram.

LESSON 8-5 Summarize Data Using Measures of Variability

Quick Review

The mean absolute deviation (MAD) describes how spread out data values are from the mean. The interquartile range (IQR) describes the difference between the third quartile and the first quartile.

Example

Find the MAD of the data set.

6, 7, 8, 8, 8, 11

Mean = 8

The absolute deviations from the mean are 2, 1, 0, 0, 0, and 3, and their sum is 6.

So, MAD $= \frac{6}{6} = 1$.

Practice

In 1–3, find the mean and the MAD for each data set.

1. 5, 12, 0, 7

2. 8, 14, 22, 16

3. 1.25, 2.5, 3

In 4 and 5, find the median, first quartile, third quartile, and IQR for each data set.

4. 10, 20, 35, 45, 45, 50

5. 24, 12, 30, 17, 32, 13, 19

LESSONS 8-6 AND 8-7 Choose Appropriate Statistical Measures and Summarize Data Distributions

Quick Review

You can summarize data by finding the measure of center and the measure of variability. Use the IQR when the median is an appropriate measure of center, and the MAD when the mean is an appropriate measure of center.

Example

Use statistical measures to summarize the data set shown.

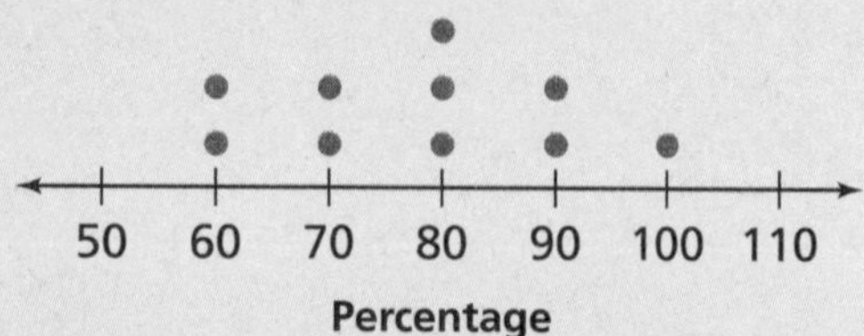

The mean and MAD are good measures to describe this data set.

The mean test score is 78 points. The MAD is 10.4, so most test scores are within 10.4 points of the mean.

Practice

In 1–3, use the data below.

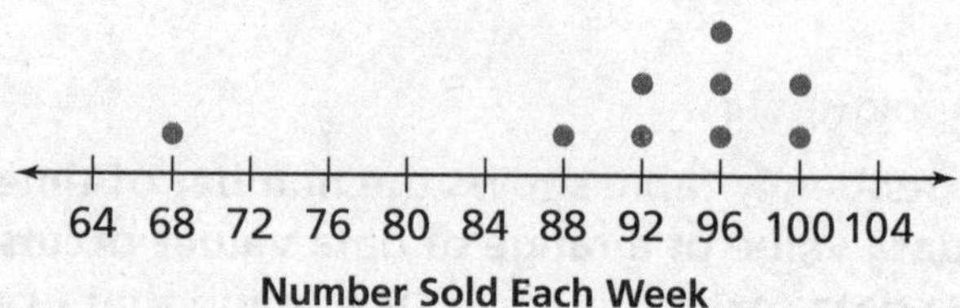

1. Describe the overall shape of the data. Include any outliers.

2. Which measure of center and measure of variability best describe the data set? Explain.

3. Summarize the data set.

Riddle Rearranging

Find each sum or difference. Then arrange the answers in order from least to greatest. The letters will spell out the answer to the riddle below.

I can...
add and subtract decimals.
6.NS.B.3

C	$14.56 + 9.471$
E	$33.582 - 2.8$
S	$8.999 + 2.3$
I	$45.74 - 22.08$
O	$1.43 + 12.89$
P	$20.4 - 11.81$
F	$25.35 - 2.5$
O	$2.456 + 7$
F	$7.074 + 12.75$
T	$80 - 66.7$

What place's name is only two words long but has hundreds of letters in it?

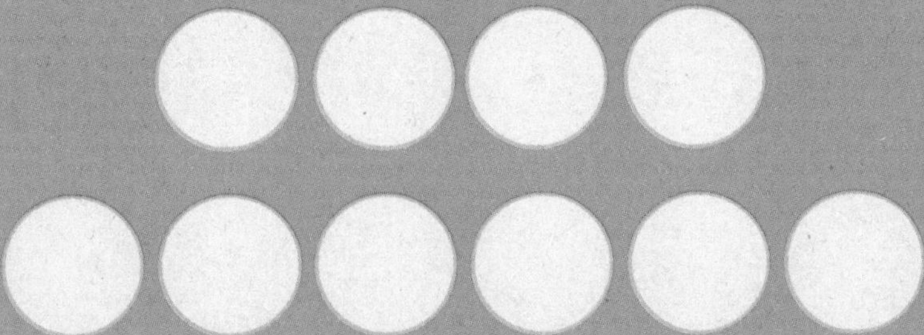

GLOSSARY

ENGLISH / SPANISH

A

absolute deviation from the mean Absolute deviation measures the distance that the data value is from the mean. You find the absolute deviation by taking the absolute value of the deviation of a data value. Absolute deviations are always nonnegative.

desviación absoluta de la media La desviación absoluta mide la distancia a la que un valor se encuentra de la media. Para hallar la desviación absoluta, tomas el valor absoluto de la desviación de un valor. Las desviaciones absolutas siempre son no negativas.

Example Data set: 0, 1, 1, 2, 2, 2, 2, 3, 3, 5, 5, 10. The absolute deviations of the values in the data set are:

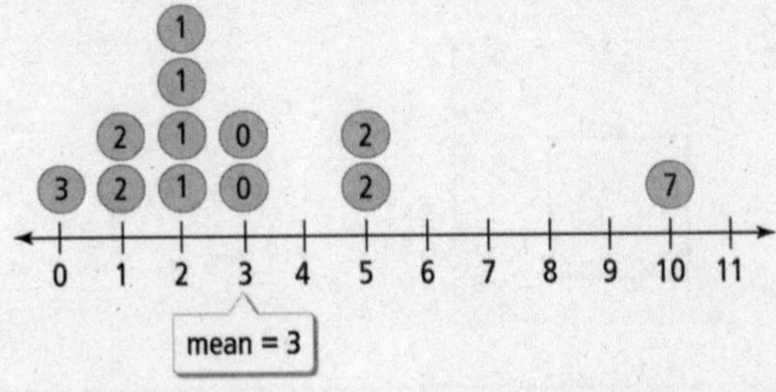

---

absolute value The absolute value of a number *a* is the distance between *a* and zero on a number line. The absolute value of *a* is written as $|a|$.

valor absoluto El valor absoluto de un número a es la distancia entre a y cero en la recta numérica. El valor absoluto de a se escribe como $|a|$.

Example -7 is 7 units from 0, so $|-7| = 7$.

---

addend Addends are the numbers that are added together to find a sum.

sumando Los sumandos son los números que se suman para hallar un total.

Example In $28 + 4 = 32$, the addends are 28 and 4.

Addition Property of Equality The two sides of an equation stay equal when the same amount is added to both sides of the equation.

propiedad de suma de la igualdad Se puede sumar el mismo número a ambos lados de una ecuación y los lados siguen siendo iguales.

Example
$$4 + 2 = 6$$
$$(4 + 2) + 3 = 6 + 3$$
$$(4 + 2) + a = 6 + a$$

---

additive inverses Two numbers that have a sum of 0.

inversos de suma Dos números cuya suma es 0.

Example 7 and -7 are additive inverses.

ENGLISH | SPANISH

algebraic expression An algebraic expression is a mathematical phrase that consists of variables, numbers, and operation symbols.

expresión algebraica Una expresión algebraica es una frase matemática que consiste en variables, números y símbolos de operaciones.

Example $x - 7$, $n + 2$, and $5d$ are algebraic expressions.

angle An angle is a figure formed by two rays with a common endpoint.

ángulo Un ángulo es una figura formada por dos semirrectas que tienen un extremo en común.

Example

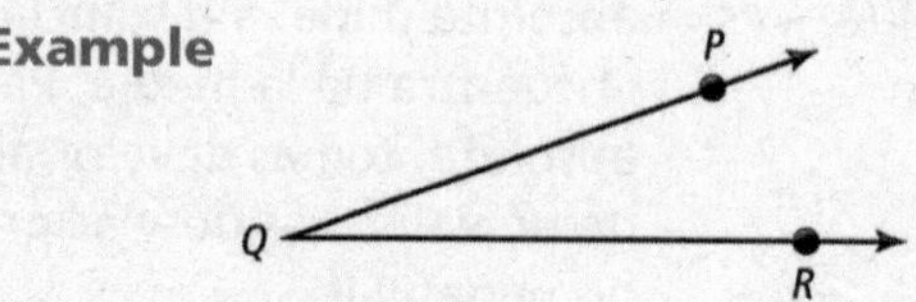

area The area of a figure is the number of square units the figure encloses.

área El área de una figura es el número de unidades cuadradas que ocupa.

Example

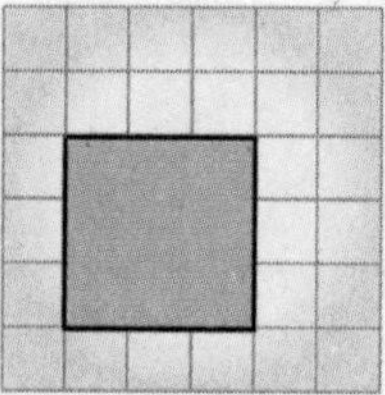

Associative Property of Addition For any numbers a, b, and c:
$(a + b) + c = a + (b + c)$

propiedad asociativa de la suma Para los números cualesquiera a, b y c:
$(a + b) + c = a + (b + c)$

Example $(3 + 25) + 4 = 3 + (25 + 4)$
$(m + 25) + 4 = m + (25 + 4)$

Associative Property of Multiplication For any numbers a, b, and c:
$(a \cdot b) \cdot c = a \cdot (b \cdot c)$

propiedad asociativa de la multiplicación Para los números cualesquiera a, b y c:
$(a \cdot b) \cdot c = a \cdot (b \cdot c)$

Example $(16 \cdot 26) \cdot 55 = 16 \cdot (26 \cdot 55)$
$(m \cdot 56) \cdot 4 = m \cdot (56 \cdot 4)$

B

bar diagram A bar diagram is a way to represent part-to-whole relationships.

diagrama de barras Un diagrama de barras es una forma de representar una relación de parte a entero.

Example

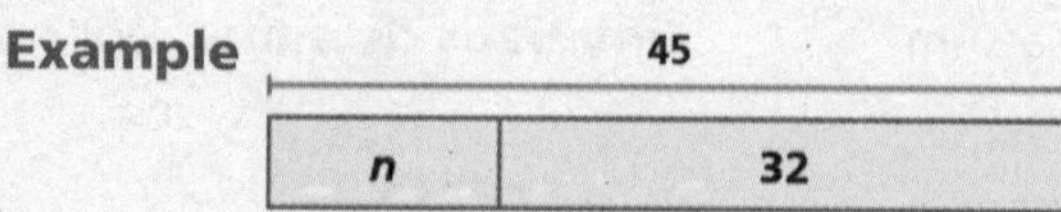

ENGLISH	SPANISH

base The base is the repeated factor of a number written in exponential form.

Example $3^4 = 3 \times 3 \times 3 \times 3$
In the expression 3^4, 3 is the base and 4 is the exponent.

base La base es el factor repetido de un número escrito en forma exponencial.

base of a parallelogram A base of a parallelogram is any side of the parallelogram.

Example

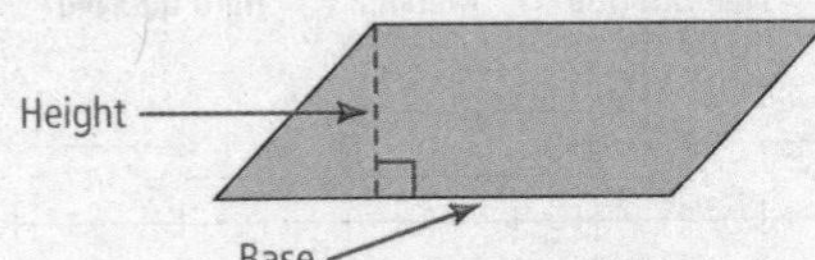

base de un paralelogramo La base de un paralelogramo es cualquiera de los lados del paralelogramo.

base of a prism A base of a prism is one of a pair of parallel polygonal faces that are the same size and shape. A prism is named for the shape of its bases.

Example

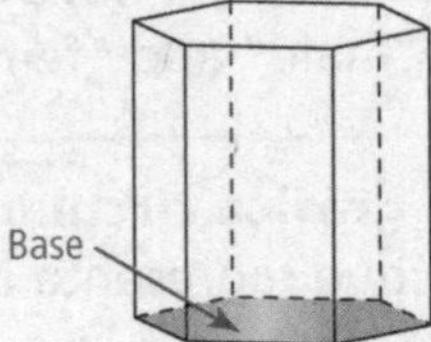

base de un prisma La base de un prisma es una de las dos caras poligonales paralelas que tienen el mismo tamaño y la misma forma. El nombre de un prisma depende de la forma de sus bases.

base of a pyramid A base of a pyramid is a polygonal face that does not connect to the vertex.

Example

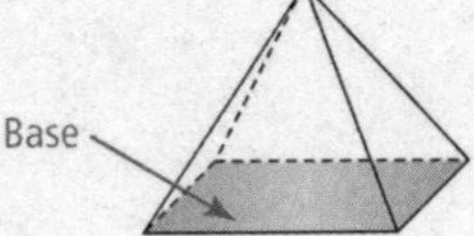

base de una pirámide La base de una pirámide es una cara poligonal que no se conecta con el vértice.

base of a triangle The base of a triangle is any side of the triangle.

Example

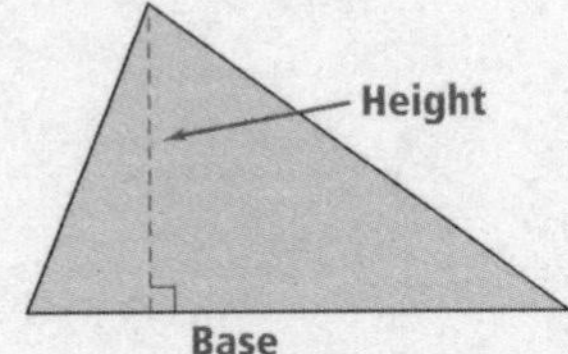

base de un triángulo La base de un triángulo es cualquiera de los lados del triángulo.

ENGLISH	SPANISH
benchmark A benchmark is a number you can use as a reference point for other numbers.	**referencia** Una referencia es un número que usted puede utilizar como un punto de referencia para otros números.
box plot A box plot is a statistical graph that shows the distribution of a data set by marking five boundary points where data occur along a number line. Unlike a dot plot or a histogram, a box plot does not show frequency.	**diagrama de cajas** Un diagrama de cajas es un diagrama de estadísticas que muestra la distribución de un conjunto de datos al marcar cinco puntos de frontera donde se hallan los datos sobre una recta numérica. A diferencia del diagrama de puntos o el histograma, el diagrama de cajas no muestra la frecuencia.

Example

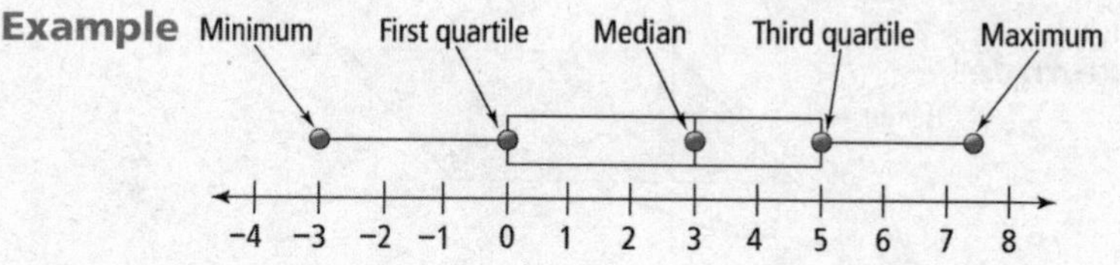

C

ENGLISH	SPANISH
categorical data Categorical data consist of data that fall into categories.	**datos por categorías** Los datos por categorías son datos que se pueden clasificar en categorías.

Example Data collected about gender is an example of categorical data because the data have values that fall into the categories "male" and "female."

ENGLISH	SPANISH
circle graph A circle graph is a graph that represents a whole divided into parts.	**gráfica circular** Una gráfica circular es una gráfica que representa un todo dividido en partes.

Example Favorite Types of Music

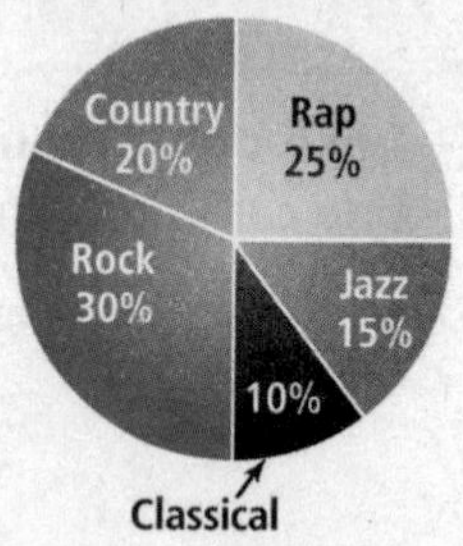

ENGLISH	SPANISH
coefficient A coefficient is the number part of a term that contains a variable.	**coeficiente** Un coeficiente es la parte numérica de un término que contiene una variable.

Example In the expression $3x + 4y + 12$, the coefficients are 3 and 4.

ENGLISH	SPANISH

common denominator A common denominator is a number that is the denominator of two or more fractions.

común denominador Un común denominador es un número que es el denominador de dos o más fracciones.

Example $\frac{5}{6} = \frac{10}{12}$ and $\frac{2}{3} = \frac{8}{12}$ and $\frac{3}{4} = \frac{9}{12}$

common factor A common factor is a number which is a factor of two or more given numbers.

factor común Factor que es el mismo para dos o más números.

Example 3 is a common factor of 6 and 9.

common multiple A common multiple is a multiple that two or more numbers share.

múltiplo común Un múltiplo común es un múltiplo que comparten dos o más números.

Example 12 and 24 are common multiples of 4 and 6.

Commutative Property of Addition For any numbers a and b: $a + b = b + a$

propiedad conmutativa de la suma Para los números cualesquiera a y b: $a + b = b + a$

Example $25 + 56 = 56 + 25$
$x + 72 = 72 + x$

Commutative Property of Multiplication For any numbers a and b: $a \cdot b = b \cdot a$

propiedad conmutativa de la multiplicación Para los números cualesquiera a y b: $a \cdot b = b \cdot a$

Example $17 \cdot 6 = 6 \cdot 17$
$47x = x \cdot 47$

compatible numbers Compatible numbers are numbers that are easy to compute mentally.

números compatibles Los números compatibles son números fáciles de calcular mentalmente.

Example When finding the quotient $206 \div 52$, you can use the compatible numbers 200 and 50 to estimate the quotient, as $200 \div 50$ is easy to compute mentally.

compose a shape To compose a shape, join two (or more) shapes so that there is no gap or overlap.

componer una figura Para componer una figura, debes unir dos (o más) figuras de modo que entre ellas no queden espacios ni superposiciones.

Example You can compose two triangles to form a parallelogram.

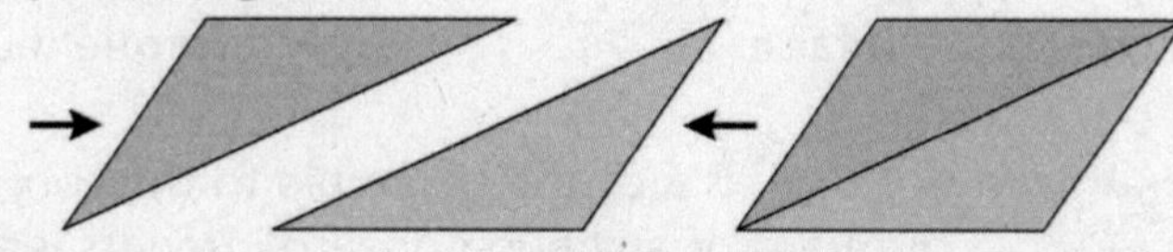

composite figure A composite figure is the combination of two or more figures into one object.

figura compuesta Una figura compuesta es la combinación de dos o más figuras en un objeto.

ENGLISH	SPANISH
composite number A composite number is a whole number greater than 1 with more than two factors.	**número compuesto** Un número compuesto es un número entero mayor que 1 con más de dos factores.

Example The factors of 15 are 1, 3, 5, and 15. Because 15 has more than two factors, it is a composite number.

conjecture A conjecture is a statement that you believe to be true but have not yet proved to be true.	**conjetura** Una conjetura es un enunciado que crees que es verdadero, pero que todavía no has comprobado que sea verdadero.

Example "The quotient of any two nonzero integers is an integer" is a conjecture. It can be shown to be false through a counterexample: $1 \div 2$ is not an integer.

constant A constant is a term that only contains a number.	**constante** Una constante es un término que solamente contiene un número.

Example In the expression $3x + 4y + 12$, 12 is a constant.

constant speed The speed stays the same over time.	**velocidad constante** Tasa de velocidad que se mantiene igual a través del tiempo.
conversion factor A conversion factor is a rate that equals 1.	**factor de conversión** Un factor de conversión es una tasa que es igual a 1.

Example $\frac{\text{60 minutes}}{\text{1 hour}}$

coordinate plane A coordinate plane is formed by a horizontal number line called the *x*-axis and a vertical number line called the *y*-axis.	**plano de coordenadas** Un plano de coordenadas está formado por una recta numérica horizontal llamada eje de las *x* y una recta numérica vertical llamada eje de las *y*.

Example

y-axis
x-axis
2
−2
O

counterexample A counterexample is a specific example that shows that a conjecture is false.	**contraejemplo** Un contraejemplo es un ejemplo específico que muestra que una conjetura es falsa.

Example $4 \div 8 = \frac{1}{2}$ is a counterexample to the conjecture "The quotient of any two nonzero integers is an integer."

ENGLISH | SPANISH

cube A cube is a rectangular prism whose faces are all squares.

cubo Un cubo es un prisma rectangular cuyas caras son todas cuadrados.

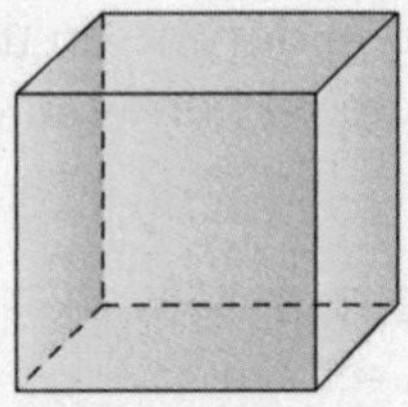

cubic unit A cubic unit is the volume of a cube that measures 1 unit on each edge.

unidad cúbica Una unidad cúbica es el volumen de un cubo en el que cada arista mide 1 unidad.

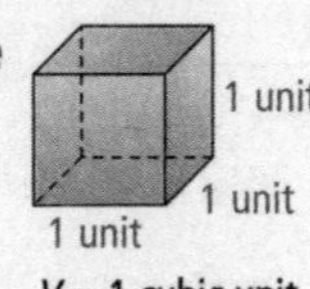

data Data are pieces of information collected by asking questions, measuring, or making observations about the real world.

datos Los datos son información reunida mediante preguntas, mediciones u observaciones sobre la vida diaria.

data distribution To describe a data distribution, or how the data values are arranged, you evaluate its measures of center and variability, and its overall shape. See distribution of a data set.

distribución de datos Cómo se distribuyen los valores.

decimal A decimal is a number with one or more places to the right of a decimal point.

Example 2.35 is a decimal.

decimal Un decimal es un número que tiene uno o más lugares a la derecha del punto decimal.

decompose a shape To decompose a shape, break it up to form other shapes.

descomponer una figura Para descomponer una figura, debes separarla para formar otras figuras.

Example

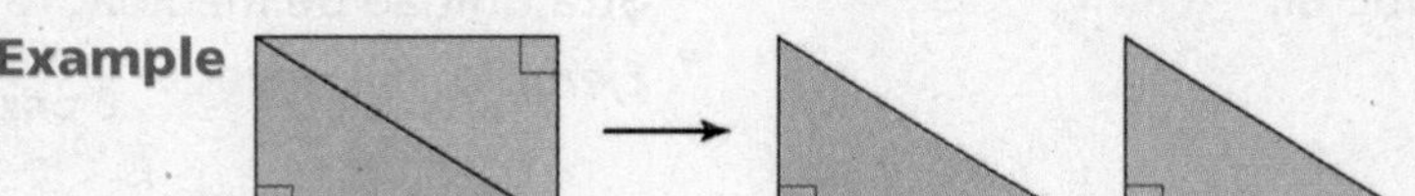

denominator The denominator is the number below the fraction bar in a fraction.

Example The denominator of $\frac{2}{5}$ is 5.

denominador El denominador es el número que está debajo de la barra de fracción en una fracción.

dependent variable A dependent variable is a variable whose value changes in response to another (independent) variable.

variable dependiente Una variable dependiente es una variable cuyo valor cambia en respuesta a otra variable (independiente).

ENGLISH	SPANISH
deviation from the mean Deviation indicates how far away and in which direction a data value is from the mean. Data values that are less than the mean have a negative deviation. Data values that are greater than the mean have a positive deviation.	**desviación de la media** La desviación indica a qué distancia y en qué dirección un valor se aleja de la media. Los valores menores que la media tienen una desviación negativa. Los valores mayores que la media tienen una desviación positiva.

Example Data set: 0, 1, 1, 2, 2, 2, 2, 3, 3, 5, 5, 10. The deviations of the values in the data set are:

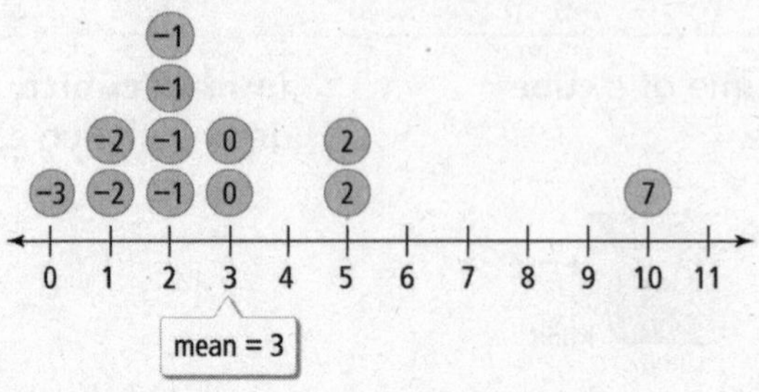

diagonal A diagonal of a figure is a segment that connects two nonconsecutive vertices of the figure.	**diagonal** La diagonal de una figura es un segmento que conecta dos vértices no consecutivos de la figura.

Example

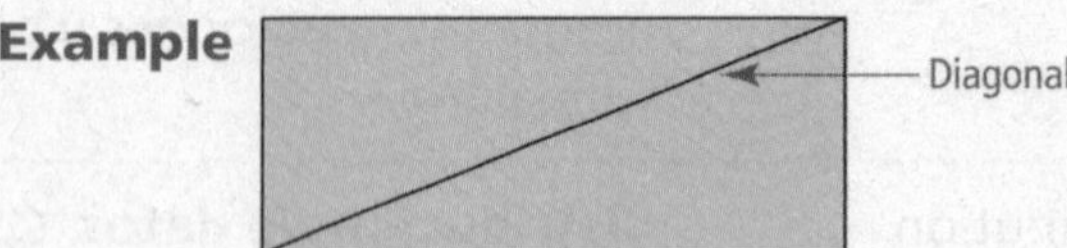

difference The difference is the answer you get when subtracting two numbers.	**diferencia** La diferencia es la respuesta que obtienes cuando restas dos números.

Example 63 − 18 = 45 (difference)

dimensional analysis A method to convert measures by including measurement units when multiplying by a conversion factor.	**análisis dimensional** Método que usa factores de conversión para convertir una unidad de medida a otra unidad de medida. *Ejemplo*: $64 \text{ \sout{onzas}} \times \frac{1 \text{ taza}}{8 \text{ \sout{onzas}}} = \frac{64}{8} \text{ tazas} = 8 \text{ tazas}$

Example $3.5 \cancel{ft} \times \frac{12 \text{ in.}}{1 \cancel{ft}} = 3.5 \times 12 \text{ in.} = 42 \text{ in.}$

ENGLISH	SPANISH
distribution (of a data set) The distribution of a data set describes the way that its data values are spread out over all possible values. This includes describing the frequencies of each data value. The shape of a data display shows the distribution of a data set. *See data distribution.*	**distribución (de un conjunto de datos)** La distribución de un conjunto de datos describe la manera en que sus valores se esparcen sobre todos los valores posibles. Eso incluye la descripción de las frecuencias de cada valor. La forma de una exhibición de datos muestra la distribución de un conjunto de datos.

Example The distribution of this data set shows that the data are clustered around 2 and 7, and there is one stray data value at 12.

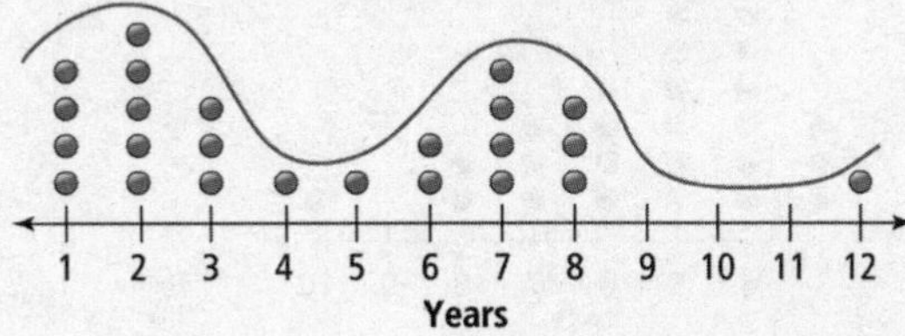

Distributive Property Multiplying a number by a sum or difference gives the same result as multiplying that number by each term in the sum or difference and then adding or subtracting the corresponding products. $a \cdot (b + c) = a \cdot b + a \cdot c$ and $a \cdot (b - c) = a \cdot b - a \cdot c$	**propiedad distributiva** Multiplicar un número por una suma o una diferencia da el mismo resultado que multiplicar ese mismo número por cada uno de los términos de la suma o la diferencia y después sumar o restar los productos obtenidos. $a \cdot (b + c) = a \cdot b + a \cdot c$ and $a \cdot (b - c) = a \cdot b - a \cdot c$

Example $36(14 + 85) = (36)(14) + (36)(85)$

dividend The dividend is the number to be divided.	**dividendo** El dividendo es el número que se divide.

Example In $28 \div 4 = 7$, the dividend is 28.

divisible A number is divisible by another number if there is no remainder after dividing.	**divisible** Un número es divisible por otro número si no hay residuo después de dividir.

Example Since $2 \times 7 = 14$, 14 is divisible by 2. 14 is also divisible by 7.

Division Property of Equality The two sides of an equation stay equal when both sides of the equation are divided by the same non-zero amount.	**propiedad de división de la igualdad** Ambos lados de una ecuación se pueden dividir por el mismo número distinto de cero y los lados siguen siendo iguales.

Example

$$4 + 2 = 6$$
$$(4 + 2) \div 3 = 6 \div 3$$
$$(4 + 2) \div a = 6 \div a$$

ENGLISH	SPANISH

divisor The divisor is the number used to divide another number.

divisor El divisor es el número por el cual se divide otro número.

Example In $28 \div 4 = 7$, the divisor is 4.

dot plot A dot plot is a statistical graph that shows the shape of a data set with stacked dots above each data value on a number line. Each dot represents one data value.

diagrama de puntos Un diagrama de puntos es una gráfica estadística que muestra la forma de un conjunto de datos con puntos marcados sobre cada valor de una recta numérica. Cada punto representa un valor.

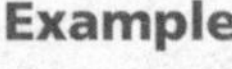
Example

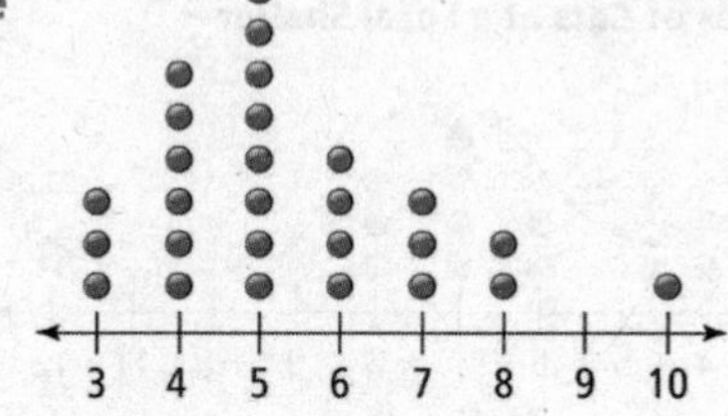

E

edge of a three-dimensional figure An edge of a three-dimensional figure is a segment formed by the intersection of two faces.

arista de una figura tridimensional Una arista de una figura tridimensional es un segmento formado por la intersección de dos caras.

Example

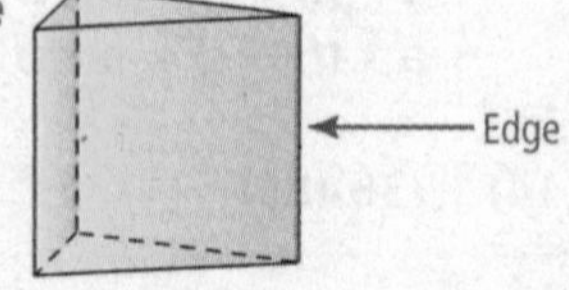

equation An equation is a mathematical sentence that includes an equals sign to compare two expressions.

ecuación Una ecuación es una oración matemática que incluye un signo igual para comparar dos expresiones.

Example $8 + 4 = 4 + 4 + 4$

equilateral triangle An equilateral triangle is a triangle whose sides are all the same length.

triángulo equilátero Un triángulo equilátero es un triángulo que tiene todos sus lados de la misma longitud.

Example

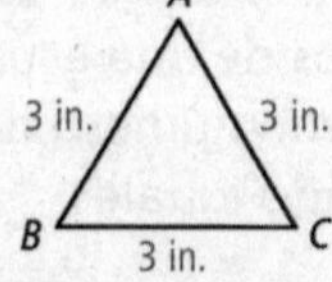

equivalent expressions Equivalent expressions are expressions that always have the same value.

expresiones equivalentes Las expresiones equivalentes son expresiones que siempre tienen el mismo valor.

Example 2(12) and $20 + 4$ are equivalent expressions.

ENGLISH	SPANISH

equivalent fractions Equivalent fractions are fractions that name the same number.

fracciones equivalentes Las fracciones equivalentes son fracciones que representan el mismo número.

Example $\frac{3}{4}$ and $\frac{6}{8}$ are equivalent fractions.

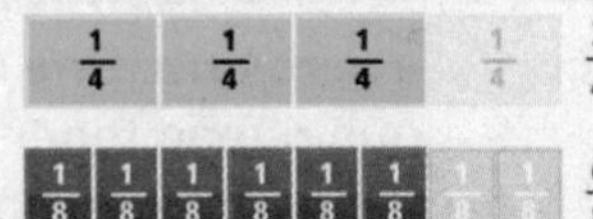

equivalent ratios Equivalent ratios are ratios that express the same relationship.

razones equivalentes Las razones equivalentes son razones que expresan la misma relación.

Example 2 : 3 and 4 : 6 are equivalent ratios.

estimate To estimate is to find a number that is close to an exact answer.

estimar Estimar es hallar un número cercano a una respuesta exacta.

Example An estimate for 28×53 is $30 \times 50 = 1{,}500$.

evaluate a numerical expression To evaluate a numerical expression is to follow the order of operations.

evaluar una expresión numérica Evaluar una expresión numérica es seguir el orden de las operaciones.

Example Evaluate the expression.

	$8 + (5 \times 12)$
First multiply (5 × 12).	$8 + 60$
Then add 8 + 60.	68

evaluate an algebraic expression To evaluate an algebraic expression, replace each variable with a number, and then follow the order of operations.

evaluar una expresión algebraica Para evaluar una expresión algebraica, reemplaza cada variable con un número y luego sigue el orden de las operaciones.

Example To evaluate the expression $x + 2$ for $x = 4$, substitute 4 for x.
$x + 2 = 4 + 2 = 6$

expand an algebraic expression To expand an algebraic expression, use the Distributive Property to rewrite a product as a sum or difference of terms.

desarrollar una expresión algebraica Para desarrollar una expresión algebraica, usa la propiedad distributiva para reescribir el producto como una suma o diferencia de términos.

Example The expression $(5 - x)(y)$ is a product that can be expanded using the Distributive Property.

$$\begin{aligned}(5 - x)(y) &= 5(y) - x(y)\\ &= 5y - (xy)\\ &= 5y - xy\end{aligned}$$

ENGLISH | SPANISH

exponent An exponent is a number that shows how many times a base is used as a factor.

exponente Un exponente es un número que muestra cuántas veces se usa una base como factor.

expression An expression is a mathematical phrase that can involve variables, numbers, and operations. See algebraic expression or numerical expression.

expresión Una expresión es una frase matemática que puede tener variables, números y operaciones. Ver expresión algebraica o expresión numérica.

Example $4 + 9$
$2x$

face of a three-dimensional figure A face of a three-dimensional figure is a flat surface shaped like a polygon.

cara de una figura tridimensional La cara de una figura tridimensional es una superficie plana con forma de polígono.

Example

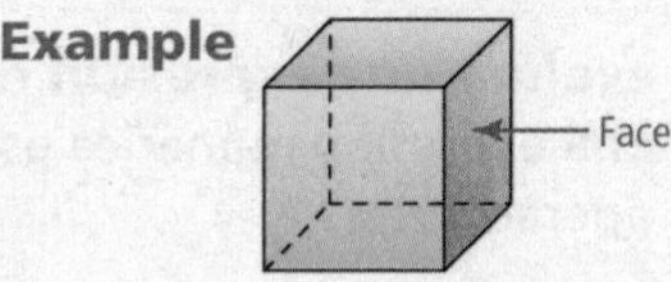

factors Factors are numbers that are multiplied to give a product.

factores Los factores son los números que se multiplican para obtener un producto.

Example In $5 \cdot 6 = 30$, 5 and 6 are factors.

factor tree A factor tree shows the prime factorization of a composite number.

árbol de factores Diagrama que muestra la descomposición en factores primos de un número.

Example

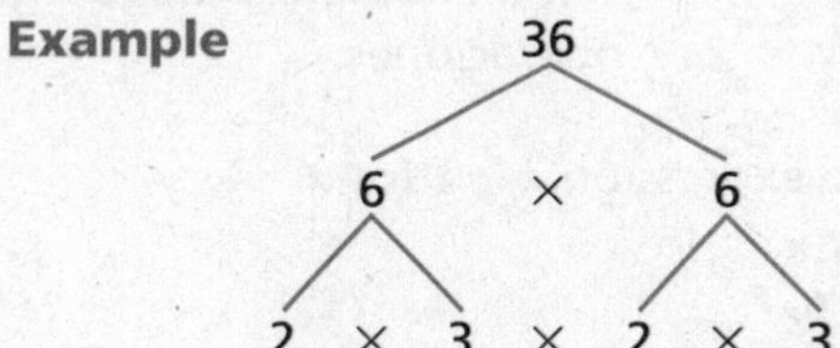

first quartile For an ordered set of data, the first quartile is the median of the lower half of the data set.

primer cuartil Para un conjunto ordenado de datos, el primer cuartil es la mediana de la mitad inferior del conjunto de datos.

Example Data set: 1, 3, (6), 10, 11, | 14, 15, 20, 23, 40

median = 12.5

The first quartile of the data set is 6.

ENGLISH	SPANISH

fraction A fraction is a number that can be written in the form $\frac{a}{b}$, where a is a whole number and b is a positive whole number. A fraction is formed by a parts of size $\frac{1}{b}$.

fracción Una fracción es un número que puede expresarse de forma $\frac{a}{b}$, donde a es un entero y b es un número entero positivo. La fracción está formada por a partes de tamaño $\frac{1}{b}$.

Example The fraction $\frac{2}{3}$ is formed by 2 parts of size $\frac{1}{3}$.

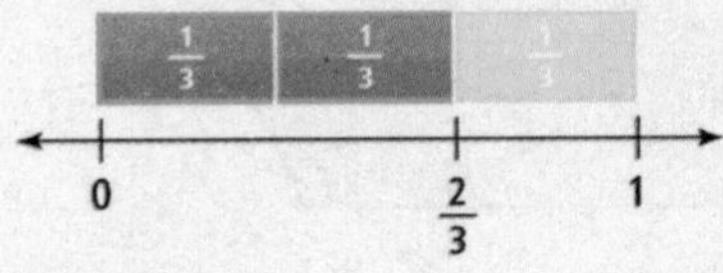

frequency Frequency describes the number of times a specific value occurs in a data set.

frecuencia La frecuencia describe el número de veces que aparece un valor específico en un conjunto de datos.

Example 1, 2, 4, 4, 5, 6, 6, 6, 7, 7, 8, 10

The value of 6 in this data set has a frequency of 3 because it occurs three times.

frequency table A frequency table shows the number of times a data value or values occur in the data set.

tabla de frecuencias Tabla que muestra la cantidad de veces que un valor o un rango de valores aparece en un conjunto de datos.

Example

Running Times	Tally	Frequency
14:00–15:59	||||	4
16:00–17:59	~~||||~~ |	6
18:00–19:59	||	2

G

gap A gap is an area of a graph that contains no data points.

Espacio vacío o brecha Un espacio vacío o brecha es un área de una gráfica que no contiene ningún valor.

Example

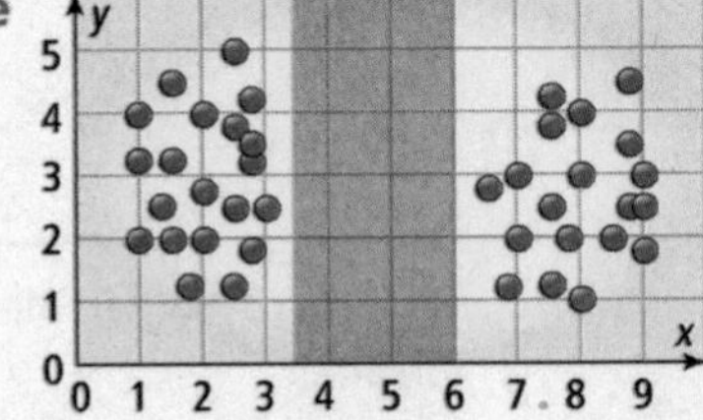

greatest common factor The greatest common factor (GCF) of two or more whole numbers is the greatest number that is a factor of all of the numbers.

máximo común divisor El máximo común divisor (M.C.D.) de dos o más números enteros no negativos es el número mayor que es un factor de todos los números.

Example The greatest common factor of 12 and 10 is 2.
The greatest common factor of 24 and 6 is 6.

ENGLISH | SPANISH

height of a parallelogram The height of a parallelogram is the perpendicular distance between opposite bases.

altura de un paralelogramo La altura de un paralelogramo es la distancia perpendicular que existe entre las bases opuestas.

Example

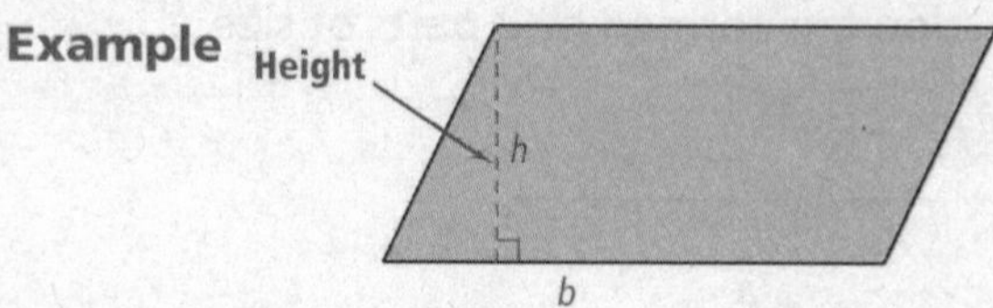

height of a prism The height of a prism is the length of a perpendicular segment that joins the bases.

altura de un prisma La altura de un prisma es la longitud de un segmento perpendicular que une a las bases.

Example

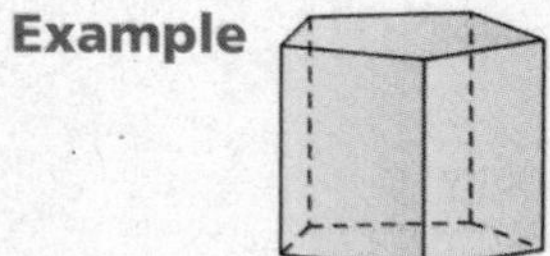

height of a pyramid The height of a pyramid is the length of a segment perpendicular to the base that joins the vertex and the base.

altura de una pirámide La altura de una pirámide es la longitud de un segmento perpendicular a la base que une al vértice con la base.

Example

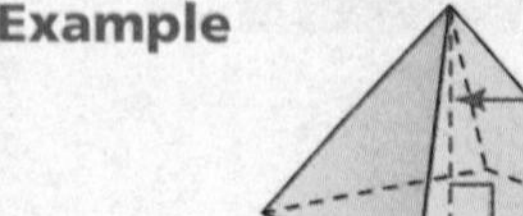

height of a triangle The height of a triangle is the length of the perpendicular segment from a vertex to the base opposite that vertex.

altura de un triángulo La altura de un triángulo es la longitud del segmento perpendicular desde un vértice hasta la base opuesta a ese vértice.

Example

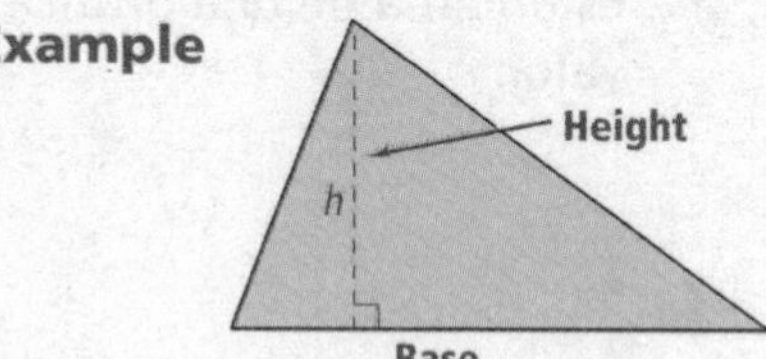

hexagon A hexagon is a polygon with six sides.

hexágono Un hexágono es un polígono de seis lados.

Example

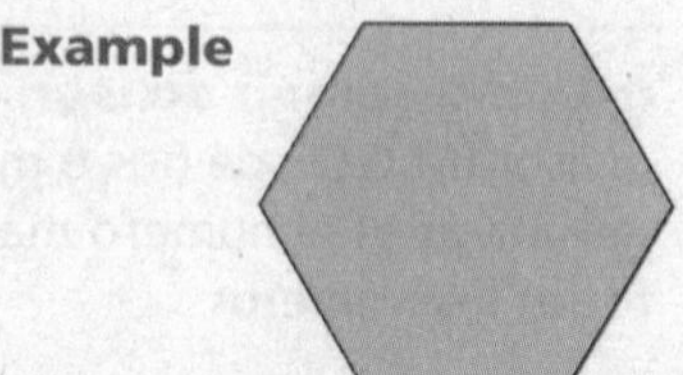

ENGLISH | SPANISH

histogram A histogram is a statistical graph that shows the shape of a data set with vertical bars above intervals of values on a number line. The intervals are equal in size and do not overlap. The height of each bar shows the frequency of data within that interval.

histograma Un histograma es una gráfica de estadísticas que muestra la forma de un conjunto de datos con barras verticales encima de intervalos de valores en una recta numérica. Los intervalos tienen el mismo tamaño y no se superponen. La altura de cada barra muestra la frecuencia de los datos dentro de ese intervalo.

Example

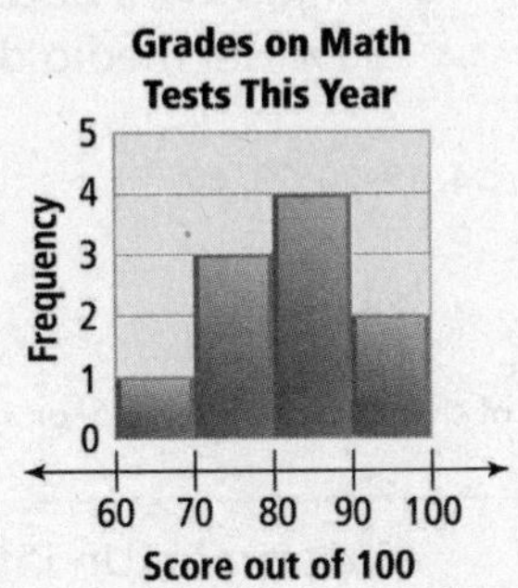

I

Identity Property of Addition The sum of 0 and any number is that number. For any number n, $n + 0 = n$ and $0 + n = n$.

propiedad de identidad de la suma La suma de 0 y cualquier número es ese número. Para cualquier número n, $n + 0 = n$ and $0 + n = n$.

Example $0 + 41 = 41$
$x + 0 = x$

Identity Property of Multiplication The product of 1 and any number is that number. For any number n, $n \cdot 1 = n$ and $1 \cdot n = n$.

propiedad de identidad de la multiplicación El producto de 1 y cualquier número es ese número. Para cualquier número n, $n \cdot 1 = n$ and $1 \cdot n = n$.

Example $1 \cdot 67 = 67$
$x \cdot 1 = x$

improper fraction An improper fraction is a fraction in which the numerator is greater than or equal to its denominator.

fracción impropia Una fracción impropia es una fracción en la cual el numerador es mayor que o igual a su denominador.

Example $\frac{4}{3}$ and $\frac{6}{6}$

independent variable An independent variable is a variable whose value determines the value of another (dependent) variable.

variable independiente Una variable independiente es una variable cuyo valor determina el valor de otra variable (dependiente).

inequality An inequality is a mathematical sentence that uses $<$, $\leq$, $>$, $\geq$, or $\neq$ to compare two quantities.

desigualdad Una desigualdad es una oración matemática que usa $<$, $\leq$, $>$, $\geq$, o $\neq$ para comparar dos cantidades.

Example $13 > 7$
$17 + c \leq 25$

ENGLISH	SPANISH

integers Integers are the set of positive whole numbers, their opposites, and 0.

enteros Los enteros son el conjunto de los números enteros positivos, sus opuestos y 0.

Example ..., $-3, -2, -1, 0, 1, 2, 3,$ ...

interquartile range The interquartile range (IQR) is the distance between the first and third quartiles of the data set. It represents the spread of the middle 50% of the data values.

rango intercuartil El rango intercuartil es la distancia entre el primer y el tercer cuartil del conjunto de datos. Representa la ubicación del 50% del medio de los valores.

Example

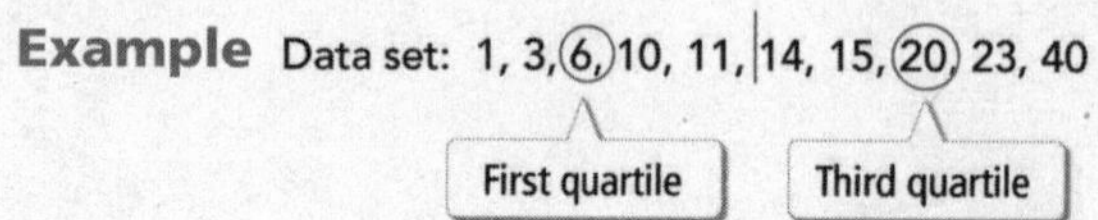

The interquartile range of the data set is $20 - 6$, or 14.

interval An interval is a period of time between two points of time or events.

intervalo Un intervalo es un período de tiempo entre dos puntos en el tiempo o entre dos sucesos.

Example A 3-hour interval is between 2:00 PM and 5:00 PM.

inverse operations Inverse operations are operations that undo each other.

operaciones inversas Las operaciones inversas son operaciones que se cancelan entre sí.

Example Addition and subtraction are inverse operations because they undo each other.
$4 + 3 = 7$ and $7 - 4 = 3$

Multiplication and division are inverse operations because they undo each other.
$4 \times 3 = 12$ and $12 \div 4 = 3$

Inverse Property of Addition Every number has an additive inverse. The sum of a number and its additive inverse is zero.

propiedad inversa de la suma Todos los números tienen un inverso de suma. La suma de un número y su inverso de suma es cero.

Example 5 and -5 are additive inverses.
$5 + (-5) = 0$ and $(-5) + 5 = 0$

inverse relationship Operations that undo each other have an inverse relationship.

relaciones inversas Relaciones entre operaciones que se "cancelan" entre sí, como la suma y la resta o la multiplicación y la división (excepto la multiplicación o división por 0).

Example Adding 5 is the inverse of subtracting 5.

isolate a variable When solving equations, to isolate a variable means to get a variable with a coefficient of 1 alone on one side of an equation. Use the properties of equality and inverse operations to isolate a variable.

aislar una variable Cuando resuelves ecuaciones, aislar una variable significa poner una variable con un coeficiente de 1 sola a un lado de la ecuación. Usa las propiedades de igualdad y las operaciones inversas para aislar una variable.

Example To isolate x in $2x = 8$, divide both sides of the equation by 2.

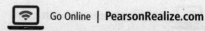

ENGLISH | SPANISH

isosceles triangle An isosceles triangle is a triangle with at least two sides that are the same length.

triángulo isósceles Un triángulo isósceles es un triángulo que tiene al menos dos lados de la misma longitud.

Example

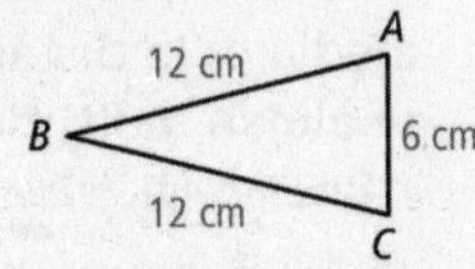

K

kite A quadrilateral with two pairs of adjacent sides that are equal in length.

cometa Cuadrilátero con dos pares de lados adyacentes de igual longitud.

Example

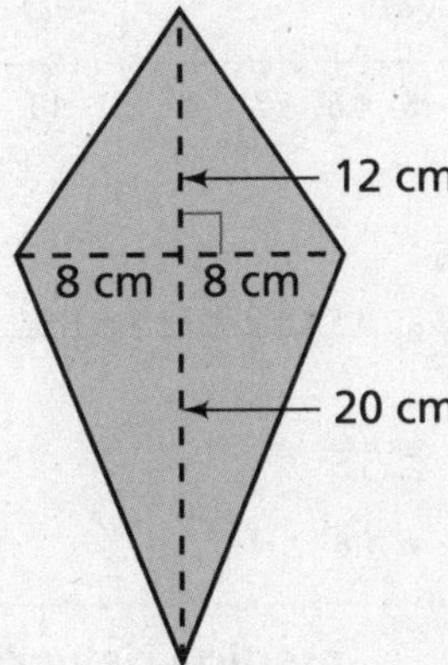

L

least common multiple The least common multiple (LCM) of two or more numbers is the least multiple, not including zero, shared by all of the numbers.

mínimo común múltiplo El mínimo común múltiplo (m.c.m.) de dos o más números es el múltiplo menor, sin incluir el cero, compartido por todos los números.

Example The LCM of 4 and 6 is 12.
The LCM of 3 and 15 is 15.

like terms Terms that have identical variable parts are like terms.

términos semejantes Los términos que tienen partes variables idénticas son términos semejantes.

Example Like terms

$y + 2.5 - 3y$

M

mean The mean represents the center of a numerical data set. To find the mean, sum the data values and then divide by the number of values in the data set.

media La media representa el centro de un conjunto de datos numéricos. Para hallar la media, suma los valores y luego divide por el número de valores del conjunto de datos.

Example Data set: 2, 4, 5, 15, 23, 12, 9

$$\text{mean} = \frac{2 + 4 + 5 + 15 + 23 + 12 + 9}{7} = \frac{70}{7} = 10$$

ENGLISH	SPANISH

mean absolute deviation The mean absolute deviation is a measure of variability that describes how much the data values are spread out from the mean of a data set. The mean absolute deviation is the average distance that the data values are spread around the mean. $\text{MAD} = \frac{\text{sum of the absolute deviations of the data values}}{\text{total number of data values}}$

desviación absoluta media La desviación absoluta media es una medida de variabilidad que describe cuánto se alejan los valores de la media de un conjunto de datos. La desviación absoluta media es la distancia promedio que los valores se alejan de la media. $\text{desviación absoluta media} = \frac{\text{suma de las desviaciones absolutas de los valores}}{\text{número total de valores}}$

Example Data set: 0, 1, 1, 2, 2, 2, 2, 3, 3, 5, 5, 10.
The mean absolute deviation of the data set is 1.8.

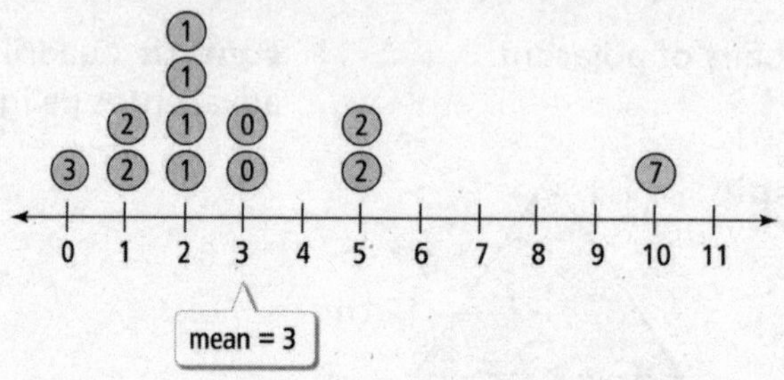

$$\text{mean absolute deviation} = \frac{3+2+2+1+1+1+1+0+0+2+2+7}{12}$$

$$= \frac{22}{12}$$

$$\approx 1.8$$

measure of variability A measure of variability describes the spread of values in a data set. There may be more than one measure of variability for a data set.

medida de variabilidad Una medida de variabilidad describe la distribución de los valores de un conjunto de datos. Puede haber más de una medida de variabilidad para un conjunto de datos.

Example Data set: 4, 5, 5, 6, 6, 7, 8, 11

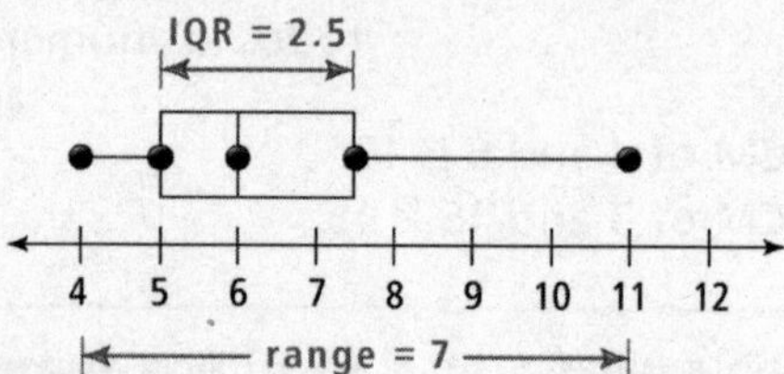

measures of center A measure of center is a value that represents the middle of a data set. There may be more than one measure of center for a data set.

medida de tendencia central Una medida de tendencia central es un valor que representa el centro de un conjunto de datos. Puede haber más de una medida de tendencia central para un conjunto de datos.

Example Data set: 4, 5, 5, 6, 6, 7, 8, 11

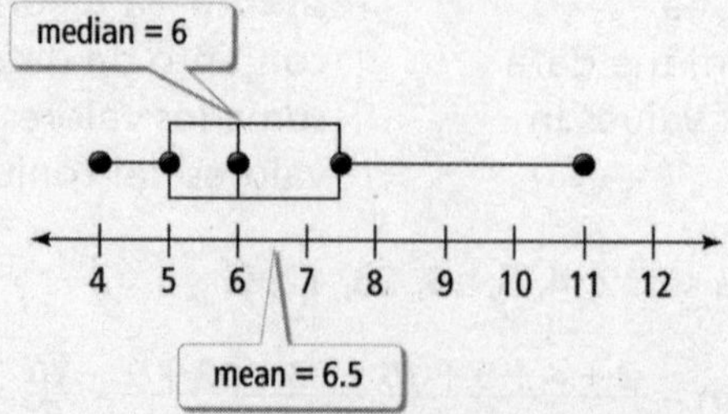

ENGLISH	SPANISH

median The median represents the center of a numerical data set. For an odd number of data values, the median is the middle value when the data values are arranged in numerical order. For an even number of data values, the median is the average of the two middle values when the data values are arranged in numerical order.

mediana La mediana representa el centro de un conjunto de datos numéricos. Para un número impar de valores, la mediana es el valor del medio cuando los valores están organizados en orden numérico. Para un número par de valores, la mediana es el promedio de los dos valores del medio cuando los valores están organizados en orden numérico.

Example Data Set A: 3, 5, 6, 10, 11, 13, 18, 21, 25
The median of Data Set A is 11.
Data Set B: 3, 5, 6, 10, 11, 13, 18, 21, 25, 30
The median of Data Set B is $\frac{11 + 13}{2}$, or 12.

mixed number A mixed number combines a whole number and a fraction.

número mixto Un número mixto combina un número entero no negativo con una fracción.

Example $1\frac{2}{3}$ and $3\frac{1}{6}$

mode The item, or items, in a data set that occurs most frequently.

modo El artículo, o los artículos, en un conjunto de datos que ocurre normalmente.

Example In a parking lot there are 18 red cars, 10 blue cars, and 12 silver cars. The mode of the data set is *red*.

multiple A multiple of a number is the product of the number and a whole number.

múltiplo El múltiplo de un número es el producto del número y un número entero no negativo.

Example The multiples of 3 are 0, 3, 6, 9, 12, ...
The multiples of 5 are 0, 5, 10, 15, 20, ...

Multiplication Property of Equality The two sides of an equation stay equal when both sides of the equation are multiplied by the same amount.

propiedad multiplicativa de la igualdad Ambos lados de una ecuación se pueden multiplicar por el mismo número distinto de cero y los lados siguen siendo iguales.

Example
$$4 + 2 = 6$$
$$(4 + 2) \times 3 = 6 \times 3$$
$$(4 + 2) \times a = 6 \times a$$

N

natural numbers The natural numbers are the counting numbers.

números naturales Los números naturales son los números que se usan para contar.

Example 1, 2, 3, ...

negative numbers Negative numbers are numbers less than zero.

números negativos Los números negativos son números menores que cero.

Example The number −5 can represent a temperature of 5 degrees below zero.

ENGLISH	SPANISH

net A net is a two-dimensional pattern that you can fold to form a three-dimensional figure. A net of a figure shows all of the surfaces of that figure in one view.

modelo plano Un modelo plano es un diseño bidimensional que puedes doblar para formar una figura tridimensional. Un modelo plano de una figura muestra todas las superficies de la figura en una vista.

Example This is the net of a triangular prism.

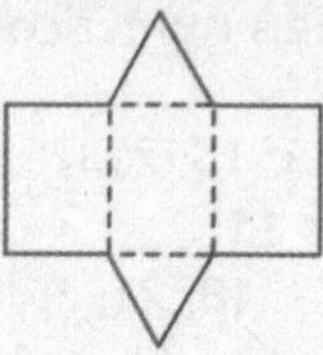

numerator The numerator is the number above the fraction bar in a fraction.

numerador El numerador es el número que está arriba de la barra de fracción en una fracción.

Example The numerator of $\frac{2}{5}$ is 2.

numerical expression A numerical expression is a mathematical phrase that consists of numbers and operation symbols.

expresión numérica Una expresión numérica es una frase matemática que contiene números y símbolos de operaciones.

Example $9 - 17$
$8 + (28 \cdot 53)$

O

octagon An octagon is a polygon with eight sides.

octágono Un octágono es un polígono de ocho lados.

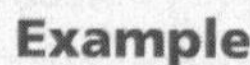

Example

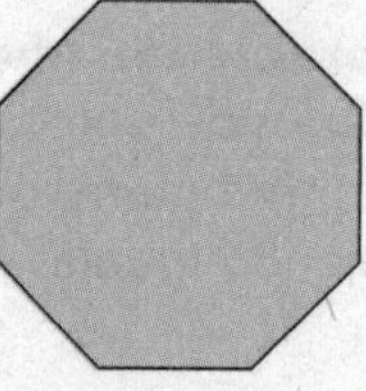

opposites Opposites are two numbers that are the same distance from 0 on a number line, but in opposite directions.

opuestos Los opuestos son dos números que están a la misma distancia de 0 en la recta numérica, pero en direcciones opuestas.

Example 17 and −17 are opposites.

ENGLISH

SPANISH

order of operations The order of operations is the order in which operations should be performed in an expression. Operations inside parentheses are done first, followed by exponents. Then, multiplication and division are done in order from left to right, and finally addition and subtraction are done in order from left to right.

orden de las operaciones El orden de las operaciones es el orden en el que se deben resolver las operaciones de una expresión. Las operaciones que están entre paréntesis se resuelven primero, seguidas de los exponentes. Luego, se multiplica y se divide en orden de izquierda a derecha, y finalmente se suma y se resta en orden de izquierda a derecha.

Example $8 - 3(9 - 7) = 8 - 3(2)$
$= 8 - 6$
$= 2$

ordered pair An ordered pair identifies the location of a point in the coordinate plane. The *x*-coordinate shows a point's position left or right of the *y*-axis. The *y*-coordinate shows a point's position up or down from the *x*-axis.

par ordenado Un par ordenado identifica la ubicación de un punto en el plano de coordenadas. La coordenada *x* muestra la posición de un punto a la izquierda o a la derecha del eje de las *y*. La coordenada y muestra la posición de un punto arriba o abajo del eje de las *x*.

Example

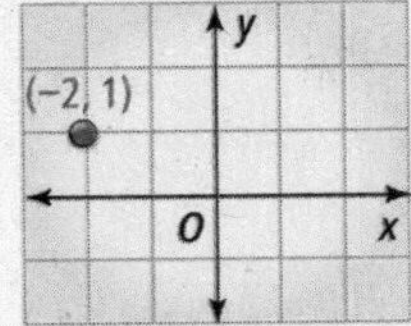

The *x*-coordinate of the point (−2, 1) is the −2, and the *y*-coordinate is the 1.

origin The origin is the point of intersection of the *x*- and *y*-axes on a coordinate plane.

origen El origen es el punto de intersección del eje de las *x* y el eje de las *y* en un plano de coordenadas.

Example The ordered pair that describes the origin is (0, 0).

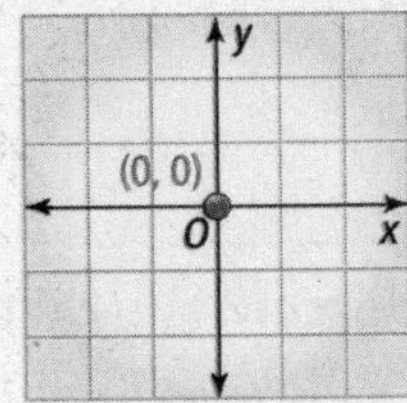

ENGLISH	SPANISH

outlier An outlier is a piece of data that does not seem to fit with the rest of a data set.

valor extremo Un valor extremo es un valor que parece no ajustarse al resto de los datos de un conjunto.

Example This data set has two outliers.

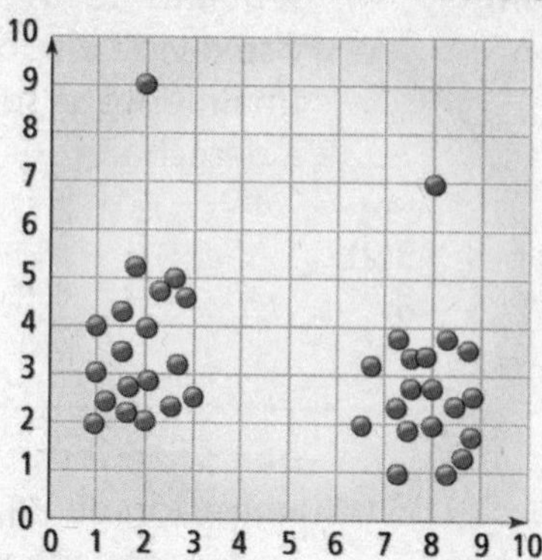

P

parallel lines Parallel lines are lines in the same plane that never intersect.

rectas paralelas Las rectas paralelas son rectas que están en el mismo plano y nunca se intersecan.

Example Line *a* and line *b* are parallel.

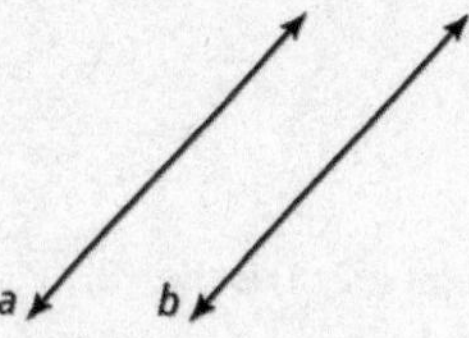

parallelogram A parallelogram is a quadrilateral with both pairs of opposite sides parallel.

paralelogramo Un paralelogramo es un cuadrilátero en el cual los dos pares de lados opuestos son paralelos.

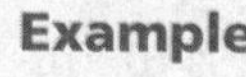
Example

percent A percent is a ratio that compares a number to 100.

porcentaje Un porcentaje es una razón que compara un número con 100.

Example $\frac{25}{100} = 25\%$

percent equation The percent equation describes the relationship between a part and a whole. You can use the percent equation (part = percent × whole) to solve percent problems.

ecuación de porcentaje La ecuación de porcentaje describe la relación entre una parte y un todo. Puedes usar la ecuación de porcentaje para resolver problemas de porcentaje. parte = por ciento • todo

ENGLISH	SPANISH
perimeter Perimeter is the distance around a figure.	**perímetro** El perímetro es la distancia alrededor de una figura.

Example

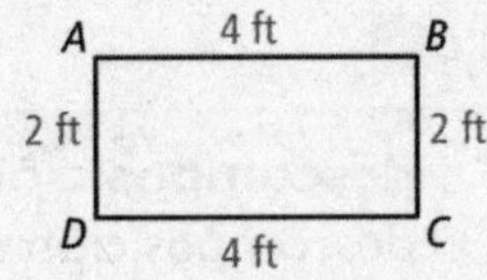

The perimeter of rectangle *ABCD* is 12 ft.

perpendicular lines Perpendicular lines intersect to form right angles.	**rectas perpendiculares** Las rectas perpendiculares se intersecan para formar ángulos rectos.

Example Line *a* is perpendicular to line *b*.

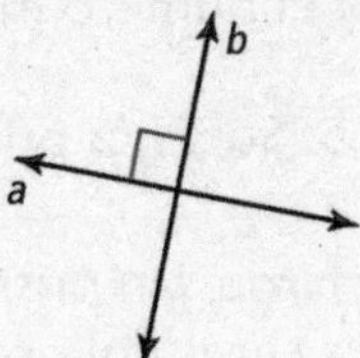

plane A plane is a flat surface that extends indefinitely in all directions.	**plano** Un plano es una superficie plana que se extiende indefinidamente en todas direcciones.

Example

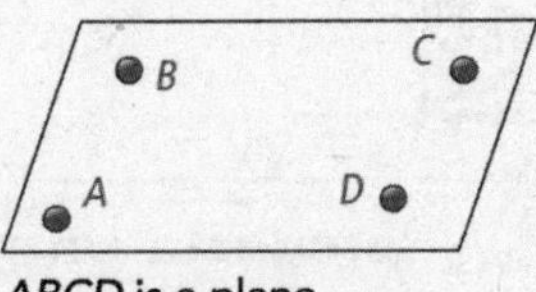

ABCD is a plane.

polygon A polygon is a closed figure formed by three or more line segments that do not cross.	**polígono** Un polígono es una figura cerrada compuesta por tres o más segmentos que no se cruzan.

Example

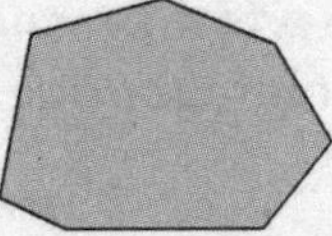

polyhedron A polyhedron is a three-dimensional figure made of flat polygon-shaped surfaces called faces.	**poliedro** Figura tridimensional compuesta de superficies planas que son polígonos.

Example A rectangular prism is a polyhedron.

positive numbers Positive numbers are numbers greater than zero.	**números positivos** Los números positivos son números mayores que cero.

Example The number +3 can represent a temperature of 3 degrees above zero. +3 is usually written 3.

ENGLISH	SPANISH

power A power is a number expressed using an exponent.

potencia Una potencia es un número expresado con un exponente.

Example 3^4 and 3^5 are powers of 3.

prime factorization The prime factorization of a composite number is the expression of the number as a product of its prime factors.

descomposición en factores primos La descomposición en factores primos de un número compuesto es la expresión del número como un producto de sus factores primos.

Example The prime factorization of 30 is $2 \cdot 3 \cdot 5$.

prime number A prime number is a whole number greater than 1 with exactly two factors, 1 and the number itself.

número primo Un número primo es un número entero mayor que 1 con exactamente dos factores, 1 y el número mismo.

Example The factors of 5 are 1 and 5. So 5 is a prime number.

prism A prism is a three-dimensional figure with two parallel polygonal faces that are the same size and shape.

prisma Un prisma es una figura tridimensional con dos caras poligonales paralelas que tienen el mismo tamaño y la misma forma.

Example

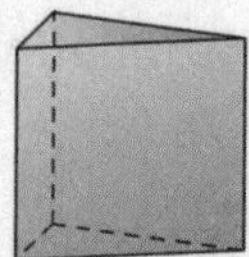

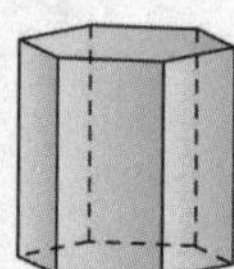

product A product is the value of a multiplication sentence or an expression showing multiplication.

producto Un producto es el valor de una multiplicación o una expresión que representa la multiplicación.

Example The product of 4 and 7, is 28 ($4 \times 7 = 28$). The expression "4×7" also may be called a "product."

proper fraction A proper fraction has a numerator that is less than its denominator.

fracción propia Una fracción propia tiene un numerador que es menor que su denominador.

Example $\frac{3}{4}$

pyramid A pyramid is a three-dimensional figure with a base that is a polygon and triangular faces that meet at a vertex. A pyramid is named for the shape of its base.

pirámide Una pirámide es una figura tridimensional con una base que es un polígono y caras triangulares que se unen en un vértice. El nombre de la pirámide depende de la forma de su base.

Example

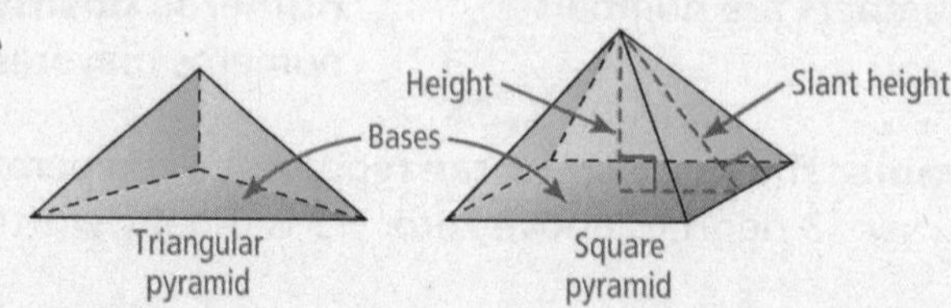

ENGLISH | SPANISH

quadrant The x- and y-axes divide the coordinate plane into four regions called quadrants.

cuadrante Los ejes de las x y de las y dividen el plano de coordenadas en cuatro regiones llamadas cuadrantes.

Example

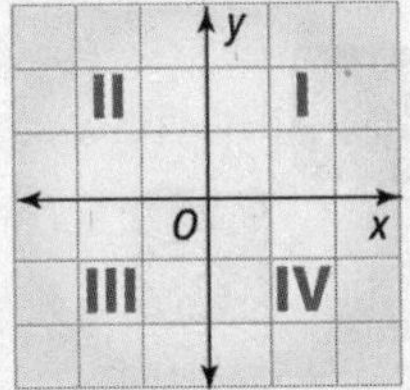

The quadrants are labeled I, II, III, and IV.

quadrilateral A quadrilateral is a polygon with four sides.

cuadrilátero Un cuadrilátero es un polígono de cuatro lados.

Example

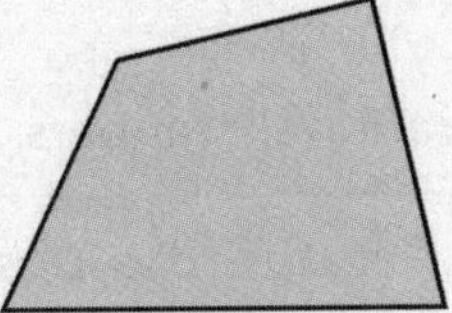

quartile The quartiles of a data set divide the data set into four parts with the same number of data values in each part.

cuartil Los cuartiles de un conjunto de datos dividen el conjunto de datos en cuatro partes que tienen el mismo número de valores cada una.

Example Data set: −5, −1, 4, 7, 8, 8, 11
First quartile: −1
Second quartile (median): 7
Third quartile: 8

quotient The quotient is the answer to a division problem. When there is a remainder, "quotient" sometimes refers to the whole-number portion of the answer.

cociente El cociente es el resultado de una división. Cuando queda un residuo, "cociente" a veces se refiere a la parte de la solución que es un número entero.

Example In $28 \div 4 = 7$, the quotient is 7.

range The range is a measure of variability of a numerical data set. The range of a data set is the difference between the greatest and least values in a data set.

rango El rango es una medida de la variabilidad de un conjunto de datos numéricos. El rango de un conjunto de datos es la diferencia que existe entre el mayor y el menor valor del conjunto.

rate A rate is a ratio involving two quantities measured in different units.

tasa Una tasa es una razón que relaciona dos cantidades medidas con unidades diferentes.

ENGLISH	SPANISH
ratio A ratio is a relationship in which for every x units of one quantity there are y units of another quantity.	**razón** Una razón es una relación en la cual por cada x unidades de una cantidad hay y unidades de otra cantidad.

Example The ratio of the number of squares to the number of circles shown below is 4 to 3, or 4 : 3.

rational numbers A rational number is a number that can be written in the form $\frac{a}{b}$ or $-\frac{a}{b}$, where a is a whole number and b is a positive whole number. The rational numbers include the integers.

números racionales Un número racional es un número que se puede escribir como $\frac{a}{b}$ or $-\frac{a}{b}$, donde a es un número entero no negativo y b es un número entero positivo. Los números racionales incluyen los enteros.

Example $\frac{1}{3}$, -5, 6.4, $0.\overline{6}$ are all rational numbers.

reciprocals Two numbers are reciprocals if their product is 1. If a nonzero number is named as a fraction, $\frac{a}{b}$, then its reciprocal is $\frac{b}{a}$.

recíprocos Dos números son recíprocos si su producto es 1. Si un número distinto de cero se expresa como una fracción, $\frac{a}{b}$, entonces su recíproco es $\frac{b}{a}$.

Example The reciprocal of $\frac{2}{3}$ is $\frac{3}{2}$.

rectangle A rectangle is a quadrilateral with four right angles.

rectángulo Un rectángulo es un cuadrilátero que tiene cuatro ángulos rectos.

Example

reflection A reflection, or flip, is a transformation that flips a figure across a line of reflection.

reflexión Una reflexión, o inversión, es una transformación que invierte una figura a través de un eje de reflexión.

Example

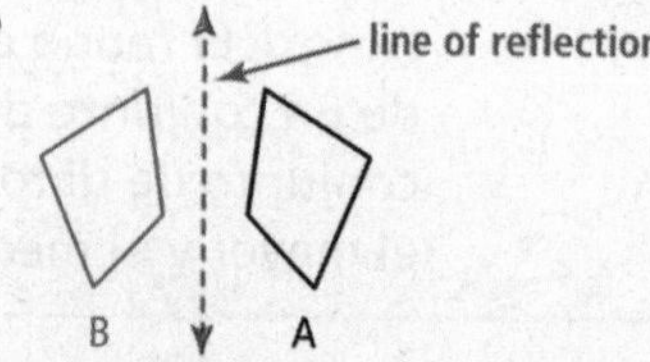

Figure B is a reflection of Figure A.

ENGLISH	SPANISH

regular polygon A regular polygon is a polygon with all sides of equal length and all angles of equal measure.

polígono regular Un polígono regular es un polígono que tiene todos los lados de la misma longitud y todos los ángulos de la misma medida.

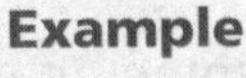

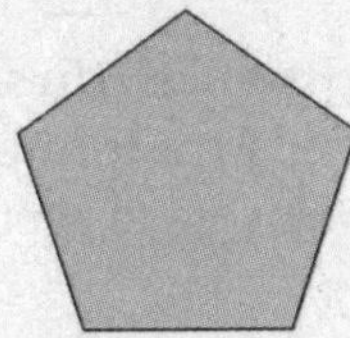

remainder In division, the remainder is the number that is left after the division is complete.

residuo En una división, el residuo es el número que queda después de terminar la operación.

Example In 30 ÷ 4 = 7 R2, the remainder is 2.

rhombus A rhombus is a parallelogram whose sides are all the same length.

rombo Un rombo es un paralelogramo que tiene todos sus lados de la misma longitud.

Example

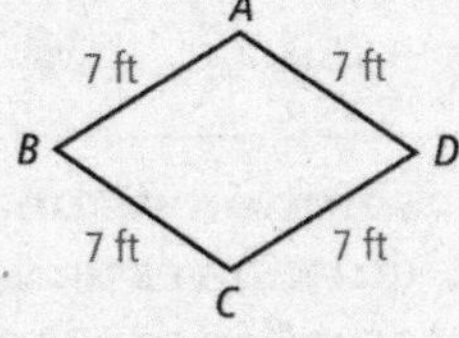

right angle A right angle is an angle with a measure of 90°.

ángulo recto Un ángulo recto es un ángulo que mide 90°.

Example

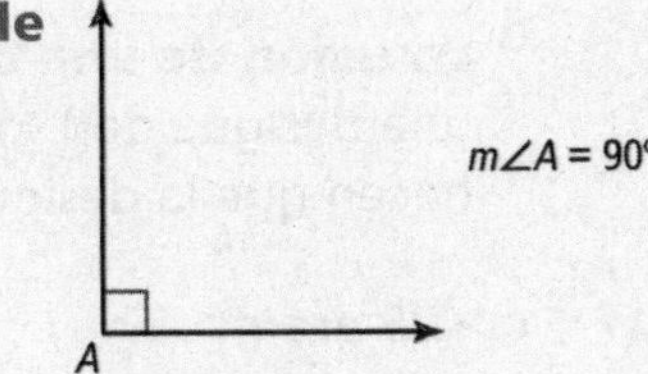

right triangle A right triangle is a triangle with one right angle.

triángulo rectángulo Un triángulo rectángulo es un triángulo que tiene un ángulo recto.

Example

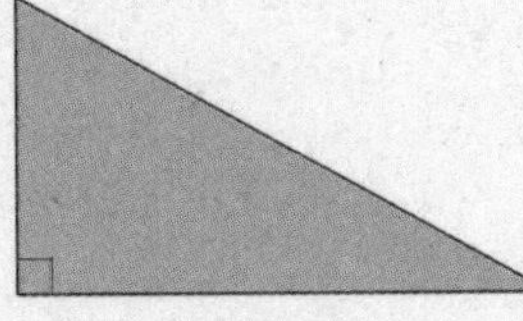

ENGLISH	SPANISH

sales tax A tax added to the price of goods and services.

las ventas tasan Un impuesto añadió al precio de bienes y servicios.

segment A segment is part of a line. It consists of two endpoints and all of the points on the line between the endpoints.

segmento Un segmento es una parte de una recta. Está formado por dos extremos y todos los puntos de la recta que están entre los extremos.

Example

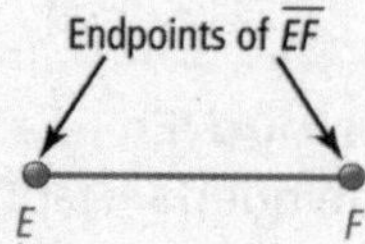

simplify an algebraic expression To simplify an algebraic expression, combine the like terms of the expression.

simplificar una expresión algebraica Para simplificar una expresión algebraica, combina los términos semejantes de la expresión.

Example $4x + 7y + 6x + 9y = (4x + 6x) + (7y + 9y)$
$= 10x + 16y$

solution of an equation A solution of an equation is a value of the variable that makes the equation true.

solución de una ecuación Una solución de una ecuación es un valor de la variable que hace que la ecuación sea verdadera.

Example The solution of $m - 15 = 12$ is $m = 27$, because $27 - 15 = 12$.

solution of an inequality The solutions of an inequality are the values of the variable that make the inequality true.

solución de una desigualdad Las soluciones de una desigualdad son los valores de la variable que hacen que la desigualdad sea verdadera.

Example The solutions of $17 + c > 25$ are $c > 8$.

square A square is a quadrilateral with four right angles and all sides the same length.

cuadrado Un cuadrado es un cuadrilátero que tiene cuatro ángulos rectos y todos los lados de la misma longitud.

Example

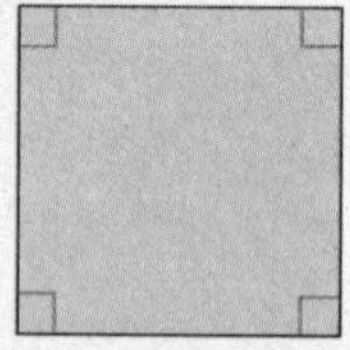

square unit A square unit is the area of a square that has sides that are 1 unit long.

unidad cuadrada Una unidad cuadrada es el área de un cuadrado en el que cada lado mide 1 unidad de longitud.

Example

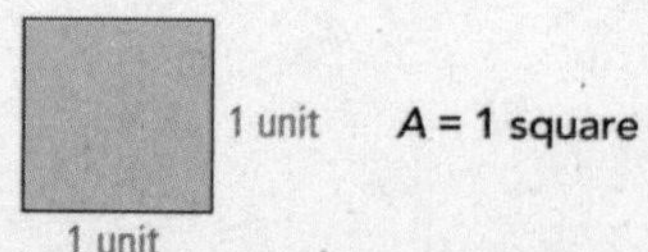

ENGLISH	SPANISH

statistical question A statistical question is a question that investigates an aspect of the real world and can have variety in the responses.

pregunta estadística Una pregunta estadística es una pregunta que investiga un aspecto de la vida diaria y puede tener varias respuestas.

Example "How old are students in my class?" is a statistical question. "How old am I?" is not a statistical question.

---

substitution To evaluate an algebraic expression, use substitution to replace the variable with a number.

sustitución Reemplazo de la variable de una expresión por un número.

Example Substitute 4 for n.
$12 + n$
$12 + 4 = 16$

Subtraction Property of Equality The two sides of an equation stay equal when the same amount is subtracted from both sides of the equation.

propiedad de resta de la igualdad Se puede restar el mismo número de ambos lados de una ecuación y los lados siguen siendo iguales.

Example
$4 + 2 = 6$
$(4 + 2) - 3 = 6 - 3$
$(4 + 2) - a = 6 - a$

---

sum The sum is the answer to an addition problem.

suma o total La suma o total es el resultado de una operación de suma.

Example In $28 + 4 = 32$, the sum is 32.

---

surface area of a three-dimensional figure The surface area of a three-dimensional figure is the sum of the areas of its faces. You can find the surface area by finding the area of the net of the three-dimensional figure.

área total de una figura tridimensional El área total de una figura tridimensional es la suma de las áreas de sus caras. Puedes hallar el área total si hallas el área del modelo plano de la figura tridimensional.

Example

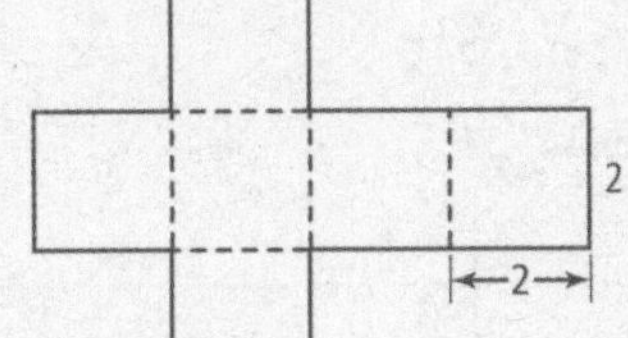

Surface area $= 6s^2$
$= 6(2)^2$
$= 6(4)$
$= 24$

T

term A term is a number, a variable, or the product of a number and one or more variables.

término Un término es un número, una variable o el producto de un número y una o más variables.

Example In the expression $3x + 4y + 12$, the terms are $3x$, $4y$, and 12.

ENGLISH / SPANISH

terms of a ratio The terms of a ratio are the quantities x and y in the ratio.

términos de una razón Los términos de una razón son la cantidad x y la cantidad y de la razón.

Example The terms of the ratio 4 : 3 are 4 and 3.

third quartile For an ordered set of data, the third quartile is the median of the upper half of the data set.

tercer cuartil Para un conjunto de datos ordenados, el tercer cuartil es la mediana de la mitad superior del conjunto de datos.

Example Data set: 1, 3, 6, 10, 11, | 14, 15, (20) 23, 40

median = 12.5

The third quartile of the data set is 20.

three-dimensional figure A three-dimensional (3-D) figure is a figure that does not lie in a plane.

figura tridimensional Una figura tridimensional es una figura que no está en un plano.

Example

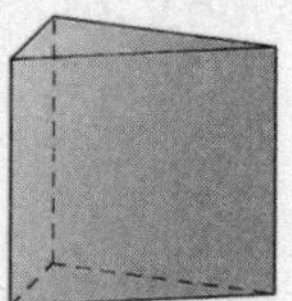

trapezoid A trapezoid is a quadrilateral with exactly one pair of parallel sides.

trapecio Un trapecio es un cuadrilátero que tiene exactamente un par de lados paralelos.

Example

triangle A triangle is a polygon with three sides.

triángulo Un triángulo es un polígono de tres lados.

Example

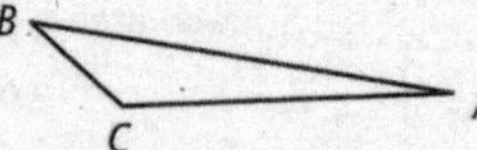

true equation A true equation has equal values on each side of the equals sign.

ecuación verdadera En una ecuación verdadera, los valores a ambos lados del signo igual son iguales.

Example $8 + 4 = 4 + 4 + 4$ is a true equation because $8 + 4 = 12$ and $4 + 4 + 4 = 12$.

ENGLISH / SPANISH

unit fraction A unit fraction is a fraction with a numerator of 1 and a denominator that is a whole number greater than 1.

fracción unitaria Una fracción unitaria es una fracción con un numerador 1 y un denominador que es un número entero mayor que 1.

Example $\frac{1}{5}$ is a unit fraction.

unit price A unit price is a unit rate that gives the price of one item.

precio por unidad El precio por unidad es una tasa por unidad que muestra el precio de un artículo.

Example $\frac{\$2.95}{5}$ fluid ounces $= \frac{\$.59}{1}$ fluid ounce, or \$.59 per fluid ounce

unit rate The rate for one unit of a given quantity is called the unit rate.

tasa por unidad Se llama tasa por unidad a la tasa que corresponde a 1 unidad de una cantidad dada.

Example $\frac{130 \text{ miles}}{2 \text{ hours}} = \frac{65 \text{ miles}}{1 \text{ hour}}$, or 65 miles per hour

variability Variability describes how much the items in a data set differ (or vary) from each other. On a data display, variability is shown by how much the data on the horizontal scale are spread out.

variabilidad La variabilidad describe qué diferencia (o variación) existe entre los elementos de un conjunto de datos. Al exhibir datos, la variabilidad queda representada por la distancia que separa los datos en la escala horizontal.

variable A variable is a letter that represents an unknown value.

variable Una variable es una letra que representa un valor desconocido.

Example In the expression $3x + 4y + 12$, x and y are variables.

vertex of a polygon The vertex of a polygon is any point where two sides of a polygon meet.

vértice de un polígono El vértice de un polígono es cualquier punto donde se encuentran dos lados de un polígono.

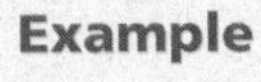

Example

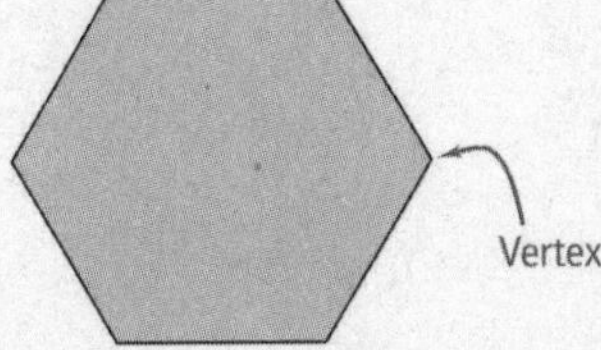

vertex of a three-dimensional figure A vertex of a three-dimensional figure is a point where three or more edges meet.

vértice de una figura tridimensional El vértice de una figura tridimensional es un punto donde se unen tres o más aristas.

Example

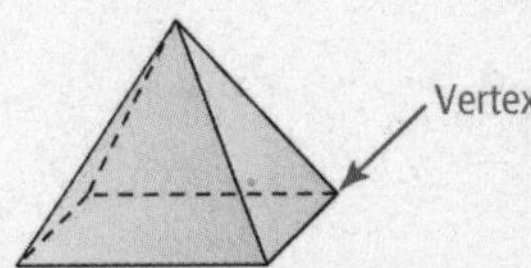

ENGLISH	SPANISH

volume Volume is the number of cubic units needed to fill a solid figure.

volumen El volumen es el número de unidades cúbicas que se necesitan para llenar un cuerpo geométrico.

Example The volume of this prism is 24 cubic units.

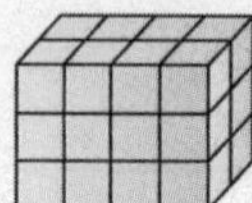

whole numbers The whole numbers consist of the number 0 and all of the natural numbers.

números enteros no negativos Los números enteros no negativos son el número 0 y todos los números naturales.

Example 0, 1, 2, 3, ...

***x*-axis** The *x*-axis is the horizontal number line that, together with the *y*-axis, forms the coordinate plane.

eje de las *x* El eje de las x es la recta numérica horizontal que, junto con el eje de las *y*, forma el plano de coordenadas.

Example

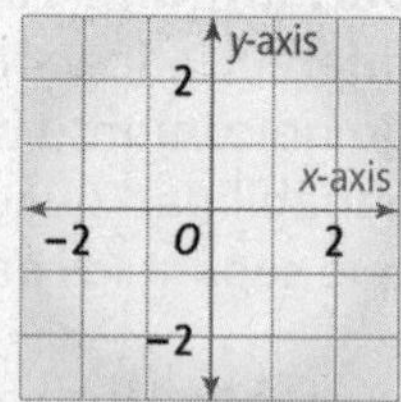

***x*-coordinate** The *x*-coordinate is the first number in an ordered pair. It tells the number of horizontal units a point is from 0.

coordenada *x* La coordenada *x* (abscisa) es el primer número de un par ordenado. Indica cuántas unidades horizontales hay entre un punto y 0.

Example The *x*-coordinate is −2 for the ordered pair (−2, 1). The *x*-coordinate is 2 units to the left of the *y*-axis.

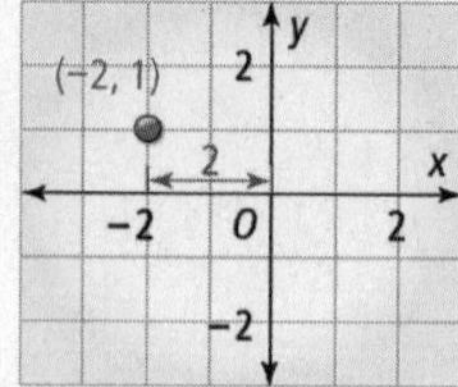

ENGLISH | **SPANISH**

Y

***y*-axis** The *y*-axis is the vertical number line that, together with the *x*-axis, forms the coordinate plane.

eje de las *y* El eje de las y es la recta numérica vertical que, junto con el eje de las *x*, forma el plano de coordenadas.

Example

y-axis
2
x-axis
−2 *O* 2
−2

***y*-coordinate** The y-coordinate is the second number in an ordered pair. It tells the number of vertical units a point is from 0.

coordenada *y* La coordenada *y* (ordenada) es el segundo número de un par ordenado. Indica cuántas unidades verticales hay entre un punto y 0.

Example The *y*-coordinate is 1 for the ordered pair $(-2, 1)$.
The *y*-coordinate is 1 unit up from the *x*-axis.

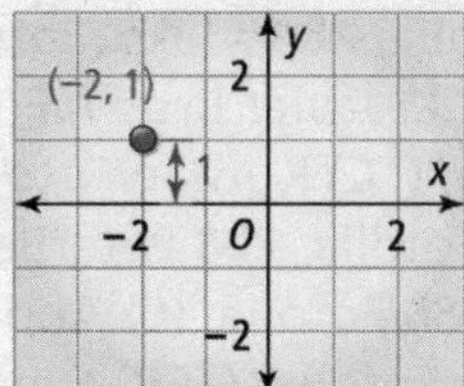

Z

Zero Property of Multiplication The product of 0 and any number is 0. For any number n, $n \cdot 0 = 0$ and $0 \cdot n = 0$.

propiedad del cero en la multiplicación El producto de 0 y cualquier número es 0. Para cualquier número n, $n \cdot 0 = 0$ and $0 \cdot n = 0$.

Example $36 \cdot 0 = 0$
$x(0) = 0$

ACKNOWLEDGEMENTS

Photographs

Photo locators denoted as follows: Top (T), Center (C), Bottom (B), Left (L), Right (R), Background (Bkgd)

Cover Jusakas/Fotolia, grthirteen/Fotolia, riccamal/Fotolia, Oksana Kuzmina/Fotolia, volff/Fotolia.

F16 Natis/Fotolia; **F17** (BL) mike166146/Fotolia, (BR) macrovector/Fotolia; **F18** Gelpi/Fotolia; **F19** blueringmedia/Fotolia; **F20** (C) piai/Fotolia, (CR) Pack/Fotolia; **F21** Taras Livyy/Fotolia; **F22** (T) duke2015/Fotolia, (TR) macrovector/Fotolia; **F23** duke2015/Fotolia; **253** Asia Travel/Shutterstock; **254** (TC) glyphstock/Fotolia, (TR) Svenni/Fotolia, (TL) Miguel Garcia Saaved/Fotolia, (TCL) vvoe/Fotolia, (CL) olly/Fotolia, (BCR) AlienCat/Fotolia, (BR) Monika Wisniewska/Fotolia, (B) yossarian6/Fotolia, (CR) donatas1205/Fotolia; **257** Marekkulhavy012/Fotolia; **258** (TCL) Pearson Education, (TC) Massimo Cattaneo/Shutterstock, (C) Ysbrand Cosijn/Shutterstock, (TC) Rebeccaashworth/Shutterstock, (TCR) Capture Light/Shutterstock, (TR) Marcel Jancovic/Shutterstock; **263** (Bkgrd) Mr Twister/Fotolia, (C) Baha/Fotolia, (TCL) Ermolaev Alexandr/Fotolia, (CL) Jovica Antoski/Fotolia, (L) Silver/Fotolia, (BCL) Carlos Santa Maria/Fotolia, (BC) Exopixel/Fotolia, (TR) Doomu/Fotolia; **264** Alekss/Fotolia; **269** (TC) Raksitar/Fotolia, (CR) Elizaveta66/Fotolia, (C) samsonovs/Fotolia; **275** (CL) Javier Brosch/Fotolia, (CR) philippe Devanne/Fotolia, (TL) Maridav/Fotolia, (C) Javier Brosch/Fotolia, (TC) Kurhan/Fotolia; **283** (C) Africa Studio/Fotolia, (CL) Okea/Fotolia; **285** Jacek Chabraszewski/Fotolia; **288** PeterBetts/Fotolia; **289** (TC) Steliost/Fotolia, (TL, TCL) Javier Brosch/Fotolia, (CL) Manati8888/Fotolia, (C) Andreacionti/Fotolia; **295** Oleksiy Mark/Fotolia; **297** (TR) Jultud/Fotolia, (TC) VTT Studio/Fotolia, (TCR) Evgenia Tiplyashina/Fotolia; **298** Anatolii/Fotolia; **301** Asia Travel/Shutterstock; **305** Library of Congress Prints and Photographs Division [LC-USZ62-113360]; **307** (CR) Injenerker/Fotolia, (TCR) Ian Maton/Shutterstock; **310** 3dsculptor/Fotolia; **311** (C) Openyouraperture/Fotolia, (CL) Amridesign/Fotolia, (TCL) Nikolai Sorokin/Fotolia, (CR) Ljupco Smokovski/Fotolia; **313** (T) Bonzami Emmanuelle/123RF, (TC) Lars Christensen/Shutterstock; **316** Hemera Technologies/PhotoObjects/Getty Images; **317** (Bkgrd) theyok/Fotolia, (C) Pete Saloutos/Fotolia, (CR) Africa Studio/Fotolia, (CL) mbongo/Fotolia; **318** kirill_makarov/Fotolia; **319** Tan4ikk/Fotolia; **331** Vixit/Shutterstock; **332** (TL) Kotomiti/Fotolia, (TC) Fenton/Fotolia, (TR) Vladimir Melnik/Fotolia, (C) tiero/Fotolia, (CR) kamonrat/Fotolia, (BR) yossarian6/Fotolia, (BCR) Yuriy Mazur/Fotolia; **341** (TL) sararoom/Fotolia, (TCL) jdoms/Fotolia; **346** afxhome/Fotolia; **347** Nattika/Shutterstock; **349** susansantamaria/Fotolia; **351** (BR) Colette/Fotolia, (BCR) Jeffrey Kraker/Fotolia; **352** PeterO/Fotolia; **355** (C) tigger11th/Fotolia, (CL) WavebreakmediaMicro/Fotolia; **360** (BR) Cla78/Fotolia, (BCR) neuevector/Fotolia; **361** Iakov Filimonov/123RF; **366** (CR) AlenKadr/Fotolia, (R) vipman4/Fotolia, (BR) Elena Milevska/Fotolia, (BCR) vipman4/Fotolia; **367** Patrick Foto/Shutterstock; **368** seanlockephotography/Fotolia; **369** Bruce Shippee/Fotolia; **373** Vixit/Shutterstock; **381** iStockphoto/Getty Images; **383** Cottonfioc/Fotolia; **384** (TR) Carolyn Franks/Fotolia, (TCR) Jaimie Duplass/Fotolia, (TC) yvdavid/Fotolia, (CL) monticellllo/Fotolia, (TL) viperagp/Fotolia, (BL) vlorzor/Fotolia, (BR) Coprid/Fotolia, (BCR) fotonen/Fotolia, (BCL) Roman Samokhin/Fotolia, (B) yossarian6/Fotolia, (C) bravissimos/Fotolia, (CR) nito/Fotolia; **392** (TR) Getty Images, (B) eboss6/Fotolia; **398** Getty Images; **401** (TCR) Budimir Jevtic/Fotolia, (TR) Roman_23203/Fotolia; **410** (CL) Jenifoto/Fotolia, (C) Ellensmile/Fotolia, (CR) Dplett/Fotolia; **413** Andreas Metz/Fotolia; **418** Zudy/Shutterstock; **419** Cottonfioc/Fotolia; **429** (C) dadoodas/Fotolia, (CL) Photocreo Bednarek/Fotolia, (CR) littlestocker/Fotolia, (TC) Sergio Martínez/Fotolia; **435** (TC) Bogdan Florea/Shutterstock, (TL) Lovely Bird/Shutterstock; **439** Pixelrobot/Fotolia; **440** Getty Images; **447** Ryan Burke/Getty Images; **449** Yongcharoen /Shutterstock; **450** (T) cunico/Fotolia, (TR) Ig0rZh/Fotolia, (CL) puckillustrations/Fotolia, (CR) andresgarciam/Fotolia, (BR) yossarian6/Fotolia, (BCR) Yuval Helfman/Fotolia; **459** (TC) Ljupco Smokovski/Fotolia, (CL) mouse_md/Fotolia; **461** Csak Istvan/123RF; **466** 3drenderings/Fotolia; **467** ki33/Fotolia; **468** (T) Racobovt/Shutterstock, (C) aleciccotelli/Fotolia; **473** bluecherrygfx/Fotolia; **492** (CR) pixelrobot/Fotolia, (R) BillionPhotos.com/Fotolia, (TR) 3dmavr/Fotolia, (TCR) alextois/Fotolia; **495** OmniArt/Shutterstock; **499** Yongcharoen/Shutterstock; **481** Gleb Semenjuk/Fotolia; **488** Pearson Education.